D0605152

DATE DUE DEC 06

GAYLORD			PRINTED IN U.S.A.

AVIATION CENTURY

WAR & PEACE
IN THE AIR

AVIATION CENTURY

WAR &
PEACE
IN THE AIR

RON DICK AND DAN PATTERSON

The BOSTON
MILLS PRESS

JACKSON COUNTY LIBRARY SERVICES
MEDFORD, OREGON 97501

A BOSTON MILLS PRESS BOOK

© Ron Dick and Dan Patterson, 2006

First printing

All rights reserved. No part of this publication may be reproduced, stored in a retrieval system or transmitted in any form
or by any means, electronic, mechanical, photocopying, recording or otherwise, without the prior written consent of the publisher.

Library and Archives Canada Cataloguing in Publication

Dick, Ron, 1931–
Aviation century war & peace in the air / Ron Dick and Dan Patterson.

Includes bibliographical references and index.

ISBN-13: 978-1-55046-430-6
ISBN-10: 55046-430-2

1. Aeronautics – History. I. Patterson, Dan, 1953– II.Title.

TL515.D517 2006   629.13'009   CS2006-901323-3

Publisher Cataloging-in-Publication Data (U.S.)

Dick, Ron, 1931-
Aviation century war & peace in the air / Ron Dick ; and Dan Patterson.

[384] p. : ill. , photos. (chiefly col.) ;   cm.   (Aviation century)

Includes bibliographical references and index.

Summary: Measures how the world has been changed by the first human flight,
examining military aviation after World War II, the safety of flight, the future of
aviation, and centenary attempts to recreate the Wright brothers' first flights.

ISBN-13: 978-1-55046-430-6
ISBN-10: 1-55046-430-2

1. Aeronautics—History. I. Patterson, Dan, 1953- . II. Title. III. Series.

629.13/009 dc22   TL515.D53 2006

Published in 2006 by BOSTON MILLS PRESS
132 Main Street,
Erin, Ontario N0B 1T0
Tel 519-833-2407
Fax 519-833-2195

IN CANADA:
Distributed by Firefly Books Ltd.
66 Leek Crescent
Richmond Hill, Ontario L4B 1H1

IN THE UNITED STATES:
Distributed by Firefly Books (U.S.) Inc.
P.O. Box 1338, Ellicott Station
Buffalo, New York 14205

www.bostonmillspress.com

Aviation Century series editor: Kathleen Fraser
Design: PageWave Graphics Inc.

Printed in China

The publisher gratefully acknowledges the financial support for our publishing program by the
Government of Canada through the Book Publishing Industry Development Program.

FRONT COVER *Main Image: An uncompromising war machine — the A-10
Thunderbolt II and its fearsome gun.*
FRONT COVER BOTTOM ROW, LEFT TO RIGHT *Polish MiG fighters outside the
Muzeum Lotnictwa Polskiego, Krakow, Poland; first steps toward an aviation
future: Margaret Patterson tackles the problems of flight; the Piaggio Aero P180
Avanti pusher turboprop executive aircraft; the flight deck of the A300 simulator
operated by UPS in Louisville, Kentucky.*
BACK COVER *This exact replica of the Wright 1902 glider flew over the sands of
North Carolina's Outer Banks in October 2002, nearly 100 years to the minute
after the Wrights had solved the question of complete control of a flying machine.*

HALF-TITLE PAGE *An iconic image of the Cold War, a Russian "Bear"
intercepted by U.S. Navy F-4 Phantom II fighters.*
TITLE PAGE *Looking straight down the nose of a USAF F-4 Phantom II fighter,
on display at the National Museum of the United States Air Force, Dayton,
Ohio.*
PAGE 3 *Burt Rutan's private space vehicle, SpaceShipOne.*
PAGE 6 *An exact replica of the 1905 Wright Flyer III, ready to fly at the Huffman
Prairie Flying Field near Dayton, Ohio.*

Dedicated to aviators,
past, present
and of the future.

Contents

ACKNOWLEDGMENTS

THE PUBLICATION OF THE fifth volume of the Aviation Century series marks the end of a project that has been a major part of the authors' lives for eight years. The help and advice given to us during that time has been remarkable.

Hundreds of organizations and individuals have been associated with the project at one time or another. Between them they comprise a significant proportion of the world's aviation museums, industries, operators and enthusiasts. Without their multifarious and invaluable assistance the series could not have been completed. Many of them have been involved in more than one of the books, and the authors are grateful for their unfailing support.

For this fifth volume, *Aviation Century War & Peace in the Air*, we also welcome many more names to the list of those to whom we are deeply indebted. We sincerely hope that every one will be remembered in our acknowledgments, but we are well aware that we are less than perfect. With the best of intentions, it is still possible that a person or organization will be overlooked, or that mistakes will be made and credit perhaps given incorrectly. If that proves to be the case, we would be glad to have the errors brought to our attention so that apologies can be offered and corrections made in future editions.

As before, the help of the aviation museums and archives of North America and Europe was indispensable in the preparation of this volume. The authors are particularly grateful to the directors and staffs of the Smithsonian's National Air & Space Museum, Washington, D.C.; the Museum of Flight, Seattle, Washington; the Virginia Aviation Museum, Richmond, Virginia: the EAA's Air Venture Museum, Oshkosh, Wisconsin; the USAF History Office; the National Museum of the United States Air Force, Dayton, Ohio; the Air Force Flight Test Center Museum, Edwards AFB, California; the Museum of Naval Aviation, Pensacola, Florida; the U.S. Marine Corps Museum, Quantico, Virginia; the American Helicopter Museum, West Chester, Pennsylvania; the National Aviation Hall of Fame; the National Transportation Safety Board; Lockheed Martin; the International Association of Eagles; Alabama National Guard, Army Aviation Support Facility, Mobile, Alabama; UPS; FedEx; the Canada Aviation Museum, Ottawa, Ontario; the Canadian Warplane Heritage Museum, Hamilton, Ontario; the Royal Aeronautical Society, London; the Imperial War Museum, Duxford, U.K.; the Royal Air Force Museum, Hendon and Cosford, U.K.; the Fleet Air Arm Museum, Yeovilton, U.K.; the Musée de l'Air et de l'Espace, Le Bourget, France; the Museo Storico Aeronautica Militare, Vigna di Valle, Italy; the Flygvapenmuseum, Linkoping, Sweden; and the Muzeum Lotnictwa Polskiego, Krakow, Poland.

Archive photographs came from the collections of Wright State University; the Smithsonian National Air & Space Museum; the Museum of Flight, Seattle; the National Museum of the United States Air Force; the National Museum of Naval Aviation, Pensacola; General Microfilm; the National Archives; Library of Congress Prints and Photographs Division; USAF photos; Ministry of Defence, U.K.; Lockheed Martin; British Aerospace; Martin Baker; Boeing; Airbus; and from the private collections of the authors. In the United Kingdom, the staffs of Key Publishing (including *FlyPast* and *Air International* magazines) and *Aeroplane Monthly* magazine were kind enough to give us access to their unrivaled archives of aviation photography.

Particular thanks go to a number of individuals for their encouragement of our efforts and for finding and providing material for this volume: John Burson, Tanya Caffrey, Francesco De Florio, Ken Ellis, Malcolm English, Michael Fopp, Hill Goodspeed, Jose Gueits, Henry Hall, Richard Hallion, Tony Harmsworth, Bill Harrell, Bob Hower, Ted Inman, Phil Jarrett, Magnus Karlsson, Mike Lee, Lydia

Matharu, David McFarland, Floyd McGowin, Graham Moffatt, Donald Nijboer, Michael Oakey, Dennis Parks, Bob Rasmussen, Karen Remaly, Mark Rogers, Nick Stroud, Katherine Williams and Kenneth Woodcock. *War & Peace in the Air* also benefited hugely from the generosity of a number of distinguished aviation artists, whose work decorates many of the pages in the book: Gil Cohen, Gerald Coulson, Jim Dietz, Sam Lyons, Paul Rendel, Chris Stone, Michael Turner and Philip West. Our particular thanks go also to Colin Hudson and Rick Taylor of Aces High Aviation Gallery. Photographic colleagues who have provided images, advice and contacts include Mariusz Admaski of Warsaw, Poland, Erik Hildebrandt, and Jay Miller.

In Dayton, Ohio, help for the final chapter came from Betty and Jack Darst, Nancy Horlacher, Ernie and Karen Sheeler, Larry Blake (Superintendent of the Dayton National Aviation Heritage National Park) and his staff, Dawne Dewey and the staff at Wright State University, Nick Engler, Mary Jane Favorite and the staff of the Wright Brothers Aeroplane Company, Walt Davis (Director of the Aviation Department at Sinclair Community College), Martha Lunken, Ron Kaplan (Executive Director of the National Aviation Hall of Fame) and his staff, the First to Fly Foundation, Lawrence Patterson and Margaret Patterson, and the Wright family, Amanda Wright Lane, Stephen Wright and Marion Wright, without whose ancestors this would have been a different story.

We would be sadly remiss if we did not conclude this eight year epic without recognizing the sterling efforts made by our publishers. When all the field work is done, the research complete, the photographs processed and selected, the text written and rewritten, and the basic design of the books mapped out, the raw material passes to the professionals. For the authors, this could be an anxious time. Will their work be properly handled? Will the end result come up to their inflated expectations? For us, the questions were superfluous. Those who proofread, suggested editorial improvements, brought life to the layouts and finally produced the books invariably calmed our fears and exceeded our hopes. John Denison, Kathy Fraser, and Noel Hudson of Boston Mills Press, and Andrew Smith of PageWave Graphics are remarkably gifted in the arts of handling difficult authors and of turning the base metal of authors' drafts into the gold of finished books.

Given the many and varied challenges faced during the eight-year gestation period of the Aviation Century series, the authors concede that they are surprised (and thankful) to find themselves still married — and to the same long-suffering ladies. In attempting to recognize the remarkable qualities of Paul and Cheryl in the previous four volumes, the authors have struggled each time to find words and phrases that could do them justice. Our wives have been described as giving us unfailing support, feeding and watering us, lifting us when we were down, following us on our peregrinations, bearing our idiosyncrasies, consoling us in failure, applauding us in success, and even carrying our bags. We have admitted that they have indulged our fantasies, boosted our confidence, discouraged stagnation, calmed rising blood pressures, tolerated eccentric behavior, borne inconvenience, smiled in adversity, dried our tears, and shouldered the burdens we have placed on them with quite remarkable grace. We have drawn attention to the way they have stiffened our backbones by their encouragement and cooled our sweating brows with their caring hands. We have even confessed that they have calmed us in times of stress, found encouraging words when progress was slow, applied restraint when ebullience threatened judgment, countered despair with patient counsel, and eased exhaustion with pleasant companionship. What more can we say, except once more to offer them our love and heartfelt thanks.

FOREWORD
Tom Burbage

THE FIRST CENTURY of manned power flight saw many dramatic advances as engineers and pioneers pushed the limits of technology, physics and courage. The evolution of four combat aircraft capabilities — performance, lethality, survivability and interoperability — was characterized by periods of gradual improvement punctuated by revolutionary breakthroughs.

Performance: Fighters evolved from single-role, daytime-only operations to multirole, day and night missions. Who can forget the mantra of recent conflicts where coalition forces "owned the night"? The next step is to "own the weather." Future fighters will be multirole, day and night, all-weather assets. Aerodynamic performance also evolved as tactical aircraft moved from canvas and glue, to aluminum, to composites and exotic metals. Flight control systems evolved from cables and pulleys, to hydraulically and electrically augmented systems, to fly-by-wire, converting aerodynamic instability into breathtaking maneuverability. Revolutionary change in combat aircraft performance came with the introduction of the jet engine, making possible the leap from incremental to dramatic improvement, more than doubling altitude and tripling airspeed.

Lethality: The capability to fire bullets and drop gravity weapons within visual range has progressed into the employment of sophisticated missiles and precision weapons from unprecedented distances. While once it was problematic even to hit an airfield, ordnance can now be placed through a specific window of a building by remote control. The number of weapons required to destroy a target has shrunk from many to one. Additionally, airborne imagery and targeting will soon be in the hands of the individual soldier on the ground.

Survivability: Early advantages in altitude, speed and maneuverability were lost as surface and air-to-air missile technology developed. Electronic warfare became the key to survivability as electronic jamming of detection systems and the employment of decoys swung the advantage back to the airplane. The revolutionary breakthrough in survivability was the advent of "stealth," dramatically reducing aircraft signature in all domains — noise, visual, infrared and others. Its effect is most profound in the radar spectra.

The SR-71 introduced first-generation stealth. Vehicle shape and special coatings to withstand skin temperatures generated by triple-sonic speeds reduced detection. Second-generation stealth came in the shapes of the Have Blue research vehicle and the F-117 Nighthawk. Faceted surfaces and special treatments prevented radar energy returning to its source. Third-generation stealth introduced curved surfaces and improved aerodynamics with the B-2. The F/A-22 represents the fourth generation, recapturing the best aerodynamic performance while designing in stealth features such as edge alignment, engine line-of-sight blockage and internal carriage of stores. American industry's research and development investment has made stealth technology easier to manufacture, own, operate and maintain. Today's newest aircraft, the F-35, incorporates fifth-generation stealth and leverages the huge advantage of tactical surprise with sensor fusion and defensive countermeasures.

Interoperability: Air combat evolved from an individual art, often done "alone and unafraid," to true joint and coalition warfare. The Information Age fueled this transformation. The next generation of fighters will be high-performance, stealthy, lethal information nodes on the Combat Global Information Grid, a prolific source and hungry user of data on the battlefield internet. With it, the United States and its allies will be able to reduce the cost to make, own, operate, maintain and sustain their forces as global battles continue to shape our world.

In this volume of the Aviation Century series, the authors succeed in bringing together the threads of aeronautical development in the jet age. It is a story well told and worth the telling, full of spectacular technological achievement, remarkable characters and extraordinary machines.

TOM BURBAGE, FORT WORTH, TEXAS, SEPTEMBER 2005

Tom Burbage is Executive Vice President and General Manager JSF, Lockheed Martin Aeronautics Company.

FOREWORD
Walter Boyne

IT IS A PRIVILEGE to be allowed to participate in even this minor way in what I believe to be the major aviation publishing event in recent history. The five volumes that comprise the Aviation Century series are a glorious tribute to the people and the technology that have made aviation such a fascinating subject. They are also a benchmark for writers, photographers and publishers for the future.

I still remember vividly the awe I felt when I saw the first book of the series, *Aviation Century The Early Years*. It was far better than any book of its kind that had ever been done before, both in conception and in execution. Author Ron Dick's text was a delight to read, extremely accurate, balanced and filled with amusing and insightful side notes. Dan Patterson's photography was superb, of the highest artistic as well as technical quality.

The authors had put many years and doubtless much expense into the development of the project, and the first book delivered handsomely. Credit goes to Boston Mills Press, as well. After so many years in the business, I really couldn't believe that there was any publisher that would have the courage and the vision to undertake so ambitious a series of books. The question that arose, of course, was if they could match the first book in subsequent volumes.

Each subsequent book, *Aviation Century The Golden Age, Aviation Century World War II, Aviation Century Wings of Change* and now, *Aviation Century War & Peace in the Air*, matched and perhaps cumulatively exceeded the quality of the very first book.

The entire effort is a tour de force, a triumph of will, energy, knowledge and devotion in an inherently noble cause. I say this because implicit in the series is a genuine reverence for the really admirable qualities that make the science, discipline, career, hobby or simple love of aviation meaningful.

The fifth book in the series must have been the most challenging for the authors, not just because the previous work had been so excellent, but because many factors in aviation have changed. One of the most prominent of changes has been the increased longevity, versatility and expense of aircraft. These have combined to reduce the

numbers required, and this in turn has led to a vast reduction in the number of companies producing them. Further, the public has become jaded as flying has become commonplace. In the Golden Age, the Cleveland Air Races were so important they knocked the World Series of baseball out of the headlines. Today the Reno Air Races get zero national attention. In a similar way, the aviation exploits of World War II had a universal appeal, while air warfare today is regarded with a calm indifference by all but the participants.

Dick and Patterson overcome these hazards brilliantly in *Aviation Century War & Peace in the Air*, recounting the swift progress of military aviation in the jet age, looking into the fascinating if sometimes frightening world of aviation safety and aircraft accidents, and finally peering into the crystal ball of the future.

Forewords rarely provide investment advice, but a canny investor might just buy four or five sets of these books, get them autographed, and then put them away as a nest egg for his or her grandchildren. They are that good.

WALTER J. BOYNE, ASHBURN, VIRGINIA, SEPTEMBER 2005

Walter Boyne is a former director of the National Air and Space Museum of the Smithsonian Institution. He enlisted as a private in the United States Air Force in 1951 and retired in 1974 as a colonel with more than 5,000 hours in a score of different aircraft, from a Piper Cub to a B-52. He has written more than 400 articles on aviation subjects and is one of the few authors to have had both fiction and nonfiction books on the New York Times *bestseller lists.*

PHOTOGRAPHER'S PREFACE
Dan Patterson

THIS FINAL VOLUME of the Aviation Century series brings to a conclusion more than eight years of shared work to create a history of aviation in the 20th century. Ron and I have adhered to our original outline as much as we thought possible. Where we have strayed from our plan has been into territory we did not even know about when we began. But we planned our travels and schedules with enough "wiggle room" to be able to react to and take advantage of great things that we knew would happen along the way, even if we didn't know where or when or how we would discover them.

Many of these serendipitous sidetracks have been associated with one of the overriding goals of our project, and that was to record a human history, especially by making portraits of a real cross section of the individuals who have been wrapped up in this amazing century of aviation history. Some of these portraits were arranged in advance, some only after many letters, e-mails and telephone calls. In most cases, once we got through the gate, the people we wanted to include in this project were happy to do whatever they could for us and ended up fascinated with what we have accomplished.

The "sidetracks" have brought to our project some memorable treasures: Larry Pisoni in Vezzano, Italy (*World War II*), the Polish warriors in Warsaw (*World War II*), Contessa Caproni in Rome (*The Early Years*), Mike Novacell (*Wings of Change* and *War & Peace in the Air*) and Neil Armstrong, a man who walked on another sphere a long way away and refers to himself as "just another aviator" (*Wings of Change*). Their faces — their expressions, the way they lift their chins, the gleam in their eyes — tell many stories. The portraits of the survivors of early flight have been most sought after, offering through their eyes an invaluable window into the time period when anyone could climb into an airplane and do something no one had ever done before. Alex Henshaw is one of those people (*The Golden Age*) and at this writing is still among us and continues to share his considerable accumulated wisdom.

We also decided to invite our colleagues who not only photograph aviation but also paint, illustrate and sculpt new visions of this rich history to participate. Those artists we asked gladly and graciously added to this body of work, allowing us to see moments in time whose only record is in the memory of the participants, in the recollections of someone waiting on the ground, or in a military debriefing, or a smudged carbon in a dusty folder. These talented friends have added their personal vision to this project, and this series is better for it.

At the end of the day — in this case, the conclusion of this adventure — it is really all about flying. Amanda Wright Lane wrote about what her uncle Orville thought about seeing the Earth from above in her foreword to *Aviation Century The Early Years*. For me, flying solo — alone in the sky — there is always a connection to the pioneers of flight. Once you get away from the airport and have the airplane trimmed for straight and level flight, once you've pulled the power back to cruise and leaned out the fuel mixture, you can look around and connect with those pioneers. The early fliers were flying solo as well. It's fun to imagine the moment when they became comfortable enough in their "aeroplane" to consider where they were and what they could see from above.

The relevance of this endeavor will take some time to sink in. As far as our initial goal, to make a history of aviation that had not been done before, we are pleased with the results. The scope of the project became wider and more far flung than either of us imagined, but our flexibility allowed that to happen, along with our very understanding and professional colleagues at Boston Mills Press. Personally, this has been a once-in-a-lifetime experience and I am just starting to come to grips with what it will be like to not have this as an excuse to not mow the lawn.

Dan Patterson
Dayton, Ohio
January 2006

INTRODUCTION
Air Vice-Marshal Ron Dick

IN 1997, DAN PATTERSON and I agreed that we would make the effort to put together a history of powered flight's first hundred years. The premise of the book was to be that aviation had changed the world more than anything else in the 20th century, and its pages were to tell the stories of the people involved as well as tracing the development of their flying machines. Given the immense scope of the project, and the knowledge that we could not really do it justice even if we produced a whole library of books, we knew that we would not have the luxury of delving into minute detail on every aspect of flight. Nevertheless, we set out to give at least some idea of how human flight had changed everyday life — technologically, militarily, economically, sociologically and politically.

At first, the plan was to pack all that material into one very large book. It became apparent that, unless it was to be sold with a wheelbarrow, that was impractical. The Aviation Century series of five volumes seemed to be a far better idea. It allowed us to stick to the original concept without compromising, while designing each book to be capable of standing alone. To ensure that the books would be as rich in content as possible, the text had to be comprehensive, it had to be well illustrated by archive images and the work of distinguished aviation artists, and it had to feature new color photography by Dan, including portraits of the people of aviation, both the famous and those with humbler aeronautical associations.

If we had grasped the true enormity of the task we had set ourselves when we began, we might have been persuaded to settle for something less demanding. The Aviation Century project has consumed a large part of our lives for eight years and taken us to nine countries. The text and captions comprise some half a million words, and Dan's cameras have captured thousands of images, with the work being done in the world's great aviation museums and with aeronautical organizations great and small. In the process, we have been privileged to meet many of the celebrated aviators who made the history recorded in these books, and we have talked to hundreds of people who may not be so well known, but whose enthusiasm for flying is an essential part of the aviation world. It has been a wonderful experience, so much so that it almost demands a book about doing the books.

This final volume of the series is arranged in three main chapters and an epilogue. Chapter 1 picks up the story of military aviation after World War II, and traces the revolutionary effects of the jet age on air-power doctrine. Everything about air forces changed with the introduction of the jet engine, not only equipment and operations but also training, logistics and administration. Aircraft played vital parts in the endless succession of major wars and minor conflicts that took place in various regions of the world after World War II, and the importance of planning and waging successful air campaigns grew as the decades of the 20th century passed. It could be claimed, however, that the significance of the particular airframe used actually declined. In between the World Wars, aircraft often reached obsolescence only a year or so after joining front-line squadrons, and the early years of the jet revolution also saw rapid equipment changes. By the end of the century, things had changed. Air forces found themselves still flying many machines designed thirty or forty years before. Some new types were introduced, but for the most part increased capability came not from new aircraft but from improvements in weaponry, avionics and aircraft systems. The successors of the basic bombers and gunfighters of the 1950s were transformed by such marvels as GPS (Ground Positioning System), FLIR (Forward Looking Infra-Red), stealth technology, and precision weapons. Although they were fewer in number than their WWII counterparts, the influence of aircraft over the battlefield was immensely greater.

Chapter 2 takes a brief look at the safety of flight, and examines some of the disasters that have shaped the way in which accidents are investigated and flight safety has been improved. Developments in this field have pulled in opposite directions. Aircraft structures are much safer than they were fifty years ago, and engine reliability is now such that failures are extremely rare events. As the machines have improved, however, they have also increased in number, introducing formidable challenges for air traffic control, especially near busy airports such as Atlanta, Chicago and London's Heathrow. From a passenger's point of view, even more powerful in its effect on the experience of flying has been the rise of terrorism. Security screening of people and their bags, sky marshals and sniffing dogs have all become accepted as necessary elements of traveling by air with a commercial carrier. These measures have added to the rising costs of operating an airline, so encouraging the trend to denser seating and the cattle-truck atmosphere of tourist class cabins. The days of strolling casually to the departure gate are already fading memories, and stories of flying boat passengers enjoying amenities such as a lounge and bar seem to be the stuff of legend. Going by air may be the safest way to travel, but it comes with a heavy burden of side effects, most of which are uncomfortable and add to the stress of flying.

In Chapter 3, we consult the crystal ball and try to discern what might happen to aviation within the Earth's atmosphere in the future. In effect, the 20th century neatly packaged the development of atmospheric aviation. Unless a form of gravity shield is discovered, it is unlikely that we will see any truly revolutionary changes to match those that followed the introduction of the jet engine. No doubt there will be improvements, but it is probable that they will merely modify or build on what is already available. Airliners may become more efficient or grow larger. There might be a return to supersonic travel once it becomes possible to design aircraft that trail less intense and therefore quieter shockwaves. Executive aircraft could experience a boom as businessmen do their best to avoid the trials of increased airline security. Airships lifted by vast amounts of safe helium, powered by steerable turbines and touting immense cargo holds, might finally bury the memory of the Hindenburg and become commercially viable.

If commercial aviation is to see real change, it must start with improvements on the ground. Security screening is here to stay, but there must be ways to make the passage from street to aircraft less painful. Self-service check-in helps, and biometric identification can speed the transition, but can airport terminals be designed so that passengers feel less like so many heads of cattle being driven to market?

Changes in military aviation could be more dramatic. Unmanned aerial vehicles will form a growing part of the front line, first with U.S. forces but increasingly elsewhere. Development of air power's unmanned element has begun and could follow a similar path to that of military flying in WWI. First comes reconnaissance, then the occasional attack, albeit this time with precision weapons rather than hand grenades heaved over the side. How long before there is aerial combat between unmanned aircraft? Will the heirs of Boelcke and Ball, Hartmann and Bong be manufactured by Microsoft? With the era of aircraft such as the B-2 and F-35, have we finally reached the zenith of costly manned aerial weapons systems?

Composite structures, ceramics, blended wings, flexible wings, scramjets, solar power, hydrogen power, collision avoidance systems, computer-driven air traffic control — there are myriad ways in which aviation could change in the decades to come. Predictions are cheap, but it is likely that, as in the past, many developments will take us by surprise.

The book ends by taking the Aviation Century series full circle and returning to powered aviation's roots. The centenary year of 2003 saw a number of commemorative ventures aimed at reproducing the Wright brothers' experience. Dan Patterson flew with them and his camera followed their activities, documenting their efforts and recording their success. The images serve to remind us how far aviation advanced in just one hundred years. They also offer a reminder of the Wrights' extraordinary achievement. On December 17, 1903, on a cold, lonely stretch of sand in North Carolina, they opened the door to the aviation century and began a process that eventually had its effect on the life of every human being on the planet. Man took flight and the world was forever changed.

Ron Dick
Fredericksburg, Virginia
January 2006

CHAPTER 1

Military Aviation in the Jet Age

As the dust settled on World War II's battlefields, and the unbridled death and destruction of global war faded into history, the principal combatants confronted the spectacle of their awesome military power and wondered what they were going to do with it. The nations involved had expended enormous resources in constructing the vast military machines needed to engage in armed conflict on an unprecedented scale. Now, with peace declared and the astronomical cost being counted, these juggernauts were suddenly an unbearable and, it was fervently hoped, unnecessary burden in a world shattered and exhausted by years of suffering and devastation. It was surely time to take off the uniforms and turn the swords into plowshares.

MANAGING THE PEACE

The air forces of the victorious Allied nations faced the peace in different ways. In September 1945, there were 2,250,000 people in the United States Army Air Force operating nearly 64,000 aircraft, over 31,000 of which were front-line combat types. In the course of the war the USAAF had taken delivery of some 159,000 combat aircraft. Almost 23,000 of these were lost in combat and perhaps as many again in non-operational accidents. The technology of aviation under the spur of wartime operations marched on at such a pace that combat aircraft rapidly became disadvantaged as one side or the other introduced new and better models, and so huge numbers were withdrawn from service as obsolete as the war dragged on. Now, the fury and the passion of the worldwide struggle spent, Americans looked at their massive armed forces in the bright light of the promised peace and thought that the services themselves were obsolete, at least in their WWII size and shape. Demobilization and disarmament followed with almost

Artifacts from the National Museum of the United States Air Force tell the stories of military aviation in the jet age. In 1947 the United States Air Force became an independent service, built upon the traditions of the U.S. Army Air Force. General Billy Mitchell's red flag is draped across a wooden ammunition crate from Operation Desert Storm. Beneath that can be seen a World War I recruiting poster and a World War II navigation map showing East Anglia, home of the Eighth Air Force in the United Kingdom. The medals of Don Gentile are at center. A desk model of an A-7 Corsair II stands on a WWII leather flying jacket. At bottom left are photos from the earliest days of U.S. military flying, showing Orville Wright demonstrating the Flyer at Fort Myer, Virginia. At bottom center is an image of a Berlin Airlift C-54.

LEFT *The Messerschmitt 262 Schwalbe (Swallow) was first flown as a pure jet on July 18, 1942, and though production was seriously delayed by Hitler's insistence that it should be used as a bomber rather than a fighter aircraft, it was the world's first turbojet aircraft to become operational. On July 25, 1944, an Me 262 was also the first jet to see combat when it attacked an RAF reconnaissance Mosquito over Munich. Once cleared for use as a fighter, the Schwalbe's superior speed and heavy armament enabled it to score heavily against bomber formations. However, hundreds of Me 262s were destroyed on the ground by the Allied air offensive, and of the more than 1,400 produced, fewer than 300 flew in combat.*
ABOVE *The Bell P-59 Airacomet was the first U.S. jet aircraft. It had relatively clean lines, but the combination of its considerable weight, thick wings and first-generation jet engines restricted its performance, which was not good enough to allow it to be developed as a front-line fighter.*

reckless haste. By December 1945, the mighty USAAF had shrunk by nearly a million and a half to 890,000 personnel, and six months later the aircraft establishment had been cut in two, leaving some 34,000 machines of all types still on strength. War fighting capability was even more severely affected. Of the 218 combat groups flying on VJ Day, only eleven were considered operational in 1946. The aviation units of the U.S. Navy and Marine Corps experienced similar, if not quite such alarming, reductions.

In Britain, the Royal Air Force moved toward demobilization more slowly. Lingering pretensions of worldwide imperial responsibility helped bring about a less rapid rundown of the armed forces. Even so, the personnel strength of the RAF fell from over a million to 300,000 between the end of the war in Europe and December 1946. At the same time, the number of squadrons in the front line went down from 487 to 100, with most of the survivors existing on single flight establishments. The Soviet Union, on the other hand, finished World War II with about 17,500 combat aircraft on strength, and by 1946 still had some 14,000 available, a figure that soon thereafter began to rise again as new types were introduced and the Soviets prepared for their confrontation with the capitalist nations of the West.

First-Generation Jets

Much of the work of modernizing and reorganizing air forces in the postwar years made little impact on the general public. The paradox of having shrinking services with expanding opportunities was not understood by many people. With the war over, the average person was content to let someone else worry about such weighty matters as military affairs and esoteric problems like high-speed aerodynamics. Nevertheless, few people were left unaware that great changes were on the wing in the world of aviation.

A host of aerodynamic problems needed solving to make the most of the jet engine's promise. Some answers were already on the way. Among the most important were those revealed at the end of World War II when the results of German research fell into the hands of the Allies. Aircraft such as the Messerschmitt 262 and Arado 234, powered by axial-flow jet engines, full of teething troubles though they were, were more advanced than anything flying elsewhere. Captured jet aircraft were studied avidly by the Allied powers, and German scientists and designers found themselves spirited away to work either in the Soviet Union or the West, depending on who had been their "liberators." Particularly significant was the work done in Germany using swept wings as a method for delaying and diminishing compressibility drag.

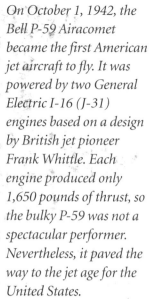

On October 1, 1942, the Bell P-59 Airacomet became the first American jet aircraft to fly. It was powered by two General Electric I-16 (J-31) engines based on a design by British jet pioneer Frank Whittle. Each engine produced only 1,650 pounds of thrust, so the bulky P-59 was not a spectacular performer. Nevertheless, it paved the way to the jet age for the United States.

ABOVE The P-59 cockpit seemed almost as conventional as its airframe, but the throttle needed careful handling. First-generation jet engines were intolerant of rapid throttle movements and flameouts could be induced easily by a heavy hand. LEFT The maximum combined thrust emerging from the P-59's jet pipes at full throttle was only 4,000 pounds, but it was sufficient to propel the straight-winged Airacomet along at 410 mph at 30,000 feet. (In 1942, the Me 262 was achieving well over 500 mph at heights greater than 20,000 feet.)

LEFT *The North American B-45 Tornado was designed before German swept-wing research became available after World War II. It first flew in March 1947 and was ordered into production as an interim stage in the USAF's conversion to a jet bomber force. The later reconnaissance version, RB-45C, proved invaluable, often crossing hostile frontiers to gain photographic and electronic intelligence of Warsaw Pact countries.* RIGHT *The XB-48 was the Martin response to a specification for a jet bomber issued by the USAAF in 1944. It was powered by six turbojets of 3,800 pounds thrust each. Only two were built, and it was canceled when it was found to be inferior to the Boeing B-47 in performance and development potential.*

Having been behind in the race to produce a jet engine, the United States was quick to make up for lost time. In September 1941, Bell Aircraft was asked by the USAAF to design a jet fighter. Just one year later, the XP-59A was ready to fly. It was a large aircraft weighing over 13,000 pounds and, powered as it was by two General Electric-built Whittle engines of a modest 1,100 pounds thrust each, it was not the answer to a fighter pilot's dream. Production variants, delivered from August 1944 onward, were fitted with GE engines of 2,000 pounds thrust, but even then they were never lively performers. Nevertheless, the P-59 opened the door to the jet age for the USAF, and much better aircraft were not far behind.

Among the earliest was one from Kelly Johnson's design team at Lockheed. They had toyed with the idea of a jet aircraft in 1939, but had abandoned it for lack of an engine and in the face of bureaucratic indifference. In 1943, the USAAF asked them to try again, replacing indifference with urgency and stipulating a time limit of 180 days between the request and first flight. Lockheed responded by having the XP-80 ready in 143 days. It first flew on January 8, 1944, and inspired enthusiasm from the start. It was a delight to fly and, even though powered by a de Havilland engine of only 2,460 pounds thrust, it was capable of exceeding 500 mph. Production P-80s were larger and heavier, but also more powerful and faster. In April 1944, the USAAF

placed orders for 1,000 P-80As, and four reached Europe before World War II was over, but too late to see any action. Lockheed's basic design would prove to be one of the most enduring of the jet age. The two-seat T-33 version, universally known as the "T-Bird," became the world's best-known jet trainer and was still in service with more than a dozen air forces over fifty years after the XP-80 first flew.

Few of the early bids to enter the jet race were nearly so successful as the P-80 and its offspring. In the rush to take advantage of the new technology, jet engines of limited thrust were often married with airframes that still lingered in the piston-engined era and the resulting performance figures were disappointing. Experimental bomber designs such as the XB-46 and XB-48 were essentially conventional aircraft fitted with jet engines. So was the North American B-45, but it was ordered into production anyway as an interim measure. Orthodox airframes persisted in the fighter world, too. Republic produced the F-84 Thunderjet, a tough and reliable single-seater that later led to greater things, and Northrop followed up the successful P-61 with the F-89 Scorpion, another large, heavily armed night fighter with a shape seemingly made to encourage drag. (The USAF replaced the P for Pursuit designation with F for Fighter on June 10, 1948.) Designers at Boeing and North American were the first to incorporate German swept-wing discoveries into their military aircraft. Both

LEFT *The Gloster Meteor was the first British jet fighter, and the first jet aircraft in the world to become operational with a front-line squadron when it reequipped 616 Squadron, RAF, in July 1944. (The Messerschmitt 262, flown by an experimental unit, was the first to see combat, also in July 1944.) Meteors were based in the United Kingdom and used against the V-1 flying bombs, destroying their first on August 4, 1944.* RIGHT *Originally known as the Spidercrab, the prototype of the twin-boomed de Havilland Vampire first flew on September 20, 1943, but Vampire 1s did not reach squadron service until they were delivered to 247 Squadron in March 1946. Smaller, lighter and less powerful than the Meteor, the Vampire was a delight to fly and was much loved by its pilots.*

companies had been working on jet designs with straight wings, but moved quickly to incorporate sweepback. The results were Boeing's B-47 Stratojet and North American's F-86 Sabre, two of the most outstanding military aircraft ever built.

Research and development in Britain was hamstrung for a while by postwar austerity measures. The government of the day was not inclined to spend money on new technologies and was generally content to see the RAF make do with what was already available. Britain's first jet fighters, the Gloster Meteor and the de Havilland Vampire, were sound enough designs but they embodied the aerodynamics of the previous generation and lacked development potential. Ironically, the widely publicized achievements of both aircraft (such as the Meteor's world speed records of 606 mph in 1945 and 616 mph in 1946, and the first jet crossing of the Atlantic by Vampires in 1948) served only to reinforce the official view that the RAF's equipment was more than adequate. As a result, the first successful British transonic aircraft, the Hawker Hunter, would not enter service until 1954, by which time the United States was already introducing the North American F-100, the first operational jet capable of supersonic speeds in level flight. Meanwhile, RAF Bomber Command was forced to soldier on with the piston-engined Avro Lincoln, which was little more than an overgrown WWII Lancaster.

Turbojet development in the Soviet Union did not really begin until after World War II, when the fruits of German and British technology became available. In the preface to the 1948 edition of *Jane's All the World's Aircraft*, the editor wrote: "Since the war, Russia has made good use of the Eastern German industry. Experimental establishments, factories, equipment, prototypes, and, in particular, technicians have all been taken over and this accession of technical equipment, knowledge and personnel, merged

The Tornado exhibited at the National Museum of the USAF is a B-45C. It was flown to the museum in 1971 and carries the markings of the 47th Bomb Group, based in the United Kingdom from 1952 to 1955.

For obvious reasons, the Swedes named their SAAB J 29 Tunnan, which is Swedish for barrel. SAAB took advantage of German research and adapted what had originally been planned as a straight-winged jet aircraft to a swept-wing design. The J 29 was Europe's first swept-wing jet fighter and became the only Swedish aircraft to see combat when five of them were used as part of a UN force in the Congo in 1961.

into Russia's gigantic aircraft industry and industrial potential, has no doubt been responsible for the remarkable progress which has taken place in recent years."

Among the first Soviet jet aircraft was the Yak-15, a hasty conversion of a piston-engined fighter, but the contemporary MiG-9 was an original straight-wing design. Both flew in April 1946 with engines based on the axial-flow Jumo 004 used in the Me 262. Neither these nor their immediate successors were considered anything more than interim fighters, and the Soviets were quick to spring a surprise on the world. In a controversial move, the British government had agreed to the export of Rolls-Royce Nene centrifugal-flow engines to the Soviet Union, and in 1947 the MiG-15 appeared, a swept-wing design built around the Nene and promising a performance to surpass anything

being flown in the West at the time. A workmanlike bomber was produced, too, in the Ilyushin 28, known by NATO as the Beagle.

The late 1940s saw a number of other countries beginning to build jet aircraft. The French aircraft industry began its peacetime resurgence with the experimental SO 6000 Triton, design studies of which were begun in 1943. By February 1949, the first of Marcel Dassault's celebrated line of fighters, the Ouragon, was flying. (Dassault had already established himself in French aviation under his original name of Marcel Bloch. He changed it on returning to France from imprisonment in Buchenwald concentration camp. It comes from the French for "attack" and was the code name of his brother Paul, who had been a leader in the French Resistance.) SAAB in Sweden converted their existing twin-boom piston-engined J 21 fighter to jet power in 1947, and went on to design the J 29, a barrel-shaped aircraft that flew in September 1948 and was the first swept-wing fighter be produced in postwar Europe. In Argentina, the Instituto Aerotecnico employed the French designer Dewoitine to design the single-seat Pulqui, which in 1947 became the first jet aircraft built and flown in Latin America. Engine industries were more difficult to establish, however, and all of these early ventures relied on Rolls-Royce to provide the power.

The Yakovlev Yak-23 was a development of earlier Yakovlev jet fighters, the Yak-15 and 17, which had in turn been derived from the piston-engined Yak-3 fighter of World War II. The principal difference in the Yak-17 and 23 was the introduction of a nosewheel undercarriage. With the appearance of the MiG-15, the Yak fighters were released for export and almost 100 were delivered to the Polish Air Force. The aircraft seen here was photographed by Dan Patterson in the Muzeum Lotnictwa Astronautyki at Krakow, Poland.

In 1944, the USAAF arranged with Douglas Aircraft to construct a new transport aircraft specifically for presidential use. Nicknamed Sacred Cow, *this VC-54C became the first military aircraft to transport a president of the United States when President Roosevelt took it to the Yalta Conference in February 1945. It is a C-54 with extensive interior modifications, including an elevator for the President and his wheelchair. The passenger compartment has a conference room with a large desk and bulletproof picture window. The* Sacred Cow *is on display in the Presidential Hangar of the National Museum of the USAF.*

American Independence

When Carl Spaatz took over from "Hap" Arnold as Commanding General, Army Air Forces, in February 1946, he was already working on how best to cope with force reduction while modernizing and reorganizing the USAAF for the future. Convinced by his own experience, Spaatz saw air power in global terms and believed that long-range bombers should form the core of U.S. air power. He also advocated of a strong Air National Guard and Air Force Reserve, emphasizing the importance of a well-funded research and development program. He worked with the confidence that independence for the Air Force could not be long delayed. In December 1945, President Truman asked Congress to introduce legislation to combine the War and Navy Departments. The completed draft of the National Security Act went to Congress at the end of February 1947. It provided for a single Secretary of National Defense and a separate Department of the Air Force, but was careful to stipulate that the Navy would retain control of its own aviation units and the Marine Corps. The bill was signed into law on July 26, 1947. Immediately after approving the National Security Act, Truman signed an executive order setting out the functions and roles of what were now three independent services. Appropriately enough, the papers were signed on board his official Air Force aircraft, the C-54 *Sacred Cow*. The Act was consummated with the formal appointment of officials — Stuart Symington as the first Secretary of the Air Force, and General Carl Spaatz as the new service's first Chief of Staff. Symington was sworn in on September 18, 1947, and that date was established as the official birthday of the United States Air Force. Billy Mitchell's vision had at last been given substance.

On July 26, 1947, VC-54C Sacred Cow *became the birthplace of the USAF when President Truman signed the National Security Act of 1947 while on board. Copies of the documents with the President's signature, together with the pen he used, are exhibited on his desk.*

A VIEW FROM THE COCKPIT

BY AUTHOR AIR VICE-MARSHAL RON DICK

IN 1952, I WAS POSTED to RAF Finningley in Yorkshire to begin my conversion to jet aircraft. Like the majority of pilots who formed the first-generation jet squadrons, I was straight from training and had little experience to fall back on. For us, the transition to the kerosene-breathing monsters was often a dramatic business — exhilarating, demanding and, on occasion, frightening. Even when the basic conversion was successfully accomplished, getting to use the beasts effectively in their operational role was something else again. In the early 1950s, most new air force pilots learned to fly in an aircraft like the North American T-6, known in the RAF as the Harvard. With all lessons learned about propellers and tailwheels, and wings duly gained, the RAF graduate of the fifties moved on to the Gloster Meteor for jet conversion in an experience fairly typical of that undergone by new military pilots everywhere. At this stage, few prospective aces had seen a Meteor or any other jet from close up. The first encounter almost invariably helped to remove some of the swagger from any young pilot's step.

For one thing, the Meteor was almost twice as long as a Harvard and three times as heavy. It had two engines, stuck well out in the wings, and the nacelle for each appeared big enough to swallow a Harvard fuselage. It seemed obvious that what was left of the wing outside the engines could not possibly be adequate for the job of getting the whole creation off the ground. After all, the span was 5 feet less than that of the Harvard, and the Harvard wing was not encum-

bered with large rotating chunks of metal. The cockpit was something of a shock, too. The trainer version of the Meteor, the Mk. 7, had its two seats in tandem. These were covered by a long and very heavy single-piece canopy, which was hinged along its right side. To get into the cockpit, we seized the canopy by handles on its left-hand edge and heaved it open. The perceived similarity to a coffin lid was immediate and unforgettable. It was not for nothing that the RAF's pet name for the Meteor was "Meatbox."

Once seated in the monster, I was not the only one to feel the first stirrings of agoraphobia. There was

ABOVE CENTER *Author Ron Dick converted to the Meteor after gaining his RAF wings in 1952.* RIGHT *Fifty years later, he renewed his acquaintance with an old friend in the RAF Museum.* OPPOSITE *The business end of the Meteor 8. Four 20 mm Hispano cannon were fitted in bays alongside the cockpit, two on each side of the nose. Meteor WH301 seen here is exhibited in the markings of 609 (West Riding) Squadron, RAuxAF, at the RAF Museum, Hendon, in northwest London.*

The Gloster Meteor 8 equipped twenty RAF Squadrons and ten squadrons of the Royal Auxiliary Air Force in the 1950s. Here the five Meteors of 64 Squadron's aerobatic team, which represented the RAF during the 1953/54 airshow seasons, turn in to begin their display.

almost nothing in front of me. Gone were the comforting curves of the cowling. It was painfully apparent that I was essentially in front of the aircraft. Far from being an integral part of anything, it appeared that I was to be separate from and pursued by this howling banshee.

Dropping my eyes, I could see that a few of the instruments were like those I had used in the Harvard, but there was also much that was unfamiliar. The altimeter had more needles, the airspeed was marked in knots instead of miles per hour, and the engine instruments looked strange. There were air brakes (oddly known as speed brakes in the United States), high-pressure fuel cocks and relight buttons. Clearly, there was a great deal with which I would have to become accustomed. Even the smell was different, and just starting the engines could be alarming. The Rolls-Royce Derwents were remarkably reliable but, as with all early examples of a new technology, they had distinct limitations and needed careful handling. When an engine start button was pressed, a low moaning began, rising steadily in pitch. Five seconds or so later, the undercarriage lights dimmed, and it was then necessary to move the appropriate high-pressure cock lever (near the floor to one side of the pilot's seat) to the half-open position. As engine rpm registered on the gauge and began to increase, the HP cock was eased slowly and steadily to the fully open position. Any tendency I might have to hurry the process was rewarded by a terrify-

ing resonance that shook the whole aircraft, a jet-pipe temperature-gauge needle that rose rapidly into the red zone, and a stream of invective from the instructor in the back cockpit. Once both engines were running, however, I found that the Meteor was a pleasure to taxi. The initial reluctance to move from standstill overcome, it rolled along quite happily with the engines at idle power, and the exposed position in the nose allowed me to find out what it was like to taxi in a straight line, instead of weaving drunkenly from side to side to see round the nose.

To those of us newly arrived from piston-engined training, the Meteor takeoff was exhilarating. Once we had the machine lined up on the runway, the engines were opened up to full power against the brakes. A final check of the engines (14,700 rpm — a startling figure after the Harvard's 2,250 rpm), then brakes off. The acceleration was quite brisk under the impulse of the two 3,500-pounds-thrust Derwents and the takeoff arrow straight. To counter the built-in tendency of piston-trained pilots to extend one leg automatically against a swing, the instructor usually had both boots clamped down hard on the rudder pedals at this stage. The nosewheel eased off the runway at 90 knots, and the Meteor took to the air at about 120 knots. Wheels had to be in the well before reaching 175 knots (or 201 mph, which was faster than most of us young pilots had ever flown, and that well before reaching the airfield boundary).

From then on, the thrill of seeing and feeling a truly dramatic expansion of the boundaries of aviation in every direction proved addictive. However, it was necessary to temper euphoria with caution. These jets were always ready to burn the casual hand, and at that time they were not fully understood, even by those who thought they knew it all. Unforgiving machines they were, yet pilots like us with a total flying time of just 200 hours or so, all on single piston-engined aircraft, were sent off for our first solo in the twin-jet Meteor after a mere 3 hours, 20 minutes dual instruction. We soon found that it was necessary to change mental gears when converting to jet aircraft. Everything happened so much more quickly, especially things like eating up distance and running out of fuel. By almost any standards the Meteor and most of its cousins became recovery emergencies not long after takeoff.

Fitted with the extra ventral tank, the Meteor's full fuel load was 595 gallons. A climb to 40,000 feet could consume almost 200 gallons of that. Minimum fuel for landing was 80 gallons, and a certain amount had to be set aside for the recovery to base. Less than half was available for the rest of the sortie. When the frequently dirty British weather is taken into account, together with the lack of radar coverage over mainland Britain and the minimal navigational equipment in the Meteor (VHF radio, G4F compass, E2 standby compass), the scale of the problem becomes evident. Those of us whose navigational training had been completed below 10,000 feet within 80 miles of base could find ourselves alone over the North Sea at 40,000 feet, 150 miles from home with 200 gallons or less left. It concentrated the mind.

One of the most significant differences between the piston engine and early jets was throttle response. The clever devices that now allow jet throttles to be slammed open or shut with impunity did not exist. Rapid movement of the throttle in either direction could lead to flaming out an engine and severe embarrassment for the pilot. This was true even at low level, and the problem became more acute with increasing altitude. Since this was combined with the absence of a foolproof engine relighting system, jet pilots who wished to survive soon developed a gentle touch on the throttle and cultivated the ability to anticipate the need

ABOVE *To a pilot trained in the T-6, the cockpit of the Meteor 8 represented a dramatic change. There were two throttles, an air-brake lever (speed brakes in the U.S.), an ejection seat, relight buttons, and an array of unfamiliar instruments.*

LEFT *Exhibited in the RAF Museum, Hendon, is a W2B engine, a reverse-flow turbojet built by the Power Jets company, founded by Frank Whittle. By 1944, it had been developed to produce 2,485 pounds of thrust. Examples were flown in Meteor prototypes, but it was a purely experimental unit that never entered mass production.*

to add power. (I should know. I was once ham-handed enough to flame out both engines at 30,000 feet over the North Sea and solid cloud cover. For a while, I was indeed seriously embarrassed.)

Another novelty was the Martin Baker ejection seat, which was still new enough to be regarded with some apprehension by most aviators. It was a long way from being the sophisticated creation of later years. For one thing, it relied on a gun rather than a rocket, so its upward acceleration was rather violent and inclined to be damaging to the user. For another, it was a "manual" seat. In other words, nothing happened automatically; the pilot was required to separate himself from the seat once clear of the aircraft. We had been trained in the routine of sliding open the canopy and bailing out, so we did not at first relish the thought of sitting on a high explosive charge as we went about our daily work, and we certainly did not like the idea of having to wrestle clear of the seat before pulling the parachute ripcord. This took time, and so it was wise to make an ejection decision with plenty of height available. Of course, that was not always possible, and many pilots were forced to take their lives in their hands quite close to the ground.

Experienced piston-engine aviators were often unsettled by the developments that accompanied the introduction of jets. The unforgiving nature of jet flight — considering the link between height and range — gave little comfort to those brought up in an age of rudimentary navigation aids when the best insurance policy was eye contact with the ground. Indeed, many of the challenges particularly associated with the early jets were in part the result of the unprecedented ease with which pilots could operate at altitudes above 30,000 feet. Rates of climb were not spectacular by later standards, but they were markedly better than the Harvard's, and jet aircraft kept climbing. The Meteor 7 could be through 40,000 feet some twelve minutes after takeoff, and I sometimes found myself as high as 46,000 feet. As the trainer version of the Meteor, the 7 was not weighed down with the luxuries carried by its day fighter sisters, such as ejection seats, guns, ammunition boxes and armor plate. It therefore was frequently used by wingmen flying in the top cover section of a squadron battle formation, simply because its performance was slightly better than the single-seaters.

The problem with that was that knowledge was patchy about the effects on aircraft or aircrew of flying at great heights. Besides having no combat equipment, the Meteor 7 lacked pressurization and yet we flew it wearing nothing more than standard flying clothing — lightweight flight suit, "Mae West" lifejacket, thin leather gloves, boots, and a soft flying helmet with a flexible, leaky oxygen mask. Not a thought was given to pressure breathing equipment, nor even to having masks that were tight and properly fitted. Limiting all Mk. 7s to a maximum of 30,000 feet might have been sensible, but nobody seemed to think that the medical reasons for doing so should be taken seriously and, anyway, the 7s were needed to fly top cover. During the Meteor 7's career, a number were lost "cause unknown" after flying at high altitude, but it is more than probable that, in most cases, the pilot had collapsed because his oxygen supply was inadequate. Many Mk. 7 aircrew (including me) suffered

Queen Elizabeth II's coronation took place on June 2, 1953. One of the day's events was a flypast over Buckingham Palace by over 600 aircraft of the Royal Air Force and Royal Canadian Air Force. Seen here are the Meteors of 64 Squadron from RAF Duxford, which led the Coronation Flypast.

In the early 1950s, RAF Fighter Command still had pairs of armed Meteors on standby at the end of the runway before dawn every day. Air traffic procedures at the time were not very sophisticated and aircraft approaching the United Kingdom were sometimes unidentified. In that event, a Dawn Patrol pair would be scrambled to intercept, and civil airline passengers were often surprised to find themselves the targets of the interceptions.

minor cases of bends and headaches, and pains in the ears were frequent, not to mention rumbling stomachs.

Flying a 7 with a cold could be excruciating. If we could not clear our ears during a descent, the Meteor did not have the fuel to allow us to take our time. More often than not, it was a case of having to keep the descent going and putting up with the pain until reaching a doctor's healing hand or, all too frequently, until the ear drum burst, bringing silence and blessed relief. Vision was a problem at altitude, too, though not generally appreciated at first. As budding fighter pilots, we were conceited about our eyesight and there was keen competition among us to see who could call in the most "bogies" during a sortie. With very little radar on the ground or in the air, sharp eyes were vital to an operational squadron. Unfortunately, later research showed

that the lack of visual cues at altitude makes most eyes drift to a resting position, focusing quite close to their owner. Aircraft several miles away, although perfectly visible under more normal circumstances, cannot be seen. Apart from the reduction in operational effectiveness, there was a hazard here. Aircraft on a collision course, particularly from head-on, could get surprisingly close before the pilots became aware of each other. Even the early jets went about their business above 20,000 feet at 8 or 9 miles a minute, so the time left for avoiding action could be brief, perhaps less than four seconds per mile of separation distance.

Of course, separation from other aircraft was the furthest thing from the minds of most of us in the years following World War II. Proximity was actively sought. Squadron and flight commanders were usually combat veterans and, for many of them, there was only one way to train fighter pilots. Aircraft had to be flown frequently, to their limits, and as often as possible in simulated combat. New boys like us, freshly arrived from training, could hardly believe the difference between the rigidly controlled and physically limited world of the Harvard and the riotous freedom of a first-generation jet squadron. Sometimes it seemed as though life was one long dogfight and, apart from the fact that the guns were not being fired, the rules were pretty loose. Rival squadrons would challenge each other and the briefing would consist of little more than an agreement to "meet at 30,000 feet with twelve aircraft each." The encounter was invariably exhilarating but it has to be said that it was unnecessarily hazardous for a peacetime air force.

The straight-winged Meteor, for one, was not always controllable at high speed. It ran into a brick wall at about Mach 0.82 and, if pressed beyond that, it resisted the experience with some spirit. The aircraft snaked, a strong nose-up change of trim occurred, and the ailerons were given to irregular snatching. Finally, one wing dropped sharply and the Meteor went off on its own for a while, deaf to the entreaties of its pilot. It was quite easy to induce this sequence of events when dogfighting at high altitude and absorbed in the thrill of the chase. Locked on to the enemy framed in the gunsight, the increasing Mach number went unnoticed until suddenly the aircraft was buffeting, the ailerons were snatching the stick left and right, and then the Meteor was on its back and heading downhill toward the comforts of thicker air and a lower Mach number. It was infuriating for us to be forced to leave a dogfight in this involuntary fashion, but nothing could be done until the aircraft had recovered its composure several thousand feet lower down.

In the absence of formal arrangements, anything that moved was fair game for a simulated attack and that included nonmilitary aircraft. Squadron briefing rooms were places to exhibit gun camera pictures of as many types as possible, and new ones, especially prototypes, were given pride of place. The Comet 1, the world's first jet airliner, caught during its initial flight trials, adorned many a crewroom wall. After some years of all this enjoyment, with several accidents and countless near misses, the boom was finally lowered and unauthorized dogfighting was banned. As air forces grew accustomed to both peace and jets, it was inevitable that airmen's egos would be squeezed and their freedoms would diminish.

However, there were plenty of other things about flying on a fighter squadron in the early 1950s that challenged a young man's moral fiber, and not all of them were reasonable or necessary. Many were just part of flying high-performance military aircraft, but others were hangovers from the way things were done in the heady days of World War II. Since the experienced squadron aviators operated that way, we new pilots gritted our teeth, copied our idols, and did not feel that we had joined the "big boys" until our flying had acquired the flair, dash and bad habits of our elders. Superficially, safety was important on a fighter squadron, but all too often it was not fully supported by the example of the squadron and flight commanders. It was too difficult to set aside those things that they had always done and that gave a bit of an edge to life. "Nobody lower than me" was the instruction given by many a leader to set a height for a low-level sortie. When he then left a wake on the surface of the sea, or passed between the hangars on a rival's airfield, most members of his squadron were too occupied with the exciting business of basic survival to pay much attention to the merging of his aircraft with its shadow.

More worrying was the formal instruction from higher headquarters that all Meteor pilots were required to complete at least five practice single-engine landings every month. This was a classic case of the problem not having been thought through. Engine failures were extremely rare and, when they did occur, a combination of adrenalin and common sense invariably ensured that the ensuing single engine landing was successful. (The Meteor was not difficult to land on one engine, especially if it was a declared emergency and everyone else got out of the way.) Practice engine failures, however, were common, and for that reason did not attract the attention they deserved, which was strange because they were real enough. In a curious hangover from piston-engine days, when single-engine landings were practiced with one propeller feathered, the rules said that the exercise in a Meteor should be carried out with the high-pressure cock closed on one engine, rather than with the engine throttled back to idle. The practice, therefore, was made real.

If one of us made a mistake on final approach (more likely than in an actual emergency, because adrenalin was

Meteors on Ice *by Chris Stone.*

was four times as high as it was for piston-engined aircraft, and there were some 200 fatal accidents each year involving the deaths of more than 300 aircrew. For a peacetime air force, these were shocking figures, and the RAF was not unique. Similar statistics were being compiled in other countries.

For those of us fortunate enough to experience the thrill of flying first-generation jets and survive, the life of a fighter pilot was exciting and a great deal of fun. The sheer exhilaration of operating high-powered machinery to its limits largely unhindered by the restraining hand of authority was a memorable experience, but there was a negative side to all this enjoyment. In an all-round comparison between the air forces of the 1950s and today, the pilots of the early jet period would probably be seen as being less professional than their modern counterparts. I would still maintain, however, that we first-generation jet pilots could fly, formate, navigate and shoot at least as well as any of our successors. Given the difficulties with which we had to cope, I believe that we could think quickly for ourselves in the air better than most. However, there is no denying that our flying discipline was relaxed, and we were seldom encouraged to develop a really deep knowledge of the many faceted business of being a fighter pilot. Even in the 1950s, there were those who had their doubts about the effectiveness of a system that purported to be training for war and produced so much uninhibited enthusiasm in its pilots while being so reluctant about turning to face the new realities of the jet age.

Early in 1953, after a live firing exercise against a towed target, one RAF fighter squadron flight commander wrote in his monthly report: "I am not sure about the squadron's ability to deal with a major attack on the United Kingdom by fast, high-flying Soviet bombers. However, if anyone dares to approach our shores towing a 30-foot-long canvas banner at 10,000 feet and 180 knots, we will probably give a good account of ourselves."

not flowing as fast) or if we were sent round again by air traffic, the need to cope with a single-engine overshoot was genuine, and, at low airspeed on one engine with wheels and flaps down, the Meteor did not always behave like a lady. It was possible to get away with it from as low as 125 knots (though the official single-engine safety speed was 155 knots) by using full rudder and a judicious amount of bank into the live engine. This was known as the "knee trembler." To hold the rudder on successfully, it was really necessary to keep the leg straight with the knee locked. The shoulder harness had to be tightened down hard, too, otherwise the rudder merely pushed the pilot back up against the canopy. A successful recovery from low airspeed on one engine left the pilot alive but with harness bruises on the shoulders and a knee given to uncontrollable bouts of trembling. All of this was probably very good for the character. Unfortunately, as a training exercise, it was unnecessary. Indeed, it is true to say that the RAF induced far more accidents from the practice of asymmetric landings than ever resulted from the real thing.

One fact about flying jets in the decade immediately following World War II is inescapable. The accident rate was appallingly high. Primitive aircraft, low experience levels, loose discipline, and "press on" attitudes combined with a lack of understanding of the need for changes led to the perpetuation of outdated techniques and practices. These elements came together to compile some horrifying statistics. In the years 1952/53, the RAF fatal accident rate for jets

SHOOTING STARS

The first operational U.S. jet fighter was the Lockheed P-80 Shooting Star, designed by Kelly Johnson and his "Skunk Works" team. It was the first production combat aircraft to exceed 500 mph in level flight, the first American jet-powered aircraft to score a victory in air-to-air combat, and was the victor in the world's first jet-versus-jet combat. It participated in the world's first operational combat mission assisted by air-to-air refueling, and a modified version held the world's air speed record for a brief time. F-80C FT-696 on display at the National Museum of the USAF is a combat veteran, having flown missions in Korea with the 35th Fighter Bomber Squadron, 8th Fighter Bomber Group. (The aircraft designation changed from P for Pursuit to F for Fighter in 1948.)

LEFT The P-80's cockpit was more complex than that of the earlier P-59. Note the ejection seat handle at lower left, and the pad on the gunsight, placed there in the hope of protecting pilots' good looks during accidents.

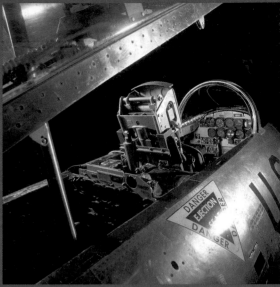

In May 1947, in response to an increasing number of P-80 accidents, Lockheed began work on a two-seat trainer version, which was designated T-33. The "T-Bird" was among the best known and most widely used of the first-generation jet aircraft. Over 5,600 were built in the United States, plus 866 in Japan and Canada. They served with the air forces of more than thirty nations, and many are still flying today in the hands of private warbird owners.

ABOVE The T-33 cockpit accommodated two pilots in tandem by adding a little more than 3 feet to the fuselage. The long and heavy single-piece canopy was hinged at the rear to ensure clean separation if it was jettisoned. The ejection seats protruded well above the cockpit rails, allowing pilots an excellent all-round view.

The Allison J-33 centrifugal-flow jet engine produced 4,600 pounds of thrust and was used to power the Lockheed P-80 and T-33. It was based on an original design by Frank Whittle.

Jet Turbulence

As the USAF wrestled with the challenges of its newly gained independence, all the major air forces were feeling the impact of revolutionary change. The jet engine had its effect, in varying degrees, on everything an air force did. Operational and training concepts, engineering practices, logistic support, equipment design and all kinds of administrative functions were reshaped by the hot breath of jet propulsion. However, it did not always happen as easily or as quickly as it might have done. Military organizations are notoriously conservative by nature and resistant to innovation. Air forces of the time generally were of the view that aircraft were aircraft, propellers or not, and they were often slow to recognize that fundamental change was being forced upon them.

For the pilot in the cockpit, the disappearance of the propeller was a considerable challenge. Many experienced aviators, seasoned by endless hours behind the pistons of World War II, found the absence of a reassuring whirling disc unsettling, and the thin whining of the new engines when heard from the cockpit was no substitute for the earthy, heart-warming roar of powerful reciprocating machinery. Nevertheless, seasoned pilots usually made light of the basic problem of converting to type. The actual flying of the airplane and adapting to the different techniques involved seemed to be a relatively simple matter. Eventually, almost anyone could get used to not having the silk scarf streaming in the breeze because the canopy was closed all the time, and could learn not to lunge forward automatically with a large bootful of rudder every time the throttle was opened. On the face of it, once a pilot gained familiarity with this strange phenomenon, the air forces' new toys could seem almost too easy to fly. Before the light dawned that jets really were different, and all the experience in the

Thousands of pilots from more than thirty countries gained their wings flying the North American T-6 Texan, known in the RAF as the Harvard. First flown in 1935, the T-6 family was by far the most important Allied training aircraft of World War II. Over 15,000 were built and hundreds were still flying in private hands seventy years after the first flight.

world counted for little unless it was accompanied by a willingness to learn, that attitude killed more than a few old, bold pilots.

"Boom"

Only days after the USAF became independent, an event occurred that excited public interest and pride in the accomplishments of America's professional military airmen. It was the first major achievement of the new USAF and it could hardly have been more auspicious in its promise for the future. During World War II, high-performance piston-engined aircraft such as the P-51 and the Spitfire sometimes reached very high speeds in dives and the pilots then encountered severe buffeting and control problems. These problems were experienced even more frequently in first-generation jets. To explore the unknown aerodynamic territory close to the speed of sound

On October 14, 1947, Chuck Yeager became the first man officially credited with flying faster than the speed of sound. His rocket-powered Bell X-1 Glamorous Glennis reached Mach 1.06 after being launched from a B-29 mothership.

where these phenomena occurred, Bell Aircraft developed the X-1, a small, bullet-shaped aircraft with thin, straight, laminar-flow wings, powered by a four-chamber liquid-fuel rocket motor. With all four chambers burning, the maximum thrust produced was 6,000 pounds and the four tons of fuel on board disappeared in only two and a half minutes. To get the most out of each flight, the X-1 was carried aloft in the belly of a B-29 and launched into free flight at 20,000 feet or higher. The initial proving flights of the X-1 were conducted by a Bell company test pilot, but when the aircraft had performed satisfactorily up to Mach 0.8, the Air Force took over the program. The pilot selected to fly the X-1 into regions unknown was Captain Charles E. "Chuck" Yeager, a man who had already built himself a considerable reputation with the P-51 in Europe. (Yeager's first flights in the X-1 took him to Mach 0.94 where his observations on elevator control led to the discovery that a "flying tail" — a moving solid slab horizontal stabilizer — offered greatly improved control at high Mach

numbers. That development later gave the F-86 Sabre a marked advantage in combat.)

On October 14, 1947, the X-1 was dropped from the B-29 over the California desert and Yeager fired up all four rocket chambers to climb away. At 36,000 feet he switched two chambers off again, and then. "Leveling off at 42,000 feet, I had thirty percent of my fuel, so I turned on rocket chamber three and immediately reached .96 Mach. I noticed that the faster I got, the smoother the ride. Suddenly the Mach needle began to fluctuate. It went up to .965 Mach — then tipped right off the scale…. We were flying supersonic!"

Chuck Yeager's achievement of becoming the first man to fly faster than sound won him both the Mackay and Collier Trophies. He had confirmed that the "sound barrier" was no barrier at all, and pointed the way for whole families of aircraft to follow the X-1 and make supersonic flight an everyday occurrence. For the USAF, it was an inspiring start to life as an independent service.

SWEDEN, ACTIVELY NEUTRAL

The displays at the Swedish Air Force Museum at Linköping tell the compelling story of the Swedish people's determination to defend their traditionally neutral status with equipment developed in Sweden. ABOVE The Saab J 21 was designed during World War II and served the Swedish Air Force from 1946 through 1954. Initially powered by a Daimler-Benz DB 605, the J 21 was converted to jet propulsion in 1947 with a de Havilland Goblin. The pusher design gave the J 21 excellent forward visibility and allowed the armament, consisting of a 20 mm cannon and four 13 mm machine guns, to be concentrated in the nose. INSET The cockpit of the J 21.

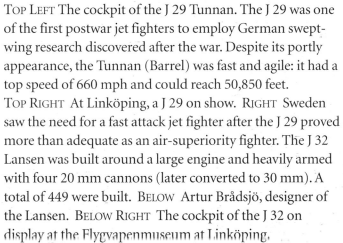

TOP LEFT The cockpit of the J 29 Tunnan. The J 29 was one of the first postwar jet fighters to employ German swept-wing research discovered after the war. Despite its portly appearance, the Tunnan (Barrel) was fast and agile: it had a top speed of 660 mph and could reach 50,850 feet.
TOP RIGHT At Linköping, a J 29 on show. RIGHT Sweden saw the need for a fast attack jet fighter after the J 29 proved more than adequate as an air-superiority fighter. The J 32 Lansen was built around a large engine and heavily armed with four 20 mm cannons (later converted to 30 mm). A total of 449 were built. BELOW Artur Brådsjö, designer of the Lansen. BELOW RIGHT The cockpit of the J 32 on display at the Flygvapenmuseum at Linköping.

The Saab J 35 Draken was designed to replace the J 29. More than fifty years later, Austria is still operating the long-serving fighter, of which 604 were built.

ABOVE The wing of the Draken is a double delta, which allows for enhanced performance characteristics at different speeds. The inner wing has a sweep angle of 80 degrees for high-speed performance, while the outer, 60-degree wing works for efficient low-speed flight, making the J 35 the ideal fighter for Sweden's well-hidden and at times short runways.

BELOW The Draken on display at Duxford in the United Kingdom.

TOP The cockpit of the Draken on display at the Flygvapenmuseum at Linköping.
BOTTOM A head-on view of the Draken reveals the low-to-the-ground layout and the mid-fuselage wing design.

TOP LEFT Erik Bratt, Saab's designer of the
J 35, has said how surprised he is that the
Draken is still in active service today.

TOP RIGHT The Saab JA 37 Viggen,
designed to replace the Draken, is a
progression of the very efficient and capable
high-speed jet fighters built by the Swedish
company. The Viggen retains the double
delta-wing shape and has added a canard
forward of the main wing.

LEFT The Saab design lineage is apparent
in this head-on view of a Viggen.

ABOVE The huge engine outlet for the
Viggen, powered by a Svenska Flygmotor
RM8B, a license-built version of the
Pratt & Whitney JT8D that powers
commercial airliners, but with an
afterburner.

THE ART OF WAR TURNS COLD
Operation Vittles

In the wider world, where the armed services functioned as instruments of international politics, headline-making achievements could not hide the USAF's shortcomings. Implicit in the Truman Doctrine was the need for an air force that could project power globally, but at the moment of its birth in 1947 the USAF's capability for fulfilling that role was severely limited. Strategic deterrence of Soviet expansionist ambitions seemed to depend solely on the U.S. nuclear monopoly and on the B-29 as a means of delivering a nuclear weapon. Respecting the weight of such a big stick, the Soviets chose to challenge the West in ways that would emphasize their strengths while minimizing the risk of a U.S. nuclear threat. In February 1947, the Czech government was overthrown in a Communist coup and the country became a Soviet satellite. Then, in the following month, the Soviets raised the stakes in Berlin. By so doing, they ensured that the first operational test of the USAF would not feature its front-line fighters and bombers. The stars of this show were to be haulers of food and fuel.

Berlin, the prewar German capital, was deep inside the Soviet zone of occupation in Germany from 1945 on. Itself divided into Soviet, American, British and French zones, Berlin was connected to the West by a number of air and surface corridors over and through Soviet-held territory. The Soviets proved uncooperative when it came to working for Germany's economic revival, and the western Allies decided to proceed with proposals affecting only their occupation zones. In March 1948, angered by what they saw as an attempt to build up West Germany into a resurgent threat against them, the Soviets began harassing Allied road and rail traffic into Berlin. By June 24, surface traffic into the city had ceased entirely. On that day the Allies received a teletyped message from the Soviet zone that read: "The Transport Division of the Soviet Military Administration is compelled to halt all passenger and freight traffic to and from Berlin tomorrow at 0600 hours because of technical difficulties."

Since blocking surface routes was a simple matter, and any attempt to force the issue on the ground was likely to be unacceptably dangerous, the Allies were left with the alternatives of withdrawing from Berlin or supplying the city by air. An airlift on that scale had never been contemplated before. It hardly seemed sensible to suggest that West Berlin, with a population of nearly two and a half million people, could be sustained by aircraft alone. Once the city's reserves had been depleted, the estimated supply lift required was thought to be about 4,500 tons per day, a figure that included not only essential food, but also large quantities of fuel, much of it in the form of coal.

Commander, United States Air Force Europe, in 1948 was Major General Curt LeMay. Soon after the Soviets began their blockade, he

The collection of items from the Berlin Airlift at the National Museum of the USAF includes coal and flour sacks, bags of beans, and packets of ready-to-eat cereal and dehydrated potato.

was called by the U.S. military governor in Germany, General Lucius Clay, and asked a simple question: "Curt, can you transport coal by air?" His answer was confident, if a little sweeping: "Sir, the Air Force can deliver anything!" By scraping together every aircraft he could lay his hands on, LeMay managed to have 80 tons of supplies flown into Berlin on June 26. It was pitifully small compared with the requirement, but it was a start. The problem was that the Allies did not have many assets immediately at hand. LeMay had about 100 C-47s and a couple of C-54s. The RAF had a few Dakotas (C-47s). Berlin needed the equivalent of 1,500 C-47 sorties per day. Even if it were possible to fly that many, there were only two airfields available for them to use — Tempelhof in the U.S. zone, and Gatow in the British zone. It seemed an impossible task, but by mid-July LeMay's transport force had increased to 54 C-54s and 105 C-47s with a daily lift of 1,500 tons. RAF Yorks and Dakotas added another 750 tons. It was still a long way from meeting the long-term need, but it was improving steadily, and it was certainly irritating the Soviets, who encouraged their fighter pilots to "buzz" Allied aircraft following the air corridors in and out of the city.

The USAF and the RAF reacted strongly to the challenge. Three B-29 groups were deployed to the United Kingdom to send the Soviets an unmistakable message, and F-80s were ordered to Germany from bases in the United States and the Canal Zone. On July 23, eight squadrons of C-54s (72 aircraft with three crews apiece) joined the airlift. Aircraft flew in from as far away as Guam and Alaska. To ensure that the growing number of transports was used as effectively as possible, an Airlift Task Force was formed, which at the end of July came under command of Major General William Tunner, a veteran of the "Hump" airlift into China. By October, Tunner was running a Combined Airlift Task Force, which merged American (USAF and two squadrons of USN R5Ds) and British efforts.

Tunner standardized everything — training, crew briefing, in-flight procedures, ground handling, aircraft maintenance, loading and unloading. What Tunner called "a real cowboy operation" was turned into an endless conveyor belt of aircraft delivering supplies with metronomic efficiency. Besides improving the organization, Tunner also pressed for bigger aircraft. The C-47s were replaced as rapidly as possible with larger capacity C-54s, about 300 of

General Curt LeMay in typical cigar-chewing pose at Tempelhof, Berlin, in 1948. Commander of USAFE when the Soviets blockaded Berlin, he initiated the Allied airlift that confronted the threat. Between June 1949 and September 1949, a total of 277,804 cargo flights were completed to save the city from Soviet domination.

which became the U.S. front line for the airlift. Some 225 were usually available to fly, with another 75 undergoing maintenance. The British had at least another 100 aircraft in operation on any given day. Specialization helped, too, with the USAF concentrating on coal and the British on liquid fuels.

Flights inbound to Berlin entered the air corridors three minutes apart, twenty-four hours a day, maintaining precise heights and speeds from one radio beacon to the next. Interspersing arrivals with departures, this meant that there was an aircraft movement every ninety seconds of the day or night at both Gatow and Tempelhof. Aircraft that missed an approach, as occasionally happened in really bad weather, were not permitted a second try. They were committed to taking their cargo back to base. Once landed and parked on the ramp in Berlin, aircrews stayed with their aircraft and were briefed for the return flight while the aircraft was unloaded, keeping the average turnaround time to thirty minutes. (Unloading could be remarkably rapid. One German team of twelve men managed to unload six and a quarter tons of coal from a C-54 in only five minutes and forty-five seconds!) Tight control of the aircraft was exercised both in the air and on the ground, with check pilots ensuring adherence to procedures, Ground Controlled Approach (GCA) operators monitoring aircraft separation, "Follow Me" Jeeps marshaling arrivals after landing, and operations officers allocating slots for each flight.

A meticulous program of aircraft maintenance was vital. The C-54 had been designed by Douglas as the DC-4, an airliner intended to fly for long periods at cruising power and to land at relatively light weights. On the airlift, they were operating overloaded, flying short legs and therefore spending more time each day at takeoff power, carrying such difficult cargos as coal or salt, which spread corrosive particles into every corner, and landing at well over the designed weight. Engines, brakes and tires suffered excessive wear and tear. Ground crews worked wonders to keep their aircraft on the line, and ex-Luftwaffe mechanics,

so recently the enemy, were hired to help out. Besides normal servicing, one of the more onerous jobs done at base was aircraft cleaning with brooms and mops to keep the grit down as much as possible. Bearing the residual scars and grime of their unexpected calling, the C-54s were withdrawn to the United Kingdom for major inspections every 200 flying hours, and at 1,000 hours they went back to the United States for a complete overhaul.

With growing confidence and experience, the Allied airlift went on without pause throughout the winter of 1948–49. Daily tonnages delivered rose above the 4,500 of the original estimate in September 1948. A third airport, at Tegel, became usable in December, and by January 1949, the daily figure was averaging more than 5,500 tons; in May it reached over 8,000. On one spectacular day of deliveries, April 15, 1949 (known thereafter as the Easter Parade), 1,398 aircraft landed in Berlin and unloaded 12,941 tons of supplies.

Impressive as the Berlin airlift was, it contained a smaller, unofficial activity, known as Operation Little Vittles, which generated almost as much publicity and at least as much affection. C-54 pilot Lieutenant Gail Halvorsen enjoyed Berlin's children and brought them candy when he could. There were always some watching the aircraft on the approach to Tempelhof, and it occurred to him that he could drop them candy as he flew by. He and his crew chief made small parachutes from handkerchiefs, hung candy beneath them, and began throwing them out of the cargo door on final approach. The small groups of children soon grew into crowds and Operation Little Vittles made news. People in the United States contributed handkerchiefs, U.S. servicemen gave candy, and safety-equipment personnel cut time-expired parachutes into smaller editions. It was both a great kindness and a public relations success. Bringing a light-hearted touch to a serious business, it was loved by Americans and watched with despair by the Soviets. If the Americans could take the time to think about

Almost two-thirds of the cargo carried during the Berlin Airlift was coal. A C-54 could carry over six tons of coal, but an energetic team could unload the aircraft in less than six minutes.

Berlin Airlift, *by Gil Cohen.*

throwing candy to kids, was it likely that they would find it difficult to keep the airlift going?

On May 12, 1949, the Soviets lifted the blockade. The airlift continued until September 30, to help in building up Berlin's stocks against possible future emergencies. On that day, a USAF C-54 completed the last of the 277,804 flights of the airlift. In all, the Allies flew 2,325,000 tons of supplies into Berlin, or almost exactly one ton per inhabitant. Of that total, 1,783,000 tons was lifted by U.S. aircraft, no less than one and a half million tons of which was coal. Given the intensity of the operation, accidents were almost inevitable, and there were losses. The USAF lost four C-47s and six C-54s, and the USN one R5D; the British, another nine transports. However, the Soviets had backed down and had been given a graphic illustration of Allied resolve and capability. The losses were sad, but relative to the immense total of sorties flown they were a small price to pay for such a major triumph.

In monetary terms, the Berlin airlift was good value. For the expenditure of some $200 million, the opposition was repulsed and the Allied air forces gained immeasurably in experience and from lessons learned. Interservice and international teamwork could not have been better. The feasibility of extended and intensive transport operations by day and night in all weathers was tried and proved. Air traffic and freight handling procedures were developed to new levels of excellence. Aircrews became expert in flying accurately on instruments for long periods and grew to trust the guidance of radio aids and approach controllers. Major General Tunner's enthusiasm for large aircraft was reinforced. As he pointed out, lifting a daily total of 4,500 tons into Berlin would have required a fleet of almost 500 C-47s flying three sorties per day. The same job was done by about 180 C-54s, with others adding a bonus. If C-74s (later C-124s) had been available, only 68 could have handled the same lift, and that would have meant fewer flights, fewer men, less maintenance and a cheaper, less hazardous operation. For their part, the Soviets learned that the West was prepared to be stubborn in Europe. Communism, it seemed, would have to try elsewhere. It would not be long before it did just that.

The continued intransigence of the Soviets and the openly threatening nature of their behavior in Czechoslovakia and Berlin brought home to the Western powers the marked disparity in conventional military capability that had arisen in Europe since the end of World War II. The Soviet Army had, if anything, increased in strength, while the West had effectively disarmed. The only clear Western advantage lay in American nuclear weapons, and it was by no means certain that this would be enough to deter a westward march of Soviet influence, either through political blackmail or direct military action. To counter the threat and provide a system of mutual support within which individual nations might build prosperous democratic societies, steps were taken that led in 1949 to the formation of the North Atlantic Treaty Organization (NATO). Twelve Western nations agreed to develop their capacity to defend themselves, and to regard an attack on one as an attack on all. There was no doubt, particularly in 1949, that the alliance depended heavily on U.S. military power, and that the USAF was a vital element of that power. The problem was that the USAF was but a shadow of its former USAAF self. Tactical air strength was generally far below what was needed for an air force with global responsibilities, and the U.S. was practically defenseless against air attack. Radar coverage was almost nonexistent,

and the available fighters were inadequate for maintaining a day-and-night continental air defense. The piston-engined F-82 Twin Mustang, armed with 0.5-inch machine guns, served on night fighter squadrons until well into the 1950s.

Strategic Air Command (SAC) was formed in March 1946. The principal mission of the command was to maintain a global nuclear deterrent force with the capability to carry out long-range aerial bombardment against any target in the world. From the outset, SAC was most favored in the allocation of the USAF's scarce funds, and by 1949 changes and improvements were beginning to show. Perhaps the most notable of these came in the person of General Curt LeMay, who assumed command of SAC in October 1948. During a remarkable tenure of nine years, LeMay imposed his steely will on his command to a degree rarely equaled in military history and built SAC into the annihilating weapon he believed a strategic striking force should be. When he took over, he was appalled by the command's lack of strategic capability and poor standards. He took an early opportunity to administer a sharp shock by ordering a bombing exercise at altitudes vastly greater than the SAC crews were used to. The results were, as he expected, abysmal. His remarks to commanders were typically blunt: "What a sorry operation. I've been telling you we were in bad shape. We are in bad shape. Now let's get busy and get this fixed." Under the driving impulse of LeMay's personality, SAC grew steadily in power and in self-respect.

If LeMay needed added fuel to stoke the fires of SAC's expansion, it came in September 1949, when the Soviet Union detonated an atomic bomb. The short-lived U.S. nuclear monopoly was ended and SAC's significance as an element of national security surged overnight. At this stage, the position of SAC as the nation's primary strategic military instrument was still a matter of ardent discussion, continuing a debate that had intensified in 1948. Driven by the interservice competition for limited funds, arguments broke out between the Navy and the Air Force over the respective merits of carrier task forces and long-range

General Curt LeMay's uniform jacket, impressively decorated, hangs behind his bronze image, its resolute gaze challenging visitors to the National Museum of the USAF as they pass by.

bombers for conducting strategic air operations. During 1949, this led to the cancellation of the USN's super-carrier, and then to Congressional hearings on the USAF's new bomber, the Convair B-36. When the dust had settled, the USAF had successfully defended both its procurement of the B-36 and its doctrine, and naval leaders had to accept that long-range bombers were going to take a large share of the defense budget in the years ahead.

TOP *The wing of the B-36 spans 230 feet, 20 feet greater than the Boeing 747. The bomber's great size was the result of a 1941 USAAF requirement for a bomber that could reach targets in Europe in the event that the U.K. fell to German invasion. It was specified that the bomber should have a top speed of 450 mph, cruise at 275 mph, reach 45,000 feet, and have a maximum range of 12,000 miles.* RIGHT *From the D model on, B-36s carried the additional power of four 5,200-pound-thrust J-47 turbojets, sleekly housed in pods beneath the outboard wing sections.* BOTTOM *The McDonnell XF-85 Goblin parasite aircraft was developed to protect a B-36 flying beyond the range of conventional escort fighters. It was intended that the XF-85 would be housed in the B-36 bomb bay. The Goblin could be lowered on a trapeze and released to combat the attackers. The fighter could then return, hook onto the trapeze and be lifted back into the bomb bay. Although the XF-85 was successfully launched from an EB-29B, it was never successfully recovered in flight or flown from a B-36.*

CONVAIR COLOSSUS

TOP The sheer size of the Convair B-36 Peacemaker is still impressive. A crew of fifteen (including a relief team of four) was housed in pressurized cells in the nose and tail, connected by a tunnel 85 feet long. Those in the nose worked on three levels, the pilots at the top, some 20 feet above the nosewheel.
BOTTOM The Peacemaker exhibited at the National Museum of the USAF is a B-36J, and was the last of the giants to fly. Power came from six Pratt & Whitney 3,800-horsepower R-4360 radials, supplemented by four General Electric J-47 turbojets of 5,200 pounds thrust each.

TOP LEFT The B-36 overlaps a standard taxiway and shows off its ten engines, six props and four jets.

TOP RIGHT The spacious cockpit of the B-36. Note six piston-engine throttles in the familiar quadrant close to the first pilot's right hand and four more in the roof for the podded jet engines.

CENTER LEFT The cavernous bomb bay of the Peacemaker, capable of carrying nuclear weapons or up to 86,000 pounds of conventional bombs.

BOTTOM LEFT The Mark 17 nuclear weapon alone weighed 41,400 pounds.

ABOVE A dazzling array of dials, switches and levers confronted the flight engineer in a B-36.

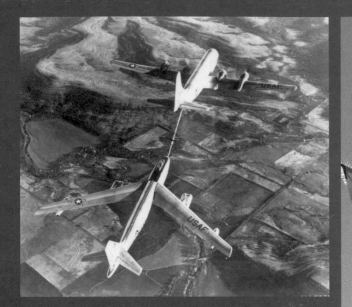

GREATER RANGE,
MORE ENDURANCE

ABOVE Air-to-air refueling gave Strategic Air Command's B-47s a much longer reach, but it was not easy for the jet bomber's pilots when the tanker was a piston-engined KC-97. The procedure was for the tanker to be held in a descent at high power so that the bomber could be flown at a comfortable airspeed.
RIGHT Boeing's development of the flying boom made air-to-air refueling less demanding than the probe and drogue system and enabled much higher rates of fuel transfer to be achieved.
BELOW Over 800 KC-97 Stratotankers were delivered to the USAF by Boeing. The example on display at the National Museum of the USAF is in the markings of the Ohio Air National Guard. Two J-47 jet engines were fitted to later model KC-97s to make them more compatible with SAC's jet bombers.

U.S. AIR FORCE

The B-36 was impressive, but it was a holdover from World War II thinking. It had been planned originally for attacks on Germany from the United States in the event that Britain was overrun by the Nazis. It met a requirement for an aircraft to operate over a 5,000-mile radius of action carrying a 10,000-pound bomb-load. With the onset of the Cold War, it was the only aircraft capable of reaching strategic targets in the USSR from U.S. bases. It was gigantic — 230 feet across the wing and with an eventual maximum loaded weight of 410,000 pounds (B-36J). Power came from six 3,500-horsepower P&W radials, later augmented by the addition of four GE jet engines of 5,200 pounds thrust each. Over a radius of 2,300 miles, the B-36 could deliver the incredible total of 72,000 pounds of bombs — far more than the B-17's maximum loaded weight. (Reporting their aircraft type to air traffic controllers, B-36 pilots took to announcing "Six a-burnin', four a-turnin'!" A contemporary piece of doggerel left no doubt about the B-36's purpose: "How dare Convair try to scare the bear / With this colossus which crosses / The globe to probe / Those gremlins in the Kremlin.")

Such startling figures aside, however, the B-36 was something of a dinosaur. Heavily armed with multiple cannon in turrets though it was, it was difficult to imagine such a lumbering monster penetrating Soviet airspace with impunity. Fighters could not escort the giant on intercontinental missions, and it was only its capacity to deliver nuclear weapons that made it a credible threat. An attempt was made to provide an escort by hanging one on the B-36 itself. The McDonnell XF-85 Goblin was a tiny parasite fighter designed to be carried in one of the B-36's bomb bays and released when needed; the XF85's chronic instability and limited endurance doomed the project.

By the end of 1949, SAC had three heavy bombardment wings of B-36s in service. There were eleven B-29/50 wings, plus two fighter and three reconnaissance wings. SAC organized these assets into three numbered air forces — the Eighth (heavy/medium bombers); Fifteenth (medium bombers); and Second (reconnaissance). Now with well over 1,000 aircraft, SAC set about making itself into a strategic force to be reckoned with, working on professionalism and readiness, and looking for ways to improve its global reach. Overseas bases in the United Kingdom and Greenland began the process of constructing a worldwide network, and plans were laid to make all SAC bombers capable of in-flight refueling. In an early demonstration of this force-multiplying technique, the B-50A *Lucky Lady II* remained airborne for ninety-four hours between February 26 and March 2, 1949, covering almost 24,000 miles and completing the first nonstop flight round the world. With the passage of time, in-flight refueling would become ever more important to USAF operations, and the tanker force would grow to impressive proportions, using at first only flexible-hose systems but soon moving to a fleet in which the more efficient Boeing flying boom predominated. Operating with tankers, SAC claimed to be able to reach targets anywhere in the world.

AGGRESSION IN KOREA
Surprise, Surprise!

In the closing days of World War II, Soviet forces invaded Korea and accepted the surrender of the Japanese in the northern half of the country. They then created the Peoples' Democratic Republic of Korea, dividing the country into two states at the 38th parallel. It was across this arbitrary partition that the Communist world next chose to challenge the democracies. At first light on June 25, 1950, North Korean armed forces swept across the frontier, intent on reuniting Korea under a Communist government. The attack achieved complete strategic and tactical surprise. Ten Communist divisions brushed aside the inadequately armed Republic of Korea (ROK) Army and raced southward. During these early hours of the war, the North Korean Air Force (NKAF) was active and effective. It operated almost 200 aircraft, mostly Russian of WWII vintage, including 70 Yak-9 fighters and 62 Il-10 ground-attack bombers. Unimpressive by Western standards, it was formidable compared to the few T-6 trainers owned by the South.

Response to the invasion was led by the United States. Reacting to pleas for help from South Korea, President

> *"Without the support of the indiscriminate bombing and bombardment by your air and naval forces, your ground forces would have long ago been driven out of the Korean peninsula by our powerful and battle-skilled ground forces."*
>
> NORTH KOREAN ARMY LIEUTENANT GENERAL NAM IL, IN ARMISTICE DISCUSSIONS WITH UN REPRESENTATIVES AT PANMUNJOM, AUGUST 1951

In the collection of the Muzeum Lotnictwa Polskiego in Krakow, Poland, is a Czech-built Ilyushin Il-10, known as the Avia B-33. The Il-10, successor to the Il-2 Shturmovik, did not appear until the last few months of World War II, but it quickly established a reputation as a formidable combat aircraft and continued to serve in front-line squadrons after the war. Avia did not begin building the B-33 until 1951, and 281 of these were exported to the Polish Air Force.

Truman pledged support and took the matter to the Security Council of the United Nations. In the fortuitous absence of the Soviet Union, whose delegation was boycotting the Security Council at the time, a vote was taken to support the South against the aggression of the North. Member nations were encouraged to "render such assistance to the Republic of Korea as may be necessary to repel the armed attack…." General MacArthur was appointed Supreme Commander, Allied Powers, and the United States set about rallying democratic nations to the flag.

As a first step, MacArthur was instructed to ensure the evacuation of U.S. citizens from Korea, covering the operation with fighter aircraft flying from bases in Japan. Once again, U.S. transport aircraft were to lead the charge in meeting an emergency. The first USAF aircraft lost in the Korean War was a C-54, strafed and burned by a Yak-9 on the first day at Seoul's airfield, Kimpo. On June 27, the NKAF hit Kimpo again, but this time there were F-82Gs from the 8th Fighter-Bomber Wing overhead. Three out of five Yak-9s were destroyed, Lieutenant William Hudson of the 68th Fighter Squadron claiming the first U.S. air victory. Later that day, eight Il-10s tried their luck and were met by F-80Cs of the 35th Fighter-Bomber Squadron. Four Il-10s were destroyed, and the rest fled. Although these encounters suggested that USAF crews and aircraft were superior, it was apparent that the NKAF did pose a threat and that it would be sensible to counter it at source. On June 30, President Truman authorized the USAF to strike targets above the 38th parallel, and within a month, attacks on air-

A Lockheed F-80C seen during a low-level attack on a North Korean position.

fields in the north by B-26s and B-29s had reduced the NKAF to impotence. (These B-26s were the Douglas A-26 Invaders introduced toward the end of WWII. In 1948, when the original Martin B-26 Marauder was phased out, the A-26 inherited the designation B-26, to the eternal confusion of aviation historians.)

Air supremacy over the whole of Korea having been so easily established, Allied army commanders may have hoped that the situation would soon resemble that in Western Europe after the Normandy invasion. If so, they were to be disappointed. The circumstances of the two conflicts were so vastly different that many of the lessons learned in World War II offered misleading guidance for combat in Korea. The resources committed to the war were never on the unlimited scale of WWII, nor was it possible for those resources available to be used without

LEFT *An LT-6G Mosquito of the 6147th Tactical Control Group rolling in to mark a Korean target with smoke rockets in July 1952.*
RIGHT *F-82 Twin Mustangs and F-80C Shooting Stars, seen here sharing a ramp at Itazuki, Japan, were the first U.S. fighters to see action in the Korean War.*

restraint. American forces went into action in Korea without preparation at a time when the U.S. military was at a low ebb, surviving on minimal funding and with its units often under strength and poorly equipped. Things would improve, but massive force, as it was understood in Europe, was never available. Air supremacy over Korea was achieved at the outset but would not last, even though the USAF was invariably able to gain local air superiority when necessary. Perhaps most significantly, political restrictions seriously limited the way in which the Korean War could be fought, reducing the effective-ness of air strikes and offering the enemy safe havens. Soviet and Chinese industries supplying the war from outside Korea were permanently out of reach, and the effective interdiction of surface communications proved almost impossible, given the USAF's limitations and the undeveloped nature of Korea. The enemy was always ready to use pack animals and manpower to keep supplies flowing over trails to the front. In short, the United States found itself involved in a limited war, a phenome-non that was to become disturbingly familiar as the 20th century progressed.

P-51 Mustangs were overdue for retirement in 1952, but they were better able than jets to cope with the primitive conditions of Korean airfields so they were hastily restored to front-line service. The 12th Fighter Bomber Squadron, operating from Chinhae near Pusan, was one of the units that gave up its F-80C jets and reconverted to P-51s.

Gaining air supremacy in the first month of the war was one thing; checking the onrushing North Korean Army was quite another. Neither the soldiers of the broken ROK Army nor the lightly equipped U.S. Army infantry units were capable of imposing anything more serious than temporary delays on their rampaging opponents. By the end of July, the South Koreans and their U.S. allies had been driven back into a small pocket no more than about 70 miles across in any direction, centered on the port of Pusan. Here the UN ground forces took their stand and hung on until early September, enduring an almost endless series of crises as the North Koreans hurled themselves against the defenses of the Pusan perimeter. On September 3, Major General William Kean of the 25th Division reported: "The

ABOVE Thunderjet in Korea, *by Gil Cohen.*
RIGHT *The cockpit of the F-84 had the haphazard look of many jets of the 1950s. F-84 pilots said they found the cockpit roomy and comfortable, with good all-round visibility. Note the red ejection seat handle to the right of the seat, and the reflector gunsight, with a dial for setting the wingspan of enemy aircraft.*

close air support strikes rendered by the Fifth Air Force again saved this Division, as they have many times before."

At the heart of the Allied air effort in Korea was the USAF's Far East Air Force (FEAF). The largest of its subordinate commands was the Fifth Air Force, described by its commander as "a small but highly professional tactical-type air force." It comprised three F-80C wings, one under-strength light bombardment wing of B-26s, and two all-weather fighter squadrons with F-82s. One wing of B-29s was drawn from the Twentieth Air Force in Okinawa, and a further two wings were detached from SAC.

Initially, the F-80Cs were a problem. Their combat radius was limited and there were no airfields in Korea capable of handling jets. As an interim solution, many F-80 pilots

reconverted to F-51s taken from storage. The Mustangs could be based in South Korea, had the endurance to allow them to fly extended armed reconnaissance sorties, and could carry bombs and napalm, which the F-80Cs could not. At a time when the ground forces were hard pressed and close air support was vital, the born-again F-51s were invaluable, in blunting enemy thrusts until army reserves could be brought into action. Even B-29s were used against battlefield targets, but with disappointing effect. Mostly, however, the B-29s pounded industrial and transportation targets north of Seoul. By September, there little was left of the North's steel plants, oil depots, railway yards and harbor facilities. Interdiction targets south of Seoul were more difficult. After the first few days, when some enemy convoys

ABOVE *A C-119 Flying Boxcar of the 314th Troop Carrier Group dropping some four tons of supplies to UN troops during the Korean War.* BELOW *The Republic F-84 Thunderjet was the first USAF jet fighter with the capability of carrying a tactical nuclear weapon. In Korea, the F-84 was used primarily for low-level interdiction missions. Railroads, bridges, supply depots and troop concentrations were attacked with bombs, rockets and napalm. The F-84E seen here is on display at the National Museum of the USAF.*

were caught in the open in daylight and severely dealt with, the North Koreans learned to move at night. Thereafter, FEAF's lack of an adequate night-tactical capability proved to be an embarrassment. The night-intruder role fell to the B-26s, but they were far from ideal since they were not fitted with radar altimeters, short-range navigation radar, or blind-bombing radar. Nor were they particularly maneuverable, which was a distinct disadvantage for an aircraft that sometimes needed to operate by night at low level through Korea's rugged terrain.

Interdiction of static targets by daylight was more successful. By mid-September, FEAF claimed that, with the help of naval aircraft, 140 bridges had been destroyed between Seoul and the Pusan perimeter, and 47 cuts had been made and maintained in rail lines. Another 93 bridges around Pusan had been rendered unusable, and hundreds of locomotives, railway cars and motor vehicles destroyed. Impressive though these figures were, it was never possible to stop the flow of North Korean supplies entirely. Pack animals, including humans, helped to keep them trickling through. Nevertheless, the interdiction campaign against the lengthening enemy logistic chain played an important part in the eventual defeat of the North Korean offensive. It is significant that North Korean prisoners taken in September admitted that the morale of their units, extremely high at the start of the offensive, was now very low. Reasons for the decline were sought during interrogation and two emerged as by far the most important — shortage of food and fear of aircraft.

MacArthur Strikes Back

When it came, the collapse of the North Korean Army was rapid. On September 15, MacArthur loosed his master-stroke, landing the 1st Marine Division at Inchon, close to Seoul and 150 miles behind the fighting around Pusan. Strongly supported by Allied carrier aircraft, the Marines advanced rapidly and within two days had recovered Kimpo airfield. The day after the Inchon landing, the 8th Army broke out of the Pusan pocket and drove north under the Fifth Air Force's umbrella. No longer capable of withstanding American firepower, and hounded from the air, the North Korean Army disintegrated, and by the end of the month had been driven from South Korea. MacArthur made it clear that he intended to seek the final destruction of the North Korean Army by continuing to advance beyond the 38th parallel. He was quite sure that the risk of Chinese intervention was minimal. On October 7, 1950, euphoria brought on by success encouraged the UN General Assembly to approve a resolution that "all necessary steps be taken to ensure conditions of peace throughout the whole of Korea." Under this thin cloak of authority, the UN troops set off for the Yalu River, the boundary between Korea and China.

If anything, Fifth Air Force support for UN soldiers was now even better than before. Since the utility of Forward Air Controllers (FACs) on the ground was limited by the terrain, North American T-6s drew an unexpected and often hazardous combat role, flying close to the battle lines with FACs on board.

Known as "Mosquitos," they kept in radio contact with both ground units and supporting fighters, marking targets with 2.75-inch rockets and controlling air attacks as necessary. Air transport came into its own, too, when C-119s and C-47s of General Tunner's new Combat Cargo Command dropped 2,860 paratroopers across enemy escape routes north of P'yongyang, the North Korean capital, on October 20. It was one of the most effective paratroop operations ever carried out, sealing the fate of the enemy forces leaving the city. North Korean resistance quickly crumbled all along the front and, by the end of October, some UN units were on the banks of the Yalu. MacArthur was triumphant. The war would soon be over and he would have brought about the unification of Korea, having given the Communists a bloody nose in the process. Such unbounded confidence was sharply checked in November, when the Chinese showed that they were not prepared to sit idly by while North Korea was forcibly gathered to the bosom of democracy.

Chinese Intervention

American forces first felt the heat of Chinese anger toward the end of October. Some forward positions were overrun by Chinese troops, and on November 1, a patrolling F-80C was shot down by antiaircraft guns firing across the Yalu. Chinese aircraft began "trailing their coats" over North Korea and, on November 8, the world's first all-jet combat took place when F-80Cs of the 51st Fighter Interceptor Wing were jumped by MiG-15s. In a brief exchange, the USAF scored first blood, Lieutenant Russell Brown shooting down one of the attackers. That early success was no indication of relative capabilities, however. It was quickly apparent that F-80Cs were no match for MiG-15s. The Soviet fighter was some 100 mph faster than the F-80C, could climb to 50,000 feet, and was armed with one 37 mm and two 23 mm cannon.

The principal protagonists in the air war over Korea were the MiG-15 and the F-86 Sabre. Both were swept-wing jet fighters capable of supersonic flight in a dive. The MiG-15 could outclimb the Sabre and was more heavily armed. However, it was more lightly built, had an inferior gunsight, was a mediocre gun platform, and had a tendency to flick out of high-G turns. The rate of roll of the MiG was relatively slow, and directional stability was poor at high altitudes and speeds. By the end of the war the overall superiority of the F-86 was reflected in the comparative losses — 792 MiGs shot down for the loss of 76 Sabres.

was more stable as a gun platform at high Mach numbers. It also had the advantage of being fitted with a radar-ranging gunsight. Equally important, the Sabre was a joy to fly, whereas the MiG-15 had a tendency to flick savagely if driven too hard in high-G turns.

A less glamorous American jet arrived in Korea in December. The 27th Fighter Escort Group brought their F-84E Thunderjets to the war. The F-84 was an aircraft that inspired more respect than affection in its pilots. It was a rugged machine, but it was underpowered for the fighter-bomber job it had to do. Fully loaded with bombs, rockets and fuel, the F-84 weighed over 10 tons. Its spidery, wide-stance undercarriage had to cope with long takeoff runs on the rough airfields of Korea, and the J-35 engine of the earlier models was apt to shed turbine blades when shaken too hard. Nevertheless, for all its shortcomings, the F-84 proved to be a fearsome fighter-bomber and the champion hauler of bombs and napalm in the Korean War. If there were people who viewed the F-84 with affection, they were the hard-pressed UN soldiers its heavy punch supported.

By the end of November, the UN forces were in trouble. Chinese ground forces estimated at more than half a million men had crossed the Yalu, and the UN forces were in disorderly retreat. Overwhelmed by sheer numbers, many units broke and ran under the shock of the massive Chinese assault. In the air, the UN air forces had nothing to match the MiG-15, and air supremacy close to the Yalu River could no longer be guaranteed. By mid-December, a measure of balance was given to the air war with the arrival in Korea of the 4th Fighter Interceptor Wing (FIW), equipped with North American F-86A Sabres. A classic fighter, beloved by its pilots, the F-86 was not quite as good in the climb or at very high altitude as the lighter MiG-15, nor did its six 0.5-inch machine guns have the hitting power of its opponent's cannon, but it was just as fast and

ABOVE *The Grumman F9F Panther first flew in 1947, powered by a Rolls-Royce Nene turbojet built under license by Pratt & Whitney as the J42. Panthers served with distinction in the Korean War as the primary Navy jet fighter and ground-attack aircraft. Panthers were withdrawn from front-line service in 1956, but remained in training roles and with the reserves until 1958.*
RIGHT *Grumman F9F-3 Panther of Fighter Squadron 52 (VF-52) taxies forward on USS* Valley Forge *(CV-45) before being launched to strike targets along the east coast of Korea, July 19, 1950.*

It was not long before the new American arrivals were in action. On December 17, Lieutenant Colonel Bruce Hinton of the 4th FIW gained the first F-86 victory over a MiG-15, the first of four achieved by his unit that day. The welcome intervention of the F-86 in the air war was short-lived, however. The Chinese ground offensive forced the UN armies back south of Seoul, thereby denying airfields to the F-86s, which retreated temporarily to the safety of Japan. With his demoralized troops facing an apparently inexhaustible Chinese Army, MacArthur came to the conclusion that Korea could not be held unless mainland China was attacked, and he advocated the use of nuclear weapons. During this unpromising phase of the war, the F-84s exerted a powerful influence on the battle, hammering the advancing Chinese incessantly and giving desperate units of the Eighth Army the chance to escape destruction. In the eastern half of Korea, salvation for the Marines also came with wings — their own close air support aircraft and FEAF's transports. Cargo aircraft kept the troops supplied during their fighting withdrawal from the Chosin Reservoir, flew out their wounded from hastily prepared landing strips, and dropped a 16-ton, eight-section Bailey bridge to aid their escape across a deep gorge. Eventually the transports completed an aerial evacuation of over 4,000 men from the Hamhung area under the noses of the Chinese.

As the bleak winter days of January 1951 passed into history, the resistance of the UN ground forces stiffened under the inspiring

new leadership of General Matthew Ridgway. By the middle of the month, with their extended supply lines relentlessly attended by Allied aircraft, the seemingly irresistible Chinese Army slowed to a halt. UN counterattacks led to the recovery of Seoul, and the F-86s were back in Korea by the end of February, albeit forced to operate at a disadvantage. Based near Seoul, the F-86s had to fly up to "MiG Alley" — northwest Korea between the Yalu and Ch'ongch'on Rivers — to meet their enemy. There they were close to the limit of their range and could not spend long in combat. They were forbidden to cross the Yalu into Manchuria. Their opponents, on the other hand, often operated within sight of their bases and could stay on their side of the Yalu until they chose to engage. The F-86s were also heavily outnumbered. During 1951, the number of MiGs available rose to over 500, opposed to 100 or so F-86s. The figures made little difference to the consistent combat superiority of the F-86. The Sabres shot down three MiGs in March and fourteen in April. In May, Captain James Jabara became the first jet ace when he downed his fifth and sixth MiGs. (Jabara went on to become the second ranking ace of the Korean War, registering fifteen victories. He also had one and a half in World War II. The leading scorer in Korea was Captain Joseph McConnell, with sixteen. Eleven pilots reached double figures.) June saw the appearance in combat of Soviet instructors, but they had little effect on the trend — forty-two MiGs were claimed destroyed in the month for the loss of three F-86s.

TOP *James Jabara was the first U.S. jet ace, shooting down fifteen MiG-15s while flying the F-86 Sabre in the Korean War. Jabara was also credited with 1.5 victories over Europe during World War II. He died on November 17, 1966, in an automobile accident.*
MIDDLE *The leading jet ace of the Korean War was Captain Joseph McConnell, Jr., who shot down sixteen MiG-15s during 1953. On the day McConnell claimed his eighth MiG, his F-86 was hit and he bailed out over the Yellow Sea. After only two minutes in the freezing water, he was rescued by a helicopter and the following day he was back in combat to shoot down his ninth MiG. On August 25, 1954, McConnell died in the crash of an F-86H at Edwards AFB, California.*
BOTTOM *John Glenn and his F-86,* MiG Mad Marine, *during his tour of exchange duty with the USAF. The future astronaut and senator shot down three MiG-15s while in Korea.*

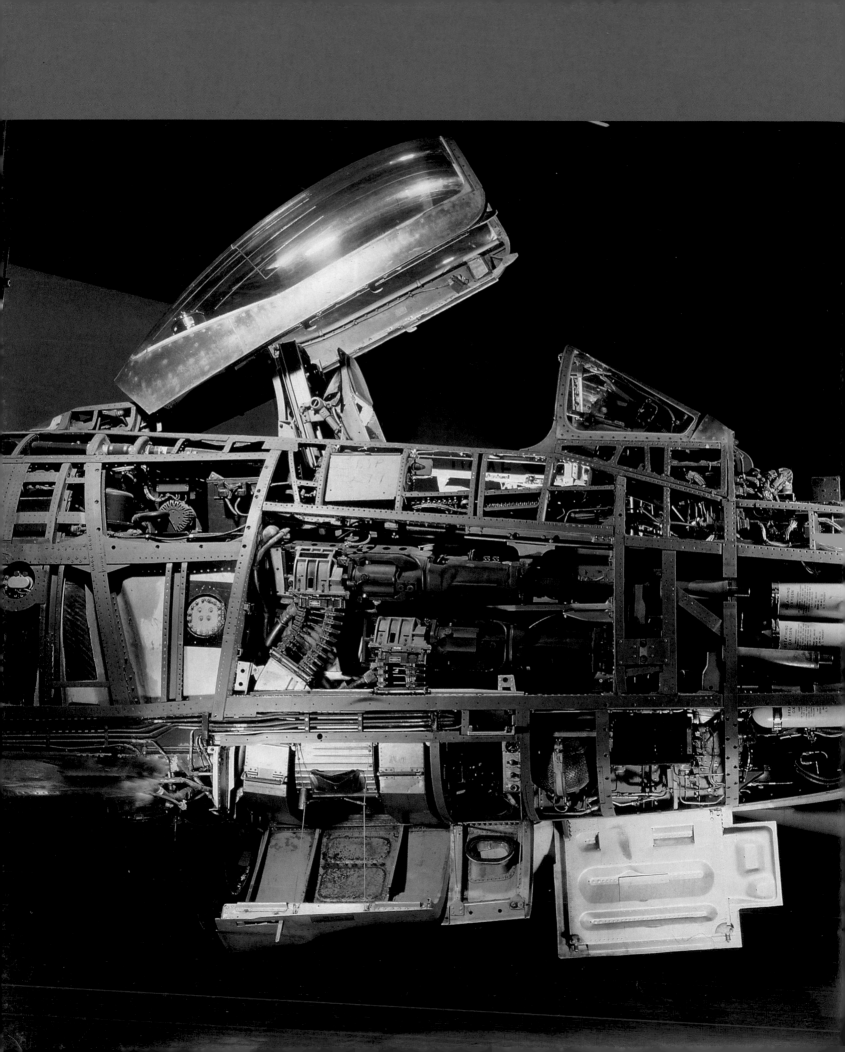

INSIDE THE SABRE

LEFT Even in early jet aircraft such as the F-86 Sabre the construction was relatively dense. (Compare the SE.5a cutaway shown in *Aviation Century The Early Years*.) The F-86H exhibited in the National Museum of the USAF is displayed without its skin and with its internal organs revealed. Among the most instantly recognizable are the 20 mm cannon and their ammunition bays.

ABOVE Walker "Bud" Mahurin, WWII and Korean War ace, thought the F-86 cockpit was "fine." He found the "controls and instruments in the F-86 close to hand and easy to reach." He compared the F-86 and MiG-15 cockpits as being like a Cadillac and an early Ford, pointing out that the MiG did not have air conditioning or boosted controls, whereas the F-86 had both.

SOVIET SURPRISE

In 1948, the Soviet MiG design bureau developed a high-performance jet fighter called the I-310. It incorporated a 35-degree wing sweep, and promised to be a sprightly performer. However, the engine was inadequate. This problem was overcome when the British government authorized Rolls-Royce to export their Nene turbojet to the Soviet Union. As soon as the Klimov engine design bureau received the Nene, they developed a copy, calling it the Klimov RD-45. The re-engined aircraft was designated MiG-15 and entered service early in 1949. Later that year, the improved MiG-15bis and a two-seat trainer, the MiG-15UTI, appeared. In 1950, the UN air forces in Korea were taken by surprise by the combat capability of the MiG-15, which was quickly seen to be superior in almost every respect to the F-80s and Meteors of the Allies. The Soviet fighter was some 100 mph faster than the F-80C, could climb to 50,000 feet, and was heavily armed with one 37 mm and two 23 mm cannon.

LEFT AND ABOVE On September 21, 1953, Lieutenant Kim Sok No defected from the North Korean Air Force and flew his MiG-15bis to Kimpo Air Base in South Korea. The aircraft on display at the National Museum of the USAF is that MiG-15bis. The young pilot said that life under Communism was slavery, and he preferred freedom. He seemed genuinely unaware that a reward of $100,000 had been offered to anyone who defected to the West with a MiG-15. In commenting on the aircraft, Kim Sok No said that the main problems were the lack of power-boosted controls, which made the MIG very heavy to fly, and the poor cockpit conditioning, which resulted in pilots experiencing extremes of temperature. As can be seen in the cockpit photograph, the control stick is long, allowing some mechanical advantage in the absence of hydraulic boosting.

ABOVE RIGHT Ex Polish Air Force MIG-15 UTI Fagot over the Mojave desert, California.

In an effort to provide effective air support for their army, the Chinese began preparing airfields in North Korea that would allow them to move fighters south of the Yalu. UN reconnaissance aircraft kept an eye on the work being done until it neared completion in April 1951. B-29 raids then destroyed the airfield facilities and cratered the runways. This sequence of events was repeated at intervals, and the Chinese never succeeded in operating MiGs regularly from North Korea. Important as this B-29 achievement was, it had a cost. On October 23, 1951, for example, about a hundred MiGs kept the escorts busy, while fifty more broke through to attack eight B-29s on their way to bomb airfields. Three of the bombers were shot down and the rest so severely damaged that they never flew again. Soon after these losses, the B-29s were restricted to night operations. Constraints of this kind, forced by enemy action, brought the USAF to the realization that air supremacy was beyond its reach over North Korea.

> *"No one who fought on the ground in Korea would ever be tempted to belittle the accomplishments of our Air Force there. Not only did air power save us from disaster, but without it, the mission of the United Nations forces could not have been accomplished."*
>
> U.S. ARMY GENERAL MATTHEW RIDGWAY'S MEMOIR, *THE KOREAN WAR*, 1967

Stalemate

On the ground, the war congealed into stalemate by mid-1951. Both sides now recognized that there could be no easy victory and armistice talks were proposed. In October the talks settled into a tedious and frustrating pattern at Panmunjom, where the chief North Korean delegate, General Nam Il, paid the UN air forces a bitter tribute: "Without the support of the indiscriminate bombing and bombardment of your air and naval forces, your ground forces would have long ago been driven out of the Korean peninsula by our powerful and battle-skilled ground forces."

As the talks assumed the character of a propaganda war, the fighting continued and the aerial struggle carried on much as before. High on the list of priorities for Far East Air Force (FEAF) was the interdiction of the enemy's supply lines, with the object of preventing the Chinese Army from building up stocks for a future offensive. Efficiently done, interdiction might even force the Chinese to think about withdrawing northward to shorten their logistic chain. Starting with Operation Strangle in May, and continuing with the Rail Interdiction Program, UN aircraft kept up a persistent day and night assault on roads and railways in North Korea throughout 1951. That it caused the Communist forces discomfort and inconvenience is certain. It did not, however, accomplish either of its main aims. The enemy was not prevented from accumulating supplies, nor was there any sign of withdrawal. On December 28, a Fifth Air Force intelligence summary acknowledged defeat: "The enemy's highly developed repair and construction capability of both bridges and rail lines has broken our blockade...."

There were several reasons for the failure of the interdiction campaigns. First, the daily consumption of Chinese divisions was small; perhaps only a tenth of that needed by their Western counterparts, particularly when they were not engaged in an offensive. Second, the enemy's large labor pool made for quick repair of damaged routes and allowed the alternative of carrying supplies over primitive tracks. Third, the USAF's global commitments ensured that FEAF would have insufficient aircraft for the task. Just as serious was the USAF's inability to replace losses as they occurred, especially once the enemy's defenses improved and FEAF's fighter-bomber loss rate rose to more than twenty a month. (In August, Fifth Air Force lost 30 fighter-bombers and had another 24 damaged. In September, the figures were 33 and 233; in October, 33 and 239; and in November, 24 and 255.) Fourth, the fighter-bombers were forced by increasing flak to resort to dive-bombing, which halved the effectiveness of their strikes. Fifth, the USAF did not have an aircraft capable of undertaking effective night interdiction, especially in an underdeveloped country such as Korea.

The frustrations of trying to fight an enemy so ready to use low-technology countermeasures did not end there. The Communist air forces, incapable of launching a major campaign against the UN's airfields, began night nuisance raids using Polikarpov Po-2 biplanes to drop small bombs or hand grenades. Only occasionally did these "Bed-check Charlies" cause any real damage, but they were intensely irritating. No sensible answer was ever found to their nightly raids, although a few were brought down, usually more by luck than judgment. Modern aircraft found it hard to cope with a wood and fabric biplane flying at 90 mph or less in the dark. One was shot down when it happened to fly in front of a B-26 preparing to land, and another was flown through by a pursuing F-94; since both aircraft were destroyed, it was a poor exchange. F-94s, only recently arrived to replace the F-82s, were equipped with the most advanced airborne radar then in existence. The Po-2 incident appeared to confirm the radar's accuracy but carried a warning about attempting radar interception of an aircraft with a maximum speed less than the interceptor's landing speed.

At the other end of the performance scale, the MiG-15s changed tactics and began to impose themselves more forcibly on the air war. Now fitted with drop tanks, they expanded their area of operations. "Trains" of MiGs, sixty to eighty strong, crossed the Yalu at high altitude and flew down the center of the peninsula, elements peeling off at intervals to challenge the patrolling F-86s. The main body continued south, converging over P'yongyang with a similar formation coming from the east coast. The resulting force of 100 or so then dropped down to medium altitude and searched for UN fighter-bombers on interdiction sorties. Losses to the MiGs were few, but the fighter-bombers often had to jettison their weapon loads under attack and, by September 1951, they were forced to restrict their hunting to areas south of the Ch'ongch'on River.

Toward the end of 1951, another pattern of MiG-15 activity was noticed. Large groups of MiGs maneuvered south of the Yalu, staying at maximum altitude and keeping well clear of F-86s. Over a six-week period, the formations became steadily bolder. Then the cycle started again. It appeared that courses were being run to provide a gentle introduction to combat for new pilots. The fighter strength in Manchuria rose to over 1,000 MiG-15s. Neither the increase nor the innovations seemed to make much difference to the way aerial battles went. During 1952, MiGs were claimed at an average rate of one per day. F-86 losses averaged one per week. The introduction of the F-86F with a redesigned wing and more powerful engine made the disparity even wider. The F-86F left the MiG-15 (even the improved 15bis) without any real advantages. In the last months of the war, from March through July 1953, there were 225 claims for MiGs shot down, while FEAF lost just ten F-86s.

In mid-1952, it was decided to use UN air power to break the stalemate at the Panmunjom talks. The "Air

Pressure" campaign, as it was known, was directed against selected targets in North Korea with the aim of making the conflict as costly as possible for the enemy. On three days at the end of June, attacks were concentrated on North Korea's capacity to generate electricity. Ninety percent of the system was destroyed, and industry was crippled all over the country. For the rest of 1952 and the first part of 1953, FEAF's bombers continued to pound at military and industrial targets but, though North Korea was badly hurt, the peace talks remained deadlocked.

Two events, one political and one military, then influenced the discussions. In March 1953, Joseph Stalin died in Moscow, after which Chinese Premier Chou En-lai let it be known that he wished to bring the talks to an end. Progress remained glacial, however, until UN aircraft attacked the North Korean irrigation system. It was a decision not taken lightly. Strikes were permitted against only those dams that, when breached, would release waters to wash away railways and military supplies. On May 13 and 16, fighter-bombers breached several dams. General Mark Clark, now the UN commander, reported that the raids were "as effective as weeks of interdiction." The Communists quickly strove to improve their position and inflict military defeat on the UN before proposing a ceasefire. Major ground offensives were launched and repulsed under the cover of massive air support. On June 27, 1953, six weeks after the attacks on the dams, agreement on a ceasefire was finally reached at Panmunjom.

NATO AND THE WARSAW PACT
Reach and Power for the USAF

Before America's involvement in the Korean War, the USAF had been caught between the nirvana of newly won independence and the perdition of shrinking defense budgets. Senior airmen knew what they wanted to do to build a global air force but there was never enough money to do it. Chinese intervention in Korea changed all that. The USAF's strength increased rapidly during the war and, with Americans generally accepting that confrontation with communism had become a fact of life, expansion continued even after the shooting stopped, albeit at a slower pace.

If any command exemplified the new Air Force, transformed by technological advances and determined leadership, it was Strategic Air Command. In 1950, SAC had 71,490 personnel and 868 aircraft. The backbone of its striking force consisted of 390 B-29s. Five years later, the personnel strength was 196,000, and there were 3,068 aircraft, including well over 1,000 B-47s backed by a tanker fleet of more than 700.

SAC's first Boeing B-47s were delivered in October 1951, bringing with them revolutionary changes in operational doctrine and in aircrew attitudes to the bombing mission. The B-47 was an extraordinary technical achievement, bearing almost no resemblance to its predecessors and pointing the way to the future for large aircraft in both military and civil aviation. Its loaded weight was half again as great as the B-29, but its size was disguised by slender lines and the novelty of a fighter-type cockpit. The normal crew of a B-47 was only three — two pilots in a tandem cockpit and a navigator hidden in the nose. Its shoulder-mounted wings were razor-edged and remarkably thin, and were swept back at the then startling angle of 35 degrees. To retain the aerodynamic advantages of thin aerofoils, the conventional practice of housing the engines, fuel and wheels in the wings was abandoned. The axial-flow turbojets were in pods hung below the wings, and fuel was stored in the fuselage. The landing gear was a pair of two-wheel trucks placed fore and aft on the fuselage centerline, with small outriggers under the inner engine pods to keep the aircraft stable on the ground. To help with the landing speeds associated with the high wing-loading (twice that of a B-29), a large brake-chute was installed. Defensive armament was limited to a remotely controlled tail turret housing a pair of 0.5-inch or 20 mm guns.

The B-47's principal limitation was its radius of action on internal fuel, some 1,500 miles, which would not allow adequate coverage of targets in the Soviet Union. Again, Boeing had the answer. The KC-97 tanker could fly fast enough, if necessary in a slight dive, to match a throttled-back B-47, and its efficient flying boom refueling system turned the bomber into an intercontinental weapon. Each B-47 wing had a complement of forty-five bombers supported by a KC-97 squadron of twenty tankers. The capabilities of the partnership were amply demonstrated in a series of record flights in the 1950s. During an intercontinental bombing trial, a B-47 flew nonstop from Hunter AFB, Georgia, to Morocco and back in twenty-four hours and four minutes, refueling four times from KC-97s. Even more remarkable, a B-47 flown by Colonel Burchinal of the

43rd Bomb Wing was caught in the air by bad weather covering the whole of Western Europe and North Africa. Burchinal elected to wait between the United Kingdom and Morocco until the weather cleared and called for tanker support. He finally landed at Fairford after nine refuelings, having been airborne for forty-seven hours and thirty-five minutes. These and other demonstrations left no doubt that the B-47 was a strategic weapon to be reckoned with.

Remarkable though it was, however, the B-47 was only an intermediate step toward SAC's long-term future. In 1955, SAC began taking delivery of the aircraft that would come to symbolize U.S. strategic air power for generations of bomber aircrew — Boeing's B-52 Stratofortress, commonly known as the "Buff" (in genteel translation: Big Ugly Fat Fellow). In 1946, Boeing's design team had begun work on a very large bomber, sketching out what was in effect a stretched B-29 with six engines. The USAF wanted higher performance, however, and Boeing finally produced the immense B-52, powered by eight jet engines hung in four underwing pods. Originally intended to penetrate enemy defenses at high subsonic speeds and altitudes above 50,000 feet, the B-52 showed enormous capacity to absorb technological developments and adapt to changes in role and tactics. Its unrefueled radius of action of well over 4,000 miles became almost unlimited with flight refueling support. Over the years its maximum loaded weight rose to nearly half a million pounds as it took on more internal fuel, increased its weapon-carrying capacity, and accumulated various navigation and electronic defensive systems.

As with the B-47, it was not long before SAC showed the world what the B-52 could do. In 1956, within a year of its arrival in the front line, a B-52 dropped a thermonuclear weapon with a yield of almost four megatons at Bikini Atoll. Global reach was demonstrated in January 1957 when three B-52s of the 93rd Bomb Wing, supported by KC-97 tankers, flew from California via Labrador, Morocco, Ceylon, the Philippines, Guam and Hawaii to complete a nonstop round-the-world flight of 24,325 miles in forty-five hours and nineteen minutes. Captain of the leading B-52, *Lucky Lady III*, was Lieutenant Colonel James Morris, who had been the co-pilot of the B-29 *Lucky Lady II* on SAC's 1949 global epic. In just eight years, Morris had seen the round-the-world record reduced by better than half.

When the B-47 Stratojet appeared in the late 1940s it shattered preconceptions of what a bomber should look like. Its futuristic design was sleek and elegant. Thin swept wings, podded axial-flow jet engines, and a fighter-type cockpit were obvious evidence of a break with the past.

After a surprisingly short operational career, some elements of the B-47 force began phasing out in 1957, but B-52s arrived at a rate of more than ten a month during the year, and the command took delivery of its first jet tanker, the Boeing KC-135. In the months that followed, KC-135s compiled an impressive list of world records for point-to-point speed, closed-circuit speeds with payload, weight-lifting, and straight-line distance flown without refueling. The KC-135 proved to powerful force multiplier for the USAF, offering greatly improved tanker performance and growing to be an indispensable part of everyday operations worldwide for aircraft in a wide variety of roles.

Other SAC records followed when the Consolidated B-58 Hustler made its appearance in 1960. The B-58 was a true delta, with a slim area-ruled ("Coke bottle") fuselage, and the USAF's first supersonic bomber, capable of Mach 2.1 at over 60,000 feet. Beneath the slender body hung a 62-foot-long payload pod, part fuel tank and part weapons bay, that was expendable when empty. The three-man crew — pilot, radar navigator / bombardier, and electronics officer — sat in separate escape capsules. In the first year of B-58 operations, numerous world records were set and a very public tragedy recorded. On May 10,

1961, a 43rd Bomb Wing aircraft flew 670 miles in just over half an hour, averaging 1,302 mph. On May 26, a B-58 covered the 4,612 miles from New York to Paris in three hours, nineteen minutes and forty-one seconds, about a tenth of the time taken by Lindbergh. Sadly, that aircraft was destroyed in an accident at the Paris airshow only a week later. Though in many ways the most advanced bomber of its time, the B-58 had a short operational career. Expensive to operate and maintain, it claimed too large a share of SAC's budget and its high-altitude penetration role was overtaken by events. The B-58 was phased out of service at the end of 1969.

In 1958, airborne alert force trials were conducted, leading to the regular practice of keeping part of the SAC bomber fleet constantly armed and in the air. Tests were carried out, using specially modified KC-135s, on the feasibility of maintaining an airborne command post that could assume control of SAC's combat forces if the ground command centers were destroyed. In 1961, SAC went to a ground alert posture for fifty percent of its force, and airborne command-post operations (code-named Looking Glass) began, each EC-135 equipped with comprehensive communications and carrying a staff headed by a general

SAC'S STRATOJET

ABOVE The Boeing B-47 Stratojet was the world's first swept-wing bomber and the first to be specifically designed to deliver nuclear weapons. In tandem under the canopy sat the pilot and copilot, and the navigator occupied a claustrophobic space beneath them in the nose. The copilot was also a gunner, and could fire the tail-guns by remote control. The crew arrangement meant that the pilots had ejection seats that fired upward, but the navigator had to leave downward.

LEFT The pilot's cockpit in the B-47. Sitting for hours strapped to an ejection seat, unable to stand up and often sweltering beneath the greenhouse of the canopy, pilots found that on long missions this could be an uncomfortable place. If the pilot adjusted the air conditioning to cool down, the navigator beneath him froze.

When production of the B-47 ended in 1957, more than 1,200 Stratojets were serving in Strategic Air Command. The B-47E on display at the National Museum of the USAF was flown as a test-bed aircraft at Wright-Patterson Air Force Base from 1967 to 1969. It was the first USAF aircraft used for trials of a fly-by-wire system, in which the pilot's movements of the control column are transmitted to the control surfaces electrically rather than by cables and mechanical linkages.

officer. Looking Glass shifts remained on watch in the air for eight hours before handing over to another team, ensuring twenty-four-hour coverage every day of the year.

While SAC was making such marked progress in the strategic arena, tactical aircraft were not forgotten. At the end of 1950, Tactical Air Command and Air Defense Command were reestablished as separate entities, and major efforts were made thereafter by TAC to enhance the overseas capabilities of its fighter-bombers. Even as preparations were underway to send F-84s to Korea, there was a large deployment of fighter-bombers in the opposite direction. In September and October 1950, 180 F-84Es were ferried in two huge waves from Bergstrom, Texas, to Furstenfeldbruck, Germany, stopping five times en route for fuel. Within two years, fighters equipped for in-flight refueling were making similar deployments to Europe and Japan much more

quickly with the aid of tankers.

At the same time that tactical aircraft were making such gains in global flexibility, they were becoming far more powerful offensive weapons. Rapid progress in nuclear weapons design allowed the production of nuclear warheads small enough to be carried by fighters. With each weapon having a yield approximating to that of Fat Man, the bomb that leveled Nagasaki, the deployment of a fighter-bomber wing represented a fearsome projection of potential destructive power.

European Air Force Nuclear Deterrents

In January 1947, the British government decided that nuclear weapons should be at the core of Britain's defense policy. With development of the weapons underway, steps had to be taken to ensure that they could be delivered. The most probable enemy was the Soviet Union, and that presented a problem. RAF Bomber Command's front line was led by the Avro Lincoln, an aircraft that was not capable of reaching most of the likely targets nor did it have much prospect of surviving if it did. Operational Requirements were issued for jet bombers that could penetrate enemy defenses at high altitude, were fast enough to evade interception, and could deliver a nuclear weapon. In the years until such aircraft became available, Bomber Command accepted a reequipment program that never promised more than makeshift solutions. From 1950 to 1954, several RAF bomber squadrons operated refurbished B-29s (known as Washingtons) on loan from the United States, and from mid-1951 the twin-jet English Electric Canberra began entering service. The Canberra was originally intended as a

replacement for the Mosquito, a fast, high-flying bomber without defensive armament. It opened the door to jet aviation for the RAF's bomber crews and, like its prop-driven forebear, it proved to be a superbly versatile aircraft, but it was not a strategic bomber. It was the mid-1950s before the RAF at last began to acquire a genuine strategic capability, and even then the first four-jet that appeared, the Vickers Valiant, was itself an interim aircraft, ordered into production as a safeguard against the possible failure of the more radical designs that were to follow.

The Valiant first flew in May 1951 and entered service with 138 Squadron in February 1955. Interim it might be, but the new aircraft offered an exhilarating jump in performance compared to the B-29s of only the year before. It could reach Mach 0.85 and had a service ceiling of 54,000 feet. The bomb bay could hold a 10,000-pound nuclear weapon or twenty-one 1,000-pound high-explosive bombs. In time, ten squadrons were Valiant equipped, and it proved a versatile performer, in due course taking on the additional roles of strategic reconnaissance and tanking. In 1956–57, Valiants of 49 Squadron were selected to drop the first British nuclear weapons on ranges in Australia and at Christmas Island. Surpassed in terms of performance by the two later members of the V-force trio, the Avro Vulcan and the Handley Page Victor, the Valiant was eventually overtaken by structural weakness, too. In December 1964, cracks were found in the wing main spar and it was decided that the Valiants had run their course. They were withdrawn from service and scrapped.

Dramatically different in their distinctive designs, the Vulcan and Victor both met the RAF's original

ABOVE *The partnership between the KC-135 Stratotanker and the B-52 Stratofortress was the basis for the air-breathing element of the U.S. deterrent triad. The jet-powered KC-135 could operate at the same speeds and heights as the bombers, and it had a fuel capacity more than three times as great as the earlier piston-engined KC-97.*

BOTTOM *From 1957 on, Strategic Air Command maintained a ground alert system to cope with the need to ensure a rapid reaction to a threat. Here crew members race from their car to their already cocked and bombed-up B-58.*

DASHING DELTA

ABOVE The Convair B-58 Hustler was capable of exceeding Mach 2 and was the first supersonic bomber to go into production. It was also the first aircraft to be constructed mainly from stainless-steel honeycomb sandwich, the first to have a separate payload pod because its body was so slim that bombs could not be carried internally, and the first to have a stellar inertial navigation system.
RIGHT The B-58's pilot, navigator and defense systems operator were housed one behind the other in separate cockpits, each of which could be ejected as a capsule in an emergency. On March 5, 1962, Captain Robert G. Sowers piloted the B-58A now in the National Museum of the USAF from Los Angeles to New York and back in four hours, forty-one minutes, setting three transcontinental records. The crew earned the Mackay Trophy, the Bendix Trophy, Distinguished Flying Crosses, and congratulations from President John F. Kennedy.
BELOW LEFT Besides its other unconventional features, the B-58 defied U.S. bomber tradition in having a fighter-type stick for the pilot.
BELOW RIGHT The B-58 was powered by four separately podded General Electric J-79-5 afterburning turbojets of 15,600 pounds thrust each. Here the streamlined shape of the finned payload pod can be seen between the stalky undercarriage legs.

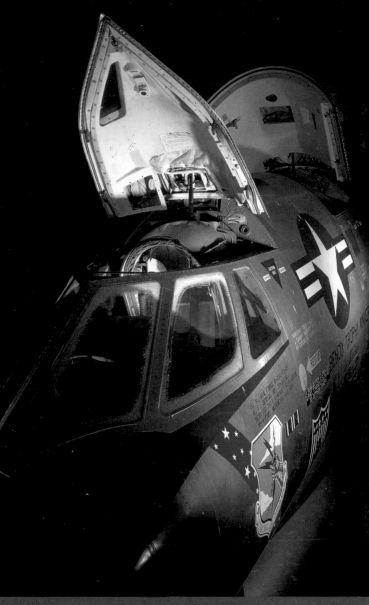

Developed during a period of parsimonious defense budgets, the Republic F-84F Thunderstreak was essentially a re-engined F-84 Thunderjet with swept wings. It filled the fighter-bomber gap until the arrival of the F-100, but it had some serious deficiencies. Problems with the engine were never wholly sorted out, and it had some unpleasant handling characteristics, especially at high speed. The example on display at the National Museum of the USAF is one of more than 200 fighters involved in a mass deployment across the Atlantic Ocean in response to the 1961 Berlin crisis.

requirement. The vast delta-wing form of the Vulcan was in marked contrast to the shark-like sleekness of the crescent-winged Victor, but both bombers could reach 60,000 feet and cruise at more than Mach 0.9. Both could deliver nuclear weapons, and a number of them were later converted to carrying the standoff Blue Steel missile, which was capable of being launched up to 150 miles from the target. For conventional bombing, the Vulcan's standard load of 1,000-pound iron bombs was twenty-one, but the Victor's bomb-bay design would have allowed it to carry as many as forty-eight. In July 1957, 83 Squadron became the first to receive its Vulcan 1s, and Victors took their place in the nuclear-strike front line with 10 Squadron nine months later. Victors also operated in the strategic reconnaissance role and soldiered on as tankers into the early 1990s. The Vulcan, much modified as the Mk. 2, remained in the front line as a bomber the longest of the three Vs, the last of them being retired in the early 1980s after being used in anger for the first and only time during the Falklands War.

Like SAC, the V-force kept a number of aircraft standing by on Quick Reaction Alert (QRA) to counter the possibility of a "bolt from the blue" nuclear strike by the Soviet Union. QRA was introduced by the RAF in February 1962, and from then on, one crew from each squadron was kept permanently at readiness to go to war when the alarm sounded. Warning was given by the radars of the Ballistic Missile Early Warning System (BMEWS) positioned in Greenland, Alaska and the United Kingdom. While they were on QRA, the V-force crews lived, ate and slept in their flying suits and were never more than minutes away from their checked and bombed-up aircraft. It was normal practice for the QRA system to be tested once every twenty-four hours with an exercise alert. Sirens and alarm bells would sound and the crews would rush to their aircraft, aiming to get to the takeoff position in less than four

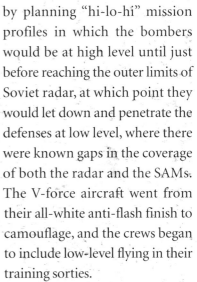

The English Electric Canberra B-2 was the principal production version (412 built) of one of the most adaptable aircraft of the jet age. More than a dozen air forces operated the type, and it was produced in several forms to meet bombing, interdiction and various reconnaissance requirements. In the United States, it was built by Martin as the B-57, which was itself much modified as the B-57F, with long wings and more powerful engines for flight at very high altitude. Here one of the B-2 prototypes is seen flying near the English Electric factory in the United Kingdom.

minutes, which was the length of time reckoned to be available before the first missiles might be expected to impact on targets in the United Kingdom. SAC crews based in the United States had the luxury of being further away and were given fifteen minutes.

When the Soviet air defenses grew more capable (as demonstrated to considerable effect by the shooting down of a U-2 near Sverdlovsk in 1960) and their high-level SAM cover more complete, it became apparent that the high-altitude penetration tactic of NATO's strategic bombers was no longer a sensible option. SAC and the V-force responded by planning "hi-lo-hi" mission profiles in which the bombers would be at high level until just before reaching the outer limits of Soviet radar, at which point they would let down and penetrate the defenses at low level, where there were known gaps in the coverage of both the radar and the SAMs. The V-force aircraft went from their all-white anti-flash finish to camouflage, and the crews began to include low-level flying in their training sorties.

While low-flying training offered more of a challenge and was more interesting, there were some additional problems associated with low-level operations. Aircraft designed specifically for high-level penetration were not ideally suited to flight at low level. The Vulcan, for example, had a huge delta wing that did not offer an easy ride through turbulence, and the bomber's lively capacity for maneuver had to be treated with care since the airframe was limited to a maximum of only 2G. The powerful Olympus 301 engines fitted to the Vulcan 2 (20,000 pounds thrust each) to allow the aircraft to operate at 60,000 feet were almost an embarrassment at low level, where they could quickly drive the airframe beyond its structural limits if left at full throttle, and their fuel consumption was impressively high. Another concern arose out of the escape facilities provided to cope with a major emergency: the two pilots sat on

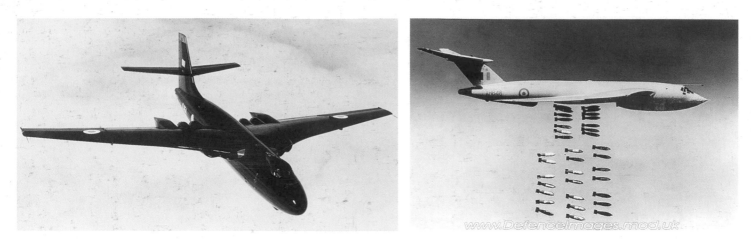

Of the three Vickers Valiant prototypes, one was for an advanced variant, the B-2, known as the "Black Bomber" for its glossy black finish. It was intended for the pathfinder role, penetrating to target at low level and marking it for follow-up strikes by other bombers. When the Air Ministry concluded that target marketing was an outdated concept, the program was canceled and only one B-2 was completed. The Black Bomber was used as a test-bed in the 1950s before being destroyed in the humiliating role of ground gunnery target.

ejection seats, but the three rear crew had to unstrap and leave through the door in the floor of the crew compartment. Many Vulcan crews were uncomfortably aware of the "us and them" situation this created, especially in the event of a catastrophic failure at low level. Whether any of this would have affected the capacity of the V-force to do its job effectively is a question to which an answer, thankfully, was never required. The fact is that nuclear conflict between NATO and the Warsaw Pact was avoided, which suggests that the deterrence triad (Intercontinental Ballistic Missiles [ICBMs], nuclear submarines, strategic bombers), with SAC and the V-force the vital airborne leg, was an insurance policy well worth the high cost of the premiums.

An extra source of concern for the Soviets was the

French "Force de Frappe," conceived as a nuclear deterrent genuinely independent of NATO. The Armée de l'Air's only strategic bomber, the Dassault Mirage IV, became operational in October 1964, and by 1966 it equipped nine squadrons. It was, in effect, a scaled-up version of the successful Mirage III fighter, and it was intended to follow a quite different strike profile from its NATO counterparts. Since the first part of the route from French bases would necessarily be through the concentrated Soviet defenses of Europe's Central Front, the Mirage IV was designed to penetrate those at low level and high subsonic speed before climbing rapidly close to the target and accelerating to carry out a sprint attack. The Mirage IV was capable of climbing to over 60,000 feet and had a maximum speed of Mach 2.2.

To improve the Force de Frappe's capability, it was supported by a fleet of Boeing C-135F tankers, and a later version of the bomber was modified to carry the ASMP standoff missile.

The Avro Vulcan was conceived as a large delta and posed many unprecedented challenges to the design team. At first the wing had a straight leading edge, but this was curved to correct buffeting in turns at high altitude. Originally painted white for the high-altitude role, the Vulcan was camouflaged when the V-force mission was changed to low level in the mid-1960s. Here a Vulcan 2 of the RAF's Near East Air Force Bomber Wing is seen crossing the coast of Cyprus in the early 1970s.

TOP *Seen from head-on, the Handley Page Victor was a dramatic sight, and in the 1950s it was so unique that it was thought the designer may have been inspired by reading science fiction. Dan Patterson photographed this survivor (serial XL231) in 2003 at the Yorkshire Aviation Museum. Victor XL231 joined 139 Squadron on February 1, 1962, was converted to become the prototype K.2 Tanker on January 23, 1972, and saw service in the Falklands War, in support of the Operation Black Buck Vulcan raid on Port Stanley.*

BOTTOM *The cockpit of XL231. As in the other V-bombers, the pilots sat on Martin Baker ejection seats, but in the ultimate emergency the rear crew had to get up and escape through the entrance door. In the center of the cockpit is a retractable panel (pushed away forward to allow pilots access) including the fuel gauges and fuel pump switches, and the autopilot controls. Top center of the instrument panel are the fire warning lights, and below them the switches for the powered flying controls.*

ABOVE *In the foreground is the domed cockpit of Vulcan B-2 XJ824, one of the aircraft in the collection at the Imperial War Museum's airfield, Duxford, near Cambridge in the United Kingdom. Seen in the background are a Spitfire, a Lancaster and a Mosquito.*
BELOW LEFT *The pilot's compartment of the Vulcan B-2, dominated by the centrally positioned throttle quadrant. Relight buttons can be seen in the tops of the four throttles. In the foreground is the fuel system tray, which was folded away forward until the pilots were safely seated. Note the fighter-type control sticks and the lambskin seat covers, added to ease the discomfort of long sorties.*
BELOW RIGHT *Normally, the Vulcan's engines were started one at a time, but to the left of the first pilot's seat was a panel that included the gang-start system. This was used when a crew was scrambled while standing Quick Reaction Alert (QRA). As the first pilot entered his seat, he hit the gang-start bar and all four engines wound up together, so saving precious minutes.*

Soviet Strategic Reach

The USAAF B-29s that diverted into Siberian airfields during the WWII air offensive against Japan offered the Soviets a shortcut to the production of a strategic bomber. Andrei Tupolev was instructed to copy the American aircraft, and by 1947 it was entering service as the Tu-4, an astonishing performance considering that everything about the B-29 had been reproduced from scratch — airframe, engines, systems, instruments and so on, to the last nut and bolt. Since that time, the Tupolev factory has been responsible for all of the significant large bombers flown by the Soviet forces. The list is impressive evidence of aeronautical achievement at the highest level. The first Soviet swept-wing jet bomber was the Tu-16 (NATO code name Badger), which first flew in 1952 and made a public appearance in 1954 with nine of them flying over the annual May Day parade in Moscow. This was followed by the Tu-95 Bear, a huge, swept-wing four-engine turboprop that entered service in 1957 and rivaled the B-52 in size. Supersonic capability was introduced in 1961 with the Tu-22 Blinder, and improved upon ten years later when the swing-wing Tu-22M (sometimes referred to as Tu-26) Backfire offered high-altitude dash speeds approaching Mach 2. In the late 1980s the Tu-160 Blackjack appeared, another swing-wing strategic bomber similar in concept to the Rockwell B-1, but larger, faster and with a greater unrefueled radius of action. All of these Tupolev aircraft were produced in quantity in both bomber and maritime reconnaissance versions, and all could be armed with either free-fall bombs or guided missiles.

The Centuries

A change of character was evident when the second generation of USAF tactical jet aircraft appeared. Agility, particularly at altitude, might have been desirable for fighting MiGs in Korea, but it was not a notable characteristic of the North American F-100 Super Sabre and the other "Century Series" fighters. Although ostensibly designed to meet a requirement for an air superiority fighter to replace the F-86, the F-100 was built in the mold of a rugged ground-attack aircraft. It was heavy and very fast, the first production fighter in the world to exceed the speed of sound in

> *"I don't mind being called tough, because in this racket it's the tough guys who lead the survivors."*
> GENERAL CURTIS LeMAY, USAF

level flight. On August 20, 1955, Colonel Horace Hanes took the official world speed record beyond the speed of sound in an F-100C, at 822 mph. The F-100C, with its strengthened wings and hard points for external stores, confirmed the USAF's intention to use the aircraft primarily in the ground-attack role, and the F-100D, the definitive variant, added the capacity to deliver nuclear weapons.

The later Century Series fighters continued the fast and heavy trend, and most variants, including those used as interceptors, were nuclear capable. McDonnell's F-101 Voodoo was originally conceived as a long-range escort fighter for SAC, but became an ADC interceptor and served in TAC both as a fighter-bomber and a reconnaissance aircraft. Powered by two afterburning Pratt & Whitney J-57s of nearly 15,000 pounds thrust each, it was slowed little by its considerable size. On December 12, 1957, Major Adrian Drew raised the world speed record to 1,207 mph in an F-101A.

Two other members of the Century Series were unashamedly of the "very fast in a straight line" persuasion, so much so in the case of Lockheed's F-104 Starfighter that it was referred to as the "missile with a man in it." Supposedly the result of talks with fighter pilots in Korea, the F-104 was offered as an air superiority fighter, but the design ensured its unsuitability for that role. Its dimensions were outrageous — 55 feet long and only 22 feet across the wing — and it was powered by a 15,000-pound-thrust General Electric J-79, which gave it a startling performance of Mach 2.2, a 50,000-feet-per-minute rate of climb, and zoom capability to over 90,000 feet. The F-104 was the first aircraft to be supersonic in the climb, and the first to hold world records for speed and height simultaneously. (On May 7, 1958, Major H.C. Johnson reached 91,243 feet in an F-104A. Nine days later, Captain W.W. Irwin recorded 1,404 mph. On December 14, 1959, Captain J.B. Jordan, in an F-104C, raised the height record to 103,389 feet. Rocket-boosted F-104s were flown higher at the astronaut training school, Edwards AFB, "Chuck" Yeager reaching an unofficial 108,000 feet in 1963.) Unfortunately, the tiny, razor-edged wings restricted both weapon load and maneuverability, problems that limited both the F-104's production run and its operational life with the USAF.

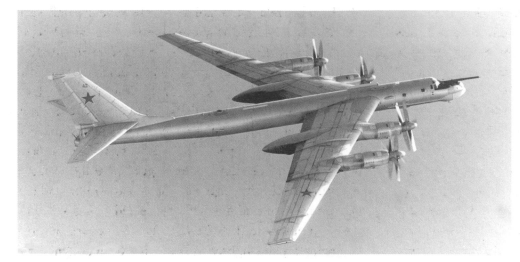

The Tupolev Tu-95MS (Bear H) was introduced during the 1980s and was the first new strike-version Bear produced since the 1960s. It was the launch platform for the long-range AS-15 air-launched cruise missile.

No such reservations were applied to Republic's F-105 Thunderchief. It was proposed in 1951 as a high-speed, long-range hauler of conventional or nuclear weapons, and it did just that extremely well. It had an internal bomb-bay, which could accommodate an extra fuel tank, and five pylons for a variety of external stores. Known as the "Thud," the F-105 was the largest single-seat, single-engine combat aircraft made, the loaded weight of later variants reaching 54,000 pounds. From the beginning it was an outstanding performer, the YF-105A exceeding the speed of sound on its first flight. Development problems held up the Thud's arrival in the front line until 1958, but it eventually proved itself operationally invaluable. The F-105D had all-weather capability and its external load for a combat sortie was impressive, typically eight 750-pound bombs, an ECM pod and an external fuel tank. A 20 mm rotating-barrel cannon was fitted, and other armament could include Bullpup air-to-surface missiles, rocket pods, napalm, and AIM-9 air-to-air missiles.

The remaining pair of Centuries to become operational originated from the urgent need to improve the defense of

ABOVE *The swing-wing Tupolev Tu-160 (Blackjack) is the Russian equivalent of the USAF's B-1B. Capable of Mach 2 at high altitude, the Blackjack can launch AS-16 short-range attack missiles (SRAMs) or AS-15 air-launched cruise missiles (ALCMs).* RIGHT *First flown in 1952, the Tu-16 (Badger) has been a most adaptable design. Over 2,000 were built in specialized variants for the bombing, reconnaissance, maritime surveillance, electronic intelligence gathering (ELINT), and electronic countermeasures (ECM) roles.*

the United States. At the time of the Soviet takeover in Czechoslovakia, North America was essentially undefended against air attack. During the 1950s, strenuous efforts were made to rectify matters by building immense transcontinental radar screens facing north across the Arctic and by acquiring jet interceptors equipped with air-to-air radar. Interim designs such as the F-86D, F-94C and Northrop's F-89D Scorpion served well enough for a while but were clearly inadequate as long-term solutions to the problem. The Convair F-102 Delta Dagger and F-106 Delta Dart were almost identical twins designed to meet a 1949 request for a "1954 interceptor." Aerodynamic problems and performance shortcomings delayed their introduction to service until 1956 and 1959 respectively, but both eventually performed well, the F-106 in particular proving itself a formidable Mach 2 interceptor for ADC, armed as it was with both conventional and nuclear-tipped air-to-air missiles. The F-106 was the closest thing to a manned robot then flying. Fitted with the Hughes MA-1, a radar developed as an automatic fire control system that could be coupled to an autopilot, it could be flown hands off to interception and missile launch.

Whatever the merits or shortcomings of the individual Century Series fighters, as a group they marked a dramatic expansion of the combat aircraft's performance envelope. The P-51D made its first appearance less than ten years before the first flight of the F-100. That decade saw fighter pilots move from general acceptance that they were confined by parameters of 40,000 feet and subsonic speed to everyday expectation of 50,000 feet plus and Mach 2. Reaching for the edge of the performance envelope had led to some sacrifice in the realm of maneuverability, and that was something the USAF would learn to live with until the next generation of fighters arrived. Fighters were growing in other ways, however. Radar was being recognized as increasingly essential to their effectiveness as weapons systems, as were guided missiles, and the additional role of ground attack had become a necessary consideration in the design of almost every fighter.

The appearance of the outstanding Soviet MiG-23 and MiG-25 fighters in the late 1960s encouraged the American development of more advanced aircraft. In reviewing its combat power, the USAF had to take account of the need both to deter (and, if necessary, to fight) the

USSR and to retain a capability to intervene in small wars affecting U.S. interests wherever they might occur. Here, at least in part, the lessons of Vietnam were invaluable. Aircrew who had been in combat usually had specific ideas about what was needed in the front line. Much as they appreciated the capabilities and toughness of aircraft such as the F-4 and A-7, they knew their limitations, too. When the F-4 first appeared in Southeast Asia, it was fast, but it was also large, not very agile, gunless, and trailed the signature of smoking engines. A strap-on cannon and the later addition of leading-edge slats helped a bit, but something better was needed. (Besides, it was time the Air Force had really capable fighters that had not been designed for the Navy!)

The perfect answer came in the shape of the McDonnell Douglas F-15 Eagle, an aircraft intended to make the most of the electronics revolution of the 1970s and designed from the outset as an air superiority fighter. The F-15 first flew in 1972 and reached front-line squadrons in 1975. Even larger than the F-4, the F-15 is immensely powerful; its two 24,000-pound-thrust Pratt & Whitney turbofans giving a clean aircraft a thrust-to-weight ratio of better than one at sea level. Its astonishing agility is born of this great power and the generous area of its delta-shaped wing. Pilots revel in the all-round visibility from the high bubble canopy, and in the systems that simplify the business of flying and fighting the Eagle — notably the head-up display and the "hands on throttle and stick" (HOTAS) arrangement of essential switches. The F-15's size allows space for the most comprehensive avionics and weapons control systems, and for an integral Vulcan cannon plus a wide variety of external stores. It also made the Eagle an obvious candidate for development as a long range, all-weather interdiction aircraft — the two-seat F-15E, capable of carrying 24,500 pounds of ordnance.

If the F-15 had a drawback, it was unit cost. Even while the Eagle was being developed, proposals were made for a lighter, cheaper fighter to complement the F-15 and allow for a larger front line. It was important to have enough aircraft to meet emergencies wherever in the world they occurred. After a fly-off with the Northrop YF-17 (subsequently produced as the McDonnell Douglas F/A-18 for the USN), General Dynamics' YF-16 was selected for development as the USAF's lightweight fighter.

THE CENTURIES

Top The sharply swept tail surfaces of the North American F-100 Super Sabre set a pattern followed by all of the Century series fighters. Tail number 41753 is an F-100C on display at the National Museum of the USAF, and is marked as an aircraft of the 452nd FDS (Fighter Day Squadron), 322nd FDG (Fighter Day Group). It was named *Susan Constant* in a 1957 ceremony celebrating the 350th anniversary of the founding of Jamestown, Virginia.

Bottom Left The F-100 was the first production aircraft capable of supersonic speed in level flight. It proved an outstanding ground attack aircraft. Here one is seen under guard at Tan Son Nhut Air Base, Saigon, South Vietnam, in May 1966.

Bottom right The F-100 cockpit layout was typical of the post-World War II period. The basic flying instruments are in the center, with engine instruments to the right. Radio and navigation aid controls are along the right console, and warning indicators are scattered around roughly at eye level. The control stick is shaped to the hand and carries buttons to transmit radio messages or drop weapons, a trigger to fire the guns, and a "coolie hat" switch on top to set the aircraft's trim.

Top The RF-101C Voodoo on display at the National Museum of the USAF was flown by the 45th TRS (Tactical Reconnaissance Squadron) of the 460th TRW in Southeast Asia. During the Vietnam War, RF-101Cs flew some 35,000 sorties; 44 were lost — 31 to antiaircraft fire, five to SAMs, one to an airfield attack, six to operational accidents, and only one in air combat. In 1957, the museum's Voodoo took part in Operation Sun Run, a transcontinental flight that established new records, including a round-trip from Los Angeles to New York and back in 6 hours, 46 minutes and 36 seconds. This aircraft flew low-altitude reconnaissance during the Cuban Missile Crisis.

Left The second Voodoo in the USAF Museum is an F-101B, the two-seat all-weather interceptor variant. The front cockpit is relatively uncluttered because the radar fire-control system instruments are in the rear, entrusted to the radar operator. Note the red tags, warnings that ejection seat safety pins must be removed before flight.

Inset The eighth F-101A produced (32425) in flight. This first version of the Voodoo was designed as a long-range escort fighter. Only 77 were built, and many were later modified as tactical reconnaissance aircraft.

RIGHT The winged sword of Tactical Air Command decorates the fin of the F-104C in the National Museum of the USAF. Starfighter 60914 was flown by the winning pilot in the William Tell international fighter meet competition in 1962.

BELOW LEFT The Lockheed F-104 Starfighter was an almost wingless aircraft and very fast, earning it the nickname of "the missile with a man in it." Powered by an afterburning J-79 engine producing up to 15,800 pounds of thrust, the F-104 could reach speeds well in excess of Mach 2.

BELOW RIGHT The cockpit of the F-104C was compact and well-arranged. Note that the throttle lever is vertical rather than horizontal and, at upper left, that there is a rearview mirror fixed to the open canopy rail. A yellow handle next to the right footwell jettisons the canopy, and pilot ejection is initiated by pulling up the black-and-yellow striped handle just in front of the seat pan.

Left The F-105D Thunderchief in the National Museum of the USAF (AF60504) is named *Memphis Belle II*. It has two aerial victories recorded over MiGs. The F-105D, a single-engined fighter-bomber, could carry over 12,000 pounds of weapons. That was considerably more than the original four-engined *Memphis Belle*, a B-17F bomber, could manage in World War II.

Below Left One of the Thunderchiefs on display at the National Museum of the USAF is a two-seat F-105G, modified for Wild Weasel operations. It served in Southeast Asia from 1967 to 1973 and is adorned with red stars recording claims for three MiGs shot down. Note the two rearview mirrors and the linear instruments fashionable at the time. The radar screen in front of the stick provided air search, automatic target tracking and terrain avoidance information.

Below Right The Republic F-105 Thunderchief (known as the "Thud") was the principal USAF strike aircraft used against North Vietnam from 1965 to 1970. In the course of those operations it suffered almost 20 percent of the USAF's total wartime losses of fixed-wing aircraft. Of the 833 F-105s of all variants built, 397 were lost in Vietnam.

Top Left and Right The F-106 at the National Museum of the USAF last served with the 49th FIS (Fighter Interceptor Squadron). During a sortie from Malmstrom AFB on February 2, 1970, it entered a flat spin, forcing the pilot to eject. Unpiloted, 80787 recovered on its own and made a gentle belly landing in snow-covered field. After minor repairs, it was returned to service. Bottom Left The Convair F-106 Delta Dart was equipped with the Hughes MA-1 electronic guidance and fire-control system. It was capable of carrying out hands-off interceptions and could launch nuclear-tipped Genie air-to-air missiles automatically. Bottom Right F-106 pilots did not have to have pointed heads, but it might have helped! Note the linear instruments and the horseshoe control stick, through which the pilot viewed the radar scope.

In the course of the years that followed, the F-16 Fighting Falcon grew in capability until it was neither as light nor as cheap as had been hoped, but there is no doubting that it became a superbly adaptable fighter. It is an electronic masterpiece, evidence of which can be seen in the head-up display and in the side-stick controller operating fly-by-wire flying controls. The computer-driven cockpit features a reclining seat, the better to help the pilot cope with the stresses of sustained 9G turns, and the wings are equipped with an array of hard points that allow for the carriage of over 20,000 pounds of external stores, a load exceeding the original empty gross weight! The F-16's dramatic performance, advanced systems and capacity to handle a wide range of weapons have made it an admirable all-weather, multi-role aircraft, capable of excelling in roles as diverse as air superiority, close air support or deep interdiction.

Canadian Contribution

The postwar expansion of the Royal Canadian Air Force was undertaken with fighters occupying center stage. In the early 1950s, the RCAF reinforced NATO by taking several squadrons of Canadair Sabres (Canadian-built F-86s) to Europe, basing them at airfields in Britain, France and West Germany. In Canada, Air Defence Command operated all-weather CF-100s from 1953. The air defense of North America became a fully integrated system in 1957, when Canadian personnel joined their U.S. counterparts at the joint North American Air Defense Command Headquarters (NORAD) near Colorado Springs. The U.S. and Canada agreed to share air defense information and to manage jointly the early warning radar chains (the mid-Canada, Pinetree, and DEW lines) built across Canada and Alaska. Canadian and U.S. squadrons then operated on a twenty-four-hour alert basis to react to any threat from across the Arctic.

Air Defense of the United Kingdom

In the early 1950s, the RAF found itself embarrassed by the pace at which its fighters were becoming obsolescent. The performance of aircraft such as the Soviet MiG-15 and Tu-16 offered unwelcome evidence that the British aircraft industry, which had been at the forefront of military jet aircraft development at the end of World War II, was lagging behind. To plug the gap until a homegrown product was available, twelve squadrons of F-86 Sabres were acquired from the United States, ten of which were based in Germany. They shared the RAF front line with Meteor 8, Vampire 5 and Venom day fighters until Hawker Hunters began arriving in 1954. Night-fighting duties were looked after by two-seat, radar-equipped adaptations of the Meteor, Vampire and Venom. The Gloster Javelin all-weather fighter became available from 1956, but it was not an unqualified success. Even with two 11,000-pound-thrust engines, its thick delta wing kept it subsonic, and it did not carry missiles as standard armament until mid-1958.

The Hunter, especially in its later Mk. 6 form, was a joy to fly, a real pilot's aircraft, but it was still a basic gun-firing, day-only fighter, incapable of flying at supersonic speeds except in a dive. (The closest a Hunter could come to the speed of sound in level flight was demonstrated when test pilot Neville Duke set a world speed record of 728 mph — Mach 0.92 — over the English Channel on September 7, 1953.) It was, however, maneuverable and extremely robust, and once the English Electric Lightning started to reach squadrons in 1960, the Hunter moved to the ground attack role, for which it was admirably suited.

The arrival of the twin-engined Lightning was a notable event for RAF Fighter Command. The spectacular advance in performance represented by the Lighting was unprecedented, as was the impressive jump in size and weight. The new fighter was 55 feet long and its loaded weight was 20 tons. Its unconventional layout gave it a startling appearance. After the graceful Hunter, the Lightning was a burly, slab-sided monster, with sharply swept, inadequate-looking wings, a great sail of a fin, and engines mounted one above the other. Impossibly thirsty, it needed the pregnant bulge of a huge ventral fuel tank and a flight refueling probe to give it time to do its job. All that having been said, the Lightning proved to be a splendid interceptor. It was the first RAF aircraft to be supersonic in level flight, and in its definitive Mk. 6 form it could achieve Mach 2.3 at 40,000 feet, a height it could climb to in two and a half minutes fully loaded; the service ceiling was 60,000 feet. Most significantly, the Lightning was the first RAF fighter designed as an integrated weapons system rather than a mere gun platform. A Ferranti air intercept radar and Firestreak or Red Top missiles were the principal elements, with two 30 mm Aden cannon in a ventral pack added as secondary armament.

The CF-105 Arrow was a delta-wing interceptor aircraft, designed and built in Ontario by Avro Canada. Seen as the crowning achievement of the Canadian aerospace industry, the Arrow first flew on March 25, 1958, and quickly showed that it had the potential to be the most advanced air defense fighter aircraft in the world. After long and bitter political debate, the program was canceled in 1959. By then, five of the six completed prototypes had flown a total of over 70 hours, achieving speeds up to Mach 1.96 and altitudes over 50,000 feet. To ensure that the Arrow program could not be resurrected, Avro was instructed to destroy the prototypes and burn the blueprints. On display in the Canada Aviation Museum are what remains of the sixth Arrow prototype, the nose section (left) and part of the fuselage, on which is clear evidence that a saw was used to cut the aircraft into pieces.

TOP *The first Avro Arrow prototype, RL 201, was rolled out at Malton, Ontario, in October 1957.* ABOVE *Referred to by its crews as "Clunk" or "Lead Sled," the Avro Canada CF-100 was arguably the best of the first-generation all-weather jet fighters and the only Canadian-designed fighter to enter full production. Nearly 700 were built.* RIGHT *For a first-generation jet fighter, the cockpit of the CF-100 was quite well laid out. However, its heating system was inadequate and the CF-100 had a reputation for freezing its crews.*

At last equipped with a formidable air defense fighter, the RAF was confounded by British government policies. A 1957 Defence White Paper said that the Lightning would be the last manned fighter for the RAF. It concluded that there could be no effective defense against nuclear missiles, and that a deterrent against attack was the only sensible counter to such a threat. For the time being, that would be the V-force bombers, but eventually they too would be phased out, to be replaced by ICBMs. Until they were, the defense of V-force bases would be the primary responsibility of a reduced fighter force, acting in concert with surface-to-air missiles. In the shadow of this misguided policy, the British aircraft industry suffered the cancellation of many advanced aircraft projects during the 1960s, and Fighter Command shrank from 600 front-line aircraft in thirty-five squadrons in 1956 to 140 aircraft in eleven squadrons in 1962.

It was not long before the idea of a 20th-century air force having no manned combat aircraft collapsed under the weight of its own impracticability. In the meantime, however, the cancellation of several aircraft programs left the RAF of the late 1960s searching for a solution to the problem of being able to meet its responsibilities effectively. At one stage, hopes had been pinned on the Hawker P.1154, a proposal for a supersonic V/STOL fighter, but that fell by the wayside in 1965, to be followed by the government decision to fill what was becoming a yawning gap in the RAF's capabilities by buying F-4 Phantoms from the U.S. and powering them with Rolls-Royce Spey engines. The ubiquitous F-4 was to be used in the air defense, strike/attack and reconnaissance roles (and by the Royal Navy) until other types, developed in Europe, became available. The first operational Phantoms (designated FGR.2 in the RAF) were delivered to 6 Squadron in May 1969, and the first pure interceptors (FG.1)

On March 30, 1962, XM967 was the first two-seat Lightning T.5 to fly. It was retired to the fire dump at Kemble airfield in December 1976.

joined 43 Squadron six months later. With the introduction of the Anglo-French Jaguar in the mid-1970s, those Phantom squadrons dedicated primarily to the attack and reconnaissance roles were released to take over air defense from the ageing Lightnings. Just two Lightning squadrons were retained until 1988.

In their turn, the Phantoms were replaced starting in 1987 by the Air Defence Version (ADV) of the swing-wing Panavia Tornado. (In the early years of the Tornado project, the fighter was known as the MRCA — Multi-Role Combat Aircraft. To those grown cynical over political mismanagement of defense matters, the initials stood for Military Requirements Come Afterwards.) Given the special needs of the U.K. Air Defence Region for a fighter that could reach out to intercept bombers such as the Backfire before they launched their standoff missiles, the Tornado ADV promised

The BAC (English Electric) Lightning exhibited at the RAF Museum, Hendon, is a Mk. 6, the final and definitive version of the type. Mk. 1s entered service with 74 Squadron in 1960, and the last Mk. 6s were retired from 11 Squadron in 1988. With two engines one above the other and additional fuel tanks mounted above the wings, the Lightning's appearance was unconventional, but beneath the slab-sided design was a powerful and capable Mach 2 air defense fighter.

good range and endurance. In a 1982 trial flown with missiles in place and two underwing fuel tanks, a Tornado flew at high level to a point 375 miles from base, descended to medium level for two hours and twenty minutes, returned and loitered near base for fifteen minutes, remaining airborne for a total of four hours and fifteen minutes. When the support of tankers is added, there is little doubt about the ability of the Tornado F.3 (the RAF designation) to function as an effective interceptor. Once early problems with the GEC Foxhunter radar had been overcome, it proved able to detect targets at 100 miles and offered both "track while scan" and "look down / shoot down" facilities. Sky Flash, Sidewinder and AMRAAM missiles can be carried and there is a 27 mm Mauser cannon built into the lower fuselage. Seven squadrons of Tornado F.3s were the United Kingdom's first line of defense against air attack throughout the 1990s, supported by an innovative arrangement in which eighty-nine of the RAF's Hawk jet trainers were modified to carry Sidewinders.

Air Defense Elsewhere in Europe

In the rest of European NATO during the 1950s and 1960s, the air forces generally relied on a mixture of British and American aircraft to take them into the jet age and provide a measure of air defense. Meteors, Vampires and Sabres flew with the air forces of Norway, Denmark, Belgium, the Netherlands, Italy and Greece. When the Luftwaffe was reborn in West Germany in 1956, the first air defense aircraft ordered were Sabres. At various times in later years most of the continental European countries became customers for export versions of U.S. fighters — the F-104 Starfighter, F-4 Phantom II, F-5 Freedom Fighter, F-16 Fighting Falcon or F-18 Hornet. One odd addition to the

TOP *The Hawker Hunter was a delight to fly, a pilot's sportscar of an aircraft. Here three Hunters of 92 Squadron complete a formation loop over the Yorkshire coast near Flamborough Head.*

BOTTOM *The Hunter cockpit was less spacious than those of contemporary U.S. fighters, but comfortably snug. The stick was shaped to the hand and carried the elevator trim switch, trigger and cine-camera button. For an aircraft of the 1950s, the general arrangement of instruments and switches was better than most. This Hunter 6 is on display at the Imperial War Museum's airfield at Duxford in the United Kingdom.*

The Panavia Tornado was produced under a joint agreement between Germany, Italy and the United Kingdom. It is a compact twin-engined variable-geometry aircraft and the first production military aircraft to have fly-by-wire controls. There are strike-attack (seen here in the markings of 617 Squadron, RAF), air defense, and electronic warfare versions in service.

NATO inventory came after the disintegration of the Warsaw Pact, when East German MiG-29s were added to the front-line strength of the unified Luftwaffe.

On Different Flight Paths

Traditionally neutral Switzerland developed a jet fighter, the P-1604, to the prototype stage in 1955, but it was not successful and reliance was placed first on Vampires and then on Hunters and F-16s. Sweden's SAAB, having had some success with the barrel-shaped J 29, went on to greater things with the J 32 Lansen all-weather fighter, and the J 35 Draken, a uniquely original double-delta design that began entering service in 1960. By the mid-1960s, the Draken had developed into a most effective interceptor, capable of Mach 2 and with armament that included both radar-guided and infrared-seeking missiles. It was followed in the 1980s with another original design, the JA 37 Viggen, the first canard-delta fighter to enter operational service. In 1993, the next step was taken with the JAS 39 Gripen, a small cropped delta with close-coupled flying canard fore-planes. (JAS is an industrial group headed by SAAB. The initials stand for Jakt/Attack/Spaning — Fighter/Attack/Reconnaissance.) The canards, together with the elevons, provide the aircraft with control surfaces both fore and aft of the center of gravity, thereby improving agility and reducing induced drag. Designed from the outset to have the growth capability to meet new threats and the changing operational and logistics requirements of an air force, the Gripen has been planned as a fighter to meet the challenges of the 21st century.

In France, the Armée de l'Air eased the postwar transition into jets with the purchase of Vampires from Britain. Home-grown Dassault Ouragans began reaching interceptor squadrons in 1952, and these were followed only three years later by swept-wing Mystère IVAs. That same year, the ultimate development of the line, the Super Mystère, flew, and on its fourth flight exceeded the speed of sound in level flight. By 1957 it was in production for the Armée de l'Air, and was the first European supersonic aircraft to serve with front-line squadrons. However, Marcel Dassault was not resting on his laurels. Work was already well underway on the first of his superb series of Mirage delta-wing fighters. In October 1958, the Mirage IIIA, powered by an Atar turbojet of 13,000 pounds thrust, exceeded Mach 2 and then, boosted by an auxiliary rocket, climbed to 82,000 feet. At the same time, it demonstrated its ability to take off and land on less than 2,500 feet of grass. This adaptable fighter subsequently appeared in many different versions, over 1,400 being built to see service with the air forces of twenty nations. In France the formidable multirole Mirage III took its place at the forefront of the Armée de l'Air's operations. It was therefore with some confidence in their front-line aircraft that French airmen faced the future when France formally withdrew its forces from NATO in 1966 and set about establishing a wholly independent defense policy.

Dassault continued to dominate French fighter production for the rest of the century with the Mirage series. Although the name was retained, the principal fighters to succeed the Mirage III in the series had little in common with their illustrious forebear. The Mirage F1, introduced in 1974,

RIGHT *A Mirage 2000 takes on fuel. The two-seat versions of Dassault's front-line fighter are the Mirage 2000N, designed for all-weather nuclear penetration at low altitude and very high speed; and the Mirage 2000D, a ground attack aircraft equipped with precision weapons and avionics that allow it to fly in any weather, day or night, and at a very low altitude, hugging the terrain.*

BELOW *Dassault fighters parade their pointed-nose pedigrees outside the Musée de l'Air et de l'Espace, Le Bourget, Paris.*

broke the delta pattern with conventional swept-back wing and tail surfaces, but the familiar delta planform returned with the next generation Mirage 2000. Developed initially as an air superiority fighter, the Mirage 2000 first flew in 1982, and deliveries to the front line began in the following year. In subsequent years, it demonstrated its versatility, being produced in various forms, including the 2000C (cannon and Matra air-to-air missiles), 2000D (up to 14,000 pounds of bombs and missiles plus cannon), and 2000N (nuclear-tipped cruise missile). The weapons could be carried on nine wing and fuselage hard points, together with ECM pods and external fuel tanks as necessary. Adoption of a fly-by-wire control system allowed the Mirage 2000 to be made inherently unstable, so dramatically improving the fighter's maneuverability while adding safeguards to prevent the pilot from losing control or overstressing the machine. Fast, capable and a pleasure to fly, the Mirage 2000 gave the Armée de l'Air a formidable combat aircraft as the spearhead of its front line for the closing years of the 20th century.

Aircraft performance is still a major factor in any combat engagement, but now it is more often the performance of the active and passive sensors, electronic countermeasures, aids to pilot situational awareness, and weapon capability that are the deciding factors in an engagement. Stealth technology is equally important. By the early 1990s, yet another Dassault delta was being tested that took all this into account. The Rafale is a twin-jet combat aircraft capable of carrying out a wide range of short- and long-range missions including ground and sea attack, air defense and air superiority, reconnaissance and high-accuracy strike or nuclear-strike deterrence. The Rafale M variant, a single-seat carrier-based version for the navy, entered service in 2001; the two-seat Rafale B and single-seat C for the Air Force followed in 2003. The cockpit has Hands-On Throttle-and-Stick (HOTAS) control, and is equipped with a head-up wide-angle holographic display from Sextant Avionique that provides aircraft control data, mission data and firing cues. A collimated multi-image head-level display presents tactical situation and sensor data, and two touch-screen lateral displays show the aircraft system parameters and mission data. The pilot also has a helmet-mounted sight and display. A camera records the image of the head-up display throughout the mission. The RBE2 radar developed by Thomson-CSF and Dassault Electronique has look-down, shoot-down capability and can track up to eight targets simultaneously. The electronic warfare system incorporates solid-state transmitter technology, jammers, and radar, laser and missile-warning systems. The range of weapons includes Mica, Magic, Sidewinder, ASRAAM and AMRAAM air-to-air missiles; Apache, AS30L, ALARM, HARM, Maverick and PGM100 air-to-ground missiles; and Exocet/AM39, Penguin 3, and Harpoon antiship missiles. For a strategic mission, the Rafale can deliver the Aerospatiale ASMP standoff nuclear missile. On reaching full combat configuration in 2005, Rafale showed itself to be a most impressive multimission aircraft.

Aviatsiya PVO

During the Cold War the Soviet air defense system faced the enormous challenge of defending a nation spread over two continents, with possible opponents at land borders as widely spread as those with Norway and Afghanistan, Turkey and China, while eyeing the U.S. across the Bering Strait and the Arctic wastes. The interceptors of the Aviation of Air Defense (Aviatsiya Protivo-Vozdushnoy Oborony, or APVO) were on constant alert, and, unlike their NATO counterparts, they were not at all reluctant to use their weapons. Enemy aircraft on reconnaissance missions might perhaps be considered fair game (and were), but there were also instances of both civil and military aircraft that had wandered off course being shot down. The most notorious incident occurred on September 1, 1983, when a Korean Airlines Boeing 747 was destroyed by missiles fired from a Sukhoi 15 Flagon after entering Soviet airspace and flying over the Kamchatka Peninsula: 240 passengers and 29 crew died.

Having surprised the West with the MiG-15 in 1947, the wizards of the Soviet aviation industry went on

The Mirage 2000 is the current front-line fighter in the Armée de l'Air. It also serves in various forms in the air forces of Abu Dhabi, Egypt, Greece, India, Peru, Taiwan and Qatar.

pulling jet-powered rabbits out of their hats. The Mikoyan-Gurevich factory improved the basic breed with the MiG-17 Fresco and the supersonic MiG-19 Farmer, before moving on to the astonishingly successful delta-winged MiG-21 Fishbed in the late 1950s. Supersonic at sea level and capable of exceeding Mach 2 at altitude, the MiG-21 was produced in numerous versions and saw service with the air forces of some fifty countries. Derivatives were still being produced in China at the end of the century. Successive machines continued to achieve remarkable performance figures. The MiG-25 Foxbat was designed to counter the U.S. SR-71 Blackbird and was capable of speeds approaching Mach 3. On July 7, 1962, Georgiy Mossolov flew a modified MiG-25 (designated E-166) to a world record speed of 1,666 mph, and on August 31, 1977, Alexander Fedotov took an E-266 to an altitude of 123,523 feet, a world record for aircraft that still stood at the end of the century. An improved version of the Foxbat that was just as fast but had much greater range was the MiG-31 Foxhound, which entered service in the mid-1980s. The Mikoyan stable also produced the versatile swing-wing MiG-23 Flogger, which became a worldwide multi-role success, and the dramatic, exceptionally capable MiG-29 Fulcrum, a Mach 2.3 fighter with an initial rate of climb exceeding 60,000 feet per minute. Its contemporary, the large Su-27 Flanker, was another surprise for NATO. It was a major advance in Soviet fighter capability — fast, agile, rapid-climbing, unusually long-ranged, and able to carry up to ten missiles, either radar- or IR-guided.

The Central Front

Nowhere was the Cold War confrontation between NATO and the Warsaw Pact more intense than on Europe's Central Front, which was the setting for the heaviest concentration of opposed military muscle the world has ever seen. In terms of numbers, the Warsaw Pact forces, led by the Soviet Union, greatly outnumbered their NATO counterparts, and their doctrine was based on "resolute attack

Bolt for the Blue, *by Gerald Coulson.*

points from the air or for the rapid deployment of airborne troops.

Knowing themselves to be considerably out-numbered, the NATO forces were forced to rely on sophisticated tech-nology and superior training to meet the challenge. It would have been quite a balancing act. The respective main battle tank strengths in the 1980s were indicative of the problem: NATO was outnumbered by almost three to one, and the antitank systems mounted on vehicles or helicopters the Warsaw Pact held a similar advantage. At the heart of NATO's defense were the West German armed forces, reborn in the 1950s. The new Luftwaffe developed quickly into a formidable air arm, its backbone initially composed of F-84Fs and later F-104Gs and F-4s capable of being used in the air defense, nuclear strike, interdiction and reconnaissance roles. The smaller central nations, Belgium and the Netherlands, also operated the F-104 for a while, as did the Canadians in Europe, who produced their own version, the CF-104. In time, Belgium moved on to the Mirage 5 and the Netherlands chose the Canadair/Northrop NF-5, before both countries elected to build F-16s under license. The French withdrew from NATO's defense councils in 1966 and thereafter presented the Soviets with a dilemma. France possessed an independent air force of notable capability, built around Dassault's Mirage fighters and the nuclear-armed Force de Frappe. Since the French would no longer act in accordance with NATO policy, would they be restrained in their use of nuclear weapons, or would they be prepared to use them immediately in any conflict?

conducted at great tempo and in great depth." If the Warsaw Pact had taken the offensive, the air forces would have led the way, with strike aircraft such as the Su-24 Fencer and the fighters of the MiG family flooding westward to attack airfields and key targets such as command and control centers. Interdiction of reinforcement and supply routes would have followed. Planning and controlling these operations was the task of Frontovaya Aviatsiya (Frontal Aviation). By the 1980s, Frontal Aviation had more than 5,000 tactical fixed-wing aircraft available, with ground-attack duties being performed by such capable machines as the MiG-27 Flogger variable geometry fighter and the Su-25 Frogfoot. Besides these there were well over 3,000 helicopters, among them fearsome creatures such as the Mi-24 Hind gunship, the Mi-28 Havoc antitank helicopter, and the Kamov Hokum, a dedicated fighter intended to take on the enemy's helicopters and close-support aircraft. Used in combination, these aircraft gave the Warsaw Pact an extremely powerful, fast-moving, flexible force with which to punch holes in enemy defenses and maintain the momentum of the armored columns on the ground. The use of large numbers of assault and gunship helicopters offered the Warsaw Pact forces unprecedented mobility, either for offensive action against strong

EUROPEAN JETS

ABOVE A Dassault Ouragan, bearing the insignia of the famous Escadrille des Cigognes, stands in front of a Mystère IVA in the Musée de l'Air et de l'Espace, Le Bourget. RIGHT Apart from the captions in French, the cockpit layout of the Mystère was very similar to those of contemporary American and British aircraft. This example can be seen at Duxford in the United Kingdom.

RIGHT Several examples of the Fiat G.91 are on display at the Italian Air Force Museum (Museo Storico dell' Aeronautica Militare Italiana), Vigna di Valle, on the shores of Lake Bracciano, north of Rome. BELOW Guarding the entrance to the Caproni Museum in Trento, Italy, is a Lockheed F-104, appropriately mounted in a steep climbing attitude. BOTTOM In the 1950s, the Fiat G.91 was the winner of a NATO lightweight fighter competition. It was operated by the air forces of Italy, Germany and Portugal. The last G.91 was finally taken out of service by Italy in 1995.

Britain's Royal Air Force introduced a new factor into the Central Front equation in 1970 when the world's first V/STOL fighter, the Harrier, became operational with 4 Squadron in RAF Germany. The Harrier's unique ability to be independent of fixed runways gives it an operational flexibility unattainable by more conventional warplanes. If war between NATO and the Warsaw Pact had broken out, Harriers could have been dispersed to presurveyed sites and housed in barns, bus stations, supermarkets, warehouses, or any other large buildings capable of rapid conversion to aircraft hangars. The equipment needed for logistics support of these sites — pillow fuel tanks, spares and munitions packs, vehicles, et cetera — comes as part of the Harrier package. Decried in its earliest form as an aircraft that could carry very little not very far, the Harrier was developed into a formidable weapons system. The RAF's night/all-weather Harrier II GR 7 version has provision for two 25 mm cannon, and is fitted with pylons capable of carrying 9,000 pounds of external stores, including a variety of bombs and rockets for close support, air-to-air missiles for intercept missions, reconnaissance pods, or nuclear weapons.

Having provided for a day when there could be no airfields left, the RAF in Germany did not neglect attack aircraft dependent on fixed bases. The Hunters and Canberras of the 1960s gave way to F-4 Phantoms and Buccaneers, and then in the 1970s to Anglo-French SEPECAT Jaguars (SEPECAT, from Société de Production de l'Avion Ecole de Combat et Appui Tactique), unprepossessing but effective little fighter-bombers with all-weather and tactical nuclear strike capability. By the mid-1980s, all of the Germany-based Jaguar squadrons had been reequipped with the Panavia Tornado GR 1. Designed from the outset as a low-level supersonic aircraft, the Tornado GR versions are capable of carrying a wide range of conventional stores,

The Polish Army Museum in Warsaw exhibits military artifacts from their long and often difficult history. The corridor through Poland has been a path of invasion for hundreds of years, the most recent being the German invasion that opened World War II. The Soviet occupation continued that oppression. Here, Napoleonic horse-drawn carts and Russian tanks and helicopters make a fascinating contrast.

including the Air-Launched Anti-Radar Missile (ALARM), Paveway laser-guided bombs (LGBs), standoff missiles and an anti-armor missile system. For self-defense, the GRs carry Sidewinder air-to-air missiles and twin internal 27 mm cannons.

From the first, the United States Air Forces in Europe (USAFE) were essential to NATO's defensive plans for the Central Region. By 1950, USAFE commanded two tactical fighter wings based in West Germany and equipped with F-84E Thunderjets. Two years later, there were eleven wings, and more airfields had been acquired in Germany, France and the United Kingdom. Following an incident in 1953 when an F-84 was shot down by MiG-15s near the Czech border, F-86s were deployed to Germany, but by the mid-1950s these were replaced by F-100 Super Sabres. In 1959, the nuclear-capable F-100 wings had to make arrangements to leave France and redeploy to the United Kingdom when President de Gaulle insisted that all nuclear weapons in France had to be under French control. After several more years of discomfort with U.S. predominance in NATO, de Gaulle finally dropped the other shoe in 1966 when he announced the withdrawal of France from the military alliance, requiring all NATO installations to be removed from French territory within one year. By the time of de Gaulle's ultimatum, USAFE included eleven tactical wings — seven Tactical Fighter Wings, three Tactical Reconnaissance Wings, and a Troop Carrier Wing. Losing the French bases was painful but hardly fatal. Three of the fighter wings (F-100s and F-4s), two reconnaissance wings (RF-101s and RF-4s) and the transport wing went to the United Kingdom, and the others moved to Germany (F-4s and F-105s).

ABOVE *Formation of eight Polish Army Mi-8 Hip helicopters.*
BELOW *The Soviet IS-2 heavy tank (46 tons) fitted with 122 mm gun was introduced by the Soviets early in 1944 and used by the Polish Army during the Cold War. IS-2s would have been high on the target list for NATO tactical fighters in the event of war.*

POLISH PURSUITS

Mariusz Adamski, of Warsaw, Poland is passionate about aviation and images of aviation. He has allowed us an insider's view of Cold War military fighters, front-line Polish Air Force MiG and Sukhoi jets, from the "other side" of the conflict. The Polish Air Force is an independent force, but was part of the Warsaw Pact before the fall of the Soviet Union and is now part of NATO.

ABOVE A Polish Air Force MiG-21MF Fishbed-J above the clouds. The MiG-21 was the first Soviet fighter to be capable of flying at more than twice the speed of sound. Over 11,000 were produced and were flown by the air forces of some fifty countries.

RIGHT Two Polish Navy MiG-21bis Fishbed-Ns in formation with three German Navy Tornados over the Baltic.

ABOVE A pair of Polish Fulcrums — a MiG-29UB closes on a MiG-29A.
BELOW The Polish Air Force was one of the customers for the Sukhoi Su-22, the export version of the Su-17 Fitter. Here the leader of a pair of Su-22M4 Fitter-Ks breaks away from his wingman.

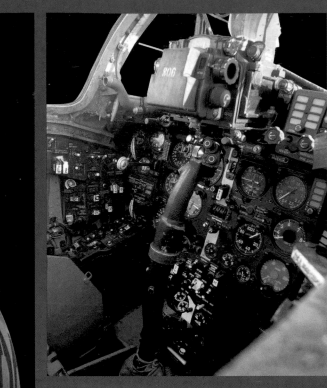

SUPERSONIC SOVIETS

LEFT The Su-7 was the first of the Sukhoi fighters (Su-7/17/20/22) known to NATO by the code name Fitter. The example on display at the Polish Aviation Museum in Krakow is an Su-7BKL, the most numerous variant, with about 500 built. Fast and maneuverable, the Su-7 was an excellent ground attack aircraft, but hampered by its notoriously short combat radius. ABOVE The Su-7's cockpit was typical of its era, with instruments and switches scattered around in an apparently haphazard manner. Pilots found that the visibility from the Su-7 cockpit was not good, especially during an approach to landing. BOTTOM LEFT Air reached the engine via a nose-mounted intake with a translating shock cone containing the SRD-5M radar. BOTTOM RIGHT A total of 1,847 of all versions were produced, 691 of which were exported to nine countries, including Poland.

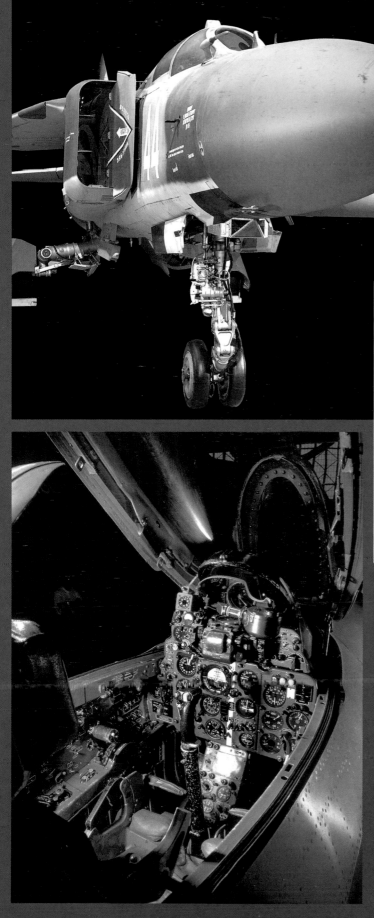

TOP LEFT The MiG-23 Flogger represented a major advance in Soviet fighter design. It was the first Soviet aircraft to have variable sweep wings, and to be fitted with a "look-down, shoot-down" radar. Powered by a Tumanski afterburning engine of 22,000 pounds thrust, the Flogger was very fast, capable of Mach 2.3 at altitude and Mach 1.2 at low level. ABOVE The most obvious difference between this MiG-21 cockpit and its Western counterparts is the bright turquoise coloring of its protective paint. Another unfamiliar feature is that the cockpit canopy is hinged at the front. Pilots complained that the seat was set too low, limiting their visibility, and that armament switches were not logically arranged. LEFT In numerical terms, the MiG-21 Fishbed is the most successful jet fighter ever produced. More than 8,000 were built and they were flown by the air forces of over thirty countries. It was the USAF's principal aerial opposition during the Vietnam War. The MiG-21F seen here is exhibited at the National Museum of the USAF.

A BRIT AND TWO BEARS

In 1994, the British Defence and Air Attaché in Moscow, Air Commodore Phil Wilkinson, was a guest on board a Tu-142 Bear F of Russian Naval Aviation during flights to and from the United Kingdom. It was a truly unique experience for a Western observer at that time. Two Bears made the trip (an Air Force Tu-95MS Bear H accompanied the Bear F) to take part in the 1994 International Air Tattoo at RAF Fairford. TOP LEFT Introduced in the 1950s, the Tu-95 Bear was the most successful Soviet bomber, and was the only operational bomber deployed by any country to be powered by turboprops, which provided long endurance at speeds only slightly less than comparable jet bombers. The variant seen here is the Tu-95MS Bear H, which became the launch platform for the AS-15 Kent cruise missile. TOP RIGHT A Tornado F3 of the Royal Air Force closes in to escort the Bear F out of U.K. airspace after the Russian aircraft's appearance at the International Air Tattoo, RAF Fairford, in 1994. For the first time, an RAF officer saw an intercepting NATO fighter from inside a Bear. CENTER RIGHT The glazed nose of the Tu-142M Bear F. Beyond is the left inboard Kuznetsov turboprop of 15,000 shaft horsepower, which drives two four-bladed contrarotating propellers. BOTTOM RIGHT Phil Wilkinson's view from the Bear H of the accompanying Bear F on the ramp at Kaliningrad during the flight to RAF Fairford in 1994.

TOP LEFT The Bear F flying over the English countryside's pathwork quilt of fields and hedgerows. CENTER LEFT Aboard the Bear F during engine start, with the first and second navigators keeping their eyes on the pilots. BOTTOM LEFT King Hussein of Jordan meets the Bear F crew at RAF Fairford. TOP RIGHT The U.K. Defence and Air Attaché settles into a sonics operator's seat aboard the Bear F. He later changed into a flight suit to look the part while occupying a pilot's seat. CENTER RIGHT The Bear F crew after landing at RAF Fairford (Air Commodore Wilkinson is fifth from left). BOTTOM RIGHT The Tu-95MS Bear H adorned with the Russian flag. The large radome houses the ground mapping and target acquisition radar. Above it is a smaller radome for a terrain-following radar.

As the decade of the 1960s ended, the impact of the U.S. involvement in Southeast Asia was all too evident in the USAFE. In 1961 the strength of the command had been some 100,000 personnel and about 1,600 aircraft. By 1970 the figures were down to 57,000 and 770. At the same time, new and far more capable aircraft were on the horizon. The first F-111 "Aardvarks" arrived in the United Kingdom in September 1970, and in 1977 the first F-15A wing was established at Bitburg in Germany. By 1983 all the F-4 wings had reequipped with F-15s and F-16s, and the specialized role of close air support on the battlefield had been given to the Fairchild A-10 Thunderbolt II, more colloquially and generally known as the "Warthog." Impressive though these new aircraft were in boosting USAFE's tactical air power during the latter part of the century, they would have been strongly and rapidly reinforced from the United States in an emergency.

The Haulers

Although TAC's image was popularly associated with its fighter squadrons, there was much more to the command than that. At the end of the Korean War, TAC controlled some 1,100 aircraft, no less than 60 percent of which were transport types, with the Fairchild C-119

A Harrier GR 7 of 20 (Reserve) Squadron, RAF Wittering. The unit is responsible for the training of all RAF pilots joining front-line GR 7 squadrons.

steadily replacing the ageing C-46. By the mid-1950s, tactical airlift aircraft were beginning to assume the practical forms that would predominate for the rest of the century — high wings, cavernous box-shaped interiors, unobstructed flat floors, and full fuselage rear doors that lowered to become ramps. Lockheed's incomparable C-130 Hercules and its smaller cousin, Fairchild's C-123 Provider, transformed the business of hauling military cargo and later proved to be superbly adaptable multirole aircraft.

The currents of technological change reached out to the other USAF commands, too, in the 1950s. Halfway through the decade, the Military Air Transport Service (MATS) fleet of over 1,400 aircraft included 610 four-engined transports. Most were C-54s, but the Douglas C-124 Globemaster, known as "Old Shaky," added significantly to the lifting capacity of the command. The huge clamshell doors in its nose made it possible to carry such bulky cargo as tanks or bulldozers, and it was capable of taking 200 fully equipped troops in its double-decked cabin. However, it was not very speedy. The solution to that failing was in sight, since the C-124 was the last piston-engined transport ordered for MATS.

Besides being responsible for its global route system, MATS operated the Air Weather Service (AWS), using aircraft to track and penetrate severe weather areas, and the Air Rescue Service (ARS), which carried out worldwide search and rescue activities over both land and water. The ARS of the 1950s was equipped with an assortment of aircraft: SB-17Gs, SB-29s, SC-54s, SA-16 Albatross amphibians, and helicopters such as the Kaman H-43A, Sikorsky H-19 Chickasaw and Vertol H-21 Workhorse.

In the late 1950s, Douglas sought to retain their prime position as supplier of large military transports with the C-133 Cargomaster, a four-turboprop aircraft capable of swallowing the Atlas and Titan ICBMs through its rear loading door. Useful as it was, the C-133 was never a great success, principally because of unexpected engine and fatigue problems. A little later, the Boeing C-137 and the Lockheed C-141 Starlifter added pure jet speed and much greater reliability. In 1970, the outsize C-5 Galaxy was introduced, with a huge "drive-through" cargo deck capable of taking main battle tanks, large helicopters, or over 300 troops. In its later C-5B version, the Galaxy can accept payloads of almost 150 tons over distances of 3,000 miles. In the early 1990s, the USAF's transport fleet was further improved by the arrival of the McDonnell-Douglas C-17 Globemaster III. Smaller than the C-5, the C-17 is still capable of taking vehicles up to the size of an M-1 tank, and has been designed to operate from what are called "austere fields."

World leadership in transport aircraft design was consolidated by the United States during World War II, and continued thereafter. However, the aircraft industries in a number of other countries began to produce independent designs after the war, many of them adapted for military purposes. In Britain, the RAF replaced the ubiquitous Dakota with the Vickers Valetta, and gave the heavy

The United Nations forces in the Korean War were kept supplied by Combat Cargo Command's transpacific air bridge. At a Japanese air base in June 1952, a C-124 disgorges supplies through its clamshell doors, a C-54 and a C-47 in the background.

transport role to the Handley Page Hastings, a C-54 contemporary of similar size that was one of the last big transports to retain the challenge of a tailwheel. In 1956, the Blackburn Beverley, at the time the largest aircraft ever to enter service with the RAF, arrived to take on heavy lifting for the military. An uncompromisingly angular monster with a wingspan of 162 feet, the Beverley was unconcerned with such niceties as streamlining. Powered by four Bristol Centaurus piston engines and sporting an impressive fixed undercarriage under its cavernous fuselage, the Beverley was slow and had limited range, but in regions such as the Middle East its ability to para-drop large loads and to operate from small, dirt strips proved invaluable.

The RAF continued to operate British designs as the turbojet era dawned. The twin-boomed turboprop Armstrong-Whitworth Argosy became the tactical transport in the 1960s, by which time the long-range duties had been taken on by the turboprop Bristol Britannia and the pure jet de Havilland Comet. Lighter loads were handled by the Hawker Siddeley Andover, a twin-engined multipurpose turboprop; some of them were used as VIP transports. The RAF's long-range capabilities were further enhanced in 1966 by the Vickers VC-10 and the Short Belfast, a large heavy-lift transport powered by four Rolls-Royce Tyne turboprops. The Belfast was the first military aircraft in the world to become operational with an auto-

matic landing system. From the late 1960s, the Hastings, Beverley and Argosy were steadily replaced in the role of tactical transport by the C-130 Hercules. In the mid-1980s, as a direct result of lessons learned during the Falklands War, the RAF took delivery of nine ex-British Airways and Pan American Lockheed Tristars, which were converted to passenger/freighter tankers, and in the specialized world of transporting VIPs, the "Queen's Flight" acquired a BAe 146.

In the medium transport range there were a number of successful aircraft produced by various countries after World War II. The French built the twin-boomed Nord Noratlas, which flew in 1950 and stayed in service for twenty years. Elsewhere in Europe there were the CASA Aviocar (Spain), Fokker F-27 Troopship (Holland), Aeritalia G-222 (Italy) and the Franco-German C-160 Transall. Kawasaki of Japan produced the twin-jet-powered C-1, and de Havilland Canada the piston-engined Caribou, later developed into the Buffalo turboprop STOL transport. One notable cooperative development undertaken at long range in the 1980s was the Airtech CN-235, a joint venture between CASA of Spain and IPTN of Indonesia. The twin-turboprop CN-235 has been a considerable success and has been sold in its various forms to some twenty countries.

The only national aircraft industry to continue to match the United States in both the size and diversity of its military transports throughout the post-WWII era was

that of the Soviet Union. Antonov, Ilyushin and Tupolev between them produced a steady stream of capable transport aircraft. The Antonov contributions have been particularly impressive, beginning after the war with the adaptable An-2 Colt single-engine biplane, of which more than 15,000 were built during the later part of the century. Turboprops have included the large An-12 Cub and the medium-sized An-26 Curl. For operations from remote, "hot and high," and unprepared fields, the turboprop An-32 Cline and its successor, the jet-powered An-72

TOP *The huge Douglas C-133 Cargomaster added new dimensions to the USAF's airlift capacity when it arrived in 1957. Always technically temperamental, C-133s were withdrawn from service in 1971 because of fatigue problems.*
LEFT *From 1965, Lockheed C-141s played a major role in airlifting supplies to U.S. forces all over the world. Early models often ran out of space before reaching their load-carrying limit, so Lockheed designed fuselage plugs to stretch the cargo hold.*
BELOW Coronet Oak, *by Gil Cohen. During Operation Coronet Oak, members of the 179th Airlift Wing, Ohio, and the 130th Airlift Wing, West Virginia, prepare for their missions while a C-130 from Rhode Island's 143rd Airlift Wing takes off from Howard Air Force Base, Panama.*

LEFT *The Handley Page Hastings entered service with 47 Squadron, RAF, in 1948. The type survived as a tailwheel transport for twenty years before being replaced by the Lockheed C-130.* RIGHT *The heavy lift requirements of the RAF were met by the Short Belfast between 1966 and 1976. It could carry 150 fully equipped troops or a Chieftain tank or two Wessex helicopters. Only ten were built and they were operated by 53 Squadron.*

Coaler, were both designed with engines mounted above a high wing that was fitted with slats and slotted flaps. At the larger end of the scale have been the An-22 Cock, a four-engined turboprop with a wingspan of 211 feet, and the gigantic An-124 Condor, the Soviet answer to the USAF's C-5. Powered by four 52,000-pound thrust jet engines, the An-124 is 240 feet across the wing and has a drive-through hold capable of engulfing 330,000 pounds of cargo, including tanks, helicopters, construction equipment, missile batteries, and so on, together with eighty-eight passengers in an upper cabin. Fully loaded, its range is almost 3,000 miles. In 1985, an overloaded Antonov 124 flown by Vladimir Tersky established a world record by lifting a payload of 340,000 pounds to an altitude of 35,270 feet. (Even larger is the An-225 Mriya, by far the heaviest and most powerful aircraft built in the 20th century. Using a stretched An-124 fuselage and larger span wings, the Mriya was powered by six 52,000-pound-thrust turbofans and had an unobstructed cargo deck 141 feet long. It was intended to carry the Soviet space shuttle on its back.)

Western Spies in the Sky

Adequate military power for the containment of communist expansion was vital to the West during the Cold War confrontation, but it was equally important to know what the other side was doing. There was a continual need for strategic reconnaissance of potential enemies and their activities. Immediately after World War II, American surveillance of the Soviet Union began with modified B-29s (F-13A, B-29F) of the 72nd Reconnaissance Squadron at Ladd Field, Alaska. Later, other units expanded the role, using RB-50s, RB-36s, RB-45s and RB-47s. It was a risky occupation, involving a limited number of high-altitude overflights for photographic coverage, but soon including sorties in which electronic sensors derived information from the opposition's radio and radar transmissions. One extraordinary development was the modification of a few B-36s (GRB-36F) to allow them to operate with RF-84Ks carried in a cradle. The huge bomber stayed in international airspace around the Soviet Union while the RF-84K was launched on a high-speed-dash reconnaissance mission and then retrieved for the ride home.

To gain maximum value from electronic surveillance, "Ferret" missions were flown. Ferret aircraft flew close enough to Soviet airspace to provoke a reaction. At first, search and height-finding radars would sweep the Ferret. If the "threat" persisted, missile guidance and ground-controlled interception radars joined in, accompanied by increased radio transmissions and message traffic, all monitored and recorded by the Ferret. Occasionally, the Soviet reaction to the Ferret was aggressive and the information hunter became the hunted. In the decade of the 1950s some two dozen aircraft of the Western powers were lost on strategic reconnaissance missions, and several others were attacked and damaged. At least eight of the losses were suffered by the USAF, including an RB-50 and four RB-29s, plus an ERB-47H of the 55th SRW (Strategic Reconnaissance Wing) shot down by MiG-19s over the Barents Sea on July 1, 1960. (The American aircraft came from the USAF, USN and CIA. Also lost were a number of British, Swedish and Chinese Nationalist aircraft.)

In an attempt to remove the risk from strategic reconnaissance, aircraft were sought that would be of such high performance that they could operate over anywhere in the world with impunity. The Martin RB-57D and F, much-rebuilt Canberras with more power and greatly increased wing area, did well in the role, and in the 1950s and 1960s two remarkable aircraft came from Lockheed's famous "Skunk Works" to meet the need. The first, the U-2, looked like a jet-powered sailplane. Even in its earliest form, the U-2 could operate up to 70,000 feet; later versions pushed this up to 90,000 feet. For a while, 70,000 feet seemed to put them out of reach of the Soviets, and in the late 1950s USAF pilots temporarily released to the CIA flew over the Soviet Union and gained much invaluable information about such things as bomber deployment, air defense systems and submarine development. However, on May 1, 1960, a U-2 flown by Francis Gary Powers was shot down near Sverdlovsk by SA-2 missiles. Chairman Kruschev used the incident to embarrass President Eisenhower and wreck a summit meeting, and penetrations of Soviet airspace were brought to a halt, at least for the time being. At

Lockheed, the "Skunk Works" was already at work on an aircraft capable of presenting the Soviets with a still greater challenge. By the mid-1960s, the United States had the SR-71 Blackbird, a strategic reconnaissance vehicle that could match the U-2's performance for range and altitude while adding the ability to sustain flight at more than three times the speed of sound.

The RAF was also involved in strategic reconnaissance. In special Anglo-American arrangements made at the highest level, British crews penetrated Soviet airspace several times in the early 1950s while flying USAF RB-45Cs temporarily painted in RAF markings, in one case drawing flak at 36,000 feet from the defenses near Kiev. One of the deepest penetrations was achieved in 1953, when a modified RAF Canberra B-2 flew to a new missile site at Kapustin Yar, near Stalingrad. Operating at heights up to 48,000 feet in daylight, the Canberra was finally intercepted and damaged by Soviet fighters as it approached its target. It managed to escape, however, and landed safely in Iran. Specialized versions of the Canberra for photographic reconnaissance soon arrived, culminating in the 1960s with the PR-9, which remained operational in the front line beyond the end of the century. Larger aircraft, modified for gathering electronic intelligence in similar fashion to the USAF's RC-135s, were the Comet and then, from the mid-1970s, the Nimrod.

LEFT *Moving the Herd, by Jim Dietz* RIGHT *The Antonov An-72 (Coaler) was designed to fly from small unprepared airstrips. The An-74 derivative is capable of operating from ice floes in the Arctic. Its most significant design feature is the use of exhaust gases blown over the wing's upper surface by the high-mounted engines to improve short takeoff and landing (STOL) performance.*

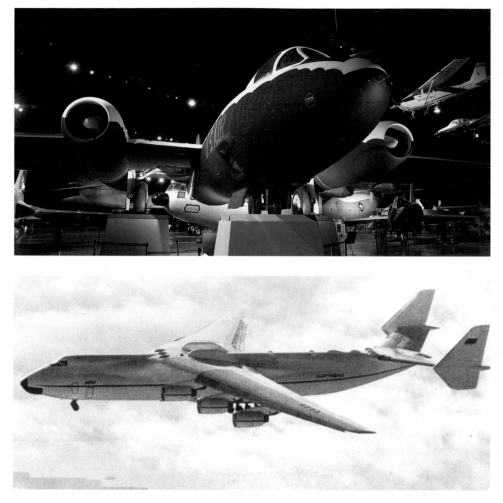

TOP *In the 1950s, the Martin RB-57D's long wings helped fill the USAF's need for a strategic reconnaissance aircraft that could fly high enough (70,000 feet) to avoid interception. Soviet protests over these missions led President Eisenhower to end military overflights of the USSR after three RB-57Ds demonstrated their capability by flying over Vladivostok in daylight on December 11, 1956. In 1960, following wing structure problems, the USAF withdrew them from the strategic role, but some were retained to fly weather reconnaissance and air defense training missions. The last RB-57D was retired in 1970. The example at the National Museum of the USAF is displayed in the markings of the 4025th Strategic Reconnaisssance Squadron (Light).* BOTTOM *The Antonov An-225 Mriya was the largest aircraft to fly in the 20th century. The weight of the Mriya at maximum load is over 1.3 million pounds; its wingspan is 290 feet; and it is supported by a thirty-two-wheel landing gear.*

Missiles on the Doorstep

When Fidel Castro scized power on January 2, 1959, Cuba joined the list of countries that were under occasional surveillance by the strategic reconnaissance eyes of the United States. After the fiasco of the Bay of Pigs invasion by U.S.-based Cuban exiles, the Soviets stepped up the supply of arms to their Cuban client, and by 1962 it was clear from photographs taken by U-2s that these included surface-to-air missiles (SAMs). It also seemed that the SAMs were placed to defend other sites intended for mobile medium-range ballistic missiles (MRBMs). High-altitude U-2 coverage of the island confirmed the assessment and revealed other sites being prepared with fixed launching pads for intermediate-range ballistic missiles (IRBMs). With these in place, nuclear warheads could be launched against U.S. targets from the East Coast to Wyoming. In mid-October, American fears were confirmed when a U-2 mission photographed a site with MRBMs deployed. Low-level reconnaissance by RF-101s and USN RF-8s followed, and President Kennedy was handed incontrovertible photographic evidence of both the presence of missiles and Soviet involvement. On October 22, Kennedy reported to the American people on the threat and the countermeasures being taken, and announced a blockade of Cuba. Three days later he warned the Soviets directly against continuing to deploy missiles.

Meanwhile, combat aircraft (F-100s, F-104s, F-105s and F-106s) packed USAF bases in Florida. In SAC, B-47s went to their dispersal bases, B-52s flew nuclear-armed airborne alert, and missile crews came to instant readiness. Tension rose on October 27 when Major Rudolf Anderson's U-2 was shot down over Cuba. Matters worsened even further the next day because a U-2 on an Arctic mission inadvertently strayed over Siberia's Chukotka Peninsula and Soviet missiles were readied. A U.S. apology for the transgression was accompanied by a steely assurance that U.S. forces were now ready to take military action in Cuba and elsewhere, if necessary. Kruschev took the hint and agreed to withdraw

LEFT *The Lockheed U-2* Dragon Lady *was first used for high-altitude reconnaissance over the Soviet Union in 1956. Fifty years later, U-2s were still invaluable reconnaissance assets, flying at altitudes above 70,000 feet to collect signals and imagery intelligence simultaneously. Several have been shot down, but the U-2 is notoriously difficult to fly, and most of the forty destroyed have been lost in accidents.*

ABOVE RIGHT *A photograph taken by a low-flying RF-101 on October 25, 1962, of a medium-range ballistic missile (MRBM) launch site at San Cristobal, Cuba.*

BELOW *The SA-2 (Guideline) missile is the most widely used air defense missile in the world. More than 13,000 have been fired in anger, one of which brought down the U-2 of Francis Gary Powers in 1960. Controlled by the Fan Song radar, the SA-2 has a range of about 30 miles, a maximum operating altitude of 80,000 feet, and speed of Mach 3.5.*

both the missiles and a number of Il-28 bombers already delivered to Cuba. The "Cuban Crisis" was over, and a salutary lesson had been given on the value of strategic reconnaissance in an age of global confrontation.

At Sea with the U.S. Super-Carriers

As Cold War tensions rose after World War II, it became clear that the Soviet Union was intent on building a blue water navy with a strong submarine fleet potentially threatening the sea lanes in both the Atlantic and the Pacific. The United States and its NATO partners perceived a need to react by ensuring that their naval forces and maritime patrol aircraft could counter the threat in either ocean. In the 1950s, as opinions in the United States were revised about the utility of large aircraft carriers, a new class of 60,000-ton ships was commissioned incorporating the latest naval engineering features, including the angled decks and steam catapults developed by the Royal Navy. Another RN device, the mirror landing system that replaced the deck landing officer and his paddles, was added in 1955. Besides being much larger ships, the new Forrestal-class vessels were far more potent than their WWII ancestors. From the outset they were conceived as a means of projecting real power to almost every corner of the globe. The WWII idea of providing floating airfields for fighters and short range attack aircraft was expanded to add the roles of long-range strike and reconnaissance, and to include an effective airborne antisubmarine capability.

After toying with the idea of a composite fighter during the end of World War II (the Ryan Fireball was powered by both a radial piston engine and a turbojet), the U.S. Navy became the first to go to sea with a fully operational jet fighter squadron when McDonnell FH-1 Phantoms joined the light carrier *Saipan* in 1948. The FH-1 was the first in the McDonnell (and McDonnell Douglas) family of jet fighter designs flown by the U.S. Navy. As the progenitor of its line, it was a transitional aircraft; within a year its successor, the F2H Banshee, was in service, together with the first of Grumman's naval jets, the F9F Panther. Both of these saw combat in the Korean War. So, too, did a bulky all-weather night-fighter, the Douglas F3D Skynight. Flown by U.S. Marine Corps squadrons, the Skynight destroyed more enemy aircraft than any other carrier-borne type in the Korean War.

With the arrival of the Forrestal class, U.S. Navy decks began hosting even larger machines such as the Douglas A-3 Skywarrior, an 82,000-pound nuclear-strike aircraft, and later the spectacular Mach 2 North American A-5 Vigilante, which served first as a bomber and then in the long-range reconnaissance role. Development of carrier-borne fighters was rapid, and a proliferation of types in a variety of shapes and sizes were produced as designers sought to take advantage of new ideas in aerodynamics and construction techniques. Some original and promising designs — the revolutionary Chance-Vought Cutlass and record-breaking Douglas Skyray among them — were quickly overtaken by events and were out of production before the end of the 1950s. McDonnell's F3H Demon, dogged by problems that killed four test pilots at the prototype stage, was another fighter taken into service even as design work was well underway on its successor, and the Grumman F11 Tiger was supplanted after little more than a year as the Navy's front-line fighter by the LTV F8U Crusader. The F8U showed its paces early when, on July 16, 1957, with the help of three in-flight refuelings, John Glenn flew a photo-reconnaissance version from Los Angeles to New York in three hours and twenty-six minutes, an average speed of 724 mph.

One factor that may have contributed to the relatively short in-service lives of many U.S. Navy and Marine Corps fighters was the adaptability required of each airframe. The search for the perfect multirole naval aircraft was pursued with vigor. Shipborne fighters were sought to match the performance of their likely land-based opposition, operate in all weathers, and carry weapons ranging from guns and bombs to air-to-air missiles. As a result, many U.S. naval aircraft were extraordinarily capable. The Crusader was a carrier stalwart throughout the 1960s, as was the Douglas A-4 Skyhawk, a diminutive delta-winged wonder originally seen as a replacement for the ageing piston-powered Skyraider in the attack role. The A-4 proved capable of absorbing perennial rejuvenation to remain an effective combat aircraft in several of the world's air forces for the rest of the century. Having first flown in 1954, the Skyhawk was in production until 1979, when the 2,960th and last was delivered to the U.S. Marine Corps. In its various forms, the A-4 came to accept weapons loads as varied as 500-pound bombs, gun pods, torpedoes, rocket packs, air-to-surface and Sidewinder missiles. Its pylons could carry ECM pods

ABOVE *North American A-5 Vigilantes stand ready on the deck of the* Ranger *(CVA-61) while a Douglas A-4C of VA-93 lands on. This photograph was taken in the South China Sea, February 22, 1965.*

LEFT *A Grumman F9F Panther of VC-61 on the hangar deck of the* Bon Homme Richard *(CV-31) off the coast of Korea, November 15, 1951.*

or extra fuel tanks that more than doubled the internal fuel capacity. An in-flight refueling probe was fitted, too, and there was the capability to act as an in-flight tanker. All this from an aircraft with a wingspan of only 27 feet, so small that it was a rarity among naval aircraft — its wings did not need to fold for storage aboard ship.

Were there a prize for "dominant combat aircraft of the 1960s and 1970s," the most obvious candidate for the title would be the McDonnell Douglas F-4 Phantom II. Originally thought of simply as a fleet air defense fighter to replace the Demon, the F-4 had exceptional capabilities that soon led it to be employed in other roles — air superiority, interdiction, close support, photo-reconnaissance — and by other services. The first major in-service variant was the F-4B, which joined Squadron VF-101 of the U.S. Navy in 1961, but the Phantom II had begun to attract the attention of the aviation world before that with a series of records — an altitude of 98,557 feet in December 1959, and a 500-kilometer closed circuit flown at 1,217 mph and 100-kilometer closed circuit at 1,390 mph in September 1960. The record-breaking did not stop there: next was a world speed record of 1,606 mph in November 1961; and an altitude of 98,425 feet reached in just 6 minutes, 11 seconds, in April 1962.

ABOVE LEFT *A barrier engagement by a North American FJ-4 Fury of VA-146 on the* Oriskany, *November 21, 1960.*

ABOVE RIGHT *The North American RA-5C Vigilante carried side-looking radar, an infrared scanner and an array of vertical, oblique and split-image cameras. With a loaded weight of up to 80,000 pounds, Vigilantes were among the heaviest aircraft to operate from carriers. They were retired from service in 1979.*

BELOW *The Vigilante at the National Museum of Naval Aviation, Pensacola, was flown by RVAH-6 during the deployment of USS* Nimitz *(CVN-68) to the Mediterranean in 1978.*

JETS AT SEA

LEFT Unconventional in appearance, the Chance Vought F7U Cutlass was not a successful naval aircraft. Its lack of adequate power earned it the nickname "Gutless Cutlass." Afterburners were required for landings, heavy takeoffs and wave-offs, and it could not be landed aboard ship on one engine. U.S. Navy test pilot Lieutenant John Moore said that "The Westinghouse J-46 engines generated about as much heat as [the company's] toasters." The improved F7U-3 was delivered to squadrons in 1954, but by 1959 the Cutlass was retired from service.

ABOVE The Cutlass exhibited at the National Museum of Naval Aviation, Pensacola, is an F7U-3M. On March 12, 1953, VA-83's Cutlasses went aboard *Intrepid* (CVA-11) armed with AIM-7 Sparrows, becoming the first squadron to deploy overseas with missiles.

ABOVE Nearly 2,000 F9F Cougars were produced for the U.S. Navy and
Marine Corps, serving in the fighter, attack, photo reconnaissance, and
training roles. The Cougar was also the first swept-wing aircraft used by
the Blue Angels flight demonstration team, during the 1955–1957 air
show seasons. The F9F-6 Cougar on display at Pensacola was flown by
VF-142 off the aircraft carrier *Boxer* (CVA-21) in 1955.

RIGHT The Director of the National Museum of Naval Aviation, Captain
Bob Rasmussen, logged over 1,000 hours in F9Fs, both Panther and
Cougar. Although he enjoyed flying the fighter, he admits to being a little
disappointed in the cockpit. He says that for him it was almost too roomy,
giving him the feeling that he was not "part of the machine," and that he
was sitting too low down, "submerged to the neck in the airplane."

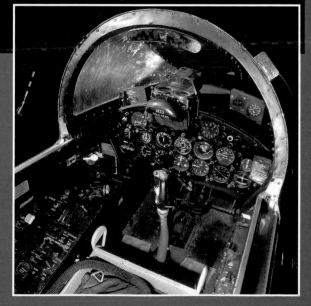

Designed to a U.S. Navy requirement for a lightweight, single-engined, carrier-based, high-performance daylight attack aircraft capable of close support, dive-bombing and interdiction roles, the prototype Douglas A-4 Skyhawk first flew in 1954 and the type entered service in 1956. By 1979, when production ended, 2,960 Skyhawks had been delivered. Built small to be cost effective and so that more could be accommodated on a carrier, A-4s were affectionately nicknamed "Heinemann's Hot Rod," after Douglas designer Ed Heinemann. Developments included adding a refueling probe, provision for antiradar missiles, and a fuselage hump accommodating an avionics pod.

Upgraded models had improved engines and a drogue parachute, new avionics displays, larger cockpit canopies, and more ammunition for the two cannons. The Skyhawk's combat career began with the first U.S. carrier-launched raids on North Vietnam, August 4, 1964. During Israel's Yom Kippur War in 1973, Skyhawks provided much of the striking power on the Sinai and Golan Heights fronts. The Navy's Blue Angels flight demonstration squadron flew the A-4 from 1974 to 1986. Skyhawks were also used by the armed forces of Argentina, Australia, Israel, Kuwait, Singapore, Indonesia, Malaysia and New Zealand, and they remained active with several air forces into the 21st century.

The A-4A (137813) at Pensacola is the first production Skyhawk.

BOTTOM RIGHT One of the most capable fighters of the post-WWII era, the Vought F-8 Crusader was a sleek design that featured a gaping jet intake beneath the fuselage and a variable-incidence wing that could be raised to enable the aircraft to land and take off at slow speeds while maintaining the fuselage parallel to a carrier deck and providing good visibility for the pilot. On August 21, 1956, Commander Robert Windsor flew a Crusader to a national speed record, averaging 1,015 mph over a 15-kilometer course, so making the F-8 the first operationally equipped jet formally recorded as flying faster than 1,000 mph.

TOP The F-8A on display at Pensacola served with VF 174 and VF11 during its career, its time with the latter squadron including a deployment on board the *Franklin D. Roosevelt* (CVA-42).

BOTTOM LEFT According to Rear Admiral Paul Gillcrist, the Crusader was "the most difficult carrier aircraft to land, ever." As a single-seat fighter, the F-8 was a large aircraft for its time (over 54 feet long and weighing up to 34,000 pounds), but the cockpit was quite small and visibility to the rear was almost nonexistent. The Crusader was the last U.S. fighter designed with guns as its primary weapon.

TOP *The first flight of the F-4J version of the McDonnell Douglas Phantom II took place on May 27, 1966. A total of 522 F-4Js were built for U.S. Navy and Marine squadrons. Typical ordnance carried was up to six underwing Sparrow II missiles or four Sidewinders. As much as 16,000 pounds of assorted ordnance could be carried on five strong points.*
BOTTOM *An LTV A-7D Corsair II of the Ohio Air National Guard seen just after releasing a Mk. 82 Ballute 500-pound parachute-retarded bomb during an exercise.*

Skyhawk. The choice fell on an LTV design with a chin intake that gave it a superficial resemblance to the F8U, but the likeness ended there. The sleek, supersonic Crusader was a very different machine from the squat, subsonic A-7 Corsair II, named by pilots (in B-52 "Buff" fashion) "Sluf" — "Short little ugly fellow." Once again, however, the USN had chosen so well that the USAF followed and acquired another type originally conceived for naval duties. The A-7 was a rugged, nimble attack aircraft, capable of carrying up to 10 tons of weapons and equipped with systems that allowed them to be delivered with remarkable accuracy.

By the late 1960s, four Forrestal and four Kitty Hawk (improved Forrestal) carriers had been commissioned. They had been joined in 1961 by the *Enterprise*, a huge nuclear-powered ship with capacity for ninety-nine aircraft and a complement of 5,500 people. In the 1970s and 1980s the Nimitz class arrived, also nuclear-powered and just as large, more than 90,000 tons at full load but still capable of steaming at 33 knots. These immense warships, over 1,000 feet long and with flight decks covering some four and a half acres, accommodated relatively large aircraft without difficulty, and the carrier air wings became in effect small comprehensive air forces, with all roles represented on board. Increasingly adaptable fighters operated alongside Grumman A-6 Intruders, awesomely capable low-level attack aircraft fitted with the Digital Integrated Attack Navigation Equipment (DIANE), a system that allowed aircrews to program missions beforehand and then fly them hands-off, from takeoff to weapon delivery. A variant of Grumman's bomber, the EA-6B Prowler, provided electronic countermeasures and, from the mid-1970s, Lockheed S-3A Vikings were taken on board to specialize in antisubmarine warfare. Airborne early warning was looked after by the

In May 1961, the Phantoms of VF-101 smashed John Glenn's transcontinental F8U record by flying from Los Angeles to New York in 2 hours, 47 minutes, an average of 870 mph, and they did it while carrying missiles and external fuel tanks. This extraordinary multirole fighting machine was so good that it outdid its more specialized counterparts at their own game and challenged airmen everywhere to rethink their ideas about how best to fight the air war. The Phantom II quickly established itself as the world's most effective combat aircraft. Besides becoming the predominant type used by the U.S. Navy and Marine Corps, it was seized upon by the USAF and flown by the air forces of a dozen other countries, including the United Kingdom, Germany, Japan, Israel, Iran, Greece, Turkey, Spain, Korea and Egypt. By the time production of the F-4 slowed in the late 1970s, over 5,000 had been manufactured.

Reluctant to believe that the ubiquitous little A-4 could go on forever, the USN began looking in the 1960s for an attack aircraft to supplement and eventually replace the

Grumman E-2 Hawkeye, which in its E-2C form could detect ships and aircraft 240 miles away with its APS-125 radar, classify contacts as friend or foe, and then simultaneously direct strike and interception forces against 250 targets. Helicopters rounded out the air wing's collection, and were seen throughout the fleet, adding their unique capabilities in the search and rescue, antisubmarine, and troop assault roles. (See *Aviation Century Wings of Change*, Chapter 4.)

The enormous cost of super-carriers, plus their air wings and escort ships, put them beyond the reach of all the naval powers apart from the United States. They are among the most complex objects ever constructed by man, providing services that make it possible to support some of the world's most sophisticated aircraft and weapons while operating in areas remote from land-based facilities. In the 1970s and early 1980s, the U.S. Navy deployed two potent new fighters, laden with state-of-the-art avionics and of extremely high performance, that demanded super-carriers as a prerequisite for their employment. Remarkable though it was, even the F-4 could not be expected to go on forever, and in 1972, USN squadrons began to receive one of the most technologically advanced fighters in the world — the Grumman F-14 Tomcat. The F-14 was acquired to fill the U.S. Navy's need for a long-range, heavily armed fighter to counter the threat of both enemy bombers and cruise missiles while retaining the ability to engage in close-quarter combat. Unusually large for a fighter, the Tomcat is nearly 63 feet long and can weigh as much as 74,500 pounds. Its swing-wing design gives it a maximum wingspan of 64 feet, but that can be reduced to 33 feet for storage. Among its wide range of weapons is one unique to the Tomcat — the Phoenix missile, which can be fired at oncoming targets from 100 miles away.

TOP *A McDonnell Douglas F-4 Phantom II of VF-92 shares deck space on board the* Enterprise *(CVN-65) with a Grumman A-6 of VA-145, December 1968.*
CENTER *A Douglas A-4C Skyhawk of VA-64, piloted by the ship's executive officer, Commander Kenneth B. Austin, ready for the first catapult launch from the newly commissioned carrier* America *(CVA-66), April 5, 1965.*
BOTTOM *Standing beside his work station, the Landing Signals Officer (LSO) of the* Constellation *(CVA-64) watches a Grumman E-2A Hawkeye in the final stages of its approach, October 1966 in the China Sea.*

TOP *A close-up view of a Grumman F-14A Tomcat of VF-84, the "Jolly Rogers."* BOTTOM *Clouds of steam billow from a catapult on the* Lincoln *(CVN-72), as an F-14A of the Jolly Rogers taxies into position.*

Hornet should be expanded to cover such diverse all-weather day/night missions as defending the fleet and Marine Corps ground forces, escorting strike aircraft, conducting attack missions and armed reconnaissance, and providing FAC (forward air control) support. It was almost inevitable in the circumstances that the decision should be taken to add another crew member to share the mission load. A two-seat Hornet, the F/A-18D made its debut in 1987. Its wide choice of weapons includes Sidewinder, Sparrow, AMRAAM, Maverick, Shrike, Harpoon, HARM, rocket launchers and an assortment of bombs, besides the M61 six-barrel cannon mounted in the wingroot.

Confusion and Change in the Royal Navy

At the beginning of the 1950s, Britain's Royal Navy had just one fleet carrier (*Implacable*) and four Colossus-class light fleet carriers (*Triumph, Vengeance, Glory, Theseus*) operational, all of them with piston-engined aircraft equipping their Fleet Air Arm squadrons, a mixture of Seafires, Fireflies, Sea Furies, Sea Hornets, Firebrands and Barracudas. As they soon discovered in the Korean War, these were no match for jet aircraft in combat. (Although one MiG-15 was promptly shot down when its pilot took on a Sea Fury in a turning dogfight.) By the end of that decade, the Fleet Air Arm had changed dramatically. Piston engines had disappeared from the front-line squadrons and the interim turbine-powered aircraft such as the Supermarine Attacker and Westland Wyvern had come and gone. By January 1960, there were five carriers operating fixed-wing aircraft — *Victorious, Ark Royal, Eagle, Centaur* and *Albion.* They had a variety of jets embarked. Some were hangovers from the first jet generation, such as the Sea Venoms and Sea Hawks, but newer aircraft were making their appearance. The Scimitar was a big day/strike fighter, and the Sea Vixen was an equally large, twin-boomed

The question of unit cost drove the USN to prepare a specification for a smaller, cheaper fighter to complement the F-14. The result was the McDonnell Douglas F-18, which itself grew more complex as the Navy and Marine Corps added multirole requirements. By the time deliveries to the service began in 1981, the new single-seater had become the F/A-18A Hornet (F/A, for fighter/attack). In time, it was thought that the remarkable capabilities of the

AIRFIELD AFLOAT

On board the USS *Lincoln* in the Persian Gulf in 2002, photographer Mariusz Adamski spent a few days capturing these iconic images of a modern warship in action.

TOP RIGHT A fully loaded F-14 Tomcat, tied down with the wings folded back to save space on deck. The F-14 has been the U.S. Navy's long-range air superiority fighter but is being phased out as the upgraded FA-18 Super Hornet fills the role.

CENTER LEFT At dusk, an FA-18 approaches *Lincoln* with the tailhook deployed for an arrested landing.

CENTER RIGHT FA-18 Hornets of the *Lincoln*'s air wing, lined up, armed and ready,

BOTTOM LEFT The FA-18 becomes a blur as it lands.

BOTTOM RIGHT One of the *Lincoln*'s E-2C Hawkeye aircraft comes aboard at sunset. The E-2C is the U.S. Navy's all-weather, carrier-based tactical airborne warning and control system platform.

In the 1970s, the Soviet Union launched three 40,000-ton ships capable of operating helicopters and vertical takeoff and landing (VTOL) aircraft. They were the Kiev, Minsk and Novorossiysk. The air wing of the Kiev class was small, consisting of a dozen Yak-38 Forger fighters and twenty helicopters. By 1994, all three ships had been scrapped.

was a useful aircraft, but it did not amount to much more than a swept-wing Skynight and it entered service nine years later.

An attempt was made to rectify the situation with the Hawker proposal for a supersonic V/STOL fighter, which was under consideration as the replacement for the Hunter in the RAF, and for both the Scimitar and Sea Vixen in the FAA. Shortage of funds and the inability of the services to agree on a compatible specification killed the project in 1964, at which point the government announced that F-4K Phantom IIs would be bought from the United States. Since the deal included the fitting of British engines and other equipment, it raised the unit cost of the aircraft by some 60 percent over the USN's F-4J, and the size of the Phantom II tied the future of the FAA to the big carrier. If there was a bright spot in the FAA story, it was the arrival in 1962 of an often underrated strike aircraft — the Blackburn Buccaneer. With an internal bomb-bay capable of taking either nuclear weapons or four 1,000-pound bombs, the Buccaneer brushed aside turbulence to maintain high subsonic speeds at very low level. In 1964, the more powerful Mk. 2 version appeared, complete with in-flight refueling probe and strengthened underwing pylons that could accommodate an additional 12,000 pounds of stores. Martel guided missiles were added in 1966.

With that, a brutal axe fell on the FAA. The 1966 government White Paper on defense canceled plans for new carriers and confidently announced that land-based air power would be able to cope with any foreseeable future conflict involving the United Kingdom. (Sixteen years later, events in the Falkland Islands would mock that assumption.) By 1972, only *Ark Royal* remained to operate fixed-wing aircraft. In December 1978 the *Ark* was decommissioned; the Phantoms and Buccaneers aboard were transferred to the RAF, and the AEW Gannets were scrapped. Six decades of fixed-wing flying by the Royal Navy came to an end. As that chapter closed, however,

all-weather fighter armed with Firestreak missiles. Portly Fairey Gannets, powered by two turboprops, looked after antisubmarine warfare.

If the 1960s began with some promise for Britain's FAA, with new jet fighters coming aboard, they ended on quite a different note as the Royal Navy faced the loss of the carriers that were at the core of its operational doctrine. The process of decline had been going on for some time. Britain's withdrawal from Empire led to drastic shifts in national policy and considerable confusion about how best to provide defense forces to meet the changed circumstances. There was a reluctance to spend money on equipment that might prove to be unnecessary, and therefore a tendency to stretch out procurement programs. As a result, costs rose and by the time equipment was brought into service it was no longer at the cutting edge of technology. When the subsonic Scimitar was introduced, it had no radar and was a generation behind the Phantom II, which was then being tested by the USN. Similarly, the Sea Vixen

British Aerospace (Hawker Siddeley) Buccaneer, *by Michael Turner. A Buccaneer of 237 Operational Conversion Unit from RAF Honington is shown at high speed over the North Sea, surrounded by a typical cloud of condensation.*

another was opening. In July 1980, the first example of a new class of ship, the light carrier *Invincible*, was commissioned. Less than 20,000 tons loaded, and therefore small by the standards of a conventional carrier, the *Invincible* was at first known as a "through-deck-cruiser" and was intended to operate only helicopters. At a late stage, fixed-wing aviation staged at least a partial comeback and a requirement was added to accommodate Sea Harrier V/STOL aircraft.

Two more ships of the Invincible class, *Illustrious* and a new *Ark Royal*, were authorized, but while they were being built the Royal Navy filled the capability gap by reviving the old ASW carrier *Hermes* with a refit that included

modifications to allow for the operation of Sea Harriers. One noteworthy addition was a prominent ski-jump ramp at the bow. It had been discovered that Sea Harriers could get airborne from a small carrier deck with a heavier load if they used partial down nozzle and had an upward trajectory at liftoff. The same load could not be lifted in a vertical takeoff and needed a much longer run if the deck was flat. The changes to *Hermes* turned out to have been an inspired move when predictions about the ability of land-based air power to cover any likely conflict proved fallacious in 1982. Only the presence of *Hermes* and *Invincible* and their Sea Harriers enabled Britain to prevail in the war with Argentina over the Falkland Islands. Fixed-wing aviation was back in the Royal Navy to stay, albeit for the time being in a different form. With the lessons of the Falklands firmly in mind, plans were laid to build two larger carriers, capable of handling 21st-century fighters, for commissioning in 2010.

LEFT *The de Havilland Sea Vixen was a twin-engined, swept-wing, twin tail-boom fighter developed as carrier-based all-weather fighter for the Royal Navy. It was a large aircraft and had a maximum speed of Mach 0.94. The Sea Vixen did not enter service until 1958, by when the U.S. Navy was already flying the Grumman F-11 and the Vought F-8, both Mach 2 aircraft.* RIGHT *The Westland Wyvern was a single-seat strike aircraft intended to operate with the Royal Navy as a daylight fighter and torpedo bomber. The aircraft was unpopular with pilots, one test pilot even calling the Wyvern lethal. Nevertheless, it served in the Fleet Air Arm from 1954 to 1958 and saw action during the Suez crisis, with 830 Squadron losing two aircraft in seventy-nine combat sorties.*

FLEET AIR ARM JETS

RIGHT The Hawker Sea Hawk entered service with the Royal Navy in 1953. It was a simple, elegant design and a delight to fly. However, its front-line career was brief. The straight-wing design was soon overtaken by more advanced, swept-wing aircraft and the last Sea Hawk squadron disbanded in 1960. Sea Hawks did see combat during the Suez campaign.

ABOVE Hawker Sea Hawk WV856 went to sea with 806 Squadron on board HMS *Centaur* in 1955. It is now on display at the Fleet Air Arm Museum, Yeovilton, in the U.K.

RIGHT BOTTOM The Sea Hawk cockpit was typical of its generation, with the standard instrument flying panel centrally placed beneath the gunsight, flap and air-brake levers close to the throttle on the pilot's left, and the corresponding emergency controls a little further forward, clearly marked in black and yellow.

RIGHT Among the peculiarities of the de Havilland Sea Vixen was the offset pilot's cockpit. The narrow canopy minimized drag, though it did have some effect on the aircraft's trim in the yawing plane, and the pilot's view to the right was somewhat restricted. The Sea Vixen was the first British fighter to have all-missile armament, a concept that was popular at the time since there was a misguided notion that the guided missiles of the time had made guns obsolete.

BELOW The Sea Vixen's cockpit was necessarily more elaborate than those of its predecessors. The central instrument flying panel has a different look, and above it are switches and indicators for managing a more complex fuel system. Behind the banks of switches at bottom right can just be seen the top of the dark space known as the "coal hole" where the observer sat well below the pilot and with an almost nonexistent view.

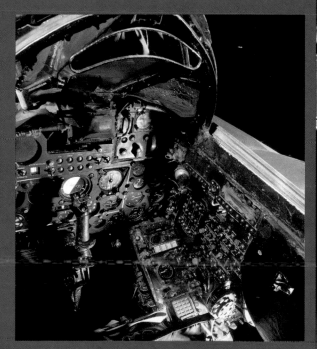

OPPOSITE *The BAe (Blackburn) Buccaneer was originally designed as a nuclear strike aircraft for the Royal Navy. With the demise of the RN carriers and the cancellation of RAF plans, first for the TSR.2 and then for the F-111, the Buccaneer was adopted by the RAF for the conventional strike role. Reluctantly accepted initially (it was said that "a buck an ear" was a hell of a price for corn), it was soon recognized as being exceptionally well suited for high-speed low-level flight. The Buccaneer S.2B at the Fleet Air Arm Museum, Yeovilton, flew with both the RN and the RAF. Now marked in naval colors, it was last operated by 208 Squadron, RAF.*

RIGHT *Author Ron Dick commanded a Buccaneer wing in the late 1970s and was comfortable in the cockpit. However, in the course of its long multiservice life, the Bucc experienced many modifications and the cockpit had become a bit of an ergonomic slum, with switches and indicators added haphazardly in whatever spaces were available. Note the mix of linear and rotary instruments. Nevertheless, the cockpit's shortcomings were forgiven once the Bucc was in the air. At 560 knots and 100 feet, its responsiveness was a joy and it shrugged off turbulence, carving through the air as if on rails.*

Carriers of Other Powers

Britain's WWII light fleet carriers were highly successful and popular ships. In the years after the war a number served as the basis for many navies attempting to found or continue naval air arms. *Colossus* became the French *Arromanches*; the Royal Australian Navy inherited *Terrible* and *Majestic* as *Sydney* and *Melbourne*; Australia also took *Vengeance* and later passed the ship on to Brazil as the *Minas Gerais*; *Hercules* went to India as the Vikrant; *Powerful* joined the Canadian Navy as *Bonaventure*; Argentina took the *Warrior* and called it *Independencia*, and then also received the *Venerable* after it had served as the *Karel Doorman* in the Dutch Navy, renaming it *25 de Mayo*.

As the years went by, few of the world's navies felt it necessary to continue funding such expensive items as aircraft carriers from their shrinking defense budgets. Some ships were not replaced as they reached the end of their useful lives, and, even when they were, cheaper options were often sought in the shape of smaller, V/STOL-capable vessels. The Dutch and the Canadians were among the earliest of those who chose not to replace their carriers, and the Argentinians retired the ageing

25 de Mayo soon after the Falklands War. India decommissioned the *Vikrant*, but replaced it with the *Viraat*, the ex-British *Hermes*, retaining the ski-jump ramp with the intention of acquiring Harriers. Later Indian plans included the proposal to buy Russia's *Gorshkov* together with some seagoing MiG-29s. In Europe, both Spain and Italy took aircraft to sea in the 1980s. The Italian *Garibaldi* and the Spanish *Principe de Asturias* are small carriers of less than 20,000 tons, built to operate Harriers in their AV8B form. In Asia, Thailand became the most recent member of the naval aviation fraternity in 1997 when another V/STOL carrier, the *Chakri Nareubet*, was commissioned to accept a complement of AV8S Harriers.

As the French economy strengthened after World War II, funds were authorized for two new aircraft carriers capable of operating jet aircraft. The *Clemenceau* and the *Foch* were commissioned in the early 1960s, both of them displacing some 32,000 tons at full load and equipped with angled decks and steam catapults. The air wings initially included Etendard and F-8E Crusader fighters, together with turbo-

TOP *The 58,500-ton* Kuznetsov *is the only operational Russian carrier. The bow slopes upward in a 12-degree "ski jump" to permit short takeoffs from the relatively small deck. The ship has the capacity to support sixteen Yakovlev Yak-41M (Freestyle) and twelve Sukhoi Su-27K (Flanker) fixed-wing aircraft and two dozen Kamov Ka-27 (Helix) helicopters.*
CENTER *The French Navy's 38,000-ton* Charles de Gaulle *is nuclear powered. The ship can operate a fleet of up to forty aircraft, including Rafale M, Super Etendard, and E-2C Hawkeye.*
BOTTOM *An F-4M Phantom II of the Royal Navy landing on the U.S. Navy's* Nimitz (CVN-68) *during joint exercises.*

prop Alizé ASW aircraft. Later Super Etendards were introduced, bringing with them Exocet antiship missiles and a nuclear strike capability. Both ships were decommissioned at the end of the century, Foch being retained until the arrival of a new carrier, the *Charles de Gaulle*, a nuclear-powered ship of 40,000 tons. The planned fixed-wing elements of the air wing on board *Charles de Gaulle* include Super Etendards, E2C Hawkeye AEW aircraft, and a new carrier-borne fighter, the Rafale M. France aims to commission a second ship of this class in 2010.

Until the 1970s, the Soviet Union had ventured into carrier aviation only with the Moskva helicopter ships. Then, in 1975, the 38,000-ton *Kiev* was commissioned, followed by sister ships *Minsk* in 1978 and *Novorossiysk* in 1982. Another ship in the class, added to the fleet in 1987, was initially named *Baku*, but later *Admiral Gorshkov*. Although four ships were built, they were only ever intended as an interim carrier design, capable of operating Yak-38 Forger V/STOL fighters alongside a squadron of ASW helicopters. A more powerful vessel, the 65,000-ton *Admiral Kuznetsov*, was commissioned in 1991, complete with angled flight deck and ski jump. It was the first full-sized aircraft carrier designed and built by the Soviet Union and it was intended to operate navalized versions of standard Soviet tactical aircraft such as the MiG-29 or the Su-27, together with helicopters and the world's first supersonic V/STOL fighter, the Yak-41/141. The *Kuznetsov* was equipped with the largest self-defense SAM suite ever fitted in a ship, besides a heavy SSM battery. Construction was started on a second similar ship, the *Varyag*, and plans were laid for even larger carriers, but none of these projects was completed. Fully operational,

such carriers would have been formidable warships, but Russian economic difficulties prevented even the *Kuznetsov* from realizing its potential.

Maritime Patrol Affairs

Aircraft carrier battle groups, for all their remarkable capabilities, cannot hope to keep watch over all the oceans of the world. The growth of the Soviet Navy, and especially the threat of its submarine fleet, drove the development in the West of a series of long-range maritime patrol aircraft. In the early 1950s the United States used the Martin Marlin flying boat, but this was seen as having limited potential compared to landplanes such as the Lockheed P-2V Neptune, over 1,200 of which were put into service by eleven countries. (On September 29, 1946, the third production P-2V, named *Truculent Turtle*, took off from Perth, Australia. Fifty-five hours later it landed at Columbus, Ohio, having covered a world record 11,236 miles.) The Neptune's successor was Lockheed's P-3 Orion, developed from the Electra airliner. Since the first production aircraft was delivered in 1962, the Orion has appeared in a bewildering array of forms for the air forces of fifteen nations, and was still being built in the 1990s. The Orion can arrange 20,000 pounds of ordnance between its bomb bay and ten wing pylons, including an assortment of mines, torpedoes, depth charges, antiship missiles and nuclear weapons. At the end of the century it remained one of the most formidable maritime patrol aircraft in service anywhere.

In the early 1950s, the RAF's maritime patrol role was filled by Neptunes and by piston-engined Avro Shackletons, aircraft only a generation removed from the WWII Lancaster bomber and bearing a distinct family resemblance. In 1969, the immensely capable Hawker Siddeley Nimrod, powered by four jet engines and based on the Comet airframe, began delivery and the Shackletons were gradually phased out of maritime patrol service. Like all modern maritime aircraft, the Nimrod is packed with sophisticated electronic equipment, including Searchwater radar, a tactical systems computer, an acoustics processor, a magnetic anomaly detector, and an infrared detection system. As a jet aircraft, the Nimrod reaches its patrol area quickly and then shuts down two engines; flying at economical cruise it can remain on task at 1,150 miles for six hours. An array of depth charges, torpedoes, sonobuoys,

A Lockheed P2V Neptune of 10 Squadron, Royal Australian Air Force, over Honolulu on May 11, 1968.

and marine markers is carried in the bomb bay or on underwing hard points. Since the Falklands War, the Nimrod has also been fitted with racks for Sidewinder air-to-air missiles, making it what its crews call "the world's biggest fighter."

The twin-turboprop SECBAT Atlantique is a multinational maritime patrol aircraft, both its design and production led by Dassault-Breguet in France. In concept and operation it follows the pattern of the Orion, a landplane designed to fly for long periods covering vast ocean areas. The tradition of using flying boats for such a purpose survived only in the Far East and the Soviet Union. The Japanese eventually turned to using the Orion, but in the 1960s the Shin Meiwa Company built the PS-1, a large amphibious flying boat powered by four turboprops. The PS-1 was withdrawn from maritime patrol duties in 1989, but a version designated US-1 continued in the long-range air-sea rescue role. Design work on a similar large amphibian began in China in 1969 at the Harbin Aircraft Manufacturing Corporation. Development was protracted and the first flight of the SH-5 did not take place until 1976. Equally lethargic production kept the Chinese Navy from operating the type until 1986.

In the Soviet Union, the Beriev design bureau specialized in the design of flying boats and amphibians. The twin piston-engined Be-6 Madge appeared in 1949 and continued in service long after the arrival of its successor, the turboprop Be-12 Mail in 1961. The Be-12 was not an aerodynamically clean design but, thanks to its 4,000-horsepower engines, had a lively performance and could carry a weapons load of 22,500 pounds. Endlessly patrolling the seas around the Soviet Union, the Madge and the Mail between them kept a close watch on NATO's maritime activities until well after the end of the Cold War. In contrast with the Be-12, Beriev's next design, the twin-turbofan-powered Be-42 Mermaid, produced one of the most elegant flying boats ever built. Originally intended as a maritime patrol replacement for the Be-12, its post Cold War duties concentrated more on the long-range air-sea rescue role.

A large proportion of the Soviet Union's (and later, Russia's) maritime patrol efforts were conducted by land-plane variants such as the An-72P Coaler, Il-38 May and Tu-95 Bear C / 142 Bear F. The Bear F was a particularly impressive aircraft resulting from a major redesign of the Tu-95 undertaken to update its equipment and improve both its takeoff performance and its resistance to the maritime environment. Its four 15,000-horsepower turboprops, fitted with massive contrarotating propellers, allowed the Bear F a maximum takeoff weight of 408,000 pounds and gave it a normal cruising speed of 440 mph. Its mission equipment included a Korshun search radar, infrared and other sensors, and a magnetic anomaly detector. Its weapons bay could hold up to 16,500 pounds of homing torpedoes, mines, depth charges and sonobuoys. On a typical fully armed mission, the Bear F could reach out to a maximum combat radius of 4,000 miles, but with one in-flight refueling this could be increased to 5,155 miles.

LOCAL CONFLICT IN ASIA
The East Indies, Malaya and Borneo

In the islands and peninsulas of Southeast Asia after World War II, the defeat of Japan was followed by more conflict. The people of the Dutch East Indies had been promised independence by the Japanese and fiercely resisted the idea that they might be returned to colonial status. On August 17, 1945, only three days after the Japanese surrender, the nationalist leader Soekarno declared Indonesia independent. Suitably aroused, the people of this aspiring nation took up arms against the occupying powers, initially the British and later the Dutch, and sporadic fighting lasted until 1949, when negotiations led to the formation of the United States of Indonesia. The new republic of 10,000 islands was anything but stable, however, and Soekarno's

BELOW LEFT *The most famous Neptune was, without a doubt, Lockheed P2V-1* Truculent Turtle, *which took off from Perth, Australia, on September 29, 1946 and flew nonstop to Columbus, Ohio, a world-record distance of 11,235 miles in 55 hours, 17 minutes. The aircraft's gross weight of 85,575 pounds at takeoff included 50,000 pounds of fuel aboard. The pilot in the crew of four (plus a kangaroo) was Commander (later Rear Admiral) Tom Davies, seen here with* Truculent Turtle, *which is now at the National Museum of Naval Aviation at Pensacola.*
BELOW *The BAe Nimrod MRA4 is the latest variant in a successful line of maritime patrol aircraft that entered service as the MR1 in 1969. Although still recognizable as a Nimrod, its more powerful and efficient engines, larger wing, and 21st-century avionics and weaponry make the MRA4 far more capable than its predecessors.*

The Japanese Shin Meiwa PS-1 antisubmarine warfare (ASW) and US-1 search-and-rescue (SAR) series of amphibious flying boats began operations in 1971, but by 1989 the ASW PS-1s had been retired. Equipped with a boundary layer control system that gives them good short takeoff and landing characteristics, the US-1s continue to provide valuable SAR service. In the last two decades of the 20th century they were credited with saving over 550 lives.

forces then had to deal with a number of rebellions by those who had no wish to exchange The Hague's colonial rule for government from Batavia. Meanwhile, across the Malacca Strait, Chinese-led communist guerillas who had fought alongside the British against the Japanese took a little longer to get properly organized and make their bid for power. It was 1948 before they began an armed campaign with the aim of ending Britain's administration of Malaya.

Aircraft were involved in all of these struggles, but in none of them could they be considered a decisive factor. In the East Indies the principal combat aircraft initially were leftovers from World War II, P-47s, Spitfires, P-51s, Mosquitos and B-25s among them. Later, when Indonesia pressed its claim to Dutch New Guinea in 1960, the Dutch deployed a squadron of Hunter 4s to the region as a precaution, but they did not see combat. In Malaya between 1948 and 1960, RAF squadrons flew thousands of sorties during the long-drawn-out anticommunist Operation Firedog. Until the early 1950s, piston-engined aircraft such as the Tempest, Brigand and Hornet were used to attack roaming bands of guerrillas with guns, bombs and rockets. Lincoln heavy bombers added their considerable weight to the bombing campaign, devastating areas where guerrillas were believed to be operating. In 1953 jet aircraft began making an appearance, at first Vampires and Meteors and then Canberras and Venoms. When Indonesian ambitions led to

what was known as a "confrontation" in Borneo between 1962 and 1966, Hunters and Javelins were deployed to the theater to counter possible threats from Il-28s and Tu-16s of the AURI (Angkatan Udara Republik Indonesia — Air Force of the Republic of Indonesia). Aerial clashes, however, were rare, and it was seldom that the effort expended anywhere in the region in attacking the presumed positions of opposing ground forces in rugged, heavily forested country was justified by the results achieved. The combat aircraft may have been full of sound and fury but they were minor players signifying relatively little in the struggles that shaped the modern states of Indonesia and Malaysia.

On the other hand, aircraft in more supporting roles were of considerable significance. Throughout the region, air transport proved to be essential to the success of military operations. C-47s and Valettas carried troops to where they were needed, dropped soldiers into the jungle and supplies into forts. Helicopters put patrols down in clearings, often taking the enemy by surprise, and performed casualty evacuation. Small piston-engined aircraft such as the Auster and the Pioneer did their share of delivering soldiers and supplies, as well as marking targets and doing visual reconnaissance. In Malaya, psychological warfare, both broadcast and leaflet, was conducted from the air to considerable effect, and photo reconnaissance, flown initially by Mosquitos and Spitfires, later by Meteors and

Canberras, made important contributions to the intelligence war. To deny the guerrillas their food supply, helicopters and Austers sprayed herbicides on crops found in jungle clearings. The principal actions everywhere in the region were fought on the ground, but the supporting cast of unarmed aircraft had significant parts to play in deciding the various outcomes.

China and Taiwan

In 1949, the Communist leader Mao Zedong crowned the success of his People's Liberation Army by founding the People's Republic of China. The defeated Nationalists retreated to the island of Formosa (Taiwan) and established the rival Republic of China. Concerned by these developments, the United States believed that Taiwan could serve not only as a valuable barrier to the advance of Communism but also as a useful strategic base. In August 1958 the PRC indulged in serious saber rattling, threatening to invade Quemoy and Taiwan. The U.S. made its position clear by deploying Marine Group 11's F4s to Taiwan and six carriers with some 500 aircraft to the South China Sea, and also by moving the USAF's Composite Air Strike Force forward to Japan with F-100s, F-101s, F-104s and B-57s. By this time the Chinese Nationalist Air Force had some 350 aircraft, including wings of F-86Fs and F-84Gs. Clashes

over the Taiwan Strait grew in intensity until there was a major air battle on September 24, with F-86s of the CNAF claiming to have shot down fourteen fighters, either MiG-15 or MiG-17s, four of them with Sidewinders. It was the first time that air-to-air missiles were used in combat. Over a six-week period, thirty-one MiGs were claimed destroyed for the loss of two F-86s. After a lull, another five MiGs were added to the score on July 5, 1959.

From 1950, the United States was involved in launching clandestine missions into China by air. A number of airlines, operated by the CIA under such names as Air America and the Air Asia and Asiatic Aeronautical Company, flew agents into China. It was an enterprise undertaken not without cost. Over 100 U.S. citizens lost their lives and as many more were captured during the early 1950s. In late 1958, when tension between the rival Chinese governments was at its height, the U.S. began basing strategic reconnaissance aircraft on Taiwan. Flown in CNAF markings by Chinese pilots, RB-57Ds kept an eye on the PRC until one was shot down on October 7. U-2s followed, but these ranged further afield, looking at such interesting places as the missile range in Kansu province and the Lop Nor nuclear research site. Although the shooting down of a U-2 flown by Gary Powers over the Soviet Union is more well known, the risks of flying over China were at least as great.

LEFT *Bristol Brigands of 45 Squadron seen over Malaya during the anti-communist campaign of the 1950s.* RIGHT *Spitfires were among the WWII aircraft still engaged in operations in turbulent areas of the Far East after 1945. Here a pilot of 60 Squadron climbs into his Spitfire FR.18 in Singapore for a fighter reconnaissance sortie over Malaya in 1950. Note the camera window behind the cockpit. The last RAF Spitfire offensive sorties anywhere were flown by the FR.18s of 60 Squadron on January 1, 1951.*

The first group of Martin RB-57D Canberras were designed as single-seat aircraft. The primary mission of these long-winged Canberras was high-altitude photo reconnaissance. Here an RB-57D is seen in formation with an RB-57A, showing the greatly increased wing area of the later aircraft. The enlarged wing suffered from frequent failures, and on more than one occasion a wing broke off on landing.

A U-2 was lost near Nanching on September 9, 1962, and this was the first of eleven shot down over China up to 1974, when an accord was reached between the United States and the PRC.

India and Pakistan

In contrast to the clashes in China and Southeast Asia, where unarmed reconnaissance and transport aircraft overshadowed the efforts of the more belligerent machines, the Indo-Pakistan wars saw combat aircraft engaged in a more prominent role. When the British Raj ended in 1947 and the Indian subcontinent was partitioned into the independent nations of India and Pakistan, many issues were unresolved between the two, among the most important the question of who was to control Jammu and Kashmir, a state with a predominantly Muslim population ruled by a Hindu Maharajah. When the Maharajah decided to join India, there was an insurrection by the population; this was supported by Pakistan and forcibly opposed by Indian troops. Later there was direct conflict between Pakistani and Indian forces, both sides using predominantly British piston-engined aircraft, including Spitfires and Tempests. After an uneasy ceasefire

was negotiated by the UN in 1949, Britain began delivering jet fighters to both air forces, Supermarine Attackers to Pakistan and Vampires, Canberras and Hunters to India. The respective air forces were then built up with aircraft from other suppliers. Pakistan gained F-86Fs, F-104s and B-57s as military aid from the United States, while India took Ouragans and Mystères from France and MiG-21s from the USSR. India also set out to build up its own capacity to manufacture military aircraft, Hindustan Aircraft Ltd. (HAL) starting to produce Folland Gnat lightweight jet fighters under license.

Kashmir was annexed by India over Pakistani protests in 1957, and the friction between the two nations continued until undeclared war broke out in 1965, with raids and counter-raids across the ceasefire line during the summer leading to major hostilities in September. By this time, the Indian Air Force (IAF) had fielded some 500 combat aircraft, and these were opposed by about 140 flown by the Pakistan Air Force (PAF). Each side concentrated most of its efforts against the other's airfields and ground forces, with the PAF adding to its front-line strength by arming its T-33 trainers for the close support role. Nevertheless, frequent dogfights occurred between the PAF's F-86s and the

Pakistani Sabres and Indian Hunters, *by Michael Turner.*

the first indigenous Indian combat aircraft had been produced, the HF-24 Marut fighter-bomber. Ground attack fighters — 175 MiG-21s and 150 Su-7s — had been bought from the Soviet Union. Meanwhile, the PAF had been affected by a U.S. arms embargo and had been scrambling to reequip with mostly outdated machines, acquiring 90 second-hand F-86s via Iran, 28 Mirage IIIs from France, and 74 Shenyang F-6s (Chinese MiG-19s).

The 1971 war grew out of the determination of East Pakistan to sever its links with the government in Islamabad and declare its independence as Bangladesh. Civil war erupted in East Pakistan in March 1971. The Pakistan Army's brutal repression of the revolt provoked the flight of millions of refugees across the Indian frontier. India intervened initially in the form of aid to the Bangladeshi rebels, but cross-border skirmishes became increasingly sharp and by December 1971 Pakistan had been provoked into taking overt hostile action. On December 3 the PAF attempted a preemptive strike by F-86s and B-57s against airfields in northwest India. The raid was ineffective and brought a prompt response from the IAF. Within days the PAF was unable to operate in the east, and was forced largely onto the defensive in the west. The conflict was fierce and brief, with Indian troops entering Dacca on December 15 and all fighting on both fronts ceasing two days later.

The two-week air campaign had been intense; in the east, the PAF managed only 30 sorties in response to the IAF's 1,978, but had opposed the IAF's 4,000 in the west with 2,840. More than 80 percent of the IAF's operations were close support or interdiction sorties. Both air forces undertook night missions against strategic targets using Canberras or B-57s, and augmented these with bombing attacks by converted transports, either An-12s or C-130s. In

Hunters and Gnats of the IAF. On one remarkably intense day of aerial combat, Squadron Leader Mohammed Alam claimed to have shot down five Hunters during a single F-86 sortie. In general, the PAF held the edge during the three-week conflict and the IAF never managed to take advantage of its superior numbers. Stalemate having been reached in the war, a ceasefire came into effect at midnight on September 22, by which time the PAF appeared to have lost about twenty-five aircraft, eleven of them in aerial combat. The IAF lost more than twice as many, twenty-five to combat, but the effect was not nearly so great on its front line. Looked at in percentage terms, there were some ominous warnings for the PAF in what they considered a victory. The PAF had never secured air superiority and its front-line strength had been reduced by some 17 percent, while the IAF had lost less than 10 percent. In a longer war of attrition, it seemed that the PAF could not win.

To some extent, the 1965 war led the PAF to sit on its laurels, whereas the IAF took note of its shortcomings and acted to put things right. By 1971, when war again broke out, the IAF had improved its training and operational readiness, and had installed a Soviet early warning radar system, together with SA-2 missiles. HAL was supplying a much-improved version of the Gnat called the Ajeet, and

Saiful Azam, from Bangladesh, is unique among fighter pilots, holding awards for gallantry in aerial combat from three countries — Pakistan, Jordan and Iraq. During the September 1965 war with India, Azam flew Sabres with 17 Squadron, PAF. In combat with Indian Air Force aircraft he earned his first victory, a Folland Gnat, and was later awarded Pakistan's Distinguished Flying Cross, the Sitara-I-Jurat. In 1966, he became an adviser to the Royal Jordanian Air Force and flew the Hawker Hunter with 1 Squadron, JAF. In two separate actions in June 1967, during the Arab-Israeli War, Azam added more victories.

On June 5, his flight of four Hawker Hunters engaged Israeli Dassault Super Mystères attacking Mafraq, the major Jordanian air base. Azam shot one down and sent another smoking towards Israel. Two days later, Azam was at a base in Iraq. During an Israeli attack, he first downed a Dassault Mirage III and, moments later, destroyed a Sud-Ouest Vautour bomber. For his actions, he received Jordan's Husame Isteqlal and Iraq's Medal of Bravery, the Noth-es-Shuja.

the course of the conflict, the hard-pressed PAF received some external reinforcement, notably a squadron of F-104s from the Royal Jordanian Air Force, and the IAF's operations were supplemented by Sea Hawks of the Indian Navy flying from the deck of the carrier *Vikrant* in the Bay of Bengal. Losses were suffered daily by both sides, but the actual figures are difficult to determine, and the claims of the opposing air forces are wildly at variance with the losses admitted: the IAF claimed 94, but the PAF admitted losing only 25; the PAF claim was for 106, against an IAF admission of 54. The actual figures probably lie between the broadcast extremes. Once again, however, the cost to the smaller PAF was relatively more severe than that suffered by the IAF, and on the larger international scene a new nation had arisen — East Pakistan had become Bangladesh.

Afghanistan

The Asian region now called Afghanistan, a nation formed from a motley collection of tribal groups in the 18th century, has been endlessly fought over since history began, both by its indigenous people and by invaders. Alexander the Great's soldiers struggled through its mountain passes, and two turbulent millennia later it was the setting for the 19th century's "Great Game" between the British and the Russians. During World War II, Afghanistan remained neutral, but in 1955 an agreement was reached with the Soviet Union that revived a 1921 treaty of friendship; arrangements were then made for the Afghan monarchy to receive Soviet economic and military aid. From that date, the Afghan forces used predominantly Soviet equipment, the Royal Afghan Air Force getting MiG-17 fighters, An-2 transports and Mi-1 helicopters. In 1973, the monarchy was overthrown and replaced by a republican government. A further series of coups then made the country critically unstable, and in March 1979 rebel forces seized the western city of Herat, in the process killing some fifty Soviet advisers and their families. The Soviet Union, alarmed at the rise of militant Muslim fundamentalism and with over 1,000 other advisers at risk in Afghanistan, now felt it necessary to intervene. By August 1979 the number of Soviet advisers in the country had risen to over 5,000, and in September plans were laid for an invasion.

As is so often the case, transport aircraft were the first air assets to make their presence felt once the Soviets decided to move. Over the Christmas 1979 period, while the Western world was effectively immobilized by seasonal celebrations, An-12s, An-22s and Il-76s flew some 5,000 troops and their equipment into Bagram, north of Kabul. The deployment

RIGHT *Two Mi-8 (Hip) helicopters of the Polish Air Force. The twin-turbine Soviet Mi-8 general-purpose helicopter has been produced in various forms since it first flew in 1961. Over 10,000 were built and have served with the forces of more than forty countries, from Afghanistan to Zambia.* RIGHT BELOW *Although used mainly in the transport role, the Mi-8 is equipped with pylons and can carry rocket pods (as here) or antitank guided weapons.*

was covered by escorting MiG-21s and 23s, and accompanied by Mi-8 and Mi-24 helicopters. On December 27, the Soviets and their allies occupied the presidential palace, killed President Amin, and installed the exiled former deputy prime minister, Babrak Karmal, in his place. The new president promptly "requested Soviet assistance," so clearing the way for 15,000 troops to cross the Aghanistan/USSR border at Termez and move toward Kabul. Their advance was covered by MiG-21 fighter-bombers and Mi-24 gunship helicopters and opposed by Afghan tribesmen, who responded to the intrusion forcibly, declaring a jihad (holy war) against the invaders.

The conflict soon developed into a bloody stalemate, with the Soviets controlling the principal cities and main roads and the rebels operating almost with impunity elsewhere. There was a tidal nature to the struggle. Soviet offensives might push the Mujahideen tribesmen out of an area, only to have them flow back once the troops withdrew. The Soviets used their air assets extensively, but found, as the United States did in Vietnam, that sophisticated weaponry is not often effective against guerrilla forces moving in difficult terrain. To complicate the problem, from the outset the Mujahideen received assistance in the form of arms contributed by the U.S. To the chagrin of the Soviets, these initially included weapons from Egypt that had been originally supplied by Moscow. Among them were SA-7 shoulder-fired missiles that were successful against many aircraft from both the Soviet and Afghan air forces. (The Afghan Air Force remained loyal to the government in Kabul, unlike many army units that defected to the rebels.)

By the time of the Soviet invasion, the Democratic Republic of Afghanistan Air Force (DRAAF) had added MiG-19 and 21s, Su-7s and Il-28s to its combat inventory. The Soviet contribution, made in considerable strength, included MiG-23s and Su-17s and 25s for ground attack, Su-24s for interdiction sorties, MiG-25s for reconnaissance, and Tu-16s and 22s, flying from the USSR, for high-level bombing. Both air forces discovered that their fast jets could play only a limited part in supporting the ground battle; using complex, high-performance aircraft against irregular tribesmen proved frustratingly ineffective and unexpectedly costly. When U.S. Stinger missiles were added to the SA-7s, it was no longer sensible to fly over Mujahideen areas without dispensing flares. Later, when the command-controlled British Blowpipe arrived, even the flares offered no protection and losses mounted. More useful than the fast jets in fighting the campaign were the Mi-8/24 helicopters, which allowed Soviet troops to respond quickly to hit-and-run attacks by guerrillas, and could also mount offensive sweeps, carry out defensive patrols, and escort army convoys. One tactic was to position rapidly moving heli-borne soldiers as "anvils" onto which other army units, swinging forward as "hammers" could drive the Mujahidden. The menacing versatility of the helicopters soon made them prime targets for the tribesmen, and losses were heavy. This led to modifications that introduced more armor and better infrared screening of helicopter engines. Decoy flares became standard stores and rearward-facing machine guns were fitted to counter the guerrilla tactic of allowing aircraft to fly past before opening fire.

Transport aircraft were absolutely essential to maintaining the campaign against the Mujahideen. In a country with very basic infrastructure, where the rudimentary roads were all but impassable because of the threat of ambush, aircraft were the only reliable method of bringing men and material into Afghanistan and of moving them around once they were there. The Soviets provided the heavy lift with Il-76s, An-12s and An-22s, while the smaller An-26s of the Afghans allowed access to basic airfields that were higher or more remote. The Mujahideen did their best to interfere with operations, positioning themselves so that they could fire missiles at aircraft taking off or landing, or mount ground assaults on the airfields themselves. Soviet defensive measures were not always effective; several transports were shot down and many other aircraft destroyed on the ground in the course of the war. Among the most damaging losses was an An-22 shot down on the approach to Kabul in October 1984 in which as many as 240 soldiers died, but a number of An-12s and 26s were similarly dealt with and one civil An-26 with 52 people on board was brought down from 9,000 feet.

By 1987 it had become clear to the Soviet government that the Mujahideen could not be defeated and that the cost of continuing the campaign was intolerably high. In a political move, President Karmal was replaced by Mohammed Najibullah, who succeeded in bringing several disillusioned tribal chiefs over to the government side and set about

The Sud-Aviation SO 4050 Vautour was a swept-wing multirole aircraft produced for the French Air Force in the 1950s. The Vautour II-B seen here was a two-seat bomber, of which forty were built.

attacking rebel base areas with renewed vigor. In Moscow, President Gorbachev, seizing the opportunity offered by these developments, announced that Soviet forces would begin a limited withdrawal in October 1987. The next year saw the withdrawal well underway, with Soviet transport aircraft flying into Kabul loaded with arms and equipment for Afghan government forces and taking troops out on the return flights. By February 1989, all Soviet forces had left Afghanistan and Moscow was left to contemplate, as the United States had after Vietnam, the hard lessons of becoming involved in a limited war against an enemy who is determined, well-armed and unimpressed by the trappings of a superpower.

Since there was no opposing air force, there was no aerial combat over Afghanistan, but there were clashes over neighboring Pakistan. Thousands of Afghan refugees were driven across the border into Pakistan by the ground war. There they set up camps from which the Mujahideen organized themselves to launch attacks against the Soviet forces. Border violations were frequent as the Soviets and their Afghan allies sought to hit back. In response, from 1986 the Pakistan Air Force began to intercept intruders. Up to the time of the Soviet withdrawal, PAF F-16s claimed to have shot down some eight aircraft, seven of them with Sidewinders, including a mixture of MiG-23s, Su-22s, and An-26s. One notable success was scored on August 4, 1988, over an Su-25 flown by Alexander Rutskoi, who survived and later became prime minister of Russia.

COLD WAR — HOT COMBAT
Indochina

The French attempt to regain their colonial grip on Indochina after World War II was not smiled upon by the United States, but the threat of Communist expansion in the area was seen as a greater evil. The Communist leader Ho Chi Minh had established himself in North Vietnam and was engaged in a guerrilla war with the aim of uniting Vietnam under a Communist government. In American eyes, that was only the first stage. According to the "domino theory," Ho Chi Minh's success in Vietnam would lead inevitably to Communist domination of Laos and Cambodia, with Burma and Thailand following soon after. Resisting the fall of the first domino was seen as essential, and, in July 1950, U.S. military personnel arrived in Saigon to form a Military Assistance Advisory Group (MAAG) offering help and advice to the beleaguered French. It was a first small and deceptively innocuous step on the slippery slope of the Vietnam War's bottomless pit.

The French will to persist in Southeast Asia was effectively broken by their defeat at the hands of Viet Minh troops at Dien Bien Phu in May 1954. At an international conference in Geneva, France accepted the inevitable. Vietnam, Cambodia and Laos were recognized as independent countries, with Vietnam temporarily divided at the 17th parallel pending nationwide elections to be held in 1956. A demilitarized zone (DMZ) partitioned North and South. The United States emphasized its partiality by offering the Saigon regime economic and military assistance, and by sponsoring the eight-nation Southeast Asia Treaty Organization (SEATO) to be the region's cloak of security against Communist expansion. From 1955 the U.S. MAAG took over training responsibility for most South Vietnamese forces, although USAF instructors for the Vietnamese Air Force (VNAF) did not arrive until 1957. At the end of 1960 there were some 800 U.S. servicemen on duty with the MAAG in South Vietnam.

By 1961, the Communist insurgency in the South had grown to critical proportions and the Soviets were publicly supporting Ho Chi Minh's efforts. Kruschev announced that the Soviet Union was wholeheartedly behind "wars of national liberation," including "the armed struggle waged by the people of Vietnam." Two weeks later, John F. Kennedy became President of the United States and made it clear that he was determined to meet the Communist challenge. U.S. involvement in Southeast Asia now began an inexorable climb toward a major regional war and the longest armed conflict in American history.

For the USAF, the air war fell broadly into five phases. The first, from 1961 until mid-1964, was ostensibly covert, with the USAF flying reconnaissance sorties over Laos, and sending whole units with their aircraft to undertake combat training duties with the VNAF. Ageing F-8 Bearcats of the VNAF were replaced by A-1 Skyraiders and T-28s. Phase two, covering the five years from mid-1964 on, saw the large-scale deployment of USAF units into Southeast Asia and their continuous engagement in air operations over South Vietnam, with frequent forays into the North and Laos. The third phase, from mid-1969 until spring 1972, was a time of retrenchment, with the USAF withdrawing many units and handing over bases to the VNAF. During the fourth phase, following the 1972 North Vietnamese spring offensive and lasting until early 1973, the USAF conducted intense strike operations, including concentrated attacks on the Hanoi/Haiphong areas. In phase five, the two years ending in May 1975, the USAF was concerned with final withdrawal from Vietnam.

The Covert USAF

Regular USAF units were operating in Southeast Asia before the end of 1961. RF-101Cs of the 15th and 45th Tactical Reconnaissance Squadrons began flying missions over Vietnam and Laos from Tan Son Nhut Air Base near Saigon in October, and F-102As were later detached from the Philippines to carry out occasional patrols against unidentified intruders over the border between South Vietnam and Cambodia. Operational missions though these were, the first experience of actual combat was reserved for other detachments of a different kind.

Responding to President Kennedy's concern about the U.S. military capability to fight limited wars or engage in counterinsurgency operations, in April 1961 General LeMay established the 4400th Combat Crew Training Squadron at Eglin AFB, Florida. Nicknamed "Jungle Jim," the unit was to develop tactics and select aircraft for the counterinsurgency role. By November, a Jungle Jim detachment was deployed under the code name Farm Gate to Bien Hoa near Saigon, to train the VNAF. Their first aircraft were

REJUVENATED RAIDER

Originally produced in WWII, the Douglas A-26 Invader returned to combat in Korea as the B-26. It was resurrected yet again for the Vietnam War. TOP The heavily modified B-26K (later confusingly redesignated A-26A) arrived in Southeast Asia in 1966 and was used for ground-attack missions along the Ho Chi Minh Trail. The B-26K version (seen here at the National Museum of the USAF) had a rebuilt fuselage and tail, strengthened wings, 2,500-horsepower Pratt & Whitney R-2800 engines, reversible propellers, and wing-tip fuel tanks. Mounted close together in the nose are eight .50-caliber machine guns. BOTTOM The B-26K can take 4,000 pounds of bombs internally and has eight wing pylons capable of carrying 8,000 pounds of mixed ordnance. Under the right wing of the museum's Invader are a pod of nineteen rockets, a bomb fitted with an extended fuze, an SUU-14/A bomblet dispenser (capped at the front, the submunitions are ejected to the rear), and a napalm tank. MIDDLE: The Invader's tall fin is seen behind the tails of the bomb and the napalm tank.

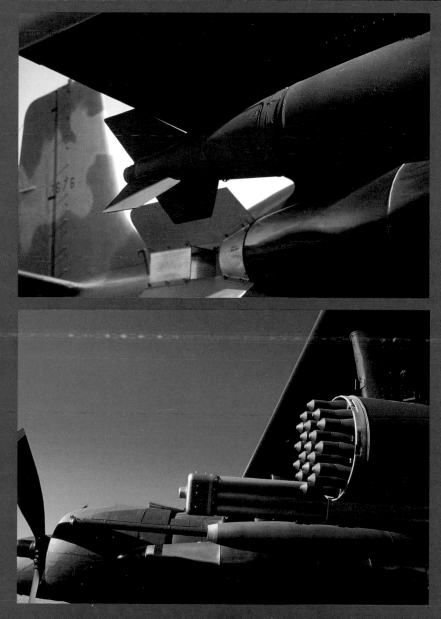

By 1964, ex-USN Douglas A-1E Skyraiders were seeing action in Vietnam, and USAF tactical instructors were flying them with South Vietnamese pilots.

four suitably modified T-28s, four SC-47s adapted for rough field operations with strengthened landing gear and JATO rockets, and four B-26 Invaders taken out of storage. For diplomatic reasons, the aircraft were flown in VNAF markings and American pilots were allowed to take part in operational sorties only if accompanied by Vietnamese. In effect, the USAF "instructors" trained their students by example while flying the missions. The official line put out for the benefit of the press was: "No USAF pilot has ever flown in tactical missions except in the role of tactical instructor." These cosmetics did not entirely hide the fact that before the end of 1961 a USAF unit had become involved in a shooting war.

Two other USAF units moved to Vietnam early in 1962, both of them equipped with C-123s. Operation Mule Train brought the 346th Troop Carrier Squadron (TCS) to Vietnam to provide tactical airlift support. More controversial was Operation Ranch Hand. UC-123Bs of the Special Aerial Spray Flight arrived at Tan Son Nhut to see whether they could defoliate the tropical jungle that hid the Viet Cong and their trails. On February 2, 1962, Ranch Hand gained the morbid distinction of suffering the first USAF casualties of the war when a UC-123B crashed without survivors.

The problem with the Farm Gate B-26s and T-28s was that they were showing their age. Corrosion was evident in elderly airframes now carrying far more than their originally designed weights of ordnance. In February 1964, a B-26 lost a wing during a combat sortie, and a T-28 suffered the same fate soon after. In recognition of its increased establishment, the Farm Gate detachment became known as the 1st Air Commando Squadron, and its disintegrating aircraft problems were dealt with by providing ex-USN A-1E Skyraiders as replacements. At first sight, the choice of one ageing prop-driven aircraft to replace another did not seem sensible. However, the A-1E proved ideal for its role. Pilots praised its capacity to absorb battle damage and swore by the accuracy of its weapons delivery. Troops were gratified to find that the A-1E could answer calls for support in weather that grounded the jets, and they admired both its weight of fire and its ability to loiter overhead for long periods.

Overt Steps

Intelligence gathering was important from the start of the U.S. involvement in Vietnam. Flying from Tan Son Nhut and Bien Hoa, EC-54s, EC-97Gs, RB-57Ds and Es, and U-2s photographed likely targets and tracked Viet Cong radio traffic. U.S. Navy reconnaissance aircraft were also active, and when a Vought RF-8A was shot down by North Vietnamese AAA over Laos on June 6, 1964, and an F-8D was lost in the same area the following day, it was decided to retaliate. On June 9, eight F-100Ds of the 511th TFS, supported by tankers, struck at AAA targets in Laos. The gloves had finally come off, and the action taken acknowledged that the United States was engaged in open, albeit limited and selective warfare with the Communists in Vietnam.

U.S. Navy ships were part of the intelligence operations, too, deployed in the Gulf of Tonkin. On August 2, 1964, the destroyer *Maddox* was attacked by North Vietnamese torpedo boats while cruising in international waters, and two days later the destroyer reported a repeat performance. Immediate retaliatory U.S. air strikes against the torpedo boat bases were followed by firm political action in Washington. President Johnson sought sweeping powers to use U.S. forces in Southeast Asia and won near unanimous support from Congress. On August 7, the Gulf of Tonkin resolution was passed, giving the President authority to use armed force as necessary to assist South Vietnam against aggression and to repel attacks on the U.S. military. Within

The primary role of the Lockheed EC-121 Warning Star (still referred to as "Connie") in the Vietnam War was to provide early warning of MiGs approaching U.S. aircraft. In October 1967, an airborne controller in an EC-121 successfully directed the interception of an enemy aircraft for the first time. Other duties undertaken by the EC-121R included tracking likely targets through sensors sown along the Ho Chi Minh Trail.

days, the U.S. forces in Southeast Asia were massively rein-forced. TAC deployed a Composite Strike Force and SAC sent more tankers. The aircraft from the Pacific Air Forces (PACAF) included B-57s, F-100Ds, and F-105Ds. A U-2 found that MiG 15s and 17s had been moved forward to Hanoi from training bases in China, which prompted General Hunter Harris, Commander of the PACAF, to request permission to destroy the new threat. At the same time, General Maxwell Taylor, now U.S. Ambassador to South Vietnam, was recommending "a carefully orches-trated bombing attack" against North Vietnam. The ideas were rejected. At this stage, President Johnson still hoped

that a mere show of force would be sufficient and that fur-ther escalation of the conflict could be avoided.

The "show of force" had little effect on the Communists. Serious political instability in South Vietnam encouraged the Viet Cong to intensify their efforts, and the flow of men and supplies down the Ho Chi Minh Trail through Laos from North Vietnam steadily increased. (President Diem was assassinated in November 1963 and a continuing struggle for power ensued.) On November 1, the Viet Cong were confident enough to strike directly at the USAF with a mortar attack on Bien Hoa airfield. Five B-57s were destroyed and fifteen others damaged. The

LEFT *The triple fins identified Connies of any version, and the distinctive "camel back" on the fuselage of the EC-121 concealed a height-finding radar. Another bulge under the fuselage held the search radar.* RIGHT *The EC-121 was powered by four Wright R-3350 turbo-compound radials of 3,250 horsepower each. This example can be seen at the National Museum of the USAF, Dayton, Ohio.*

A Ranch Hand UC-123 spraying defoliant on the jungle in Vietnam in an attempt to uncover the trails used by the Viet Cong.

USAF withdrew some of its deployed units to PACAF bases for safety. The U.S. Joint Chiefs of Staff urged that the riposte should be swift and tough. They had no faith in State Department arguments that the United States should follow a scale of graduated response, believing that an escalating campaign would be taken by the North Vietnamese as a sign of weakness and would hand them the initiative, allowing them to choose the time and place of the next step. General LeMay, the USAF Chief of Staff, believed that North Vietnam should be subjected to a punishing bombing campaign, with the promise of more to come if negotiation was refused. The JCS agreed. (During Pentagon war games on the situation in Southeast Asia, General LeMay was reported to have complained about restraints on military action. It was his opinion that the U.S. should use every available resource against North Vietnam. With typical bluntness, he summed up views by saying that, if necessary, "we should bomb them back to the Stone Age.") The President rejected the JCS proposals, preferring the State Department's "tit-for-tat" option. However, in view of the deteriorating political and military situation, he agreed that some limited action should be taken immediately. Operation Barrel Roll, begun in December 1964, was less than direct. It allowed bombing missions over Laos with the principal aim of assisting Laotian forces against Communist insurgents. President Johnson felt that the strikes would serve to signal his determination to counter mounting Communist aggression against South Vietnam.

Far from being countered, the aggression increased, often targeted specifically at Americans. On Christmas Eve 1964, a bomb exploded in the Brink Hotel, Saigon, which was being used as U.S. officers' quarters, killing two and wounding over seventy. On February 7, 1965, Viet Cong infiltrated a U.S. Army base and raided a nearby U.S. advisers' compound at Pleiku, in the central highlands. Army aircraft were destroyed and there were over 130 American casualties, including eight dead. Washington reacted by ordering raids on North Vietnamese barrack areas, President Johnson remaining concerned about "sending the right signal to Hanoi." In his turn, Ho Chi Minh signaled the Viet Cong to increase their efforts, and on February 10 they blew up another American hotel, this time in Qui Nhon. Twenty-three Americans were killed and twenty-one wounded. Further retaliatory strikes on North Vietnamese barracks followed, and this time there was more to come.

The direct attacks on Americans had been accompanied by a sharp rise in the pace of the Viet Cong offensive elsewhere. In the face of these unpalatable facts — the weakness of the Saigon regime, the success of the Viet Cong, and the willingness of Hanoi to meet U.S. challenges head on — the mood in Washington hardened and a turning point was reached. Any talk of negotiated U.S. withdrawal was swept aside by warnings that U.S. prestige was at risk and by demands that military deployments to Southeast Asia should be increased. Bombing the North was seen as essential to halting Communist erosion of the

The Republic F-105 Thunderchief was known to its pilots as the "Thud," a nickname chosen because of its ability to deliver a heavy punch. F-105D 81173, seen here loaded with sixteen 500-pound bombs, demonstrated that ability during armament trials in 1962.

South, and the JCS persisted in advocating a short, unrestrained air campaign to force Hanoi out of the war. President Johnson remained fearful of the possible consequences of such a drastic step, believing that it might bring Chinese or Soviet forces into the struggle. His authorization was for limited air operations against the North, which he intended to be conducted within well-defined and closely controlled parameters. The decision was announced in a cable to Ambassador Taylor: "We will execute a program of measured and limited air action against selected military targets in North Vietnam remaining south of the nineteenth parallel…. These actions will stop when the aggression stops." The campaign was to be carried out under the evocative code name Rolling Thunder.

Rolling Thunder

The method of conducting the air war against North Vietnam was always a source of intense frustration to those local U.S. commanders responsible for carrying out operations. President Johnson insisted on retaining such close control of the campaign that no significant target in the North could be struck without his personal approval. His targeting decisions were passed through Secretary of Defense Robert McNamara to the JCS, and were then issued as directives to CINCPAC, who allocated targets and routes to the USAF, USN and VNAF. Local air commanders responded to these orders, but had also to be aware of their responsibilities to the Commander, Military Assistance Command, Vietnam (MACV), and to the U.S. ambassadors in Saigon and Vientiane. The system was necessarily

inflexible and incapable of reacting quickly to developing situations. It also created safe havens for the North Vietnamese within which their assets could not be attacked.

Initially, Rolling Thunder objectives were selected from a fixed list of ninety-four targets, principally bridges, railways and roads. Notification was given of those which could be struck during a given week, and the number of sorties to be flown was specifically authorized. The restrictions were copious. Paramount was a concern for local civilian casualties, but Soviet and Chinese citizens were equally sacrosanct. Hanoi and Haiphong were protected areas, as was a buffer zone along the Chinese border. Ports could be neither bombed nor mined because of the danger to neutral (including Soviet) shipping. To avoid damage to crops, the dikes around the rice paddies could not be struck, a rule which led to them becoming favorite sites for antiaircraft batteries. Worse still, for fear of hurting Soviet and Chinese advisers, MiG bases and SAM sites could suffer nothing more intrusive than reconnaissance while they were being built and equipped. USAF pilots had to watch as they were completed and their crews trained, knowing that they would soon become lethal threats.

Rolling Thunder began on March 2, 1965, with an attack delivered just 35 miles north of the DMZ. Forty-four F-105Ds, forty F-100Ds, twenty B-57Bs, and seven RF-101Cs, supported by tankers and rescue helicopters, struck at the Xom Bong ammunition storage area. In post-flight debriefing, aircrew suggested that the force's 120 tons of bombs had been dropped on target, but indicated that the antiaircraft fire had been unexpectedly fierce. Many of the attacking aircraft bore scars of battle and six had been shot down. Sterling work by helicopters had saved five of the pilots, but one, Lieutenant Hayden Lockhart, had ejected from his blazing F-100 to become the first USAF prisoner of war in Vietnam.

The Douglas EB-66 Destroyer provided threat warnings and jamming protection against gun-laying radars and surface-to-air missiles (SAMs) for U.S. aircraft during the Vietnam War. Here an EB-66 acts as escort for F-105s as they release bombs over North Vietnam.

As the weeks went by, the pace of Rolling Thunder increased and the North Vietnamese air defenses stiffened. The U.S. strikes moved further north and on April 3 an attack was launched on the Ham Rong "Dragon's Jaw" Bridge across the Song Ma River at Than Hoa, halfway between Hanoi and the start of the Ho Chi Minh Trail. It was North Vietnam's sole north-south road and rail bridge and the only available route for the rapid movement of military supplies to the south. As such, it was understandably high on the U.S. priority list of interdiction targets. This attack was to be the first of many in a frustrating series lasting through seven years, until 1972.

The mission, led by Lieutenant Colonel Robbie Risner of the 67th Tactical Fighter Squadron (TFS), was intended to be decisive. The force was composed of forty-six F-105s, twenty-one F-100s, two RF-101s, and ten KC-135

tankers. The F-100s were to provide top cover and flak suppression for the main strike force of F-105s, sixteen of which carried Bullpup missiles while the rest had eight 750-pound bombs each. Well planned and executed though it was, the mission was the first of many failures. Good hits were scored on the bridge, but the 250-pound warheads of the Bullpups appeared to bounce off and the bombs merely punched easily repairable holes in roads and rail lines. The robust main structure of the bridge was unaffected. To suffer this disappointment, pilots faced intense flak that claimed an F-100 and an RF-101 besides damaging many others.

Another strike was ordered for the following day. This time the lightweight Bullpups were left behind and all forty-eight F-105s carried eight 750-pound bombs. It was estimated that the bridge and its approaches were hit by over 300 bombs, but still it stood, badly scarred but basically intact, a massive monument to over-engineering. One F-105 was lost to flak before MiGs claimed their first victims of the war. In a high-speed attack, four MiG-17s burst out of low clouds and swept through a formation of heavily laden F-105s waiting their turn at the bridge. Firing their 20 mm cannon, the MiGs shot down two on the first pass and kept going to ensure their escape.

The unwelcome intervention by the MiGs on a murky day suggested two things — that they intended to use hit-and-run tactics, and that they were under radar control for interceptions. U.S. countermeasures included the positioning of EC-121s over the Gulf of Tonkin to control traffic and warn of approaching MiGs, and the deployment to Southeast Asia of F-4C Phantoms. For their part, the North

Vietnamese understood the importance of bridges as choke points and quickly made the approaches to each of them a briar patch of antiaircraft guns. Nevertheless, by late April, USAF and USN attacks had destroyed twenty-six bridges and seven ferries. The U.S. leadership believed that such disruption in a rudimentary transportation system must have a crippling effect on the struggle in the South and must weaken the determination of the North to continue the war. The bitter lessons of Korea seemed already to have been forgotten.

In March 1965, U.S. Marines were landed at Da Nang to secure U.S. installations there. This deployment of U.S. troops to South Vietnam and the Rolling Thunder attacks on the North served to heighten public nervousness about the conflict both internationally and in the United States.

The intakes of the F-105 do not look as if they could gulp enough air to hurl the big fighter along at more than Mach 1 at low level. Their narrow reverse-angle openings were designed to provide a double shockwave at supersonic speeds, so slowing the air to a velocity that would not choke the compressor of the Pratt & Whitney J-75 engine. The red stars record this aircraft's two aerial victories over MiGs, and Memphis Belle II *turns coyly away from visitors to the National Museum of the USAF.*

The F-105G in the National Museum of the USAF is marked as it was when assigned to the 561st Tactical Fighter Squadron based at Korat, Thailand, in 1972–1973. In 1970 it was fitted with electronic countermeasure equipment and joined the 388th Tactical Fighter Wing for Wild Weasel duty, attacking enemy SAM (surface-to-air missile) sites. In 1972, the aircraft was modified to the improved F-105G Wild Weasel configuration. The large missile prominent here is an AGM-78 Standard ARM (anti-radiation missile).

To allay these fears, President Johnson made a speech in which he promised to engage North Vietnam in unconditional discussions and offered Ho Chi Minh a billion-dollar economic development program for his country if he would stop the aggression in South Vietnam. Hanoi's strident response left no doubt that they were not interested, and suggested that not only had their attitude been hardened by the bombing but that they had taken note of the increasing public criticism of government policy in the United States. They insisted that there must be an American withdrawal from Southeast Asia and that Vietnam's problems should be settled by the Vietnamese people alone.

In Washington, it was felt that such obduracy could be met only by an intensification of the bombing and the commitment of more U.S. combat troops to South Vietnam. However, it was also thought that there should first be a pause in the bombing to pursue the possibility of

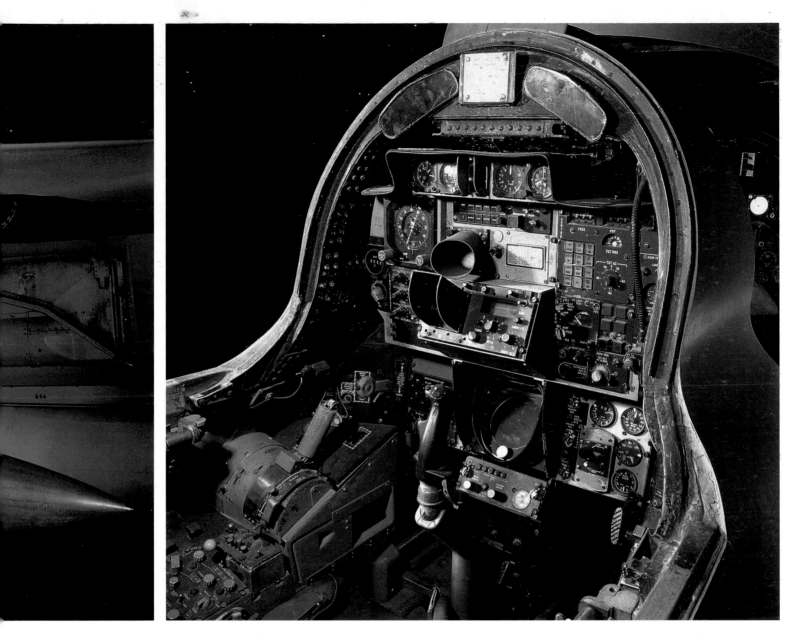

The visibility from the rear cockpit of the F-105G is very poor, but in a combat area, the EWO (Electronics Warfare Officer) in the rear seat was not looking out. He mostly kept his head down monitoring the radar scope and the assorted electronic warning displays. Just in case the pilot was incapacitated, however, the rear cockpit was equipped with a second throttle and control stick.

negotiations, if only, in Secretary of State Dean Rusk's words, "to meet criticisms that we haven't done enough." On May 10, the President cabled Ambassador Taylor, telling him that the forthcoming bombing pause was intended to "clear a path toward peace or toward increased military action."

A bombing halt was announced on May 12, 1965, but the North Vietnamese were not to be tempted. Diplomatic rebuffs led President Johnson to order the bombing resumed and the second phase of Rolling Thunder opened

after a pause of only five days. New targets were authorized, including some as far north as the rail lines linking Hanoi with China. Offensive sortie rates against the North rose, reaching 4,000 for the month of May. Armed reconnaissance missions were more frequent, with the aim of harassing targets of opportunity such as trains and trucks. As in Korea, this proved an unrewarding operation, since the North Vietnamese increasingly abandoned movement by day or on main roads.

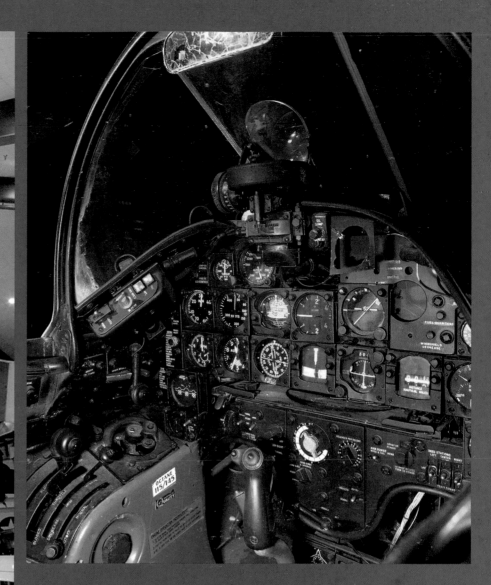

HEAVY HITTER

When it entered service in 1946, the Douglas Skyraider was the most powerful carrier-based attack plane ever produced. This single-engined aircraft with its three fuselage stations and six racks on each wing could carry a greater weight and assortment of bombs, rockets, mines, torpedoes or napalm than most WWII four-engined bombers. More than 3,100 Skyraiders were built, and the final versions of the aircraft operated until 1968. The A-1H at Pensacola flew with VA-25 "Fist of the Fleet" and was the last Skyraider to fly in the attack role in combat. From 1965 through 1968, VA-25 deployed to Southeast Asia three times, flying their A-1s from the deck of the *Coral Sea* (CVA-43). During this period, the squadron flew over 3,000 combat missions, dropping more than 10 million pounds of ordnance on enemy targets.

ABOVE There were several things jet pilots making the transition to the piston-engined Skyraider had to get used to. One was the noise, a second was the restricted visibility over the nose, and a third was the increased workload associated with the throttle quadrant. In a jet, there was just the throttle lever, but a Skyraider pilot had to juggle another two to control the propeller and fuel mixture (see lower left).

BLADE SER. NO. 153044
BLADE ASSY M20A2-162-0
ANGLE LOW AT 42 IN. STA. 27.5
ANGLE HIGH AT 42 IN. STA. 67.5
TOTAL OPPERATION HRS. 2354.3

ABOVE Power for the Skyraider came from a huge Wright 3350-26 two-row radial of 3,050 horsepower. It could pull the rugged airframe along at over 300 mph and gave it the strength to lift more than 4 tons of external stores.

RIGHT Viewed from almost any angle the Douglas A-1E Skyraider (often known by its nickname "Spad") is an impressive sight. With its uncompromisingly muscular lines it is the epitome of a rugged warplane, and its array of ordnance can be fearsome. The message on the underwing pod suggests that it is not a good idea to walk in front of a 7.62 mm gun.

M117 GENERAL PURPOSE BOMB

The M117 is a 750-pound general purpose bomb which may be employed in several different configurations. The basic M117 dates from the Korean War and uses a low-drag tail fin for medium and high-altitude deliveries. The M117R (Retarded) uses a special fin assembly providing either high-drag or low-drag release options. For low altitude deliveries, the tail assembly opens into four large drag plates which rapidly slow the bomb and allow the aircraft to escape its blast. The M117 (Destructor) looks similar to the M117R but uses a magnetic influence fuze which enables the bomb to

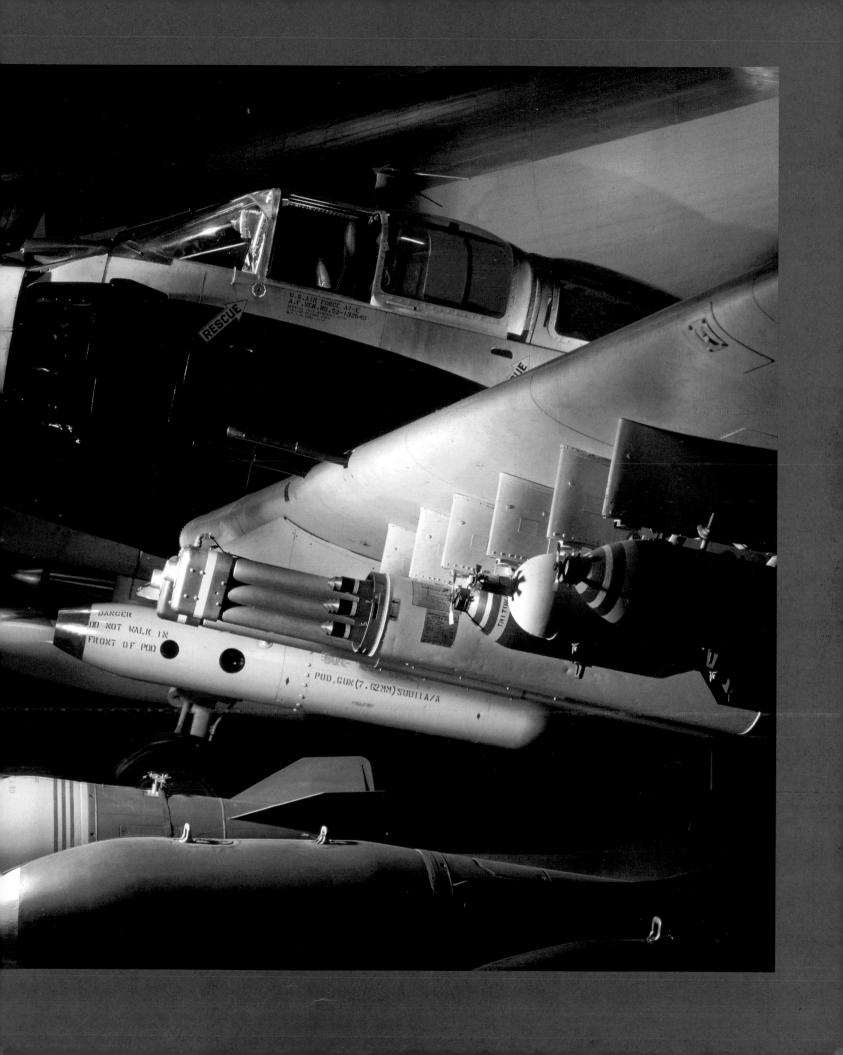

ABOVE The A-1E had seats for two but was often flown solo. Note that the flight instruments are clustered in front of the left seat.

LEFT The Skyraider exhibited at the National Museum of the USAF, Dayton, and shown on these pages in Dan Patterson's photographs is a rare example of a combat aircraft, complete with battle scars. It is the two-seater flown by Bernie Fisher on March 10, 1966, when he landed under fire in South Vietnam's A Shau Valley to rescue "Jump" Myers. They are seen after the rescue with the A-1E in the background. Bernie Fisher was awarded the Medal of Honor for his courageous action.

The first USAF loss to a SAM occurred on July 24, 1965, when an F-4C flying MiGCAP (top cover) for some F-105s northwest of Hanoi was struck by what one of the pilots described as "a flying telephone pole." It was a Soviet SA-2, a two-and-a-half-ton missile guided by a Fan Song radar. The SA-2 could reach 60,000 feet and travel at Mach 2.5. By the end of 1965, 180 missiles had been fired to shoot down eleven U.S. aircraft, five of them from the USAF. Although not the most destructive of North Vietnam's defensive systems, the SAMs did force the U.S. attackers into taking a number of countermeasures. Violent evasive maneuvers were devised to defeat the missile's ability to correct its tracking, and missions in SAM areas were flown at low level to stay below the SA-2's effective envelope. Unfortunately, low-flying aircraft came within reach of the lethal light antiaircraft guns that proliferated in Vietnam. Technological measures against SAMs included the introduction of Douglas EB-66s to detect and jam enemy radars, and the more aggressive response of finding, engaging and destroying SAM sites with specially equipped fighter-bombers, a method that came to be known as Wild Weasel.

Four two-seat F-100Fs initiated the seek-and-destroy operations. Using aircraft fitted with the Radar Homing And Warning (RHAW) system, a detachment from the USAF's Tactical Warfare Center arrived in Vietnam and began flying combat trials alongside F-105s. They were not only able to warn strike aircraft of imminent SAM firings, but also to home on the Fan Song radar's signals and either carry out or direct strikes against the enemy site. Later, modifed EF-105Fs and Gs took over as the principal Wild Weasels in missions during which they sought deliberately to draw SAM fire. They then reacted with AGM-45 Shrike missiles that followed the Fan Song beam to its source.

> "When I took over my wing [in Vietnam], the big talk wasn't about the MiGs, but about the SAMs.... I'd seen enemy planes before, but those damn SAMs were something else. When I saw my first one, there were a few seconds of sheer panic, because that's a most impressive sight — to see that thing coming at you. You feel like a fish about to be harpooned. There's something terribly personal about the SAM; it means to kill you and I'll tell you right now, it rearranges your priorities.... We had been told to keep our eyes on them and not to take any evasive move too soon, because they were heat-seeking and they, too would correct, so I waited until it was almost on me and then I rolled to the right and it went on by. It was awe inspiring.... The truth is you never do get used to the SAMs; I had about two hundred fifty shot at me and the last one was as inspiring as the first. Sure I got cagey, and I was able to wait longer and longer, but I never got overconfident. I mean, if you're one or two seconds too slow, you've had the schnitzel."
>
> GENERAL ROBIN OLDS, USAF

In their turn, the North Vietnamese showed their adaptability. They built SAM sites in profusion, many of them either unoccupied or fake. They showed how quickly they could move from one site to another after a reconnaissance aircraft had seen them, and they developed sophisticated camouflage to make the sites look like villages or clumps of trees. Fake sites, equipped with dummy missiles and transmitting Fan Song signals to draw in U.S. pilots, were surrounded by dense concentrations of guns known as flak traps. On September 16, 1965, a flak trap claimed the F-105 of one of the USAF's most celebrated airmen, Robbie Risner, condemning him to over seven years as a prisoner of war. Risner's rank and reputation ensured that he would be singled out by his captors for special treatment. (Lieutenant Colonel Risner had been featured on the cover of Time a few months before he was shot down.) He was forced to endure the pain of physical torture and the deprivation of solitary confinement during his long incarceration.

By the end of 1965, so-called "fast-mover" squadrons of the USAF in Southeast Asia were spread among bases at Takhli, Korat, Ubon and Don Muang airport in Thailand, and Tan Son Nhut, Da Nang, Bien Hoa and Cam Ranh Bay in South Vietnam. Six squadrons had F-4Cs, which had begun to make their presence felt in the air-to-air war on July 10, 1965, when the combination of Phantoms and Sidewinder heat-seeking missiles accounted for two MiG-17s in a brief dogfight. Five more squadrons were equipped with F-105s, four with F-100s, one with F-102s, one with B-57s, and one with F-5As. Other jet aircraft operating in support included RF-101s, KC-135s, RB-66s, and the Wild Weasel F-100s. Special detachments were flying the RB-57E and the U-2C. Added to all these were the USN squadrons flying from three carriers stationed in the South China Sea.

The increasingly hazardous air environment of Vietnam was revealed in the rising numbers of aircraft

As an F-86 pilot during the Korean War, Robbie Risner shot down eight MiG-15s. Called to combat again in the Vietnam War, he commanded the 67th Tactical Fighter Squadron, flying F-105s. In 1965, he was shot down twice, and the second time was taken prisoner. His rank (lieutenant colonel) and his celebrity (he had recently been on the cover of Time magazine) ensured that he would endure particular hardship during his seven years as a prisoner of war in Hanoi. His stoicism and courage under torture were an inspiration to his fellow prisoners. Robbie Risner retired from the Air Force in 1976 as a brigadier general.

being destroyed. Of 273 U.S. fixed-wing aircraft lost to enemy action in 1965, 158 belonged to the USAF. No fewer than 139 of the USAF's losses, including 54 F-105s, were attributed to AAA and small arms fire; there were now more than 2,000 radar-directed AAA guns in North Vietnam.

On December 24, 1965, President Johnson ordered a ceasefire over the Christmas period. For air operations, this was extended into a prolonged bombing pause. A "peace offensive" was launched, offering the withdrawal of U.S. forces from Vietnam but refusing to accept the participation of the Viet Cong in a coalition government in Saigon. Ho Chi Minh's rejection of the offer denounced it as "deceitful," and on January 31, 1966, President Johnson opened the third phase of Rolling Thunder. Unwilling to accede to JCS requests for an increase in the tempo of the bombing and for the mining of enemy harbors, and still wanting to leave the door open for the North Vietnamese, the President kept a tight grip on air operations, and phase

three was less intense than phase two had been. However, by the end of March, the intransigence of Hanoi led to a recommendation from McNamara that the bombing should be intensified and that the target list should be widened to include oil. Reluctantly, the President agreed, and phase four of Rolling Thunder began in June 1966, now under the operational control of Seventh Air Force, commanded by General William Momyer.

For the remainder of 1966, U.S. aircraft flew extended armed reconnaissance missions throughout the North (always excepting the Hanoi/Haiphong sanctuaries), attacked the rail links with China, and made a determined effort against oil targets and the infiltration routes north of the DMZ. The pace of the air offensive was sharply increased, with U.S. aircraft reaching a peak of 12,000 sorties over North Vietnam in September. In spite of frequently poor weather and concentrated defenses, the damage done by the campaign was clearly substantial. Countless trucks and railway wagons were destroyed, and cuts made everywhere in road and rail networks, with hundreds of bridges demolished. It was estimated that two-thirds of the North's oil storage capacity no longer existed. These considerable efforts forced the North Vietnamese to improvise. Oil was stored in barrels rather than large tanks, and dispersed in hundreds of minor dumps. Perhaps 300,000 people were diverted into repair work and into moving supplies, on foot or by bicycle if necessary. This they were evidently prepared to do, and the ground war in South Vietnam gave no sign of slackening.

By the end of 1966, there were at least 150 SAM sites operating in North Vietnam, and the first MiG-21s had made their appearance carrying infrared homing missiles.

They could be seen flying from five airfields in the Hanoi area, but the bases were not on the list of targets for U.S. aircraft. A typical execution order of the time included the instruction: "Not, repeat not, authorized to attack North Vietnamese air bases from which attacking aircraft may be operating." At least a partial answer to the MiG problem came in Operation Bolo. Colonel Robin Olds, commander of the 8th Tactical Fighter Wing (TFW) flying F-4Cs, planned a mission to lure the MiGs into battle. On January 2, 1967, a force composed predominantly of F-4Cs approached the Hanoi area in a formation normally associated with a standard F-105 strike package. Cloud covered Hanoi and Olds had to trail his coat over the enemy airfields three times before MiG-21s began popping up on all sides. In the frenetic combat of the next few minutes, seven MiGs were shot down for no loss.

An extract from Colonel Olds' report of the action describes one success: "[I] fell in behind and below the MiG-21 at his seven o'clock position at about .95 Mach. Range was 4,500 feet, angle off 15. The MiG-21 obligingly pulled up well above the horizon and exactly down sun. I put the pipper on his tail pipe, received a perfect growl, squeezed the trigger once, hesitated, then once again. The first Sidewinder leapt in front and within a split second turned left in a definite and beautiful collision course correction…. The missile went slightly down, then arced gracefully up, heading for impact. Suddenly the MiG-21 erupted in a brilliant flash of orange flame. A complete wing separated and flew back in the airstream, together with a mass of smaller debris. The MiG swapped ends immediately, and tumbled forward for a few instants. It then fell, twisting, corkscrewing, tumbling, lazily toward the top of the clouds. No pilot ejection occurred…."

The determined enemy air defense efforts in 1966 led to a sharp rise in U.S. fixed-wing combat losses to 465, of which 296 were USAF. AAA and small arms accounted for 265 USAF aircraft, and again the F-105 suffered most heavily — no fewer than 103 Thunderchiefs had fallen to the guns.

A six-day truce on the occasion of the 1967 Lunar New Year (Tet) marked the end of Rolling Thunder, phase four. Phase five began on February 14 and lasted until Christmas 1967. During the year, the target list was expanded to take in the previously forbidden Hanoi/ Haiphong area. Among the most significant new items was an industrial complex at Thai Nguyen where the country's only steel mill was situated. Ringed with ninety-six AAA batteries and several SAM sites, it was a formidable challenge. Leading the first raid on March 10 were four F-105s, two of them equipped as Wild Weasels. On the run in, the lead aircraft was shot down and his wingman severely damaged. The remaining pair, led by Captain Merlyn Dethlefsen, set about the job of eliminating a SAM site that would threaten strike aircraft bombing the steel mill. MiGs closed and attacked; Dethlefsen dived into the intense flak barrage to brush them off. The F-105s were hit repeatedly, but turned back into the flak twice more to drop bombs and finish off the site with 20 mm cannon. Dethlefsen's fierce determination was rewarded with a Medal of Honor. He made light of his gritty persistence under fire: "All I did was the job I had been sent to do," he said. "I expected to get shot at a lot."

The McDonnell Douglas F-4 Phantom II was all brute power and awkward angles. In aerial combat with MiGs during the Vietnam War, Phantoms scored 145 kills and achieved a kill/loss ratio of 3.73 to 1.

FIGHTER LEADER

TOP RIGHT *Air Force Col Robin Olds, Commander 8th Tactical Fighter Wing,* by Fred Mason. (From the USAF art collection)
TOP LEFT In October 1996, Brigadier General Robin Olds once more sat in the cockpit of the F-4 in which he scored two aerial victories over MiGs on May 20, 1967.
BOTTOM The bottom edge of the pilot's scope for the APQ-100 radar can just be seen beneath the shroud at the top of the F-4's front cockpit instrument panel, with two columns of engine instruments off to the right. To the right of the seat are the hoses that take air to the G-suit and oxygen to the pilot's mask. The black and yellow ejection seat handle is at the front of the seat.

ABOVE The McDonnell Douglas F-4 Phantom II was the most significant Western combat aircraft to appear in the 1960s. It weighed nearly 30 tons at full load, of which some 8 tons could be ordnance of various kinds. The Phantom II made its mark in a number of roles — air superiority, strike, reconnaissance, and the specialized Wild Weasel mission. The F-4C in the National Museum of the USAF is displayed with AIM-9 Sidewinder missiles on its racks.

RIGHT Two red stars decorate the plate that prevents turbulent boundary layer air from entering the left engine. They identify this F-4C as the aircraft that Colonel Robin Olds and Lieutenant Stephen Crocker were flying when they destroyed two MiGs on May 20, 1967.

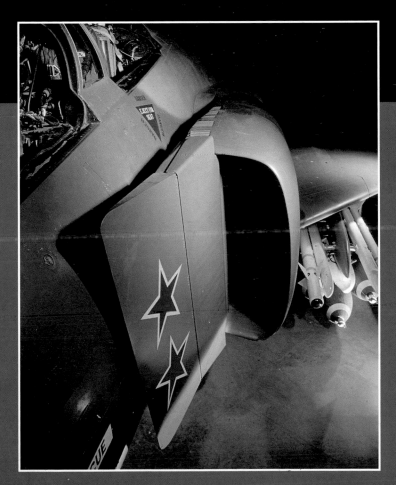

ABOVE LEFT Commander Randy "Duke" Cunningham was America's first pilot ace of the Vietnam War. Crewed with Lieutenant Willy Driscoll as his radar intercept officer, he shot down five MiGs in 1972, three of them in a single engagement on May 10. Following the third victory of that mission, Cunningham and Driscoll were forced to eject over the Gulf of Tonkin when a SAM hit their Phantom. They were rescued by a Marine Corps helicopter. "Duke" Cunningham is the holder of the Navy Cross, two Silver Stars, fifteen Air Medals, and the Purple Heart.

ABOVE RIGHT Charles DeBellevue was the first U.S. Air Force weapons systems officer (WSO) to become an ace during the Vietnam War. In 1971–72, DeBellevue logged 550 combat hours in 220 combat missions with the 555th "Triple Nickel" TFS, scoring four aerial victories while crewed with Steve Ritchie and two more with John Madden. His total of six was the most earned by a U.S. airman during the Vietnam War. Colonel DeBellevue retired from active duty in January 1998, after thirty years of military service. Among his many awards, he holds the Air Force Cross, the Silver Star with two oak leaf clusters, the Legion of Merit and the Distinguished Flying Cross with five oak leaf clusters.

OPPOSITE In afterburner, 17,000 pounds of thrust came from the huge jet pipes of the F-4C's General Electric J-79 engines, pushing the aircraft along at speeds up to Mach 2.3 at altitude and Mach 1.2 low down. The contrast with the small Sidewinder tails alongside is dramatic. Between the jet pipes is an arrester hook, a reminder of the F-4's naval heritage.

Other targets hit successfully by U.S. aircraft in and around Hanoi/Haiphong in 1967 were power plants, the provoking MiG airfields, and the Paul Doumer Bridge across the Red River in Hanoi. Several spans of the bridge were dropped at the first attempt with the help of 3,000-pound bombs. Elsewhere, strike operations expanded into the buffer zone with China, and rivers south of the 20th parallel were mined. As offensive operations were stepped up, the air-to-air war moved increasingly in favor of the United States. The F-4D Phantom and the AIM-4 Falcon missile were delivered to the 555th Tactical Fighter Squadron (TFS), the combination scoring its first victory over a MiG on October 26. By the end of the year, 75 MiGs had been shot down for the loss of 25 U.S. aircraft (USAF ratio 59 to 22), and American airmen had gained virtual air supremacy over North Vietnam. The year as a whole had seen U.S. fixed-wing combat losses peak at 515: of those, 325 were USAF, 252 attributable to AAA and small arms fire.

The year 1967 was one during which the results of Rolling Thunder were subjected to close scrutiny in a number of studies. The bombing campaign was credited with having hurt Hanoi's military-industrial base (such as it was) severely. Nevertheless, the conclusions drawn in Washington were that Ho Chi Minh's strategy appeared to be unwavering, that there was every indication that the North Vietnamese people would continue to resist, and that the ability of the North to carry on the war remained little changed. What was more, in the balance-account terms of Secretary McNamara, the bombing was costing the United States at least ten dollars for every dollar of damage inflicted. Even so, the factor in the equation that might conceivably have made the difference, the severance of North Vietnam's principal life-line to the Soviet Union by the mining of Haiphong and other harbors, was still denied to U.S. military leaders by President Johnson because he believed the possibility of damaging Soviet shipping to be an unacceptable risk.

Following the 1967 Christmas bombing pause, Rolling Thunder entered its sixth phase. It did so without McNamara, who was replaced as Secretary of Defense by Clark Clifford early in 1968. On March 31, 1968, Lyndon Johnson suspended all bombing north of the 20th parallel and announced that he would not be seeking a second term as President of the United States. To almost everyone's surprise, the North Vietnamese reacted by announcing that they would be willing to engage in peace talks. Later in the year, with the talks underway in Paris and on the eve of the Presidential elections, Johnson halted the bombing of North Vietnam altogether. Forty-four months and over 300,000 sorties after it began, Rolling Thunder rumbled away into history.

The "In-Country" War

As the United States moved inexorably toward open involvement in Vietnam in 1964, the requirement for VNAF personnel to fly on all USAF operational sorties was reconsidered. On February 18, 1965, it was rescinded, and the government of South Vietnam officially requested the USAF to fly "in-country" combat missions. B-57s struck at a guerrilla concentration the next day, and other U.S. combat aircraft became engaged in operations soon thereafter because a threatened coup in Saigon kept the VNAF otherwise occupied, standing by to intervene. By March 6, Washington accepted the inevitable and removed all restrictions on the use of U.S. aircraft in South Vietnam. With the restrictions lifted, USAF units poured into the country and a crash program of airfield construction was undertaken. By the end of 1965, the USAF had more than 500 aircraft and 21,000 men stationed at eight major air bases in South Vietnam.

Once airborne, combat aircraft were often handed over to a forward air controller (FAC). Mostly former jet pilots, the FACs spent much of the war flying the Cessna O-1 Bird Dog, a single-engined light plane capable of 115 mph flat out and unarmed except for target-marking rockets. Bird Dogs lacked even the minimal protection of armor and self-sealing fuel tanks. Since it was necessary to make visual contact with the enemy from low level, and then to hang around marking targets and directing strikes, FAC missions were among the most challenging flown by the USAF. Later, the O-1 was supplemented by the larger, twin-engined Cessna O-2 and the more capable North American OV-10, which had both armor and self-sealing tanks and carried powerful armament of its own. The job, however, was always hazardous. As one Skyraider pilot put it: "You've got to hand it to those guys.... Just a light plane, a pair of good eyes, and guts." During the war, 122 O-1s, eighty-two O-2s,

Mike Jackson served in the United States Air Force from 1968 to 1991, and flew 210 combat missions as a forward air controller (FAC) in Vietnam during 1971–72. He took part in the fight against the North Vietnamese Army during the 1972 Easter Offensive and was part of the FAC team in the remarkable BAT-21 mission to rescue Lieutenant Colonel Iceal Hambleton in April 1972.

and forty-seven OV-10s were lost in combat. Two FAC pilots, Captain Hilliard Wilbanks and Captain Steven Bennett, were awarded posthumous Medals of Honor for their persistence and self-sacrifice.

FACs controlled a formidable array of strike aircraft and weapons. Fast movers such as F-100s, F-4s and B-57s could respond to calls for support with general-purpose bombs or fragmentation bombs, cluster-bomb units, a variety of rockets and missiles, gunfire, and the ground forces' weapon of choice — napalm. Soldiers liked napalm not only because it could be guaranteed to penetrate thick jungle foliage, but also because, since it created no shrapnel, it could be used close to hard-pressed friendly troops. If the ground forces had a favorite aircraft, it was not among the jets. It was the prop-driven A-1 Skyraider. It could carry an

incredible amount of ordnance, over 4 tons on fifteen attachment points beneath the wings and fuselage, and it could stay in contact for long periods while its thirsty jet cousins came and went. Four 20 mm cannon made the A-1's strafing attacks lethal, and heavy armor-plating helped it to resist small arms fire. It was particularly suited for giving covering fire during rescue missions for downed aircrew, a task known as Rescue Combat Air Patrol (RESCAP) operating under the call sign "Sandy." By the end of the war, "Sandies" had assisted in the rescue of over 1,000 airmen.

On March 10, 1966, an outpost in the A Shau Valley manned by 375 Montagnard irregulars and twenty U.S. Green Beret advisers called for help against a force of 2,000 North Vietnamese. Close air support was made difficult by thick, low clouds covering the rugged terrain, but

Low-level FAC missions in the Cessna O-1E Bird Dog were extremely hazardous, but the presence of an FAC to call in air strikes was often the difference between life and death for U.S. or South Vietnamese ground forces in contact with the enemy.

four A-1Es led by Major Bernard Fisher found a way into the valley through a gap in the overcast. Running the gauntlet of AAA and small arms fire from the valley slopes, they heard radio calls saying that the camp was being overrun. As they strafed the attackers, two of the Skyraiders were hit hard by enemy fire. One pulled up and made for home, but the other, piloted by Major "Jump" Myers, lost its engine and burst into flames. Myers bellied the aircraft onto the camp landing strip, exploding his external fuel tank in the process. He leapt clear into a ditch as flames enveloped his A-1E. Seeing that Myers was alive, Fisher called for a rescue helicopter before joining his wingman and two other newly arrived Skyraiders in strafing enemy troops trying to reach the downed pilot. However, the helicopter was at least twenty minutes away, the A-1Es were out of ammunition, and Fisher realized that the North Vietnamese would reach Myers before he could be rescued. Rather than run that risk, he decided to

do the job himself. As the others made dummy runs overhead to distract the enemy, he landed his aircraft under fire on the shell-torn strip. Myers sprinted out of the ditch and dived into the cockpit as Fisher opened up and roared away, dodging debris on the runway and climbing into the safety of the clouds. Fisher's Skyraider bore the scars of many hits, but made it back to base. For this breathtaking exploit, Bernard Fisher was awarded the Medal of Honor.

On countless occasions, close support aircraft answered desperate calls for help from besieged troops and made the difference between survival and destruction. However, more than half of the operational sorties flown over South Vietnam were planned attacks on suspected guerrilla strongholds and supply routes. Such strikes were intended to deny the Communists safe havens and storage areas, and they were carried out by both day and night. In 1966, the ground-based Combat Skyspot MSQ-77 radar was introduced, which could guide bombers to a precise release point, so allowing tactical strikes to be made on selected targets at any time and in any weather.

The firepower for tactical operations was vastly increased in June 1965 when SAC's B-52s were made available to Military Assistance Command Vietnam (MACV) to fly combat missions under the code name Arc Light. It was a surprising shift, but one that underlined the flexibility of air power. Strategic operations were conducted against the North by fighter-bombers, while aircraft designed to promote the strategy of nuclear deterrence were tasked to meet tactical needs in the South. The B-52Fs that flew the first Arc Light missions from Guam were modified to enable them to carry twenty-seven 750-pound bombs internally and twenty-four more on external racks. Later, B-52Ds went through a Big Belly modification that allowed them to load the astonishing number of eighty-four 500-pound bombs in the bay, while retaining the external capacity for twenty-four 750-pound bombs. It was often claimed that such profligate use of air power was wasteful, since the intelligence that selected targets for the B-52s was in many cases less than certain and, in view of the B-52s' understandably slow reaction to a situation, seldom timely. Nevertheless, though B-52 raids sometimes struck at empty forest, captured Viet Cong usually reported that they were the thing they most feared. The destructive power and scale of B-52 bombing patterns was awesome, and morale suffered because it was never known where or when the earth would next erupt. With the bombers operating at 30,000 feet, nothing was seen or heard before hundreds of bombs arrived, obliterating everything over a huge area. For those who had seen the results of a B-52 raid, or had survived the experience, wondering when the heavens would open again could concentrate the mind and weaken the spirit.

In 1967, part of the B-52 force moved to Thailand, from where they could reach their targets more quickly and without refueling. By then, the B-52's contribution to the war had become considerable. A little less than two years after Arc Light began, the 10,000th B-52 combat sortie was flown, and the big bombers were being increasingly relied on to break up enemy troop concen-

> *"The debate went on until the end of the war. It was about whether bombing was a political signal or a military means to political ends."*
> THE PENTAGON PAPERS, 1971

> *"Only you can prevent forests."*
> SIGN IN THE CREW ROOM OF A UC-123 DEFOLIANT SPRAYING SQUADRON, USAF, VIETNAM

trations. At the time of the Tet offensive in 1968, a major assault was launched on the U.S. Marines' base at Khe Sanh, 6 miles from the Laotian border and 14 miles south of the DMZ. General Westmoreland believed that "the enemy hoped at Khe Sanh to obtain a climacteric victory such as he had done in 1954 at Dien Bien Phu." The U.S. base was surrounded by 20,000 North Vietnamese regulars and remained under siege for seventy-seven days. Operation Niagara was devised to provide the Marines with air support and the USAF's General Momyer was given temporary command of all U.S. air assets operating at Khe Sanh. Hundreds of sorties were flown every day, with a C-130 command center handing off incoming fighter-bomber sorties to one of up to thirty FACs in good weather and letting Combat Skyspot radar guide them in when clouds were heavy.

Vital though these missions were, it was the B-52s that most impressed the enemy. Missions were arranged so that a formation of three B-52s arrived over Khe Sanh every ninety minutes to bomb at Combat Skyspot's direction. Initially, a buffer zone was established that allowed the B-52s to bomb no closer than 3,000 yards from the forward Marine positions. However, when enemy troops developed extensive bunker complexes closer in, the Marine commander agreed to reduce the buffer to 1,000 feet. Ensuing strikes devastated enemy positions and lifted the spirits of the Marines. A captured North Vietnamese soldier estimated that one strike alone had killed 75 percent of an 1,800-man regiment. There was ample reason to believe his story. By the time the siege was broken, the countryside around Khe Sanh had been transformed into a lunar landscape, scarred as it was by endless overlapping bomb craters. During Niagara, U.S. aircraft had dropped almost 100,000 tons of bombs, and two-thirds of them had fallen from B-52s. Intelligence estimates suggested that two North Vietnamese divisions had been effectively destroyed as fighting units. It was hardly surprising that General Westmoreland later gave credit to the B-52s for preventing the large-scale buildup of forces needed by the enemy to overrun Khe Sanh.

POINT AND SHOOT

ABOVE The twin-boom North American Rockwell OV-10 Bronco was acquired by the USAF as a forward air control aircraft. Sponsons projecting from each side of the fuselage housed four 7.62 mm M60 machine guns and had four weapons attachment points. In this case, a rocket pod can be seen alongside the extra fuel tank hung below the fuselage centerline.

RIGHT The seat pan in the OV-10 sits level with the cockpit rail, giving the pilot the maximum amount of canopy to look through and a good view over the nose. The gunsight hangs down from the windshield arch, above the instrument panel.

ABOVE The large canopy of the OV-10 gave exceptional visibility to the crew, who were situated in tandem on ejection seats. Power came from two Garrett T76 turboprops of 715 ehp (effective horsepower).

INSET The Bronco was the third generation FAC aircraft used in Southeast Asia. Unlike its predecessors, the much faster OV-10 was designed to face the hazards of the job with armor plating, self-sealing fuel tanks, and substantial firepower.

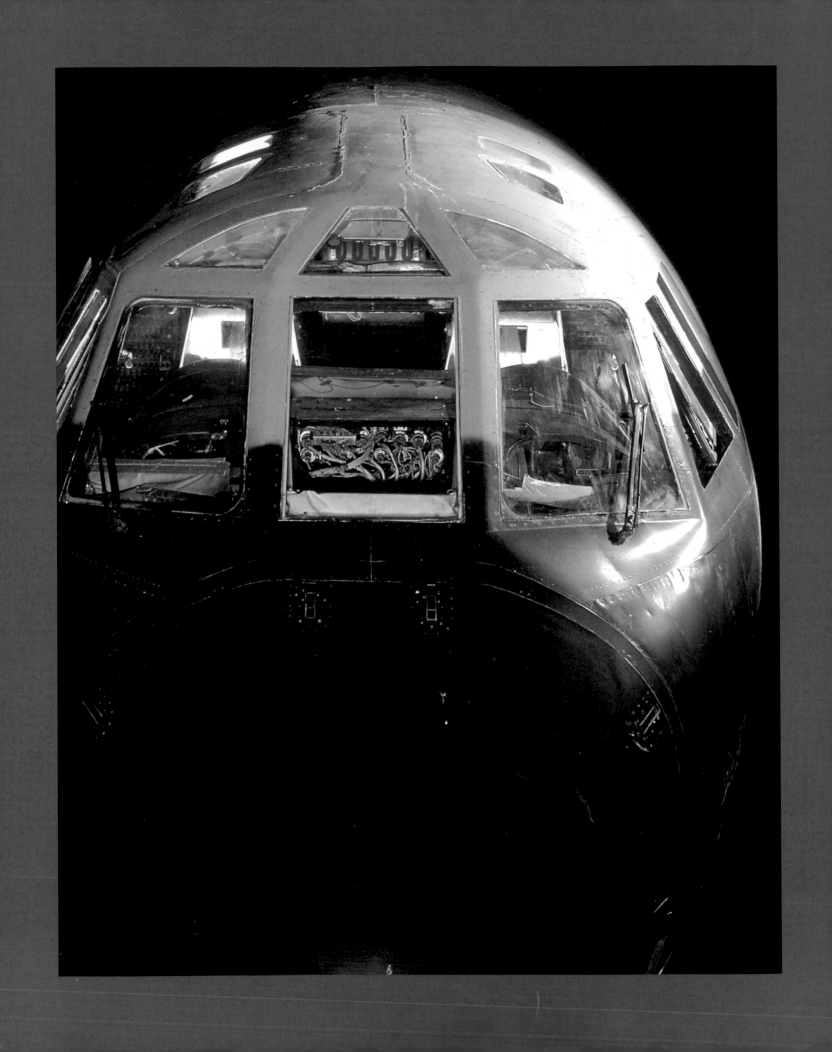

OPPOSITE The Boeing B-52 Stratofortress (nicknamed the "Buff") is the longest-lived combat aircraft ever, having been in the front line in various forms since 1955. A B-52 made the first drop of a hydrogen bomb over Bikini Atoll on May 21, 1956. In June 1965, B-52s entered combat when they began flying missions in Southeast Asia. By August 1973, seventeen B-52s had been lost to enemy action in the course of flying 126,615 combat sorties. The B-52D on display in the National Museum of the USAF is a dominating presence. It bears the scars of severe damage inflicted by an enemy SAM on April 9, 1972. Transferred from the 97th Bomb Wing, Blytheville AFB, Arkansas, it was flown to the museum in November 1978.

ABOVE Two tails and a contrast in firepower. In the rear, the B-17's twin .50-caliber machine guns were manually aimed and fired. B-52s before the G model still had .50s, but there were four of them and they tracked attacking aircraft by radar.

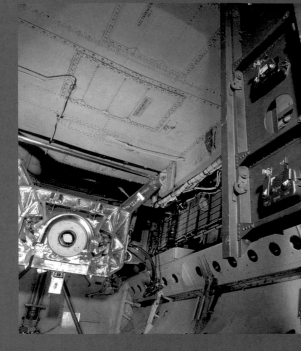

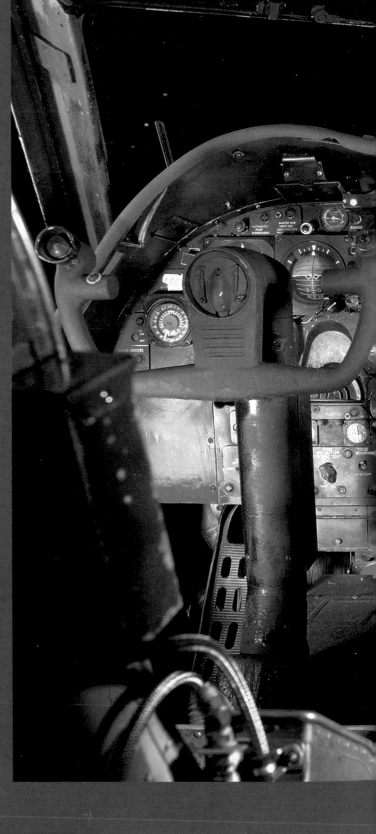

ABOVE The bomb bay of the B-52D could hold eighty-four 500-pound bombs.

RIGHT The eye-catching features of the B-52 cockpit are the fistful of throttles and the associated rows of engine instruments. Each throttle lever has two white knobs, which makes it easier to control engines separately if necessary. At the top of the instrument panel, red warning lights signal engine fires and can be pushed to initiate extinguishers. With little room left on the panel, the engine oil pressure gauges are placed above the windshield. Behind the throttle quadrant is a rotary control that allows the main undercarriage trucks to be offset before landing in a crosswind. To the left of the throttles is the elevator trim wheel, and the drag chute lever is to the right.

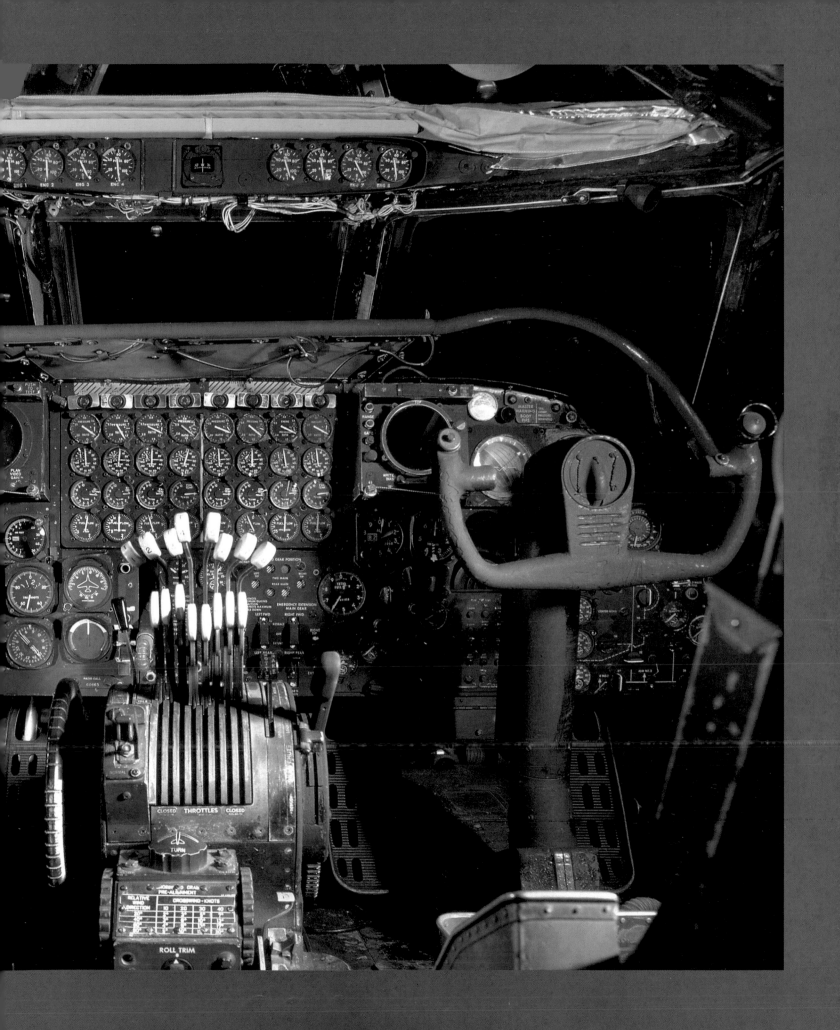

The torrent of bombs that fell from the B-52Ds made the "Buff" the USAF weapon most feared by the Viet Cong and the North Vietnamese Army.

On the Trail

Although combat operations against the enemy's fighting forces, both North Vietnamese and Viet Cong, were an essential part of the war, they did not strike at the root of the problem — how to deprive the Communist insurgency in South Vietnam of its lifeblood. From the outset, the vast network of rough roads and tracks through Laos, known collectively as the Ho Chi Minh Trail, was used to sustain the Viet Cong with a flow of supplies that grew steadily over the years to the proportions of a flood. The prime movers employed on the Trail were thousands of Soviet ZIL-157 trucks. Stopping the movement of these trucks became a paramount concern of U.S. leaders.

Supplies from North Vietnam usually crossed into Laos and entered the Ho Chi Minh Trail system through two passes: Mu Gia, about 75 miles north of the DMZ, and Keo Neua, which was twice as far north. Much of the Trail offered its users the natural concealment of a thick forest canopy, but there were open spaces that provided opportunities for movement to be detected and for tactical aircraft to make visual attacks. Once U.S. aircraft began operating over the Trail, traffic moved at night through these vulnera-

ble areas. The first operations aimed specifically at interdicting the Trail in southern Laos were code-named Steel Tiger. They began in April 1965, using roving F-100s and F-105s by day, and B-57s accompanied by C-130 flareships by night. The poor flying weather associated with the monsoon badly restricted operations until October, but over 1,000 Steel Tiger sorties per month were flown, nevertheless. Even with the help of ground reconnaissance teams to plot traffic on the Trail, results did not match the effort expended and it became obvious that improved interdiction methods would have to be developed.

The first step was the preparation of a systematic campaign against the Trail in the areas of Laos contiguous with South Vietnam. The plan, code-named Tiger Hound, combined U.S. Air Force, Navy, Marine and Army air resources with those of the Royal Laotian Air Force. UC-123s sprayed defoliants on the forest obscuring the Trail, and an airborne command post was established using C-47s and C-130s to control strike operations. FACs roamed the area, and RF-4Cs combed the Trail with infrared sensors and sideways-looking radar. F-100s, F-105s, B-57s, A-1Es, carrier aircraft and Laotian T-28s were on call for strikes; night operations added

C-130 flareships and Army OV-1 Mohawks. Later, resurrected A-26Ks took on the night interdiction role, as they had in Korea, and there were even C-123s carrying special detection devices and dispensing cargo-hold loads of bomblet canisters. By 1966, the B-52s had joined in, operating with the aid of Combat Skyspot radars, and then came the sophisticated B-57G, fitted with low-light television, infrared sensors, forward-looking radar and laser target-marking.

Aircrews were sometimes aided in their search for targets by an electronic anti-infiltration system. Small air-dropped sensors were sown along the Trail to detect the movement of troops and trucks. The information was transmitted to a monitoring aircraft, such as the EC-121R, which made assessments and recommended targets. Some of the weaponry used on the Trail was also unusual. Besides the conventional array of bombs, rockets and guns, there were land mines, incendiary clusters, fuel-air explosive munitions, and even canisters of riot control gas. This remarkable combination of air power instruments seemed impressive enough, but the most effective truck killers were found elsewhere, drawn from the unlikely ranks of the tactical transports. They were transport aircraft modified into forms that Admiral Nelson would have understood: "gunships" capable of firing broadsides of terrifying destructiveness. The first of the gunship line was the AC-47,

Douglas's venerable "Gooney Bird" in yet another role. Known to the media as "Puff, the Magic Dragon" but to ground forces by the call sign "Spooky," AC-47s were armed with three 7.62 mm mini-guns that fired sideways from cargo door and windows. Targets were attacked by flying an orbit around them and holding them centered in a sight placed to the left of the pilot in the cockpit window. Later gunships included the AC-119K Shadow, and several variants of the C-130 Hercules, the most advanced of which was the AC-130E Spectre. The Spectre was heavily armored and equipped with a multitude of sensors, including one that could detect running truck ignition systems. Its battery consisted of paired mini-guns and Vulcan 20 mm cannon, a 40 mm cannon and a 105 mm howitzer, all fired with the aid of a computer. A broadside from a Spectre was memorably devastating.

Gunships were as useful in South Vietnam against the Viet Cong as they were on the Trail, giving timely aid to hard-pressed ground units on many occasions, their murderous fire destroying the cohesion of countless enemy attacks on army bases and outposts. Impressive as the statistics of their destructive powers were, however, with literally thousands of trucks wrecked each year, even the mighty gunships could not bring the flow of supplies along the Ho Chi Minh Trail to a complete halt, and the Viet Cong resolutely continued to increase their capability to operate in the countryside of South Vietnam throughout the 1960s.

"Puff, the Magic Dragon," call sign Spooky. The venerable Douglas C-47 donned new clothes in Vietnam to become the fearsome AC-47 gunship, equipped with 200,000-candlepower flares to light up the night and three mini-guns each able to fire 6,000 rounds per minute (every fourth a red tracer). Captured Viet Cong North Vietnamese Army documents referred to the gunship's reputation, containing orders specifically to "not attack the Dragon because it would only infuriate the monster."

Fetchers and Carriers

As is always the case in war, it was the men and machines engaged in front-line combat that took the eye and monopolized the headlines. Behind them and their activities there were a host of specializations without whose services the armed warriors could not have operated. The contributions made by transport aircraft in World War II and Korea were essential to the conduct of the various campaigns, but in Southeast Asia their work was perhaps even more significant. The airbridge built across the Pacific by the Military Air Transport Service (Military Airlift Command from 1965) was massive. In the absence of adequate ports and infrastructure in South Vietnam, it needed to be. In the early days, the bulk of the transoceanic traffic was handled by C-124s. MATS had twenty-one squadrons of them, backed up by three of C-133s, seven of C-130s, and three of C-135s. The limitations of this force were soon exposed by the fact that MATS still had to provide a service for the U.S. military elsewhere in the world. Only the C-124s and C-133s had the capacity to cope with such large items of equipment as tanks and bulldozers, but the C-124s were agonizingly slow and the C-133s technically temperamental. (The C-124 took almost two weeks to make the round-trip between the U.S. and Southeast Asia, accumulating some ninety-five flying hours in the process.) Although help came from aircraft of the Air Force Reserve and Air National Guard, mostly ageing

C-97s and C-119s, the airbridge did not gain enough strength to take the strain fully until the appearance of the Lockheed C-141 Starlifter in 1965. The C-141A's ability to carry its maximum payload of 67,000 pounds for 4,000 miles cruising at 440 knots was a quantum jump over the C-124's 25,000 pounds for 2,300 miles at 200 knots. Even so, the C-141's cargo bay was neither as high nor as wide as the C-124's, and it was not until Lockheed's giant C-5A Galaxy started operations into Southeast Asia in 1971 that the United States had a true strategic airlifter capable of handling the bulkiest military loads.

MAC's airlift capacity improved in other ways besides that of acquiring better aircraft. The demands of the Vietnam War forced the development of a whole new air transport system. Established transpacific routes grew from one to more than a dozen, and airfields both en route and in Southeast Asia gained longer runways and better facilities. Aircraft utilization rates rose and freight priorities were set; the Red Ball Express system guaranteed shipment of vital spares within twenty-four hours of receiving the request. MAC also demonstrated an impressive capacity to react quickly in an emergency. For example, in 1967, C-141s and C-133s moved 10,335 paratroopers of the 101st Division, plus 5,118 tons of equipment (including thirty-seven helicopters), from Fort Campbell, Kentucky, to Bien Hoa between November 17 and December 29. The average aircraft unloading time for this operation was just seven and a half minutes. Even faster overall was the response to the Tet offensive in February 1968, when a brigade of the 82nd Airborne at Fort Bragg, North Carolina, and a regiment of the

Troops and vehicles of the 1st Cavalry Division, U.S. Army, with a C-130 Hercules of the 834th Air Division. The versatility of C-130s was invaluable during the Vietnam War, when they operated as strategic and tactical transports, tankers, gunships, command posts, rescue aircraft, drone controllers, and even occasionally as specialized bombers.

appear in 1964, and in 1967 the U.S. Army transferred its force of de Havilland C-7 Caribous to the USAF. Small as it was, the C-7 proved to be invaluable. Simple and rugged, it could get in and out of very short, rough strips, and its sortie rate under primitive conditions was remarkably high. In terms of lifting capacity, however, the C-130 had no competition. It was the most important theater transport aircraft for bulk movement, registering a high figure of 69,499 tons transported in one month. (The highest totals for other types were 16,643 for the C-123 and 10,264 for the C-7.) The ubiquitous C-130 was also involved in many other missions. Besides its gunship and aerial command post roles, it was used to start forest fires by dropping oil drums (Operation Banish Beach), for sowing antipersonnel mines during the interdiction of the Trail in Laos, and for clearing instant helicopter landing zones in the forest with huge weapons such as the 15,000-pound BLU-82 bomb (Operation Commando Vault).

On May 12, 1968, Lieutenant Colonel Joe Jackson answered a call for help from a special forces camp at Kham Duc. An evacuation of the garrison had earlier been carried out under fire by C-130s and C-123s. Two C-130s had been lost and a third badly damaged in a desperate operation. Unfortunately, three members of a USAF control team had been left behind and were in imminent danger of being overrun by enemy infantry swarming over the camp. Joe Jackson was flying a C-123 unsupported by attack aircraft. However, he judged that the Americans on the ground could not afford to wait. Approaching at 9,000 feet, he made a steep descent and slammed the C-123 down on the runway. Braking to a halt, he reversed the props and backed up to a point near where the men were taking cover. Guns, rockets and mortars engaged the aircraft while the control

5th Marine Division at Camp Pendleton, California, together with 3,500 tons of equipment, were deployed to South Vietnam in only twelve days. Outbound from Vietnam, MAC's transports performed services that were equally essential. They took troops on rest and recuperation leave, evacuated the wounded, and carried the sad coffins of the dead. When it was all over, they went back to fetch those who had survived as prisoners of war and flew them home.

For tactical transports employed within the theater of operations, war had always held its hazards. In Vietnam, the risks were vastly more severe. In a country where there were no front lines and the enemy could appear almost anywhere, the tactical transports operated all the time in a combat zone. U.S. and ARVN troops in scattered outposts relied on them for supply. They carried men and equipment quickly into areas for search and destroy operations, and they were involved in paratroop assaults. To keep the soldiers supplied, they landed on makeshift airstrips under fire, or delivered loads using either the Low Altitude Parachute Extraction System (LAPES) or the Ground Proximity Extraction System (GPES) while flying through just above the runway. Deliveries could also be made by parachute, even when the drop zone was obscured, using either on-board or ground-based radar.

At first, the aircraft used were C-47s and C-123s, but the immensely capable Lockheed C-130 Hercules began to

ABOVE *Beginning in 1965, Lockheed C-141 Starlifters played an increasingly significant role in the airlift of personnel and supplies across the Pacific and within Southeast Asia. Evacuation of the wounded was especially important. Between 1965 and 1972, C-141s flew over 6,000 medical evacuation missions out of Vietnam. Here a C-141A loads a medical vehicle at Cam Ranh Bay in April 1969.* RIGHT *A Fairchild C-123 Provider at low level over South Vietnam in 1965.*

team scrambled aboard and the C-123 roared back into the air. For the daring rescue Joe Jackson was awarded the Medal of Honor, a rare recognition of a "trash hauler" pilot.

Joe Jackson's exploit was extraordinary, but it was not unusual for unarmed "trash haulers" to brave enemy fire. During the siege of Khe Sanh, the surrounded Marine garrison was supplied entirely by air throughout, the C-123s and C-130s making 601 parachute drops and 460 landings between them. Transport crews operated daily into the besieged base, knowing that they would be exposed to anti-aircraft fire on the approach and over the field, and to mor-

tar fire on the ground. To reduce the exposure time as much as possible, even those aircraft that had to land were often unloaded on the move, resulting in an average touchdown-to-takeoff time of three minutes. Including those shot down or destroyed in attacks on Khe Sanh and other bases, the USAF lost fifty-five C-130s, fifty-three C-123s, and twenty C-7s during the Vietnam War.

It is rare for a transport pilot to receive his country's highest award for gallantry. Joe Jackson gained that distinction for his actions on June 13, 1968, while flying a C-123 over Vietnam. He volunteered to attempt the rescue of three men from a special forces camp at Kham Duc. Hostile forces had overrun the outpost and established gun positions on the airstrip, raking the camp with small arms, mortars, automatic weapons, and recoilless rifle fire. Ammunition dumps were exploding and littering the runway with debris. Eight U.S. aircraft had already been destroyed, one of which was still on the runway, reducing its usable length to only 2,200 feet. Fully aware of the extreme danger, Lieutenant Colonel Jackson proceeded to land his aircraft near where the men were reported to be hiding. While on the ground, his aircraft was subjected to intense hostile fire. With the men aboard, Jackson succeeded in getting airborne through ferocious fire directed across the runway. For completing an extraordinary rescue without regard for his own safety, Lieutenant Colonel Jackson was awarded the Medal of Honor.

Other Helping Hands

The combat aircrew who delivered the weapons and fought the enemy directly were only too well aware of the debt they owed to those in supporting roles, without whom their task would have been much more difficult and their chances of survival considerably reduced. The labor of the technicians who serviced the aircraft was especially close to their hearts, but the work of logisticians, air base defense teams, medical personnel, and many others was equally essential, though not often fully recognized. In the air, there were reconnaissance crews who sought out enemy defenses and likely targets, those who detected and countered enemy electronic transmissions, the ever present "tankers"' with their life-saving fuel, and the courageous men of the search-and-rescue squadrons.

Throughout the war, the USAF gathered copious information from many sources — visual observation, aerial photography, electronic surveillance and infrared detection.

The aircraft used were as varied as their intelligence activities. At one extreme was the Lockheed SR-71 Blackbird, and at the other was the Cessna O-1. In between were jet aircraft such as RF-101Cs, RF-4Cs, RB-57Es, RC-135s and U-2s, plus an assortment of Remotely Piloted Vehicles (RPVs). Even for the faster aircraft gathering information was not a risk-free exercise. In all, thirty-three RF101s and seventy-six RF-4s were lost in combat. Nor was the task a simple one. Visual and photographic reconnaissance were often foiled by triple-layer jungle, bad weather, and the preference of the enemy for movement by night. During emergencies such as the siege of Khe Sanh, the demands placed on the reconnaissance forces were overwhelming. As a measure of the effort, less than ninety days of Operation Niagara at Khe Sanh involved the flying of almost 1,400 reconnaissance sorties.

Much valuable reconnaissance work was done by units such as 4025 Reconnaissance Squadron (RS), which was responsible for a variety of RPVs, or "drones," such as the Ryan AQM-34 series. Launched from a C-130, they were capable of covering a very wide range of missions, including photography, television (with real-time transmission), ELINT(electronic intelligence), SIGINT (signal intelligence), jamming, and leaflet dropping. Although programmed for a particular profile, their progress was monitored and could be adjusted by the controller in the

WAR & PEACE IN THE AIR   173

C-130 as necessary. On return to a friendly area, the drone deployed a parachute and was snared by a recovery helicopter. There were 3,435 drone missions flown and 578 RPVs lost.

Electronic Support and Electronic Counter-Measures (ESM and ECM) aircraft became increasingly important as the war went on. As the North Vietnamese defenses became more electronically sophisticated, so the U.S. services responded with more competent electronic warfare systems. Most specialized of the USAF's aircraft in this role were the EB-66s, which were large enough to have four radar receiver positions for detecting and identifying enemy signals, and nine jammers for deceiving and disrupting enemy defensive systems.

If there had ever been any doubt about the value of having a tanker force, it was entirely dispelled in the skies over Southeast Asia. Whenever there were combat aircraft in action, there were tankers on station. They proved their worth repeatedly both as force multipliers and as aerial life-guards. In the knowledge that a tanker would be waiting, aircraft could be given maximum weapon loads for takeoff and then filled up with fuel at the top of the climb. On the way home after a strike, the tankers would refresh those who might otherwise die of thirst. The KB-50Js originally in Southeast Asia were permanently grounded at the end of 1964. From then on, SAC took over the aerial refueling responsibility and deployed its KC-135s in support of PACAF. Some tankers were positioned in Okinawa, Guam, Taiwan and the Philippines, principally to look after deployments from the United States and to aid B-52 operations. Others were moved forward into Southeast Asia to support the fighter-bombers. Since the tankers were such highly valued assets, it was not thought wise to have them in South Vietnam, and they were based in

The Ryan AQM-34 Firebee was air-launched and controlled from a DC-130 director aircraft. After a mission, the Firebee UAV was directed to a safe recovery area, where it deployed its parachute and was picked up by a helicopter. From October 1964 to April 1975, AQM-34 Ryan Firebee UAVs flew in excess of 3,400 operational surveillance missions over Southeast Asia.

Thailand. The peak KC-135 strength, spread across the region between Kadena and Bangkok, reached 172 in 1972, and there were then twenty-eight regular refueling stations established over the countries of Southeast Asia, with seven more tracks in the area of the Philippines. In a little more than nine years of operating in support of the air war in Vietnam, SAC tankers gave away almost nine billion pounds of fuel in the course of 813,878 refuelings.

Spectacular though these figures are, they cannot begin to tell the whole story. On countless occasions, tankers were there to aid damaged or fuel-starved aircraft that would otherwise have been lost. Pilots often left the tanker with the heartfelt message: "Thanks, tank, you can count this a save." Some of the saves were dramatic, with fighters losing fuel so fast from battle-damaged fuel systems that they had to stay hooked up and be towed back to base on the end of the tanker's boom. Others were stunningly complex, particularly one flown by a crew from the 902nd Air Refueling Squadron off North Vietnam on May 31, 1967. While engaged in refueling two F-104Cs, the tanker crew was asked to help a number of USN aircraft that were in dire straits. The first to arrive were two A-3s, both themselves equipped as tankers but desperately short of fuel. As the A-3s each took a quick drink, two F-8s arrived, equally poorly placed. One latched on to the first A-3, while the other, so short of fuel that he could not afford to wait, hooked up with the second A-3, which was still attached to the KC-135. Further refuelings took place in a complicated shuffle, including more for the original pair of F-104Cs, before two Navy F-4s were taken on. The KC-135's own fuel supply was now so depleted that it was forced to divert into Da Nang, having transferred nearly 50,000 pounds of fuel in fourteen contacts and saved eight aircraft in one sortie. In recognition of this remarkable achievement, Major John Casteel and his crew were awarded the 1967 Mackay Trophy for the most meritorious USAF flight of the year.

There were other airmen who regularly saved lives, but in a different way. The motto of the search-and-rescue (SAR) squadrons was "So That Others May Live." In pursuing this goal they routinely risked their own skins for anyone downed in enemy territory. In the course of the war, it grew to be generally understood by all aircrew that, if they were shot down, SAR teams would make every effort to get them out, regardless of the location or the risk. Such a policy did wonders for the morale of crew members being asked to face some of the most effective air-defense systems in the world. Unfortunately, once the opposition recognized what was happening, it also meant that any downed flier was used by the enemy as a lure around which they could gather a flak trap. Rescue missions therefore tended to increase in danger as time went by. Before it was all over, three Medals of Honor were earned in the course of rescue operations, two by helicopter pilots (Captain Gerald Young and Lieutenant James Fleming) and one by the pilot of a RESCAP A-1H (Lieutenant Colonel William Jones III).

In the early days, the few helicopters available for rescue in Southeast Asia were provided by Air America. It was not until mid-1964 and the open commitment of U.S. forces to combat that the USAF deployed twin-rotor Kaman HH-43Bs and a few Grumman HU-16B amphibians specifically for rescue duties. Designed for local rescue in the United States, the HH-43B was not ideal for a combat area. It lacked armor, armament and self-sealing fuel tanks, and it was short-ranged. As an interim solution, armored HH-43Fs were introduced, but the range problem remained. In 1965, matters improved with the arrival of Sikorsky HH-3Es, large, well-armored helicopters with a range of over 600 miles. Fitted with a refueling probe, they could reach anywhere in Southeast Asia. Before long, the jungle camouflage of the HH-3E had gained it the nickname "Jolly Green Giant." Two years later, the even more capable HH-53C "Super Jolly Green" made its debut and proved one of the great successes of the war. Nearly twice as large as the HH-3E, the "Super Jolly" was faster, more heavily armored,

> "Superior technical achievements — used correctly both strategically and tactically — can beat any quantity numerically many times stronger yet technically inferior."
> ADOLF GALLAND, LUFTWAFFE

and formidably armed with three 7.62 mm mini-guns.

As it developed, the SAR business became a highly organized operation. In 1967 it was renamed the Aerospace Rescue and Recovery Service (ARRS) and missions into enemy territory were conducted by a rescue package of aircraft. By 1969, the mission commander was usually flying in an HC-130P equipped as a tanker and carrying an aerial tracker system for locating downed airmen. Escort was provided by A1E/H "Sandies" (later A-37Bs or A-7Ds could be included), and top cover by F-4s. Help might be added in the shape of gunships. The "Jolly Green" carried a pararescue jumper, trained as a scuba diver and medic, who was ready to jump or be winched down to the assistance of grounded aircrew. The helicopter's winch had 240 feet of cable ending in a heavy jungle penetrator, so that rescues could be accomplished through the jungle canopy.

The crowning glory for the helicopter crews should have been a daring rescue of POWs from a camp outside Hanoi on November 21, 1971. The raid was brilliantly executed. One HH-3E full of U.S. Rangers deliberately crash-landed inside the prison compound while five CH-53Cs waited outside. Sadly, the cupboard was bare. The prisoners had been moved to another site some time before. Out-of-date intelligence had led the rescuers to a rare failure. However, in this attempt and in more conventional rescues, it was clear that the rescue teams were dedicated to their task. An example of their determination not to abandon aircrew to their fate was the rescue of Lieutenant Colonel Iceal Hambleton, the sole survivor from an EB-66 shot down on April 2, 1972. Hambleton avoided capture by the enemy for twelve days under an umbrella of A-1Es, OV-10s and an assortment of jet fighters and helicopters. Before he was recovered, concern for Hambleton's safety had cost several more aircraft, but there was never any consideration of giving up the effort as long as he was free.

From almost any point of view, the creative innovation demanded by the rescue challenge and the massive effort expended were worth it. No service was more respected, and perhaps none more rewarding. By the end of the war, the ARRS had successfully recovered 3,883 men. It was not done without cost. In the process, forty-five rescue aircraft were lost and seventy-one men gave their lives.

EYES IN THE SKY

OPPOSITE Seen from the front, the Lockheed SR-71A Blackbird looks more like a piece of avant garde sculpture than an aircraft of dramatic performance. Cruising speeds above Mach 3 and heights of 85,000 feet were part of its operational reconnaissance profile. Equipped with a variety of sensors, the SR-71 could survey an area of 100,000 square miles in an hour. Skin temperatures reached as much as 300 degrees Centigrade in flight, causing the 107-foot-long aircraft to stretch by almost a foot. The SR-71's fuel was JP-7, a special kerosene that doubled as a heat sink to absorb some of the excessive heat. BELOW The SR-71A in the National Museum of the USAF is the aircraft flown by Majors Jerome O'Malley and Edward Payne on the first operational SR-71 mission on March 21, 1968. It was the most productive of the SR-71 fleet, flying 942 sorties, of which 257 were operational missions. It is seen here arriving at the museum in March 1990. BOTTOM LEFT At first glance, the cockpit of the SR-71 looks typical of its era. There were significant differences, however. The pilots had very limited visibility, because they wore pressure suits with helmets and the cockpit windows were small. The thick glass windscreen could reach 370 degrees Centigrade, so the coaming was often used to warm squeeze-tube food. On the console to the pilot's right are the auto-navigation system controls. Pilots could not fly the aircraft smoothly enough to ensure the high-quality imagery required from the cameras. Next to the yellow drag chute handle (top left of the instrument panel) is a red warning light bearing the comforting message "RSO EJECTED." BELOW The first models of the U-2 high-altitude reconnaissance and surveillance aircraft began operations in the early 1960s. The U-2 of the 21st century is 40 percent larger than the original version and carries four times the payload weight. It is more flexible than a satellite and is deployable anywhere in the world. BOTTOM RIGHT The distinctively flat camera nose identifies this McDonnell Voodoo as an RF-101C. This particular aircraft used its cameras to good effect during the Cuban Missile Crisis, keeping an eye on the Soviet missile sites and helping to confirm that they were being dismantled.

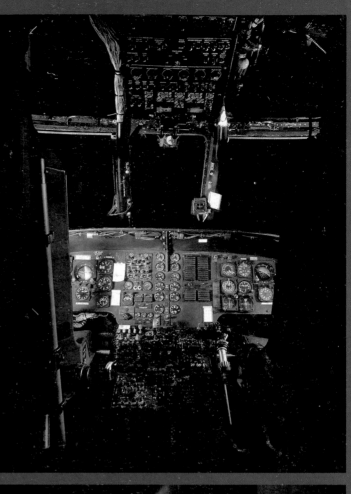

CLANDESTINE CHOPPER

OPPOSITE The Sikorsky CH-3E is a big helicopter, with an all-up weight of more than 22,000 pounds. Powered by two General Electric T58 engines of 1,500 shaft horsepower, it could achieve almost 180 mph. The later HH-53 version used in Vietnam rescue missions was known as the "Jolly Green Giant." The all-black CH-53E in the National Museum of the USAF was flown by the 20th Helicopter Squadron in Southeast Asia on clandestine missions and was known as "Black Maria."

ABOVE LEFT Evidence that CH-53E "Black Maria" operated in harm's way can be seen in the patched bullet holes on the fuselage.

TOP RIGHT As befits a big helicopter, the CH-53E's cockpit is roomy, with large flat glass windows giving excellent visibility.

RIGHT A vital asset for any combat helicopter is the winch. The CH-53E's winch could lift up to 2,000 pounds. Beyond is the rear cabin, which could accommodate thirty troops or 5,000 pounds of cargo.

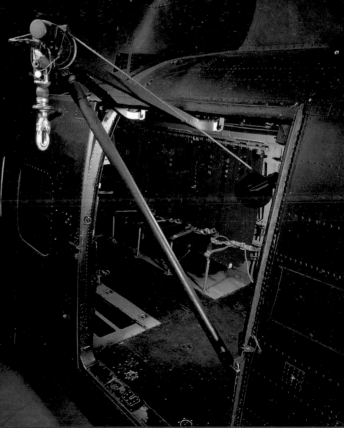

ABOVE AND BEYOND THE CALL OF DUTY

BELOW RIGHT As a forty-one-year-old USAF Reserve lieutenant colonel and ex-B29 pilot, Mike Novosel was deemed to old to do more than fly a desk in the Vietnam War. He therefore resigned his commission and enlisted in the U.S. Army to fly helicopters. He completed two combat tours in Vietnam as a Huey Dustoff pilot, and was credited with evacuating over 5,000 wounded from the battlefield. On October 2, 1969, Chief Warrant Officer Novosel got word of wounded South Vietnamese soldiers being pinned down by a large enemy force. Flying without gunship cover and exposed to machine gun fire, he repeatedly circled the battle area, flying at low level under continuous heavy fire, to attract the attention of the scattered friendly troops. Six times he and his crew were forced out of the battle area by intense enemy fire, only to circle and return from another direction to land and extract additional troops. Near the end of the mission, a wounded soldier was spotted close to an enemy bunker. CWO Novosel took the helicopter backward into heavy enemy fire to rescue the man. Although the helicopter was damaged and he was wounded, he persisted and completed the rescue. In all, fifteen extremely hazardous extractions were performed in order to remove wounded personnel. As a direct result of his selfless conduct, the lives of twenty-nine soldiers were saved. For his extraordinary courage, CWO Novosel was awarded the Medal of Honor. TOP RIGHT Mike shows the Medal of Honor he was awarded for his actions on October 2, 1969. Mike Novosel died in April 2006.

NICK COSCO'S VIETNAM ALBUM

Nick Cosco of Dearborn, Michigan, attended the Aeromechanics High School at the Detroit City Airport and wanted to be an aircraft mechanic, working on military aircraft in a combat situation. According to Nick, "The U.S. Army obliged me on all counts." He volunteered for duty in Vietnam, and served there from January 1964 through July 1965. Nick was a member of the 145th Aviation Battalion in the 98th CHFM (Cargo Helicopter Field Maintenance) Detachment at Tan Son Hut Air Force Base.

FIRST ROW LEFT: Replacement of tail boom assemblies.
CENTER: Piasecki CH-21 C Gunship *Wild Aces*. RIGHT: Sergeant Orville G. Black, trooping the line, before departing for the U.S. Nick Cosco is driving the jeep.
SECOND ROW LEFT: Aft rotor maintenance on an H-21.
CENTER: Tracking the blades of an H-21. RIGHT: Rotor maintenance of HU-1-B "Huey."

THIRD ROW LEFT: A Sikorsky H-52 Mojave. This enormous helicopter was powered by two Pratt & Whitney R-2800 radial engines (one in each pod) and, according to Nick Cosco, was "a solution looking for a problem." CENTER: U.S. Army Cessna *Bird Dog*, used by Forward Air Controllers, at rest while its tail wheel assembly receives attention. RIGHT: Piasecki CH-21 *Taxpayers Regret* and a young Nick Cosco.
FOURTH ROW LEFT: The entrance to the 145th compound at Tan Son Hut. CENTER: Behind these U.S. Army soldiers, a lineup of OV-1 Mohawks. The Mohawk was a photo observation and electronic reconnaissance airplane.
RIGHT: Nick Cosco in a more recent photo. He came back to the U.S. and was an engineer at the Ford Motor Company for over thirty years.

HUEY OVER VIETNAM

TOP *The Ride Back,* by Sam Lyons.
RIGHT Captain Bobby G. Walls, Commanding
Officer 98th CHFM, flight-testing a Huey
recently returned to service after field
maintenance. According to Nick Cosco, who
made this photo, Captain Walls was always
happy to see the mechanic who had just worked
on the helicopter he was about to fly willing to
ride along.

LEFT *It was the Boeing KC-135 Stratotanker that made possible air operations of the extent undertaken by the U.S. armed forces during the Vietnam War. The crews of offensive aircraft could take off carrying the maximum amount of ordnance, knowing that they could top up with fuel on the way to their targets, and aircraft returning short of fuel or with battle damage could be met on the way home. Here a tanker streams a drogue from its boom in preparation for receiving a customer equipped with a probe.*
RIGHT *F-4Cs wait their turn to refresh themselves from the boom of a KC-135 tanker over Southeast Asia in 1966. The nearest Phantom (37544 of the 366th TFW) was shot down by friendly fire near Da Nang on December 9, 1966. The crew ejected safely.*

The Beginning of the End

The bombing halt ordered by President Johnson as he came to the end of his term of office in 1968 was confirmed by President Nixon in January 1969. At that time, the personnel strength of the U.S. force in Vietnam had reached 536,000. Before the year was out, Nixon announced a program of "Vietnamization" and initiated a steady U.S. withdrawal from Southeast Asia. In April 1970, U.S. troops joined with the South Vietnamese in an invasion of Cambodia to attack enemy bases and supply routes, but within months the U.S. Congress had banned the use of U.S. ground forces in Laos or Cambodia. All of these steps gave great encouragement to North Vietnam. In addition, for more than three years after taking office, Nixon maintained the ban on bombing the North, and the North Vietnamese took advantage of the respite to build up their forces and prepare for an invasion of the South. Industries revived and power stations were rebuilt. Bridges, roads and railways were repaired. Soviet and Chinese supplies poured into the country and the NVA undertook exhaustive training exercises. All this was watched by U.S. reconnaissance aircraft, which continued to fly over North Vietnam and continued to suffer losses, in spite of agreements made at the Paris talks supposedly guaranteeing them safe passage.

Tit-for-tat strikes were made by U.S. tactical aircraft, which targeted air defense sites. A series of strikes carried out at the end of 1971, aimed at airfields, SAM sites, oil storage areas and truck parks, was intended to deter the buildup of Hanoi's forces, but it had little effect.

On March 30, 1972, the North Vietnamese invaded the South, sending large forces across the DMZ and developing other thrusts out of Laos and Cambodia. With U.S. military strength now down to less than 100,000, the North Vietnamese expected to overwhelm Saigon's forces, and Hanoi banked on Nixon's reaction being limited by antiwar feeling in the United States. Really effective response from the U.S. air forces was no longer possible. Fewer than 100 USAF combat aircraft remained in South Vietnam, and the total in the whole of Southeast Asia was down to 375. In any event, the invasion was launched during the cloudy northeast monsoon, and the weather kept most aircraft from interfering with the ground battle. Those pilots who did make contact with North Vietnamese troops found that they were well covered by antiaircraft systems. Large numbers of AAA and mobile SAMs were evident, and there was a new threat in the form of the shoulder-launched SA-7, a portable heat-seeker that could reach out to 8,000 feet. FACs and the A-1s of the VNAF, operating at relatively

Vietnam War artifacts held by the National Museum of the USAF include many items contributed by American POWs. Examples seen here include manufactured sandals, a T-shirt, a bowl and a spoon. Shown with them are the flight jacket worn by Steve Ritchie during the tour in which he was credited with shooting down five MiGs, and the shirt and dog tags of Airman First Class William Pitsenbarger. On April 11, 1966, Pitsenbarger was lowered from a helicopter under fire to tend to a group of wounded soldiers who had been ambushed. When the helicopter was damaged and had to retreat, he chose to stay with the wounded. His body was recovered next day, one hand holding a rifle and the other a medical kit. For his bravery and sacrifice, he was posthumously awarded the nation's second-highest military decoration, the Air Force Cross. On December 8, 2000, Pitsenbarger was also awarded the Medal of Honor after case review and additional eyewitness testimony was taken into account. After his death, he was promoted to staff sergeant.

slow speeds and low levels, were particularly vulnerable.

Since there was no possibility of reintroducing ground forces to Vietnam, it was recognized that U.S. assistance to South Vietnam in repelling the invasion would have to come from the air. Accordingly, the USAF, USN and USMC redeployed substantial numbers of aircraft to Southeast Asia. By midyear, the USAF had almost 900 strike aircraft available, and the total number from the three services was up to 1,380. To begin with, strike operations against the North, conducted under the code name Freedom Train, were restricted to areas south of the 20th parallel, but the alarming success of the invading forces led President Nixon to abandon the peace talks in Paris and to authorize operations on a more ambitious scale. Mines were at last laid in and around North Vietnam's harbors, and a comprehensive campaign against a wide range of targets in the North was cleared by Nixon on May 8, 1972. It was called Linebacker.

Linebacker was not Rolling Thunder revived under a different name. It is true that there were still some restrictions on target selection. Deliberate attacks could not be made on sensitive targets, such as anything close to the Chinese frontier, or in densely populated areas of Hanoi, for instance. However, U.S. air power generally was no longer micro-managed from the White House. Air Force commanders were allowed to use their judgment in seeking to destroy the transportation system, air defenses and stocks of military supplies in the North. Immensely adding to the weight of the campaign, B-52s were allowed north of the 19th parallel for the first time, and from September, F-111s were available to add their all-weather capability. Operationally, the crews of the fighter-bombers were greatly aided in their offensive by "smart" bombs that markedly increased the effectiveness of their strikes.

Systematic attacks were made on the bridges of North Vietnam by F-4s carrying Mk. 84 2,000-pound and Mk. 118 3,000-pound bombs fitted with laser-seeking heads and control surfaces. The results were spectacular. On May 13, sixteen F-4s delivered twenty-four "smart" bombs between them against the infamous Than Hoa bridge, wrecking a target that had defied U.S. airmen for years. (By contrast, during the attack against the Than Hoa bridge on April 3, 1965, 638 750-pound bombs were dropped and 298 rockets fired, but the bridge remained standing.) By the end of June, more than 400 bridges in North Vietnam had been destroyed or badly damaged. North Vietnamese use of more basic forms of transport, such as bicycles and small boats, ensured that their supply system did not grind to a complete halt, and it was never possible to achieve an irreparable break in their logistical chain. Nevertheless, the flow south became a trickle and, together with the effective mining of North Vietnam's harbors, it was apparent that Linebacker was hurting the enemy's attempts to maintain the scale and pace of the offensive in the South.

On Yankee Station, by Bob Rasmussen.

For the USAF, the Linebacker campaign provided a serious challenge. The air defenses of North Vietnam had stiffened in the years since Rolling Thunder, and by 1972 the Hanoi/Haiphong region was one of the best defended areas in the world, bristling with AAA and SAM sites. Nearby, the VNAF had a force of well over 200 MiG 17s, 19s and 21s, and many of the pilots were old hands who had survived earlier battles. By contrast, USAF aircrews were generally younger than they had been in the 1960s, and the majority had never been in aerial combat. The MiGs now represented a formidable threat and, for a while, the kill/loss ratio swung in their favor. During Rolling Thunder, 85 percent of the U.S. aircraft downed were lost to AAA fire. Of the forty-four USAF aircraft lost on Linebacker operations, twenty-seven were shot down by MiGs.

Instrumental in turning the situation round was "Teaball," a control center based in Thailand that coordinated all the information on VNAF operations from radar and various intelligence-gathering sources. This was passed via command aircraft to airborne missions to give them up-to-the-minute warning of the enemy's activities. Thus prepared, USAF crews began to give a better account of themselves, positioning their aircraft to meet approaching threats, and using the F-4's radar and its great speed and power to advantage in countering the MiG's superior agility. In this environment, the USAF gained its only aces of the war. On August 28, 1972, Captain Steve Ritchie of the 555th Tactical Fighter Squadron, piloting an F-4E, shot down his fifth MiG-21. In the weeks that followed, two weapons systems officers, both F-4 back-seaters, also became aces. Captain Charles De Bellevue of the 555th TFS raised his score to six MiGs (four with Ritchie), and Captain Jeffrey Feinstein of the 13th TFS claimed five.

The offensive against the North was massive. Between April and October 1972, 155,548 tons of bombs fell on North Vietnam. Technology ensured that most of them were delivered with considerable accuracy. Successful though it was in the end, the campaign did not have any immediate effect on the invading North Vietnamese forces in South Vietnam. They had built up huge stockpiles of supplies to ensure that the invasion could be sustained. For the first few weeks, the NVA maintained relentless pressure on its ARVN opponents, threatening to provoke their complete collapse. Quang Tri fell, and the cities of Hue, Kontum and An Loc seemed about to

Screaming Eagle, *by Philip West. On May 6, 1972, Lieutenant Commander Jerry "Devil" Houston and Lieutenant Kevin Moore of VF-51 (the Screaming Eagles) shot down a MiG-17 with an AIM-9 missile. Here they return from the mission and bring their F-4B onto the centerline of the USS Coral Sea.*

Lone Star Lady, by Philip West. In December 1972, the USAF launched the Linebacker II campaign against North Vietnam. For the first time, B-52s targeted Hanoi and the North Vietnamese leaders experienced the awesome destructive power of the big bombers for themselves. At the same time, the B-52 crews had to face Hanoi's impressive defensive system. In eleven days the B-52s flew 729 sorties and dropped over 15,000 tons of bombs. The North Vietnamese fired 1,242 SAMs and the USAF lost fifteen B-52s.

follow. On all fronts, it was air power that blunted and then smashed the Communist offensive, giving the ARVN time to recover and launch a counteroffensive. Besieged garrisons were reinforced and supplied by the tactical transports, and thousands of fighter-bomber and gunship sorties were flown against the NVA forces. The number of fast-mover sorties flown jumped from 247 in March to 7,516 in May. However, it may have been the B-52 attacks that proved decisive. Unlike the elusive Viet Cong, the NVA offered plentiful, recognizable targets in the shape of concentrations of troops and armor, and lengthy truck convoys. On numerous occasions, B-52s caught the enemy in the open and effectively destroyed whole units, sometimes breaking up attacks less than half a mile in front of friendly forces. General Vogt, Commander Seventh Air Force, said that facing regular mechanized army units "permitted air to put fire-power in on good worthwhile targets instead of little huts in the jungle and a few scattered guerrilla bands…. After a good dose of [U.S. air power] for several months, the enemy ranks were so badly decimated that they lost all their offensive punch…."

By the middle of June it was apparent that the North Vietnamese invasion had stalled. The ARVN went over to the offensive, and on July 13 the Paris talks were resumed. The last U.S. ground forces left Vietnam in August, and, on October 8, after the North had suffered a particularly concentrated period of bombing, Hanoi's representatives in Paris put forward new proposals. Within days, the prospects for an agreement seemed promising, and on October 23, President Nixon terminated Linebacker. All bombing north of the 20th parallel was brought to a halt. Unfortunately, it was soon seen that North Vietnam was once more engaged in delaying tactics and using the time to restore its forces. When the North Vietnamese walked out of the talks on December 13, Nixon ordered a resumption of the bombing. There followed an eleven-day campaign, code-named Linebacker II, which was the most intense aerial assault of the war. It was intended to bomb North Vietnam back to the negotiating table.

The Way Out

From December 18 to December 29, 1972, by day and night, U.S. aircraft pounded airfields, military bases, power stations, rail yards, oil storage and port facilities in and around the Hanoi and Haiphong areas. Most significantly, B-52s joined the attacks on the North Vietnamese capital. For the first time, Hanoi's leaders felt the crushing weight of conventional strikes from the big bombers for themselves, and the B-52s were exposed to the serried ranks of SA-2s defending the city.

The General Dynamics F-111A Aardvark did not have a successful introduction to combat when it arrived in Southeast Asia in 1968. By the time of the Linebacker campaigns, however, it was a much more capable aircraft and made a significant contribution to the struggle. The Aardvark in the National Museum of the USAF is an example of the much later F-111F, a dramatically improved version that made its mark in later conflicts. This particular machine was the lead fixed-wing aircraft for both Operation Eldorado Canyon, the raid on Libya, and Desert Storm against Iraq.

Ahead of the first B-52 raid, F-111s hit the MiG airfields and F-4s sowed chaff corridors to screen the bombers. The protective effort was not entirely successful. High winds dispersed the clouds of chaff and the SAM sites fired over 200 missiles, shooting down three B-52s and damaging three more. After three days, the B-52 squadrons had flown 300 sorties, but had lost nine aircraft. Although three percent was a figure judged acceptable in World War II, it could not be long supported in a limited war, especially when the aircraft being lost were such valuable assets as B-52s. It was also ominous that six aircraft had been shot down on the third night, suggesting that worse might be to come. SAC took a close look at the tactics being employed and realized the need for a change. B-52Gs, not yet fitted with

The two-man crew of the F-111 stayed together whatever happened. In a major emergency, escape was effected by ejecting a cockpit capsule. Large parachutes lowered the crew to the ground still strapped to their seats. Airbags were deployed to cushion landing impact or to serve as flotation gear in water. The module could also serve as a survival shelter.

it was thought that they might be hoping to shoot down more B-52s and so make the cost of continuing too high for the American public to bear. Destroying the air defenses would remove that possibility and leave them vulnerable to whatever further operations U.S. air power chose to undertake. On December 26, B-52s and F-111s blasted the MiG airfields, SAM and radar sites, and command and control centers, but perhaps the decisive blow was finally struck by F-4s that used the Loran navigational system to destroy the main SAM assembly area in Hanoi. At the end of the day, the North Vietnamese condemned the "extermination bombing" but let Washington know that they were ready to resume the talks. The bombing continued until the arrangements were finalized, but on December 29, Linebacker II was over. The B-52s had flown 729 sorties in eleven days and had dropped over 15,000 tons of bombs. Another 5,000 tons had been added by the fighter-bombers. The North Vietnamese had fired 1,242 SAMs and the USAF had lost twenty-six aircraft, including fifteen B-52s.

the upgraded ECM of the B-52Ds, were to be kept away from Hanoi. The raids were to be more concentrated in time, and B-52s would bomb from varying heights and different directions. Steep escape turns after bombing were to be avoided, because they produced large radar returns, and crews were authorized to make random altitude changes to confuse the SAM operators. Using these new tactics on the four remaining nights up to Christmas Eve, only two more B-52s were lost.

After a pause for Christmas Day, it was decided to make an all-out attack on Hanoi's air defenses. With most other targets already hard hit, but the North Vietnamese still giving no indication that they were ready to sign an agreement,

There can be little doubt that the Linebacker campaigns together were instrumental in bringing the North Vietnamese back to the conference table in a frame of mind to sign an agreement. Peace talks were resumed on January 8, and the ceasefire document was signed on January 23, 1973. That took care of U.S. combat activities in Vietnam, but not in Laos or Cambodia. USAF bombing operations against Communist forces continued there in response to requests from the beleaguered governments. The last sorties were

About 1,400 U.S. Army pilots flew air ambulance (Dustoff) missions during the Vietnam War. Forty were killed and another 180 were wounded as a result of hostile fire. Forty-eight more were killed and some 200 injured as a result of non-hostile crashes on evacuation missions, many at night and in bad weather. This casualty figure of over 33 percent was suffered equally by Dustoff crew chiefs and medics. The danger of their work was evident in the fact that the helicopter loss rate during Dustoff missions was almost three and a half times that of all other forms of helicopter operations in the Vietnam War. Approximately 120,000 of the 390,000 Army patients carried to a medical facility by air ambulances were battle casualties.

flown in Laos in mid-April and in Cambodia in mid-August, when Congress reacted to an escalation of the bombing by cutting off all funds for the air war.

The sad aftermath came in April 1975, when North Vietnam concluded a whirlwind campaign of conquest in the South, and the U.S. set in motion its emergency evacuation plan, Frequent Wind. On April 1,

USAF C-130s and C-141s began airlifting Americans and South Vietnamese refugees out of Tan Son Nhut airport, Saigon. Load restrictions were removed on April 20, and the transports began setting records. A C-141 recorded 316 people on board, and C-130s took as many as 260. (Normal limits were 94 and 75.) As the airfield came under fire during the final days, the operation shifted

The ubiquitous Douglas A-1 Skyraider was manufactured until 1957, a total of 3,180 being produced and serving in various forms with the U.S. Air Force, U.S. Navy, U.S. Marine Corps, Royal Navy, and the air forces of Sweden, South Vietnam, and France. The A-1's roles included nuclear and conventional strike, close air support, ASW patrol, armed reconnaissance, rescue support, in-flight refueling, and aerial mining. A number of French Skyraiders were passed on to Cambodia, Chad and the Central African Republic.

to helicopter evacuation from the U.S. Embassy compound. Fighters and gunships provided escort, and were forced to attack enemy radars and gun batteries to preserve the American lifeline. With the triumphant North Vietnamese on the doorstep, the last helicopter lifted away from the Embassy on April 30, ending an operation in which U.S. aircraft had brought out over 57,000 people from Saigon.

The Final Cost

In terms of the expenditure of national treasure, the air war in Southeast Asia was an expensive exercise for the United States. Combat over Southeast Asia between 1962 and 1973 cost the USAF alone 1,679 fixed-wing aircraft and 58 helicopters. A further 495 fixed-wing aircraft and 18 helicopters were lost in accidents, bringing the total USAF loss to 2,250 of all types. (The fixed-wing loss for all U.S. services in combat was 2,561, with another 1,158 lost in accidents. Helicopter losses for all services were a dramatic 4,869, a figure reflecting in part the hazards of the U.S. Army's operations in support of troops. However, it should be noted that 2,282 of these were recorded as "operational [non-combat] losses.") Over six million tons of air munitions were expended, which was about three times the amount for all theaters in World War II. By far the most successful of the enemy's defenses were AAA and small arms fire, which accounted for 1,459 of the USAF aircraft. SAMs felled 112 and MiGs downed 63. A further 103 aircraft were lost

during enemy attacks on air bases. Of the USAF aircraft involved, the fast movers understandably provided most of the combat losses, with 379 F-4s (plus 76 RF-4s) and 334 F-105s at the top of the list. Some way behind were 198 F-100s and 153 A-1s.

Given that more than five million sorties had been flown, it could be claimed that the casualties suffered were not too excessive. There were 2,118 airmen known to have been killed and 3,460 wounded. The number of prisoners was never established with such precision. At the end of the war, there were 588 Americans acknowledged by the North Vietnamese as being held in captivity, plus another three in China: 472 of those were airmen from all services. Other airmen fell into the "missing" column, leaving an open wound of uncertainty.

The living conditions of the U.S. prisoners had been

The Portuguese Air Force used Fiat G-91s in their campaigns against independence movements in Angola and Mozambique.

stark and their treatment often barbaric. It was a tribute to their collective spirit that so many survived their ordeal and emerged unbroken. To them, the sound of B-52s over Hanoi in 1972 was a message of hope. Colonel Robbie Risner, incarcerated for over seven years, felt that his lengthy trial was about to end: "We saw a reaction in the Vietnamese that we had never seen under the attacks from fighters. They at last knew that we had some weapons they had not felt, and that President Nixon was willing to use those weapons to get us out." Colonel Jon Reynolds agreed: "For the first time, the United States meant business. We knew it, the guards knew it, and it seems clear that the leaders of North Vietnam knew it."

CONFLICT IN AFRICA AND THE MIDDLE EAST
Troubles in Africa

Since World War II, Africa and the Middle East have been in constant turmoil, and air power has had a significant part to play in the innumerable conflicts suffered by the people of the region. Much of the disturbance has centered on the endless confrontation between Israel and the Arab states, but aircraft have been involved in a great many other struggles that have held less prominent places in the world's headlines. Africa has been a tortured continent, with the post-WWII liberation struggles of the European colonies rewarded by still more unrest once independence was achieved. The often chaotic conditions then generated by despotic rulers led to bloody internal strife, with the new nations, arbitrarily confined within European contrived frontiers, riven by tribal or religious disputes.

For the most part, the aircraft that made a significant impact on wars in the African continent were those capable of carrying troops and supplies. There was generally little air-to-air combat, and where weapons were used against ground targets, they seldom had a significant effect on the outcome of the struggle. The respective air forces were relatively small and never possessed overwhelming striking power, equipped as they were with a bewildering variety of U.S., Soviet, British, French, Chinese, Swiss, Dutch and Swedish machines and hindered by the problem of keeping such diversity serviceable. In Algeria, Morocco, Chad, Ethiopia, Somalia, Sudan, Kenya, Uganda, Rhodesia, Angola, Mozambique, Namibia, Nigeria and the Congo, the aircraft in action came from both sides of the Cold War as the rival systems sought to advance their cause by proxy. Changing political circumstances sometimes led to air forces switching suppliers, with the result that An-12s and MiG-21s might be seen operating in the same colors as C-54s and F-5s. In these small wars, it was the transport aircraft and helicopters that dominated the air effort, moving troops and equipment into position with unprecedented speed, both for the combatants and for UN peacekeepers whenever they became involved.

This is not to say that combat aircraft were not used. In Kenya, for example, the Mau Mau rebellion of the Kikuyu tribe in the early 1950s was overcome with the help of a bombing campaign, the RAF flying aircraft as diverse as Harvards and Lincolns against terrorist camps. The French forces in Algeria developed COIN (counterinsurgency) tactics using primarily piston-engined aircraft such as the T-6, T-28 and AD-4N Skyraider. Other Armée de l'Air units, flying Mirages and Jaguars, were also involved in Morocco flying alongside the F-5s and Alpha-Jets of the Royal Moroccan Air Force against the Polisario rebels, and in Chad, where they helped to oppose intrusions by the Libyans.

Further south, during the late 1960s and early 1970s, the Rhodesians quickly found that their Hunters and Canberras were not suited to antiguerilla operations, but they acquired some Cessna 337s and SIAI-Marchetti SF-260s and modified them to carry guns and rockets. In Angola and Mozambique, the Portuguese Air Force attacked independence movement soldiers with the ubiquitous T-6, together with an assortment of PV2 Harpoons, F-84Gs, B-26s and Fiat G-91s. Perhaps the most confusing region was the Horn of Africa, where Ethiopia, supported in turn by the U.S. and the Soviet Union, was embroiled for years with Eritreans and Somalis in a series of struggles across ill-defined frontiers. Canberras, F-5s and MiG-21s were among the combat aircraft used, many of them flown by Cuban or Pakistani pilots. MiG often fought MiG and there were significant losses. In the end, however, the aircraft that had the most impact on events in the Horn of Africa were the transports that brought in relief supplies for the starving population during the recurrent bouts of famine.

In the 1960s, the South-West Africa People's Organization (SWAPO) began a campaign aimed at taking power in Southwest Africa (Namibia). This was opposed by forces from South Africa, a commitment that mounted in scale when the Portuguese withdrew from their African colony and SWAPO was able to establish bases in Angola with the support of the country's new Marxist rulers. The ensuing bush war saw the South African Air Force become heavily involved in attacking the SWAPO bases in both Angola and Zambia, and in supporting the operations of South African ground forces. Strike missions were undertaken by Canberras and Buccaneers, and close-support sorties were flown by Mirages and the Atlas Impala, a South African-built variant of the Italian MB-326. There was aerial combat between SAAF Mirage F-1s and MiG-21s and 23s flown by Cuban and East German pilots, and by the mid-1980s the SAAF was having to face an impressive array of SAMs, said to be the most sophisticated Soviet-built air defense system outside the Warsaw Pact. To help in countering the increasing capability of the opposition, the South African Atlas Aerospace Company produced a formidable new fighter, the Cheetah C, which was a complete rebuild of the ageing Mirage III, designed with Israeli help and armed with South African weapons. The SAAF's fixed-wing combat aircraft played an important part in the bush wars, but as in other parts of Africa it was the capacity to move troops quickly that proved even more significant. Puma and Alouette helicopters were always essential parts of South African military operations.

Israel and the Arabs

When the British mandate in Palestine came to an end on May 15, 1948, the tensions that had been growing between Jews and Arabs over the creation of the state of Israel quickly broke into open conflict. Surrounded by hostile neighbors, the Israelis hastened to create an effective air arm, and on May 31 the Israeli Air Force was officially established, its front line anchored by a squadron of Avia S-199s, Junkers Jumo-engined versions of the Bf 109G that the Czechs were anxious to be rid of because of their unpleasant handling characteristics. In July, three B-17s arrived to form the basis for a strike force. Given that the Jewish state was actively opposed by Egypt, Jordan, Syria, Lebanon and Iraq, it was fortunate for Israel that the Arab air forces were just as limited. Jordan and Lebanon had no offensive aircraft, while Syria had only a few armed T-6s. Iraq had both T-6s and some Hawker Fury biplanes. Egypt's front line included fifteen Spitfire IXs, four Lysanders, and a Hawker Fury demonstrator. Outbursts of fighting interspersed with fragile truces lasted through 1948, by which time the Israeli Air Force had strengthened considerably; its offensive aircraft now included five

Dassault Ouragans were flown by the Israeli Air Force in the abortive Suez campaign and during the Six Day War in 1967.

Six squadrons of Hawker Sea Hawks took part in the Suez campaign of 1956, two from each of the carriers HMS Eagle, *HMS* Albion *and HMS* Bulwark. *The Sea Hawks were used in the ground-attack role, in which they excelled, causing immense damage to a variety of Egyptian targets. The military aspect of the Suez Campaign was a successful operation, unlike the disastrous political outcome.*

Beaufighters, four P-51 Mustangs, one Mosquito, and almost fifty Spitfires. The Jewish ground forces were even more formidable, and in 1949 the Arabs accepted the inevitable in a series of armistices. The consequences for the Arab leaders were dire. The prime minister of Iraq resigned, the Emir of Transjordan was assassinated, and there were military coups in both Syria and Egypt. So the die was cast in the Middle East. In six months of existence, Israel had become a state to be reckoned with, and continued Arab hostility to that fact ensured that unrest and armed conflict were established as endemic to the region.

The Suez Debacle

In 1956, President Nasser of Egypt overrode Anglo-French interests and nationalized the Suez Canal. In a poorly judged piece of international intrigue, France and Britain connived with Israel to create an incident that could provide the excuse for a Franco-British intervention with the aim of taking over the Canal. On October 29, Israeli forces launched what initially appeared to be a lone preemptive strike against the strongest of its enemies, crossing into Egypt and advancing toward the Suez Canal and into Sinai.

C-47s dropped some 1,600 paratroopers near the important Mitla Pass east of Suez, and French Noratlas transports followed up with their heavy equipment. The next day, France and Britain issued a prepared ultimatum to both sides, demanding a withdrawal to 10 miles east and west of the Canal in the interests of protecting an international waterway. As anticipated, the Egyptians refused, so precipitating the intervention the Allies required.

An important element of the Allied agreement was that the Israeli Air Force (Chel Ha'Avir) would not have to concern itself with a counter air strike against the Egyptian Air Force. In the first phase of the joint operation, the destruction of the EAF was entrusted primarily to the British, allowing the Israelis to concentrate on a ground campaign in the Sinai. Flying from bases in Malta and Cyprus, RAF Canberras and Valiants bombed Egyptian airfields from high level, and these attacks were followed up by British and French aircraft operating from aircraft carriers and bases in Cyprus. Sea Hawks, Sea Venoms, Wyverns, Corsairs, and F-84Fs were among those aircraft strafing and bombing from low level. French F-84Fs fitted with long-range tanks reached south to Luxor and destroyed the EAF's Il-28 bombers. On the ground, an Israeli armored assault forced the Egyptians to withdraw from Sinai. Only occasionally harassed by EAF MiG-15s and Vampires, the Israeli commanders were quick to give credit to their own air force, saying that "the IAF saved the ground forces several days of battle and many casualties." In the battle for Sharm-El-Sheikh at the southern tip of Sinai, "Two days of air strafing was more than he [the Egyptian commander] could stand; the rockets and the napalm did him in."

On November 5, British and French paratroops led an invasion of Egypt at Port Said and the northern end of the Canal. Hastings and Valetta transports dropped vehicles, guns and assorted supplies, while naval aircraft flew "cab rank" patrols, attacking targets on request. Whirlwind and Sycamore helicopters ferried troops ashore and evacuated the wounded. With the Allied position established, Egyptian resistance crumbling, and follow-up forces standing by to reinforce the landings and take the Canal, it became clear that the international pressure for a ceasefire, led by the United States, could not be ignored. The Soviet Union went so far as to threaten nuclear strikes on London and Paris if the French and British did not withdraw. By November 7 the fighting had stopped and a month later most of the Allied troops had gone home, replaced at key points by UN peacekeepers.

It had proved to be a fruitless operation. Western credibility in the Arab world suffered damage that would not be repaired for years, and the Anglo-American "special relationship" was strained to its limits. Oil from the Middle East now had to be shipped round Africa by the Cape route because the Suez Canal was blocked by ships scuttled on the orders of President Nasser, and the Syrians had blown the land pipeline. Compared to these catastrophes, the military cost had been slight. The Franco-British air forces had lost a Canberra, a Venom, two Sea Hawks, two

Wyverns, two Whirlwinds, a Corsair and an F-84F, mostly to ground fire. The IAF admitted losing one Mystère, two Ouragans, ten Mustangs, and two Piper Cubs. Although they fought hard, the Egyptians had been overwhelmed by the combined assault, and had lost over 200 aircraft on the ground, besides several in combat over Sinai. The combatants parted in mutual enmity and an uneasy truce followed, broken as the years went by with increasing frequency by Arab raids across Israel's borders, mainly from Jordan and Syria. Tension in the Middle East rose steadily until the mid-1960s, by which time the air forces of the Arabs and the Israelis were far more formidable than they had been in 1956.

The Six Day War

By 1967 the Israeli Air Force had almost 300 combat aircraft on strength, a formidable mix of Dassault Mirage IIIs, Super Mystère / Mystères, Ouragans, and Sud-Ouest Vautour bombers. To help in directly supporting the army, there were also 76 armed Fouga Magister jet trainers. It was a far cry from the desperate days of 1948 when a few Avia S-199s represented the whole of the IAF's front line. On the face of it, however, the Egyptians had the Middle East's most powerful air force, with about 450 combat aircraft supplied by the Soviet Union — including 120 MiG-21s, 80 MiG-19s, 150 MiG-15s and 17s, 30 Su-7s, and some 70 Il-28 and Tu-16 bombers. The Syrians, Jordanians and

Westland Belvedere, *by Michael Turner. A Belvedere of 26 Squadron, based in Aden, lifts a 105 mm howitzer into position for J Battery, Royal Horse Artillery, during operations in the Radfan, South Arabia, in 1964.*

LEFT *An Israeli Air Force Vautour flies over tanks during the buildup to the Six Day War in 1967.*
ABOVE *The French SO 4050 Vautour was built in three versions — a two-seat all-weather fighter, a single-seat ground-attack aircraft, and a two-seat bomber. By the time of the Six Day War, only one Israel Air Force squadron, the "Knights of the Heart," was operating the Vautour. Eight of the squadron's nineteen aircraft were lost during hostilities.*

Iraqis could add perhaps another 170 machines, MiG-21s and Hunters among them. Arab antiaircraft defenses had also been massively reinforced with Soviet SAMs, guns and radars.

During 1966 and early 1967, there were a number of border clashes between the air forces, with several Arab fighters shot down. Syrian guns shelled Israeli villages from the Golan Heights. The withdrawal of the UN peacekeepers from Sinai led to the closure of the Gulf of Aqaba to Israeli shipping. As tensions rose, both sides mobilized. Given the imbalance of numbers, the Israeli government decided on a preemptive strike to neutralize the Arab air forces. On the morning of June 5, 1967, the IAF employed almost all its available combat strength to hit the Egyptian airfields, leaving only twelve Mirages behind to defend the skies over Israel. The first wave was timed to catch the EAF's early-morning patrols after they had landed. Lacking aids for accurate navigation and maintaining strict radio silence, the IAF aircraft flew west over the featureless Mediterranean before descending and turning south to cross the Egyptian coast beneath radar cover. Combining skill and luck, the first wave's flights of four found their targeted airfields, bombed and strafed them, and were followed at ten-minute intervals by two further waves. The attackers then went back to base, refueling and

rearming to continue the assault. In the course of a three-hour pounding the EAF had almost 300 aircraft destroyed or disabled on the ground for the loss of nineteen IAF fighters.

Their mission against the EAF accomplished by late morning, the Israelis turned to face their other enemies. Both the Jordanians and the Syrians had launched attacks on targets in Israel by the time the IAF was in a position to respond, but the response when it came was massive, effectively eliminating the Jordanian Air Force and destroying two-thirds of the Syrian front-line strength. Not until the following day, during an attack on an Iraqi airfield, did the IAF meet significant resistance in the air, when Hunters flown by Iraqi and Jordanian pilots accounted for several of the attackers. Nevertheless, the IAF had accomplished its aim; for the time being, at least, Israeli pilots ruled the skies of the Middle East. They had achieved this in the last major air operation to carry echoes of WWII fighter sweeps, using basic navigation, guns and iron bombs. Sophisticated navigation aids, electronic warfare, smart weapons and air-to-air missiles were luxuries of the future.

Their essential duty achieved, the IAF concentrated on supporting the ground war. Unlike many other air forces, the IAF never embraced the term "close air support." As their commander in the Six Day War, Major General Mordechai Hod, said, "We have never believed in close air support…we talk of participating in the ground battle." An earlier commander, Major General Dan Tolkovsky, was more specific: "Interdiction is God's gift to the Middle East…close support, by definition, gives up the basic, inherent capability of air forces to move in depth." In keeping with this doctrine, from June 6 the IAF struck at targets beyond the lines, at supply columns and reinforcements, destroying hundreds of tanks, guns and trucks. It was not completely one-sided. Israeli troops, too, suffered from the occasional attentions of MiGs, but the EAF was no longer able to hit back with any great strength and those few air-

craft that did get through were often shot down. Denied air cover, the Egyptian soldiers still fought hard and, despite their avoidance of the phrase "close air support," the IAF found it necessary to intervene in the land battle in direct support of their soldiers, rocket-firing Magisters joining the faster jets in attacking tank concentrations and artillery positions. Where Arab resistance was particularly strong, heli-borne assaults were launched behind the lines on both the Egyptian and Jordanian fronts to initiate breakthroughs. By the time the UN ceasefire took effect on the morning of June 10, the Israelis had won a resounding victory on all fronts, seizing control of the Sinai Peninsula, the Gaza strip, the West Bank, the Arab section of Jerusalem, and the Golan Heights, but their success imposed only a temporary solution. There was to be no lasting peace. As soon as they could, both sides began replacing their losses to get ready for the next time.

LEFT *A Tupolev Tu-16 (Badger) of the Egyptian Air Force. The Egyptians acquired thirty-five Badgers from the Soviet Union and operated the bombers from 1962 to 1997.*
BELOW *Designed under the guidance of Kurt Tank (Focke-Wulf Fw 190 in WWII), the HAL-24 Marut (Wind Spirit) was India's first indigenous combat aircraft. The prototype flew on June 17, 1961, and the Marut entered service with 10 Squadron, IAF, in 1967. Two other squadrons, 31 and 220, were equipped with the type, which remained in the front line until 1990.*

Only a month after the end of the Six Day War, artillery duels began across the Suez Canal, and there were frequent instances of aerial combat around the fringes of the new Israeli empire, with the IAF claiming eleven Arab MiGs by the end of the year. Replacement of the IAF's overworked fighters was becoming a priority, but the French had decided to embargo the arranged delivery of fifty Mirages so the Israelis had to look elsewhere. The U.S. agreed to release fifty new A-4 Skyhawks and then followed those up with a further twenty-five from the U.S. Navy. In 1969, Israel ordered fifty-six F-4 Phantoms, confident that the McDonnell Douglas fighters would preserve the IAF's superiority over its neighbors. At the same time, Israel's indigenous aviation industry set out to manufacture fighters of its own, producing improved versions of the Mirage III and V, named Nesher and Kfir respectively.

In March 1969, the Israelis completed the Barlev Line, a system of fortifications on the eastern side of the Suez Canal, and President Nasser announced that there was to be a "war of attrition." "What was taken by force," he said, "must be restored by force." Egyptian artillery barrages across the Canal became a regular event, to which Israel responded with air attacks on Egyptian radars and artillery positions, in the process shooting down twenty-one EAF aircraft for the loss of three of its own by the end of May. During the later months of 1969, the IAF took delivery of its first F-4s, and in January 1970 they began striking deep into Egypt, destroying targets in both the military and the national infrastructure. Cairo became a blacked-out, sand-bagged city, its people under aerial siege, and the EAF withdrew its bomber squadrons to safe havens in Libya and Sudan. Alarmed, Nasser asked for help from the Soviet Union. Egypt had already begun to install SA-2 missile batteries along the Canal, but now a division of Soviet-manned SA-3 batteries was added and three Soviet MiG-21 squadrons were deployed near Cairo, Aswan and Alexandria by March.

With the arrival of the Soviets, the nature of the Arab/Israeli confrontation changed. In effect, the Soviet Union took responsibility for the air defense of Egypt. More MiG squadrons arrived and construction began on hundreds of new SAM sites. The IAF did its best to destroy the sites before they became operational and Egyptian fighters carried out an increasing number of hit-and-run raids across the Canal. Both sides suffered losses in the exchange, something of a climax being reached when five MiG-21s were shot down in a dogfight with Skyhawks and Phantoms on July 30, and five Phantoms were lost to missiles only three days later. Long-standing international concern at the escalating conflict now had an effect, and a UN-brokered ceasefire was declared on August 7, 1970. President Nasser died of a heart attack a month later. The terms of the ceasefire included a restriction on placing missiles closer than 30 kilometers to the Canal, but that provision was ignored by the Soviets. Within days it was apparent that a massive buildup of SAM sites was in progress on the west side of the Canal.

Fighter pilots such as Uri Even-Nir, who had been striving to keep the missile threat in check for months, were appalled: "We were fighting a centipede — you hit it here and two more legs grow in its place. We were fighting an enemy that seemed not only irrational but with unlimited resources. It was like trying to empty an ocean with a bucket. By the middle of the summer we were marathon runners, hoping just to be around at the finish. We then ended the fighting saying that the missiles wouldn't move an inch toward the Canal, but they moved, grew, multiplied, and came right up to the water line; they couldn't get any closer — and then we did nothing."

In time, an impressive air defense system was built up on the Egyptian side of the Canal, an interlocking arrangement of SA-2 and SA-3 missiles, supplemented by mobile SA-6s and shoulder-launched SA-7s, nearly 3,000 launchers in all. There were almost as many antiaircraft guns, including the radar-predicted ZSU-23/4, a rapid-fire, four-barrel 23 mm weapon effective against low-flying aircraft up to 2,000 yards. With these antiaircraft systems in place, covering between them slant ranges up to 25 miles and heights from the surface to 50,000 feet, the Egyptians had the capability of achieving air superiority over the Canal battlefield without their fighters engaging in air-to-air combat, an aspect of warfare in which they had been forced to recognize their inferiority. The IAF, on the other hand, still basking in the glow of past victories, had come to feel that it was almost invincible. In the uneasy peace that lasted until 1973, Israeli airmen remained wonderfully self-confident, complacent about their ability to defend their homeland against any Arab incursion. Their confidence was encouraged by the statements of Ariel Sharon, who went so far as to describe Israel as "a military superpower" able to "conquer in one week the area from Khartoum to Baghdad and Algeria." Such assurance was to be severely tested when the Arabs set out to recover the lands they had lost in the Six Day War.

Yom Kippur

With the help of a barrage of threats and repeated military exercises during 1973, Egypt's President Anwar Sadat lulled Israel into thinking he was all bluster and would never act. In fact, he agreed with Syria that the two Arab nations would strike as the Jews celebrated the annual religious holiday of Yom Kippur (the Day of Atonement). At 1405 hours on October 6, 2000, Egyptian guns opened fire on the Barlev Line as EAF fighter-bombers swept forward to attack Israeli positions and Tu-16 bombers launched Kelt missiles at more distant targets, such as Tel Aviv. Spearheaded by heli-borne commandos, the Egyptian Army followed, crossing the Canal and overrunning a number of Israeli strong points. At the same time, 900 tanks led the Syrian assault in the Golan Heights. Caught by surprise, the IAF was nevertheless able to react fairly quickly. Within half an hour, the first waves of Skyhawks and Phantoms were off the ground and rushing to the fight. They soon found that this would be a far more difficult struggle than 1967 had been. The layered air defense screen over the Canal proved to be very effective, breaking up the IAF attacks and shooting down ten fighter-bombers in the first half hour. Persisting in its attempts to destroy missile sites and interfere with the Egyptian Army's Canal crossings, the IAF lost over fifty aircraft in four days. Beneath such an effective shield, the Egyptians were able to establish a number of well-defended bridgeheads on the eastern side of the Canal. Not until they tried to advance beyond its cover was there a

> *"Early in the 1967 war General Benjamin Peled [Commander, Israeli Air Force] attended a briefing given by Moshe Dayan [Minister of Defense] to the Israeli press. Peled reported on the air war and mentioned the loss of an Israeli aircraft that morning, the crew of which was missing. While he was speaking a note was passed to him. He read it and commented, 'Interesting.' Looking up, he said that the missing pilot and navigator had been rescued and were on their way back to their airfield. At this point Dayan interjected that the pilot was Peled's son. 'Yes,' said Peled, adding with an expressionless face, 'and tonight they will be in action again.' It was a war of fathers and sons."*
>
> CHAIM HERZOG (MAJOR GENERAL; PRESIDENT OF ISRAEL 1983–93)

sharp reversal of fortune when they clashed with Israeli armor operating under an IAF umbrella no longer harassed by a hail of missiles. In some cases, the IAF alone was sufficient, as Egyptian Chief of Staff General Saad ad Din Shazli reported about the attempted advance of a brigade along the Red Sea shore: "In open country, outside the protection of our SAMs, the brigade was routed by the enemy air force. The mauling destroyed it as a fighting unit for several days."

Severe though the Egyptian threat was, the Israelis concluded that they could afford to give ground in Sinai while they confronted the Syrians, who were menacing the borders of Israel itself. Over the Golan Heights, the IAF ran into another wall of Soviet missiles and lost even more heavily than they did over the Canal — twenty-five Skyhawks and five Phantoms down in the first two hours of the war. Seeing the extravagant use of missiles by the Syrians, the Israelis made a conscious decision to "draw out the maximum amount of missiles from their batteries, to drain them dry…by noon Monday [October 8] they stopped shooting…. Then the air force started to be effective in the ground battle." Before more missiles could be deployed, the IAF had destroyed enough radars and missile sites to make it impossible for the Syrians to recreate an integrated, interlocking system, and Israeli armor, strongly supported from the air, drove the Syrian Army back beyond its start points. The IAF also managed to regain air superiority over the Golan Heights battlefield, engaging the Syrian MiGs (reinforced by MiG-21s and Hunters from Iraq) and overcoming them in aerial combat. With the Syrian threat contained, Israel could turn south and concentrate its efforts on the Egyptians.

On October 14, the Egyptians, responding to a cry for help from Syria, launched an armored assault beyond their integrated SAM umbrella. They lost over 200 tanks and were forced to withdraw. Seizing their opportunity, the Israeli Army followed up during the hours of darkness,

F-15 Eagles of 133 Squadron, Israeli Air Force, in formation.

that perhaps as much as 20 percent of Arab losses were due to friendly fire from their own SAMs. Such severe penalties resulted from the lack of an effective IFF system.) Hard lessons had been learned about the need for effective ECM gear and "smart" weapons. The importance of having good up-to-the-minute intelligence was also emphasized, and that pointed the way to the increased use of drones and RPVs over the battlefield rather than expensive manned aircraft. Above all, Israel was reminded of the vital role the IAF plays in national defense. Without a strong, well-equipped professional air force, it would be difficult for Israel to survive against an all-out Arab assault. The air power issue was also significant in determining the direction of Egyptian politics after 1973. Egypt's break with the Soviet Union came about in large part because the Soviets refused to supply new aircraft on credit. Evidence of a marked shift in international alignment was the key provision of the Camp David Accords that the United States agreed to supply modern fighters to Egypt.

The Long Reach of the IAF

Since 1973, the IAF has flown well beyond Israel's air space more than once to carry out some impressive operations. On June 27, 1976, Palestinian terrorists hijacked Air France Flight 139 en route from Tel Aviv to Paris and took the aircraft to Entebbe, Uganda, where President Idi Amin allowed them to hold ninety-seven Jewish passengers and the French crew hostage. The Israeli response was swift and spectacular. On July 3, four IAF C-130s and two Boeing 707s took off from Ophir at the southernmost tip of Sinai and set off down the Red Sea. One 707, equipped as a hospital, landed at Nairobi, Kenya, and stood by to deal with casualties. The other circled over the Red Sea, functioning as an airborne command and control center for the operation. The C-130s flew on, over Ethiopia and Kenya, and approached Entebbe at midnight. Once on the ground, they disgorged commandos, together with a black Mercedes and escorting Land Rovers identical to those used by Idi Amin and his bodyguards. Outside the old terminal where the hostages were being held, the Ugandan

when the IAF's support was not critical, and by first light on October 17 they were across the Canal in force, together with some tanks and heavy artillery. These turned their attention to the SAM sites and blasted a huge hole in the missile screen. At the same time, the IAF was made better able to take on the SAMs that remained. Both sides had been massively resupplied with aircraft and weapons by their superpower sponsors, and among the equipment delivered to the IAF by USAF transports were ECM pods, "smart" bombs, Shrike antiradar missiles, Maverick TV-guided missiles, and Rockeye cluster bombs. Exposed to both assault from the ground and an array of new air-to-ground weapons, the Egyptian SAM umbrella began to come apart, allowing the IAF to operate more freely in support of the Israeli Army and to penetrate into Egypt, striking airfields and infrastructure targets at will.

Diplomatic pressure to end the fighting finally took effect on the evening of October 24, with the Israeli forces in firm command of the situation. The losses to both sides had been severe. In the air battle, the Arab air forces are reported as having lost at least 442 aircraft (Egypt 242, Syria 179, Iraq 21), and the IAF 115, including 53 Skyhawks out of 170 and 33 Phantoms out of 177. (It has been estimated guards saluted the convoy and were summarily dealt with by commandos, who rushed into the building to take on the terrorists. Other soldiers fanned out and destroyed eleven Ugandan MiGs to forestall any possibility of pursuit. Eighteen minutes after the first commandos jumped from their aircraft, six terrorists and twenty Ugandan soldiers were dead and the hostages were on board C-130s starting for home. Three hostages and the commander of the raid, Lieutenant Colonel "Yoni" Netanyahu, were killed during the action. (Yoni was the elder brother of Benjamin Netanyahu, later Israel's prime minister.) It was a dramatic demonstration of Israel's determination to protect its people, no matter what the circumstances.

Five years after Entebbe, in June 1981, the IAF carried out a long-range mission of a very different kind. Iraq was within weeks of bringing on line a nuclear power station capable of producing weapons-grade plutonium. Since Israel believed that it would be the prime target for any Iraqi nuclear weapons that might be assembled, a stark choice was presented — either do nothing and risk eventual annihilation, or act to eliminate the threat. As it happened, the IAF had the tools for the job. Its front-line fighters by this time were F-15s and F-16s, both of which had the range to reach the Iraqi reactor at Osirak, well over 600 miles from Israel. On June 7, eight F-16s armed with two 2,000-pound bombs apiece took off from Etzion air base, accompanied by six F-15s as top cover. Flying at low level through Arab (Jordanian and Saudi Arabian) air space all the way, the

F-16s delivered their bombs and saw the reactor building collapse, leaving Iraq's nuclear potential in ruins. The surprise was complete. No MiGs were scrambled and the response from antiaircraft defenses was feeble. All the IAF aircraft returned safely to base. Official international reaction to the raid, even from Israel's friends, was harshly critical. President Reagan went so far as to suspend a delivery of F-16s from the United States, and Britain's Margaret Thatcher said that the attack was "a grave breach of international law." Nevertheless, there was unspoken relief in many quarters that Iraq's nuclear program had been checked, and no doubt was left in anyone's mind that Israel had shown both the will and ability to strike at anything that posed a threat to its national security.

Four years later, the IAF was called on to strike again, this time in the belief that terrorist acts merited retaliation. Following the murder of three Israelis aboard a yacht off Cyprus by PLO terrorists, an attack was planned on the PLO headquarters in Tunis, over 1,200 miles from Israel. The raid was launched on October 1, 1985. Ten F-15s flew the length of the Mediterranean, refueled by Boeing 707 tankers, before identifying the PLO buildings and hitting them hard. Again Israel rode out the international storm, firm in the resolve that, whatever the political cost, the IAF was ready to strike at foes wherever they were, carrying the message that no enemy could expect to take aggressive action against Israelis without suffering severe consequences.

Israel launched the IAI Lavi program in 1980 to develop a multirole combat aircraft to replace the A-4 Skyhawk, F-4 Phantom II and IAI Kfir. Up to 40 percent of the development costs were paid by the U.S. government. In the mid-1980s, it became clear that the United States was no longer prepared to provide technology and funds for an aircraft that could rival the F-16C/D and the F/A-18C/D on the export market. Israel could not finance the project without U.S. support and canceled the Lavi in August 1987.

Since 1973 the Israeli Air Force has received twelve C-130Es, ten C-130Hs and two KC-130Hs. They are operated by 131 Squadron (Yellow Birds) and 103 Squadron (Elephants). In 1976, C-130s transported Israeli commandos to Entebbe, Uganda, to rescue hostages from a commercial flight hijacked by Arab terrorists.

In between these long-range missions, the IAF flexed its muscles somewhat closer to home, in the skies over Lebanon. When Egypt and Israel signed the historic Camp David agreement in 1978, Syria and the PLO were left as Israel's main opponents. Almost immediately, the PLO stepped up the pace of its attacks on Israel from Lebanon, itself torn by civil war. The IAF responded by attacking the PLO camps, and Syria moved troops into Lebanon, ostensibly to keep the peace but clearly in support of the PLO. Between 1979 and 1982, at least twelve Syrian MiGs were lost in clashes with the IAF, which flew regular reconnaissance sorties over Lebanon to keep an eye on developments. In 1982 the PLO's shelling of Israeli villages increased in tempo, and Israel looked for an excuse to send troops across the border. On June 3, 1982, an assassination attempt was made on Israel's ambassador to the United Kingdom, and by June 6 the Israeli Army, supported by the IAF, was moving toward Beirut, sweeping aside the PLO in the process.

With 60,000 Israeli troops and 500 tanks charging into Lebanon, the Syrians felt it necessary to intervene, at first attempting to intercept the IAF's F-16s and then launching strikes against Israeli armor. To ensure their freedom of action, the IAF set out to establish air supremacy over Lebanon, and this meant eliminating nineteen Syrian SAM sites in the Beka'a Valley, to the north of the Golan Heights.

The IAI Kfir (Lion Cub), which entered service with the Israeli Air Force in 1974, was based on the design of the Dassault Mirage 5. It was built around a General Electric J-79 engine and had a canard added to improve aerodynamics. It could achieve Mach 2.3 at altitudes above 50,000 feet.

Under the Peace Marble Foreign Military Sales program, Israel has acquired several batches of F-16s, with deliveries between 1980 and 2008 totaling almost 300 aircraft. In June 1981, F-16 fighter-bombers destroyed the Osiraq nuclear research reactor near Baghdad.

On June 9, assisted by numerous reconnaissance drones, a strong force of F-4Es and Kfirs attacked the SAMs with anti-radar and air-to-surface missiles. Surface-to-surface missiles were fired into the valley by Israeli ground forces, and Syrian radars were hampered by Boeing 707 jamming aircraft. Further attacks were made using guided and cluster bombs, and by the end of the day, seventeen SAM sites had been put out of operation. The remaining two were destroyed the next day, together with a number of mobile SA-6 launchers. Ground fire accounted for the IAF's small losses.

High above the fury in the Beka'a Valley, the IAF's F-15s and F-16s clashed with Syrian MiG-21s and MiG-23s. Now untroubled by SAMs and kept informed of enemy activity by the radars of patrolling E-2C Hawkeyes, the highly motivated and well-trained IAF fighter pilots had all-aspect Sidewinder and Shafir missiles to add to their considerable advantages. The Syrians carried Soviet Atolls and Aphids, infrared weapons that were ineffective outside the rear quadrant of an opponent's aircraft. In seven days of air-to-air combat, the IAF's superiority in training, weapons and situational awareness proved decisive. The fight above the Beka'a was one of the most one-sided in aviation history, resulting in the destruction of eighty-two Syrian MiGs without loss to the IAF. The victory over the Beka'a Valley's SAMs and fighters

conclusively established the IAF as the Middle East's dominant air force, and for the remainder of the century there were no major challenges to Israel's aerial supremacy. As had been the case throughout the period since the birth of Israel in 1948, air power continued to have a major role to play in establishing national prestige and determining the direction of politics in the Middle East.

Sunnis and Shias

In 1980, long-standing frontier quarrels between Iran and Iraq, exacerbated by the mutual enmity of the respective regimes, burst into open conflict. On September 22, Iraqi troops crossed the disputed borders. (Iran's hard-line Shia Muslim leaders had little in common with Iraq's ruling Baath Party, in which Sunni Muslims led a state avowedly secular.) Pre-invasion attacks on Iranian airfields were ineffective for a number of reasons, including the mediocre avionics of Iraq's MiGs, their lack of advanced munitions, the dispersal of Iranian aircraft in hardened shelters, and poor pre-strike intelligence. The Iranian Air Force responded by attacking Iraqi airfields with F-4s and F-5s, again without much success. Given that both sides had powerful air forces, the air activity at this stage was relatively limited, but that did not prevent extravagant claims

being made about the number of aircraft being shot down; Iraq claimed 140 enemy aircraft, and Iran 68. Neither country used its air arm with much determination, and losses soon induced Iran to back away from the idea of a counter air offensive, moving instead to strategic strikes against Iraq's cities and oil production facilities. Bombs were dropped on Kurdestan, too, in the hope of provoking a Kurdish uprising against the Baath regime. Iraq also treated oil as a major target, and this led to dogfights between Iranian F-4s and Iraqi MiG-21s.

By November 1980, the air war had settled into a pattern, with both sides launching "nuisance raids" on cities by pairs of aircraft, the Iraqis often using Tu-22 Blinders for such missions. Occasionally, intensive ground-attack operations were flown in conjunction with an army offensive,

the Iraqi Air Force sometimes flying as many as 400 sorties in a day, but generally the soldiers' battles were grinding affairs, fought without much close air support. Attacks on oil targets remained a priority for both air forces, and the Iranians went so far as to strike Kuwait's oil facilities on the grounds that they were handling the enemy's oil. The Iraqis fired Exocet missiles at the main Iranian oil terminal on Kharg Island, and widened the war still further by sinking a Greek tanker in November 1983 and a British tanker in February 1984. Iran responded in kind by using its F-4Es to fire Maverick missiles at tankers leaving Kuwaiti and Saudi Arabian ports. This brought retaliation from Saudi F-15s, which claimed to have shot down two F-4s on June 5. By the end of 1984, sixty-seven large ships had been hit by one side or the other, and the pace increased as the months passed. In 1987, Iraq began reaching far down into the Persian Gulf, flying Mirage F-1s refueled by AN-12s converted to the air tanker role. That year 178 ships were hit, twice the number struck in 1986, a disturbing development that alarmed the international community.

Another shock came during the ground war. In an attempt to counter Iranian "human wave" attacks, Iraq began to use chemical weapons. Delivered primarily from aircraft, they produced dense white clouds and inflicted

SR-71s operating from European bases were among the reconnaissance aircraft that flew intelligence sorties before the USAF attack on Libya in April 1986.

During the evening of April 14, 1986, the United States launched Operation El Dorado Canyon, a series of air strikes against targets in Libya. Twenty-eight KC-135s and KC-10s left their bases in the United Kingdom to rendezvous with twenty-four F-111s. The refusal of France to allow overflight added about 1,300 miles each way to the flight, and required a tremendous amount of additional refueling support from tanker aircraft. The Eighth Air Force tankers refueled the F-111s four times outbound and twice more during the return. The mission took 14 hours and was the longest combat mission ever accomplished by tactical aircraft.

mass casualties. The Iranian government reported the attacks, but were at first reluctant to retaliate with chemicals of their own. However, in the face of continued provocation, Iran did deliver chemical weapons against troop concentrations on a few occasions without significantly affecting the outcome of the struggle.

As the number of attacks on oil tankers rose, Kuwait reregistered some ships under U.S. or Soviet flags and called on the U.S. Navy for protection. The involvement of U.S. warships led to a disastrous incident on July 3, 1988, when the USS *Vincennes* fired SAMs at a target identified as a hostile F-14, only to find that an Iran Air Airbus A300 had been shot down, killing all 290 people on board. It was a sad postscript to a brutal and costly war that dragged on for eight long years and during which air power was seldom used to best effect. On July 19 a UN resolution calling for a ceasefire was accepted. There had been more than a million casualties, but neither Iran nor Iraq made significant territorial or political gains, and the fundamental issues dividing the countries remained unresolved at the end of the war.

Desert One Disaster

At intervals during the 1980s regional disturbances and Cold War skirmishes involved the U.S. military in relatively limited ways. It was unfortunate that the first of them, a joint operation, should carry the same sense of unnecessary failure that lingered after Vietnam. In November 1979, Islamic militants in Iran, protesting the sanctuary being given the deposed Shah in the United States, occupied the U.S. embassy in Tehran and took sixty-six hostages. As tedious and fruitless diplomatic negotiations dragged on, plans were made for U.S. forces to attempt a rescue.

After a period of planning and training, special forces were assembled on two principal bases — the aircraft carrier USS *Nimitz* at the mouth of the Persian Gulf, and Masirah Island airfield, off the coast of Oman. The operation began on April 24, 1980, when eight USN RH-53D helicopters left *Nimitz* for an abandoned airstrip southeast of Tehran, code-named Desert One. There they planned to join six USAF C-130s bringing the 132-man rescue team and all the necessary equipment from Masirah. (They were MC-130Es with the special forces, AC-130Es for fire support over Tehran, and EC-130Hs to provide communications and helicopter refueling.) Ill luck dogged the mission from the start, with only six helicopters managing to reach Desert One more than ninety minutes late after struggling through a sandstorm. Of the missing two, one made it back to the carrier, but the other was left in the desert. Another helicopter then developed hydraulic failure at Desert One, leaving five for the operation. Since it was judged that six was the minimum number required, the mission was aborted. The five serviceable RH-53Ds began refueling from the EC-130H tankers for the return flight. In lifting away to make room for the next in line, one helicopter allowed its rotor to strike a tanker's rear fuselage. Fire and explosions followed, and flying debris damaged the remaining RH-53Ds. Eight men were killed and a number of others burned. The survivors boarded the C-130s and withdrew, leaving the helicopters behind. At a cost of seven RH-53Ds, one EC-130H, eight dead and many wounded, it was a failure dearly bought and a savage reminder that the unexpected can defeat even the best equipped forces. The hostages were not released until the following year.

Lashing Out at Libya

After a series of incidents between Libyan forces and the U.S. Navy in the Mediterranean in early 1986, a bomb was exploded in a Berlin discotheque used by U.S. servicemen. There was evidence of Libyan involvement, and President Reagan decided to retaliate. Operation El Dorado Canyon was planned as a combined USAF/USN strike against military and terrorist targets in Libya, the USAF being responsible for those near Tripoli and the USN for others in the Benghazi area. Initial USAF intelligence sorties were flown by SR-71s, TR-1As, U-2Rs and RC-135s operating from bases in the United Kingdom, Greece and Cyprus.

On the evening of April 14, 1986, eighteen F-111Fs of the 48th Tactical Fighter Wing, based at Lakenheath in England, set off for Libya. The mission was to be exhaustingly long because the USAF aircraft had been denied the right to overfly France. Spain declined, too, so a circuitous route via Gibraltar had to be flown. Support was provided by KC-10 and KC-135 tankers, an E-3A AWACS, an EC-135E tactical command center, and EF-111As for electronic defense suppression. After four refuelings on the outbound leg, the F-111Fs crossed the Libyan coast west of Tripoli just before midnight to sweep round and approach their targets from the south. Using their Pave Tack laser marking systems, they aimed 2,000-pound Paveway bombs at the military side of Tripoli airport and at Al Aziziyah barracks, where the Libyan leader Gaddafi had his quarters. Considerable damage was done to the barracks and a number of Libyan aircraft were destroyed. Unfortunately, several Western embassies also suffered damage. One F-111F was lost in the Mediterranean after the attack. Although at the time El Dorado Canyon was judged only a qualified success, the performance of the USAF crews was acknowledged as praiseworthy. Completing a round-trip of 5,500 miles with multiple refuelings to attack pinpoint targets at night was a considerable challenge, and the achievement gained respect from military aviators worldwide. As time passed and Libya's terrorist excesses were seen to have been restrained, the accomplishments of the operation could be seen in their true light.

AIR POWER IN THE AMERICAS
Skirmish and Rebellion

South and Central America were blessedly free of major international conflict for most of the 20th century. Nevertheless, the region was continually racked with instability and plenty of blood was shed in border skirmishes, rebellions and civil wars. Aircraft were used in many of these disturbances, but they seldom had any decisive effect, and only helicopters could claim to have been invariably useful. In shows of power during military coups in Argentina and Venezuela in the 1950s, and in Chile in 1973, aircraft made passing attacks on the seats of government, and incipient rebellions in Paraguay in 1959 and in Venezuela in 1992 were defeated with the help of air force units. A clash involving Ecuador and Peru in 1981 and 1995 saw Ecuadorian Mirages and Kfirs claim two Peruvian Su-22s and a Cessna A-37. The last dogfights between piston-engined WWII fighters occurred during the "football war" between Honduras and El Salvador in 1969, when Honduran pilot Fernando Soto scored the only aerial victories ever recorded by a Central American air force. On July 17, flying a Vought F-4U Corsair, Soto shot down a P-51D on one sortie and added two Goodyear FG-1 Corsairs later in the day. (Fernando Soto had a long career in aviation, accumulating some 24,000 hours while flying with both the Honduran Air Force and Servicio Aereo Honduras S.A. In 1983, he flew the Pope during his tour of Central America. Soto eventually became Director of Civil Aviation for Honduras.)

The bloodiest 20th-century conflicts in the Americas were the civil war in El Salvador and the confrontation between the left-wing Sandanista government of Nicaragua and right-wing U.S.-backed "Contra" guerrillas. Other destructive guerrilla struggles went on in Peru (the "Shining Path" rebels), Colombia (the drug cartels), and Bolivia, where in the 1960s Che Guevara led a revolt against the right-wing dictatorship of General Barrientos. In all of these, where the rapid insertion of soldiers into difficult, heavily forested country was often necessary, the most significant aircraft were the helicopters. Che Guevara was hunted down in 1967 by helicopter-borne troops, and two years later a twist of fate killed his enemy, Barrientos, in a helicopter accident. Against the Contras in Nicaragua, the Sandanistas used heavily armed Soviet Mi-8s and Mi-24s to give their troops the necessary mobility, and in El Salvador the United States supplied the government with UH-1s that proved invaluable in combating guerrilla activity, carrying soldiers swiftly into areas often inaccessible by land.

U.S. Interventions

In October 1983, U.S. forces mounted a joint service operation on the Caribbean island of Grenada. Reacting to a blatant attempt to usurp the government and turn Grenada into a Cuban satellite, the U.S. intervened to eject Cuban forces and restore democratic rule. On October 24, Operation Urgent Fury began with MC-130Es dropping small detachments of SEALS and Delta Force into Grenada to reconnoiter key areas. In the early hours of October 25, more MC-130Es dropped two Ranger battalions onto the main airport at Point Salines under covering fire from AC-130H gunships. With the airfield secured, C-141s and C-130Es brought in elements of the 82nd Airborne Division, and U.S. forces moved out to capture strong points and ensure the safety of some 1,000 American students at the university. AC-130Hs and naval attack aircraft were used to suppress opposing fire. At the same time, C-5As flew into nearby Barbados with heavy equipment, including the Army's UH-60A helicopters. An E-3A and an EC-130E cruised over the Caribbean to monitor the situation. Although resistance was often stiff, the Cuban headquarters at Calvigny was overcome on October 27. Minor mopping-up operations continued for several more days. Urgent Fury proved to be more costly than had been hoped, with nineteen U.S. servicemen dead, 116 wounded, and at least seven Army helicopters lost, but it was a success. The U.S. military had

prevailed, Cuban prestige had suffered, and Communism had been handed a setback in the Caribbean.

Confrontations between warring factions in Central America attracted U.S. concern in the 1980s, but American involvement was generally limited to providing military training and equipment to those opposing the spread of Communism, whether they be governments or rebels. USAF reconnaissance aircraft kept a close watch on events in Nicaragua and El Salvador, and AC-130Hs occasionally set out to track down arms smugglers, but overt intervention by U.S. forces in the region did not occur until 1989, when Manuel Noriega went too far to be ignored in Panama. In December 1989, after Noriega had installed himself as dictator and directed bellicose remarks at the United States, Panamanian soldiers murdered a U.S. Marine Corps officer. Operation Just Cause was launched in response. Before dawn on December 20, USAF AC-130 gunships attacked Panamanian positions in support of an assault by Navy SEALS and Army Rangers. Other USAF aircraft used were MC-130s, and two impressive helicopters — the MH-53 Pave Low and the MH-60G Pave Hawk, both fitted with all the electronic magic necessary to operate in all weathers, by day or night, at low level. Later, when the first dust had settled, C-141s flew in troops of the 82nd Airborne Division. Effective resistance was ended within forty-eight hours. Noriega sought sanctuary in the Vatican Embassy for a while, but surrendered on January 3, 1990. A USAF MC-130 crew had the pleasure of flying him to Florida to stand trial on drug charges.

Almost unnoticed, an extraordinary aircraft made its operational debut during Just Cause. Rio Hato airfield was attacked by a pair of Lockheed F-117 Nighthawks. Their efforts were not particularly noteworthy, but the mission served as a muted prelude. The complete Nighthawk work with full fortissimo orchestration followed only two years later in the Middle East.

The Dassault Super Etendard is a carrier-based single-seat strike fighter first introduced into service in 1978. Fourteen were sold to Argentina. Armed with Exocet missiles, the Super Etendard proved its combat effectiveness during the Falklands War in 1982.

FRACAS IN THE FALKLANDS
Galtieri's Gamble

On April 2, 1982, Argentine forces landed on the Falkland Islands, overcame the resistance of the small Royal Marine detachment, took down the British colors and raised the flag of Argentina. The dependent island of South Georgia was taken the following day. They were aggressive acts taken against the background of sovereignty claims and counter-claims stretching back over more than two centuries. Whatever the rights and wrongs of the competing historic claims might be, among the considerations pressing most heavily upon Argentina's President Galtieri when he ordered the 1982 invasion were that there was an urgent need for some action that would help to subdue rising internal unrest in his country, restore the reputation of armed forces tainted by stories of atrocities and disappearances during the nation's "dirty war," and establish the authority of the military junta. (In 1982 Argentina was ruled by a three-man military junta — General Galtieri of the army, installed as president; Admiral Jorge Anaya of the navy; and Brigadier Basilio Lami Dozo of the air force.) The resurrection of the Falklands issue to fill these needs was encouraged by Britain's apparent apathy over the future of the islands. There had been no British attempts to foster their development, and there was every indication that Britain was anxious to divest itself of the last vestiges of colonial responsibility. Lack of funds had brought on announcements that the British Antarctic Survey was to close its South Georgia station and HMS *Endurance*, the last Royal Navy vessel with duties in the South Atlantic, was to be withdrawn. It seemed that Galtieri was being offered a heaven-sent opportunity to make his mark on history and consolidate his position with a minimum of risk. It was unfortunate that he then chose to brandish the fact of the Falkland Islands invasion in the face of Prime Minister Margaret Thatcher, a leader with firm views about military dictatorships and implacable when it came to the usurpation of the rights of people who had voted to remain British citizens. In a statement to the House of Commons on the day after the Argentine invasion, she announced that "a large task force will sail" and that its objective would be "to see the islands returned to British administration."

In a remarkable effort to keep the prospective belligerents apart and arrive at a peaceful solution, the U.S. Secretary of State, Alexander Haig, began an epic of shuttle diplomacy, using a Boeing 707 equipped with bunks, writing desks, copying machines and radio telephones. On April 7 he left Washington for London and talks with Thatcher. By April 19 he had flown to Buenos Aires, back to London, then to Washington and Buenos Aires again before concluding that there was no compromise which could satisfy the two sides. The British were implacable in their determination and the Argentines still refused to accept that their opponents really intended to fight. Haig gave up and went back to Washington. By the time he got there his Boeing 707 had covered some 33,000 miles in twelve days. His shuttle diplomacy had not been crowned with the success he had hoped, but it had been a worthy attempt and his face-to-face meetings with the respective governments had at least ensured that all concerned had argued their case and knew that their views had been transmitted to the other side. In the days before jet airliners, not even that could have been achieved. Exhausted by his efforts but now clear in his own mind, Haig arrived home to recommend that the United States should come down firmly in support of the British position. A democracy was surely preferable to a military dictatorship, after all.

No Easy Task

It was clear that Operation Corporate, as the mission to recover the Falklands was known, would have to be led by the Royal Navy. The objective was in the southernmost reaches of the South Atlantic and there was no prospect of finding a mounting base closer than Ascension Island, a British-administered morsel of rock separated from the Falklands by 4,000 miles of open and often unfriendly ocean. The other services would have vital parts to play, but without ships there could be no operation at all. Any attempt to recover the islands would have to be launched and nurtured from ships at sea, and this gave rise to two major areas of concern. First there was the sheer scale of the logistic effort needed to accomplish the task with no support base close at hand, and second there was the question of how best to deal with the enemy's forces, which on paper seemed capable of being formidable opponents and likely to outnumber the British considerably, especially in the air.

Intelligence reports suggested that the Fuerza Aérea Argentina (FAA, the Argentine Air Force) and the

Alférez Jorge Barrionuevo and his A-4 Skyhawk. He was involved in the attack by Zeus flight that sank HMS Coventry on May 25, 1982.

Aeronaval Argentina had some 256 aircraft between them — 112 jet fighters and bombers (Skyhawks, Daggers, Mirage IIIs, Super Etendards, Canberras), 34 short-range attack aircraft (Pucarás, Turbo-Mentors, Macchi 339s), 14 reconnaissance aircraft (Boeing 707s, Learjets, Neptunes, S-2 Trackers), and 96 others (transport aircraft, helicopters, et cetera, including Hercules and Sea Kings). As it started south, the Royal Navy's defense against aerial attack comprised its own shipborne guns and missile systems, and just twenty Sea Harriers aboard two light carriers — HMS *Invincible*, one of the new "Harrier carriers," and HMS *Hermes*, an old ASW carrier modified and fitted with a ski jump to assist Harrier operations. Since the scrapping of HMS *Ark Royal* (the last British carrier capable of handling F-4s) in the late 1970s, the Royal Navy had been focused on NATO operations within reach of land-based air support. Little provision had been made for out-of-area operations, and as well as its shortage of fighters, the task force was without airborne early-warning cover, a lack of capability for which the British would pay dearly.

On the face of it, besides suffering from early-warning blindness, it seemed that the Sea Harriers were out-matched, both in terms of numbers and performance. The Mirages/Daggers and A-4s together outnumbered them by more than four to one, and the Mirages/Daggers were Mach 2 aircraft, much faster than the subsonic Sea Harriers. On the other hand, the Sea Harrier's V/STOL capabilities offered the possibility of being able to fly in weather conditions too hazardous for conventional jet fighters, and added the dimension of VIFFing (using Vectored thrust In Forward Flight). A Harrier pilot involved in aerial combat might choose to change the direction of his engine's thrust, either to bring the aircraft's nose up quickly to get off a shot, or to cause an opponent to overshoot during an attack by inducing rapid deceleration and an increased rate of turn. Since any use of VIFFing would be accompanied by a drastic loss of airspeed, it was a technique to be employed rarely, perhaps only in desperate situations, but it was comforting to have the option. The Sea Harrier's air-to-air weapon, the AIM-9L Sidewinder, held the more certain advantage of being an all-aspect missile — it did not have to be fired from an enemy's rear quarter.

Wideawake

Ascension Island's ability to act as a mounting base depended on Wideawake Airfield, a U.S. facility built up by agreement with the United Kingdom to support a satellite tracking station on the island. Accustomed to seeing only the occasional U.S. transport aircraft, Wideawake was soon handling aircraft at a dramatically increased rate, up to 400 movements a day at the height of the war. With the hastily

ABOVE *The BAe Nimrod is the only jet-powered maritime patrol aircraft in military service. During the Falklands campaign Nimrods covered the Royal Navy task force as it sailed south, and patrolled close to the coast of Argentina, keeping a watch on Argentine fleet movements. Some Nimrods were armed with Sidewinder missiles for self-defense, making them "the world's largest fighters."*

RIGHT *Handley Page Victor tankers performed sterling service during the Falklands War, notably in support of the Vulcan Black Buck bombing missions. For the first Black Buck, fifteen Victors were needed to get one Vulcan over Port Stanley.*

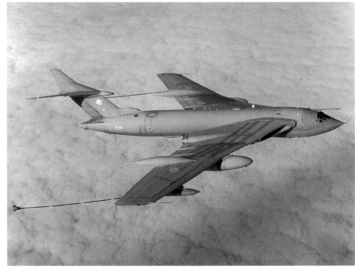

assembled fleet of warships on the way, transport aircraft (VC-10s and Hercules) began shuttling additional men and stores to Ascension. Wideawake's capacity to cope with the situation was improved by the arrival of RAF air traffic control staff and equipment, and huge portable fuel storage bags to amplify the island's meager tankage. Large though they were, they were not adequate. U.S. tankers arrived every few days with bulk aviation fuel and then sat offshore like outsize filling stations, pumping fuel into the bags as they were emptied by the insatiable thirst of more and more aircraft. RAF aircrew, soon flying at rates they had never before experienced, at first lived in tents pitched on lava. It was hot and there were generators running continuously nearby. The lack of adequate rest became a very real problem, so prefabricated aircrew accommodation units (known as "Concertina City") were borrowed from

the USAF and flown in by C-141s from Holloman AFB, New Mexico.

By April 6, RAF Nimrods had begun to fly maritime patrol sorties from Wideawake, and the first Victor tankers had arrived, some equipped for radar reconnaissance. On April 20, a Victor, supported by three others, flew over 7,000 miles in reconnoitering the area round South Georgia. The crew's report that there was no sign of enemy shipping gave the go-ahead for a Royal Navy force to move in to the island and land commandos. Appalling weather, with whirling snowstorms and winds up to 100 mph, threatened the landings with disaster. Two helicopters were lost in crashes, but there were no casualties, and after some softening up by naval bombardment, the Argentine garrison surrendered to the

British marines. In the process, the helicopters accounted for an enemy submarine that was caught on the surface and so damaged by depth charges and an AS-12 guided missile that it had to be beached and abandoned.

Surprise at Port Stanley

As the British task force plowed its way through the South Atlantic, the Argentine troops dug into defensive positions on the Falkland Islands. At the same time, the FAA deployed the bulk of its short-range attack aircraft on three island airfields — Port Stanley, Goose Green and Pebble Island — and defended them with Tigercat and Roland SAMs, and light antiaircraft guns. The first belligerent move against the growing strength of the Argentines was made by the RAF. On May 1, a single Vulcan of 101 Squadron attacked Port Stanley airfield. The mission (code-named Black Buck) was flown from Wideawake. Fifteen Victor tankers were involved in getting the bomber to its target and back. At the time, the 7,860-mile round-trip was the longest operational bombing sortie ever flown. Twenty-one 1,000-pound iron bombs were dropped on radar from 10,000 feet and a large hole was blown in the center of the runway. Since the task force was now within range, follow-up low-level attacks on Port Stanley and Goose Green were flown from HMS *Hermes* by Sea Harriers of 800 Squadron.

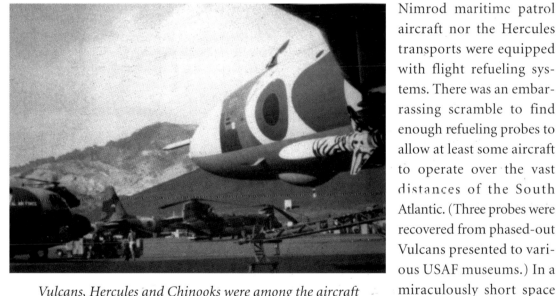

Vulcans, Hercules and Chinooks were among the aircraft crowding Wideawake Airfield on Ascension Island as British forces concentrated for Operation Corporate to recover the Falkland Islands.

The damage to the Port Stanley runway prevented, at least for a while, any move by the Argentines to deploy their more capable fast jets forward to the islands and so resolve their radius-of-action problem, though the amount of effort expended to get one Vulcan over its target seemed out of proportion to the result achieved. However, that proved not to be the main effect of the raid. That the RAF had heavy bombers that could reach the Falklands came as something of a shock to Argentina's leaders, and the thought occurred to them that the British might take it into their heads to bomb Buenos Aires. With that possibility in mind, an order went out restricting the Mirages, the FAA's only specialized interceptors, to the air defense of mainland Argentina. It was a decision that had significant implications for the air war over the Falklands.

It's a Long Way to Argentina

By the time Argentine forces invaded the Falklands, the RAF had almost abandoned its ability to fly over very long distances. The Vulcans, the RAF's last strategic bombers, were being phased out of service, and the few that remained were no longer fitted with refueling probes. Neither the Nimrod maritime patrol aircraft nor the Hercules transports were equipped with flight refueling systems. There was an embarrassing scramble to find enough refueling probes to allow at least some aircraft to operate over the vast distances of the South Atlantic. (Three probes were recovered from phased-out Vulcans presented to various USAF museums.) In a miraculously short space of time, the Vulcans had their probes replaced, flight refueling systems for the Nimrod and the Hercules were designed, built, fitted and tested, and the crews trained in the art of flight refueling. Nimrods began flying reconnaissance sorties covering over 8,000 miles to keep an eye on the Argentine Navy, and the Vulcans flew several more Black Bucks, on one of which a Skyguard radar was damaged by an AGM-45 Shrike. More specialized ELINT (electronic intelligence) sorties were flown by Nimrod R-1s and Canberra PR-9s from bases in a neutral South American country.

First Blood

It did not take long for the Argentines to respond to the first British strikes. Attacks on the British task force were made on the afternoon of May 1 by Skyhawks, Daggers and Canberras. Three ships suffered slight damage, but the attackers lost two Mirages, a Dagger and a Canberra to the Royal Navy's fighters. The Sea Harrier's first success was scored by Flight Lieutenant Paul Barton, an RAF officer on exchange duty with the navy, who described the shattering effect of his Sidewinder on a Mirage: "The missile hit him on the port side of the fuselage, then the whole rear half of the aircraft disappeared in a great ball of flame. The front half went down burning fiercely, arcing toward the sea." Barton was sure that the pilot could not have survived, but Lieutenant Carlos Petrona managed to eject when his Mirage broke up round him. He came down by parachute in shallow water just off the coast of West Falkland and waded ashore. His flight leader, Captain Garcia Cuerva, was not so fortunate. With his Mirage severely damaged by a missile from Barton's wingman, Lieutenant Steve Thomas, Cuerva struggled toward Port Stanley. As he approached the airfield, he was fired on by every available Argentine gun and hit several times. The Mirage crashed to the ground, finished off by friendly fire. Cuerva did not survive.

To the northwest, another Argentine threat was in the making. The aircraft carrier *25 de Mayo* and its escorts reached a point some 200 miles from the British task force and prepared to launch its Skyhawks. To his frustration, Rear Admiral Juan Lombardo found himself in an area of no wind, which meant that he could not catapult his aircraft off with the necessary fuel and weapons loads to carry out their mission. Another planned naval attack, by two land-based Super Etendards carrying Exocet missiles, was defeated when an attempted flight refueling failed and the aircraft had to turn back. Nevertheless, the naval threat to the British task force was very real. Another group of Argentine ships, led by the cruiser *General Belgrano,* was patrolling off to the southeast, waiting the call to join in any surface action should the carrier's strikes be successful. To diminish the threat, the nuclear submarine HMS *Conqueror* attacked the enemy cruiser. Two torpedoes struck home and the *General Belgrano* sank a short time later with the loss of over 300 men. The remaining Argentine ships, including the *25 de Mayo*, immediately withdrew to coastal waters and took no further part in the war.

Enter the Exocet

To this point, the Argentine forces had been taking most of the punishment. Now the British began to share the pain. On May 4, three Sea Harriers of 800 Squadron carried out a low-level attack on Goose Green airfield. One was hit by ground fire and crashed, killing the pilot. A few hours later, the Argentines struck a much greater blow. Refueled by a

C-130 tanker and guided to their target by a patrolling Neptune, two Super Etendards fired Exocet missiles at blips on their radars. One missile fell harmlessly into the sea, but the other hit HMS *Sheffield*, a Type 42 destroyer, amidships. It did not explode, but the impact of the half-ton missile traveling at 680 mph caused massive damage, and unburned rocket fuel started an intense fire that ignited insulating material, producing choking clouds of acrid smoke. It proved impossible to save the ship, which was abandoned and sank while under tow in heavy seas six days later. The suspected vulnerability of existing warships to sea-skimming missiles had been powerfully confirmed. It was fortunate for the Royal Navy that the Argentine stock of Exocets was only five.

Bad weather reduced air activity for a few days, though the Sea Harriers were able to maintain their combat air patrols (CAPs) over the task force. In a notable demonstration of one of the advantages of V/STOL, the Sea Harriers showed that, unlike their more conventional counterparts, they could operate even when the ships were steaming downwind or shrouded in fog. Landing on in heavy seas was a simpler matter, too, with the Harrier able to match its speed to that of the ship before settling on to the deck at the midpoint, where the motion was at a minimum. When the weather cleared on May 12, the Skyhawks struck again, attacking HMS *Glasgow* and *Brilliant* off Port Stanley. *Glasgow* was effectively put out of action after being hit by a 500-pound bomb that failed to explode. The Skyhawks paid for their success, losing four of their number, two to Seawolf SAMs from *Brilliant*, one to their own overeager gunners in Port Stanley, and another that just flew into the sea.

Helicopter Ups and Downs

The British helicopter force, operating intensively in all weathers, had mixed fortunes. There had been some extremely long sorties flown on antisubmarine duties, one Sea King staying airborne for over ten hours, refuel-

In May 1982, Harriers GR 3s of 1 Squadron, RAF, were deployed to the carrier HMS Hermes *to join the Royal Navy task force sent to recapture the Falklands Islands. The Harriers performed attack sorties from the carrier, and later from basic landing strips on the islands, often in conditions that would have grounded conventional aircraft. Three GR 3s were lost to the intense antiaircraft gunfire.*

ing in flight from nearby frigates. Other Sea Kings put special forces on to the Falklands where they remained undetected, passing back information on Argentine dispositions and preparing for diversionary attacks aimed at masking the eventual landings of the main British invasion force. On May 12, a Sea King crashed after engine failure, and five days later two more were lost, one to radar altimeter failure and the other when it came down in Chile, packed with special forces soldiers, and was burned by its crew. Yet another went down in the sea following a bird strike, killing twenty-one soldiers. On a better day for the SAS, troops were put ashore at Pebble Island, where they destroyed six Pucarás, four Mentors, and a Skyvan before being lifted off without loss.

Helicopters were an essential part of the British plan for recovering the Falkland Islands, so each loss noticeably affected the capability of the task force. During the early part of the campaign, helicopters were involved primarily in operations from the ships, but it was obvious that once the main body of troops was ashore on islands bare of infrastructure the ability of the force to move effectively would depend heavily on rotary-winged "trucks." On May 25, the Argentines struck a telling blow at that element of the task force, although they did not know it at the time. Among the largest and most heavily laden of the British supply vessels was the *Atlantic Conveyor*, a container ship of 15,000 tons that was steaming with the two carriers and their escorts some 70 miles northeast of the islands. The week before, eight additional Sea Harriers and six RAF Harrier GR 3s had been flown off the *Atlantic Conveyor*'s deck and delivered to

the carriers, but the rest of the vessel's valuable cargo remained on board.

In an attempt to break the back of the British campaign by inflicting mortal damage on the carriers, two Super Etendards, each carrying an Exocet, took off from Rio Grande air base on the afternoon of May 25. They flew well to the north of the Falklands, refueled from a KC-130 tanker, then turned south toward the area where the carriers were thought to be, attacking from an unexpected direction. The frigate Ambuscade, on the northern edge of the task force, was the first to detect radar transmissions from the Super Etendards. Alerted, the warships in the fleet fired chaff rockets and Lynx helicopters fitted with missile decoy equipment were scrambled. Soon afterward, an Exocet appeared, low over the sea, and smashed into the side of the *Atlantic Conveyor*. A huge fire was started that spread rapidly through the ship. Twelve men died and it proved impossible to rescue any of the cargo. The ship drifted on for another five days before sinking. Besides a supply of cluster bombs, quantities of aircraft spares, dozens of vehicles and thousands of tents, ten

helicopters (three Chinooks, six Wessex, and one Lynx) were lost. It was a shattering blow to British plans. If there was any good news for the British forces in all this, it was that the other Exocet had not found a target, the carriers were intact, and one Chinook had been flown off Atlantic Conveyor just before the attack. It was to perform prodigiously in the days to come.

Maximum Effort at San Carlos

The main British landings on East Falkland went ashore in San Carlos Water, at the western end of the island, before first light on May 21. The Sea Harriers flew CAPs continuously, and the GR 3s attacked Argentine positions, including a concentration of helicopters near Mount Kent, where a Chinook and two Pumas were destroyed by cannon fire. Pucará ground-attack aircraft interfered with the landings and two were shot down, one by a Sea Harrier and the other by a Stinger missile. In reply the Argentine troops claimed two Gazelle helicopters and a Harrier GR 3 of No. 1 Squadron, from which the pilot, Flight Lieutenant Jeff Glover, ejected and was taken prisoner.

The heaviest air fighting of the war took place between May 21 and 25. In that period, the Argentine air arms flew 180 fighter sorties, of which 117 were reported to have reached their targets. In response, from half as many aircraft, the British carriers succeeded in generating some 300 Sea Harrier and GR 3 sorties. Nineteen of the 117 attackers were destroyed — twelve fell to Sea Harriers, five to SAMs or guns, one was shared between the guns and a Sea Harrier, and one was an Argentine "own goal." It was a loss of more than 16 percent, a crippling rate for any attacking force to suffer, especially when the front-line strength available is limited from the outset. In the face of this punishment, the Argentine airmen continued to press home their attacks with great courage and determination. They scored repeated hits on the British ships, which saved themselves from being even more savagely treated than they were by the ferocity of their defense, forcing the attackers to fly at very low level, and often to release their bombs at a height so low that there was not time for them to arm.

Operating at extreme range, without modern avionics,

On May 4, 1982, HMS Sheffield was struck by an Exocet missile. The warhead failed to go off, but the fires started by the missile's fuel led to the loss of the ship six days later.

and needing to drop bombs fused for delivery no lower than an uncomfortably high 150 feet, the Argentine airmen nevertheless proved themselves a force to be reckoned with, sinking some ships and holing many more. Between May 21 and 25, the list of British ships hit lengthened at an alarming rate — two destroyers (*Antrim* seriously damaged by a 1,000-pound bomb that failed to explode; *Coventry* sunk by three bombs); five frigates (*Argonaut* seriously damaged by two unexploded bombs; *Ardent* hit on three separate attacks and sunk; *Antelope* damaged by two unexploded bombs, one of which later exploded and sank the ship; *Brilliant* damaged by strafing; *Broadsword* damaged by strafing and then by an unexploded bomb); and three fleet auxiliaries (*Sir Galahad, Sir Lancelot,* and *Sir Bedivere* all damaged by unexploded bombs); plus the sinking of the *Atlantic Conveyor.* It was an impressive achievement in five days, even at the cost of nineteen fighter-bombers, and at the end of that period it was the

British commanders who were beginning to wonder if they could stand the pace. However, although it was not apparent at the time, the war had taken a turn in Britain's favor by May 25. There were fewer attacks on British ships, and the troops ashore, by then well established in their bridgehead, were ready to move out and retake the Falklands.

Over Peat and Rock

On the morning of May 26, British commandos and paratroops began moving out of the San Carlos beachhead. For the next twenty days they walked (or "yomped" as they called it) over endless miles of soggy peat bog broken occasionally by rock, weighed down by weapons and equipment and enduring the extremes of winter in the South Atlantic, for the most part without benefit of shelter. In between times they fought fierce battles at such out of the way places as Goose Green, Mount Longdon, Wireless Ridge and Tumbledown Mountain. The clear weather that had marked the period of

Dassault Super Etendards of the Argentine Navy's 2nd Fighter/Attack Squadron flying from Rio Grande, Argentina, twice used their Exocet missiles to great effect during the Falklands War. The Royal Navy destroyer Sheffield *was hit on May 4, 1982, and the cargo ship* Atlantic Conveyor *on May 25. Both ships were sunk.*

aerial combat over San Carlos gave way to gales and storms, and air activity slowed. The tireless helicopters flew on, often in almost impossible conditions, and when there was a break the Harrier GR 3s added their support to the soldiers' efforts, silencing enemy guns and softening up strong points with rockets and cluster bombs.

The sole surviving Chinook helicopter, with no servicing manuals, spares, or special tools available since the loss of *Atlantic Conveyor*, performed valiant service, flying in all weathers and almost always grossly overloaded. On one sortie it lifted eighty-one troops with their weapons to a forward position, and on another, undertaken at night with low cloud obscuring the hills, it flew to Mount Kent carrying twenty-two soldiers and two 105 mm guns internally, with a third gun slung underneath. Returning from delivering this heavy load, flying the Chinook low and fast with the aid of night-vision goggles, the pilot entered a snow shower. Momentarily unable to see where he was going, he felt the helicopter shudder as it struck something. The nose was well up and the back end of the machine had hit the surface of a creek. The flat bottom of the Chinook skated across the water, throwing up spray that flooded into the engine intakes. The engines began to wind down and the hydraulically assisted power controls reverted to manual. Both pilots combined to heave the big helicopter clear of the surface, the spray stopped and the engines wound up again. The "waterskiing trials of the Chinook," as they were called, had lasted about twelve seconds.

The Westland Sea King proved remarkably durable and versatile during the Falklands War, in roles as diverse as searching for submarines, transporting troops, replenishing supplies, and inserting special forces behind enemy lines. British troops out on the wintry landscape of the Falklands were glad to hear the sound of the Sea King's rotor blades.

It's Not Over Till It's Over

With the British troops closing on their goal of Port Stanley, the end of the war seemed to be at hand, and the combination of Sea Harriers and bad weather appeared to have reduced the aerial threat to bearable proportions. However, the Argentine airmen still had some unpleasant surprises in store for their enemies. On June 8 they launched their Daggers and Skyhawks once more. Five Daggers went to Falkland Sound, where they attacked the frigate HMS *Plymouth*. None of the four bombs that struck *Plymouth* exploded but one of them set off a depth charge, starting a serious fire. The frigate limped into San Carlos Water and lived to fight another day.

On the other side of East Falkland, the Landing Ships Logisitic (LSL) *Sir Tristram* and *Sir Galahad* were stationary off Fitzroy, where they were waiting under clear skies to land units of the Welsh Guards. For once, they were without adequate cover against air attack, since the Sea Harrier CAP had chased off to deal with the aircraft attacking Plymouth, and the accompanying Rapier missiles had not yet been set up ashore. Just after 1 P.M. four Skyhawks of the FAA's Grupo 5 found them and attacked, unhindered by the usually effective defenses. Bombs struck both ships and detonated. Fierce fires broke out and the ships were quickly enveloped in thick smoke. Fifty-one men were killed and forty-six injured, many of them seriously burned. It was the worst single incident for the British forces in the whole campaign. Having demonstrated conclusively that they were still weapons to be feared, the Skyhawks flew back untouched to their base.

Later in the day, the Sea Harriers exacted some retribution from Grupo 5. Two fighters of 800 Squadron were patrolling over Choiseul Sound to the south of East Falkland just as dusk was falling. Flight Lieutenant Dave Morgan saw Skyhawks attacking a small landing craft and, together with his wingman, Lieutenant Dave Smith, he dived to intercept. He was quickly in behind his targets and: "I locked up my missile at about 1,500 yards and fired at 1,000 yards. My missile did a quick jink, then went off after him and exploded near his tail; there was a huge fireball and wreckage began to fall into the water." Morgan turned toward another Skyhawk and fired again: "The explosion took off everything behind where the fin joined the fuselage, then the front end yawed violently and dropped into the water." Dave Smith fired next and: "Then the darkness was lit up by another fierce flash and a fireball." He must have been flying so low that the missile impact and ground impact seemed almost simultaneous." The fourth Skyhawk pilot escaped to take the news of the death of his three comrades back to Grupo 5.

IAI Daggers, acquired from Israel, were flown by Argentina's air force (Fuerza Aerea Argentina) in low-level attacks on the British fleet during the Falklands War. Here a Dagger of Grupo 6 hurtles through San Carlos Water at low level on the morning of May 24, 1982. The supply ships Stromness *(in the background) and* Resource *(bow only) are ignored as the Argentine pilot looks for Royal Navy warships.*

The Falklands Recovered

In the closing days of the Falklands War the fighting for control of the high ground to the west of Port Stanley intensified. In the air, the Army's light Scout helicopters distinguished themselves, bringing out wounded under fire and attacking Argentine troops with SS-11 wire-guided missiles. The seventh and final Black Buck sortie was flown by a Vulcan from Ascension that attacked the Port Stanley airfield with air burst bombs. An FAA Learjet was shot down during a high-altitude reconnaissance sortie by a Sea Dart missile fired from HMS *Exeter*, and the same ship repeated its success when a Canberra attempted a night raid on the British positions near Mount Kent. The fifth and last Exocet was fired from a makeshift ramp near Port Stanley on June 13; it hit the destroyer HMS *Glamorgan* and caused serious damage, again without exploding. On June 14 two GR 3s took off from HMS *Hermes* to attack Argentine troops on Sapper Hill with laser-guided bombs; they were recalled as they approached their target because white flags were flying from the Argentine positions. The war was over.

It had been a war in which first the sailors and then the soldiers occupied center stage, but in which the airmen had vital roles to play throughout the conflict. A number of military aviation firsts were recorded in the air — the use of V/STOL aircraft in combat; the sustaining of a ground force advance almost entirely by helicopter; the firing of sea-skimming missiles by aircraft against warships; and the regular use of flight refueling by both sides. Operational sorties were completed that were longer than any ever flown until that time, by large aircraft such as the Nimrod, Vulcan and Victor, and also by the RAF's reinforcement Harrier GR 3s, which flew nonstop from the United Kingdom to Ascension, and then from Ascension to the task force, where the pilots accomplished their first ever landings on a ship after eight and a half hours in the air.

Things might have been different if a plentiful supply of Exocets had been available to Argentina, and there is little

Triumphant return. HMS Hermes *returns to Portsmouth from the Falklands on July 21, 1982, after 108 days at sea. Argentine reports had more than once claimed the carrier to have been sunk.*

doubt that the British campaign could not have been conducted without the Sea Harrier / Sidewinder combination, which fought with great success, despite the lack of an early warning system and the small number of fighters engaged. (There were never more than 25 Sea Harriers on the line at any one time.) For their part, suffering crippling losses though they did, Argentina's airmen reminded sailors everywhere of the risks involved in operating surface ships within reach of land-based air power, sinking six ships and damaging ten more. The aerial balance sheet showed that Argentina lost 102 aircraft from all causes (including accidents and 32 captured after the surrender) against a British loss of 34. Most notable were the Sea Harrier's figures — 25 aircraft shot down without loss in aerial combat.

THE GULF WAR
A Case for the UN

The Cold War was over and there was much to celebrate, but as the world entered the 1990s, it was made uncomfortably aware that postwar fruits often bear the seeds of other problems. With the principal adversary no longer able to take the field, the solid template against which NATO's force structure had been designed and shaped over many years faded to insubstantial shadow. Consequently it became less simple to define roles for air forces in the post Cold War era. Given the previous experiences of politically limited war in Korea and Vietnam, predictions of possible future employment in trouble spots around the world were not encouraging. However, the USAF in particular was equipped to meet any global challenge, and in 1990 it was ready when the world witnessed blatant aggression on the shores of the Persian Gulf. Saddam Hussein of Iraq instructed his forces to invade Kuwait, thereby setting the scene for a limited conflict in which air power advocates would see their cherished convictions amply vindicated. Early in the morning of August 2, 1990, the Iraqi Army burst across the frontier with Kuwait in great strength. More than 100,000 troops and several hundred tanks brushed aside such little resistance as they encountered and within hours the tiny Gulf emirate was firmly in Saddam's grasp. The world's fourth-largest army now stood on Saudi Arabia's doorstep, and Saddam Hussein appeared poised to become the man dominating Middle East oil. Reverberations from Iraq's action shook the world's economic foundations and international reaction was immediate. The UN Security Council condemned the invasion and President George Bush ordered U.S. Navy units into the region.

Desert Shield

By August 6, the UN had authorized worldwide economic sanctions against Iraq, and President Bush had announced the movement of U.S. Army and Air Force units to the Middle East in Operation Desert Shield. Initially, the aim of the U.S. forces was to defend Saudi Arabia against the further ambitions of Saddam Hussein. Communications and surveillance satellites were maneuvered into positions from which they could better support any U.S. operations, and Military Airlift Command got ready to undertake the largest airlift in history.

On August 7, within eighteen hours of the President's order, MAC's C-141s and C-5s began the deployment of the 82nd Airborne Division's "Ready Brigade" and the supporting elements of the 1st Tactical Fighter Wing's F-15 squadrons. The forty-eight F-15Cs of the wing were on their way, too, flying nonstop from Langley AFB, Virginia, to Dhahran, Saudi Arabia, refueling seven or eight times during a flight averaging over fourteen hours. In confirmation of allied solidarity, the United Kingdom deployed RAF Tornados on the following day. By the middle of the month, other USAF squadrons of F-15Cs and Es, F-4G Wild Weasels, A-10s, and F-16s joined these trailblazers in Saudi Arabia, and E-3 AWACS aircraft began a continuous patrol over the troubled area. On August 21, twenty-two F-117 Nighthawk stealth aircraft took off from their base in Nevada to exchange the desert surroundings of one continent for those of another. While all this was happening, USAFE F-111s and F-16s arrived at bases in Turkey, and SAC deployed its U-2R/TR-1A reconnaissance assets and moved B-52s forward to Diego Garcia in the Indian Ocean.

Looked at in terms of scale, rate or distance, the U.S. military buildup in Saudi Arabia was impressive. The air bridge was particularly remarkable. Once established, it spanned nearly half the globe and saw a cargo aircraft landing somewhere in the Middle East every ten minutes or so. By the end of the campaign, the USAF's strategic airlift had recorded 20,500 missions (a mission being a completed movement from origin to destination, regardless of intermediate stops), carried 534,000 passengers, and hauled 542,000 tons of cargo. The airlift totaled 4.65 billion ton/miles, which compared to just under 700 million for the sixty-five weeks of the Berlin Airlift in 1948.

From the USAF's point of view, the operation was a timely vindication of the case for maintaining a truly balanced air force, capable of accomplishing tasks across the whole wide spectrum of air power and of responding swiftly to an emergency anywhere in the world. The projection of global power could not have been done without the fleet of large-capacity cargo and tanker aircraft in the USAF's inventory, nor without the ready availability of well-trained Reserve and National Guard personnel to fill gaps in the front line. Given Iraq's considerable forces and their aggressive intent, good reconnaissance was essential too, and on the assumption that Saddam was not going to back down and withdraw from Kuwait, aircraft were needed for every combat role, from air superiority through conventional bombing to tank-busting. Behind this aerial armada there had to be

the supporting services that enabled it to fight — command and control facilities, maintenance, armaments, food, accommodation, medical services, administration, et cetera. During the months following the President's launching order, the personnel and equipment to make such a force function were uprooted from their U.S. bases, transported many thousands of miles to work in unfamiliar (and often basic) surroundings, and asked to create an air force that was instantly combat-ready and capable of defeating any opposition it met. That all this was done, and done superlatively well, is a tribute to the professionalism that had been achieved in the USAF during the 1980s.

After August, the momentum in the Gulf changed hands. The Iraqis became more concerned with the defense of their ill-gotten gains than with posing an offensive threat to Saudi Arabia. By mid-January 1991, they were well dug in, but the Coalition forces opposing them were strong enough to undertake the recovery of Kuwait with confidence. The UN call for troops had been answered by twenty-two nations, and the U.S. contingent had risen to more than 400,000. The overall commander of the Coalition forces was General Norman Schwarzkopf, U.S. Army, though all Arab national forces remained under the operational control of the Saudi Chief of Staff, Prince Khalid. Deputy to Schwarzkopf, and theater air forces commander, was Lieutenant General Charles Horner, USAF. From the beginning, it was apparent that the mistakes of Vietnam were not going to be repeated. There would be no micromanaging from Washington. The President, the Secretary of Defense and the Chairman of the Joint Chiefs of Staff would decide policies and set goals, but the planning and execution of operations would be left to the discretion of the theater commander.

On November 29, 1990, a UN resolution was adopted that approved the use of "all necessary means" to remove Iraqi forces from Kuwait if they did not leave voluntarily by January 15, 1991. Saddam remained recalcitrant. He would not leave what he called his nineteenth province, and he assured the Coalition that he would order the use of chemical weapons in repulsing attacks on his forces. On January 12, with the UN's deadline approaching and Iraq's leaders still unmoved by universal condemnation of their aggression, the U.S. Congress gave President Bush the authority to go to war. In the desert, nearly one million soldiers and airmen faced each other and prepared themselves for what

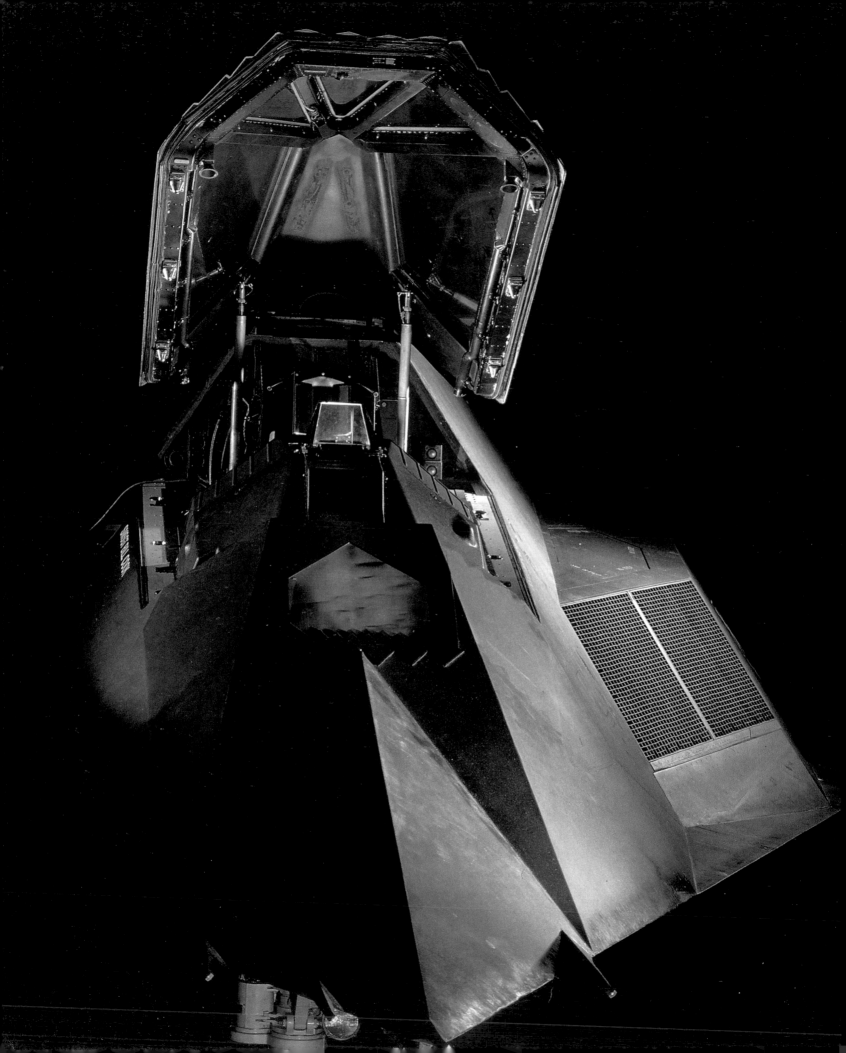

OPPOSITE *The many-faceted fuselage of the arrowhead-shaped Lockheed F-117A Nighthawk is designed to reflect radar signals at different angles, and the aircraft's exterior is manufactured from radar-absorbent materials. The engine intakes on either side of the nose are covered by grills with strips closer together than an enemy's radar wavelength. In front of the cockpit, a fine mesh covers the forward-looking infrared sensor. The first operational mission of the stealthy F-117A was carried out during Operation Just Cause in Panama in 1989. It was later used more extensively in the Balkans and the Middle East.*

Saddam had promised would be the "mother of all battles." The Coalition's generals had every reason to believe that he was right, and that the recovery of Kuwait was not going to be an easy matter. The Iraqi forces had spent five months preparing a defensive line in Kuwait that included bunkers, berms, minefields, masses of razor wire, and oil-filled ditches ready for burning. General Tony McPeak, USAF Chief of Staff, described Iraq's protection against air attack as "a first class air defense, not a featherweight opponent." It was indeed formidable, with advanced aircraft such as the MiG-29 among those equipping the Iraqi Air Force's thirty-nine fighter squadrons, and ground defenses that included some 9,000 AAA guns and perhaps 17,000 SAMs, all backed by modern radars and computer data links.

If Saddam Hussein had hoped for an early commitment of ground forces in an assault on his fortress, he was disappointed. The first blows, and most of those that followed, were struck from the air. By mid-January 1991, the 690 combat aircraft of the Iraqi Air Force were outmatched in both quality and quantity by those of the Coalition air forces. Ten countries had contributed units to raise the front-line strength of the Coalition in the Gulf region to almost 2,500 fixed-wing aircraft. Of these, the USAF provided 50 percent, the USN 16 percent, the USMC 7 percent, and allied air forces 27 percent. The air plan of campaign was split into four phases. In Phase 1, Coalition airmen were to gain air superiority over Iraq and Kuwait, destroy Iraqi strategic attack capability, and disrupt the enemy command and control system. Phase 2 would suppress the air defenses around Kuwait, and Phase 3 would see the weight of attack shifted to the Iraqi Army deployed around Kuwait, while continuing to pursue the objectives of Phases 1 and 2 as necessary. Phase 4 was concerned with air support for ground operations as and when they took place. As it happened, the air strength available to the Coalition commanders was such that it was possible to run the first three phases concurrently.

TOP *GBU-12 Paveway II 500-pound bombs were used by F-117As and a variety of other attack aircraft during Operation Desert Storm.* BOTTOM *F-117 tail number 781, now on display at the National Museum of the USAF, was an aerodynamic test aircraft, first flown on September 24, 1981. In the interests of security, the original surface was replaced by a layer of black paint, and the exhaust ports were faired over to prevent anyone from peering inside to see the details of how the exhaust was constructed.*

To Iraqi early-warning radar operators, the returns they saw on their screens during the early morning hours of January 17 at first looked no different from those they had grown used to seeing for months. AWACS aircraft and F-15 combat patrols were orbiting just inside Saudi Arabian airspace as usual. But this would not be just another quiet night for Iraq. What the operators could not see were hundreds of aircraft forming into strike packages outside the range of their early-warning cover. Nor did they realize that their units were at the top of the Coalition target list. The first shots of the Desert Storm campaign were fired at two radar sites by a special team of U.S. Army AH-64 Apache helicopters, led into position by MH-53J Pave Low helicopters of the USAF. Hellfire laser-guided missiles and 2.75-inch rockets from the Apaches destroyed the sites, punching a hole in the Iraqi air defense screen through which the initial waves of strike aircraft could flow unseen.

At about 1 A.M. local time, as the Apaches were making their way to their targets, tankers from the USAF, USN and RAF got airborne to establish their refueling stations. Combat air patrols were strengthened with more F-15s, USN F-14s, Canadian CF-18s and RAF Tornado F.3s. Strike aircraft began taking off from bases in Saudi Arabia and Turkey, and from aircraft carriers in the Persian Gulf and the Red Sea. At 3 A.M., all hell broke loose over Iraq. From the ships in the Gulf came the first of a barrage of Tomahawk missiles, which led the attack on Saddam Hussein's capital of Baghdad. In the course of the longest bombing raid ever, a thirty-five-hour mission from Barksdale AFB, Louisiana, B-52Gs launched AGM-86C ALCMs at Baghdad's power stations and communications facilities.

The nose of Ol' Rigor Mortis, *the Apache helicopter flown by Lieutenant Colonel Dick Cody in the early hours of January 17, 1991, when he led the attack on Iraqi air defense radar sites and opened the way for the air assault on Baghdad.*

Confusing the issue for the defenders in the early stages of the attack were almost 200 pilotless decoys. These drew the attention of antiaircraft radars, which thereby exposed themselves to the HARMs (High-speed Anti-Radiation Missiles) of predatory Wild Weasels.

At about the time that the Apaches were turning away from reducing their targets to rubble, the F-117A Nighthawks made their surreptitious entrance, first attacking radars close to Baghdad and then a communications center in the city. Before the night was out, the Nighthawks had hit thirty-four targets, using a variety of laser-guided bombs. The F-117A's low observable technology (commonly called "stealth") allowed it to operate in Iraqi airspace at night with impunity. It was used to attack high-value targets, especially those in heavily defended areas where precision was vital and it might be necessary to orbit while identifying the aiming point. Command centers, control bunkers, chemical/nuclear facilities, critical bridges and the like were almost invariably struck with startling accuracy.

As the follow-up raids approached their targets, it was apparent that Iraq's defensive system was crumbling from the effects of the earlier strikes. F-111s, F15Es, F/A18s, and RAF and Saudi Tornados went after air bases, SS-1 (Scud) missile sites, and more radars. They were supported by EF-111 Ravens, jamming whatever electronic emissions survived the onslaught. One EF-111 scored a defensive victory after dodging a missile fired by an Iraqi Mirage. The Raven's tight diving turn behind a screen of chaff and infrared decoys finished just above the desert, but the chasing Mirage did not pull out. The EF-111's crew reported: "We got so low, he couldn't hack it and smeared into the ground behind us." It was the first Iraqi aircraft destroyed during Desert Storm air combat.

The first conventional air-to-air "kill" was achieved by an F-15C pilot, Captain Steve Tate of the 1st Tactical Fighter Wing. Alerted by AWACS to the presence of a "bogey" approaching his flight, Tate confirmed it as "not friendly" and loosed off an AIM-7 Sparrow at 12 miles range. The weapon struck an Iraqi Mirage, which disappeared in a huge fireball. It was a rare encounter. Not many Iraqi Air Force aircraft got airborne and contacts with those that did were few and far between. For their part, the ground-based defenders fired copious quantities of AAA and SAMs, but got little return for their efforts. Over 670 sorties were flown by Coalition aircraft that first night, without loss. (Initially, the Iraqis claimed that over 100 Coalition aircraft had been shot down. It may have been so. Over 100 decoys went down in or around Baghdad and might have either fallen or been shot down. It was not the first time that small aircraft falling to earth in the middle of an intense antiaircraft barrage had been claimed by the defenses. The same thing happened during the first night of the German V-1 attack on London in 1944. It was not initially understood by the gunners that the V-1 was accomplishing its mission if it fell to earth.)

General Dick Cody seen in 2005 with three members of his 1-101st Aviation Regiment team that fired the first shots of Operation Desert Storm. From left to right: Chief Warrant Officer Greg Turberville (Battalion Standardization Pilot); Lieutenant Colonel Doug Gabram; General Cody; Chief Warrant Officer Tim Vincent (Battalion Master Gunner). General Cody was a lieutenant colonel during that action. He is now Vice-Chief of Staff of the United States Army

By midnight on the first day, Coalition aircraft had flown over 2,100 sorties and the Iraqi air defenses were severely degraded. During the hours of daylight, the Coalition suffered its first losses — an F/A-18 and an A-6E of the USN, a Kuwaiti A-4, and three Tornados, one Italian and two British. Since the Iraqi Air Force had flown only twenty-four fighter sorties, it was not surprising that none of the Coalition losses came in air-to-air combat. The Iraqis lost eight fighters, five of them to the F-15Cs of the 33rd TFW from Eglin AFB, Florida. The almost clinically impersonal nature of late-20th-century air warfare was summarized by one of the victorious F-15C pilots, Captain Charles Magill, a Marine exchange officer flying with the 33rd TFW: "When you get down to the bottom line, everything was incredibly basic. Weapons system set up just right, shoot your ordnance at the first opportune moment, watch the MiG blow up, and get the hell out."

Unable to withstand the Coalition's aerial onslaught, Iraq hit back in the only way guaranteed to cause international alarm. After dark on January 17, a Scud ballistic missile was fired at the Dhahran air base, but was claimed destroyed by a U.S. Army Patriot SAM before reaching the ground. Soon afterward, however, several more Scuds were fired at Tel Aviv and Haifa in Israel, causing casualties and some local damage. Militarily, the Scud was of little consequence. With its small warhead, limited range, and lack of accuracy, it was a minimal threat to the Coalition's operations. Even used with chemical warheads, it could not have affected the outcome of the struggle. However, fired at noncombatant Israel, the ineffective Scud became a political instrument of disturbing power. If Israel could be provoked into striking back, it was Saddam's hope that the fragile Coalition would break up, since the Arab allies would not wish to be seen fighting on the same side as their traditional enemy. Intense U.S. political pressure and the rapid deployment of Patriot batteries to Israel defused the crisis, and Israelis gritted their teeth to suffer in silence through a barrage of forty Scuds in the course of the conflict. Forty-six more Scuds were fired at Saudi Arabia, one of which demolished a U.S. barracks, killing twenty-eight Army reservists.

The business end of the McDonnell Douglas AH-64 Apache. Aerodynamic cleanliness is not a requirement in a battlefield helicopter. The lumps of the Target Acquisition and Designation Sight (TADS) sprout from the nose of Ol' Rigor Mortis, and Forward Avionics Bays (FABS) cling to the fuselage beneath the pilots on either side. Two General Electric T700-GE-701 turboshaft engines of 1,600 shaft horsepower bulge out behind the cockpit. General Dick Cody can be seen in the rear (pilot's) seat.

Another significant weapon against the Scuds was Boeing's E-8A Joint STARS, two prototypes of which were rushed to the Gulf to boost the Coalition's surveillance effort. Still in the development stage of the J-STARS battlefield control system, the E-8As were a great success. Their huge side-looking radars could detect stationary armored vehicles and provide an accurate plot of slow-moving objects.

Up to January 26, the main aims of the Coalition's air offensive were to ensure air supremacy and destroy Iraq's command and control system, with the Scud hunt as an unlooked-for complication. Some USAF strikes against Iraqi troop concentrations had been made in the early stages with A-10s and B-52s, and after January 26 these were stepped up, with other attack aircraft joining in. F-16s and A-10 "Warthogs" were the most numerous types deployed to the Gulf, some 200 of each seeing combat, and they were principally employed against Iraqi troops and vehicles. In close encounters, the A-10s used their 30 mm cannon to fearsome effect. One pair of Warthog pilots from the 23rd TFW claimed twenty-three tanks between them in one day, and two others, from the 10th TFW and the 926th Tactical Fighter Group and Air Force Reserve (TFG, AFRes), destroyed enemy helicopters, claiming the first ever air-to-air successes for the A-10.

Initially, B-52 missions were flown from the island of Diego Garcia in the Indian Ocean, but other bases in the United Kingdom, Spain and Saudi Arabia were used during the conflict. The bombers were B-52Gs, carrying

The political danger from the Scuds was such that considerable effort was devoted to finding and destroying them, diverting Coalition strike aircraft from other tasks and effectively forcing the extension of the planned period of Desert Storm air operations from thirty to thirty-nine days. Fixed Scud sites were quickly dealt with, but mobile launchers were more difficult. The "Great Scud Hunt" began on the night of January 18. The principal USAF hunters were F-15Es of the 4th TFW from Seymour Johnson AFB, North Carolina. They flew in pairs at about 15,000 feet, generally with the leader carrying four GBU-10 laser-guided bombs and the wingman armed with six CBU-87 cluster bombs. Sweeping ahead with their Low Altitude Navigation and Targeting Infrared for Night equipment (Lantirn), they searched for signs of mobile Scud missile launchers, attacking in sequence when a site was found.

loads of fifty-one 750-pound bombs to strike at soft targets, paying particular attention to the Republican Guard troop concentrations in the desert west of Basra. Flying in flights of three, they achieved coordinate releases of 153 bombs at a time, carpeting an area one and a half miles long by a mile wide. Apart from the damage done by such a weight of explosive, it had a marked psychological effect on troops. The morale of many Iraqi units was shattered by the B-52 attacks, which were instrumental in persuading large numbers of soldiers to surrender as soon as the Coalition ground offensive was launched.

As well as carrying out direct attacks on Iraqi Army units, Coalition aircraft struck at military storage areas and supply routes, aiming to weaken the enemy's fighting capability before the ground offensive. This did not mean that earlier targets were left untouched. Raids were still made deep into Iraq, searching out command and control centers and ensuring that the comatose air defense system did not get a chance to rise again. Many of the surviving elements of the Iraqi Air Force fled to safe havens in Iran, but the occasional contact was still made with enemy fighters in the air. On January 27, two F-15Cs of the 36th TFW from Bitburg AB, Germany, were vectored toward an enemy formation by a patrolling AWACS. In the hectic seconds after making contact and closing to firing range, the USAF pilots launched a rapid combination of AIM-7s and AIM-9s to shoot down three MiG-23s and one Mirage F-1.

On the night of January 27, the USAF struck an important blow for environmental causes. The Iraqis had seriously damaged Kuwait's oil fields, and were deliberately allowing two pumping stations to spill oil into the Persian Gulf. Three F-111F "Aardvarks" of the 48th TFW, RAF Lakenheath, U.K., made a precision attack on the pumping stations involved. The weapons were GBU-15 laser-guided bombs, tossed from two of the F-111Fs flying supersonic at 20,000 feet. The third "Aardvark," tracking parallel with the coast some 50 miles out to sea, guided the bombs onto their targets. Direct hits were scored on both stations and the flow of oil stopped. Success in such a newsworthy effort offered a rare moment of recognition to the crews of the F-111Fs. Dogged by their sometimes checkered past and overtaken in the public eye by newer types, the Aardvarks in the Gulf went about compiling the most impressive record of any strike aircraft in the war. By the time it was over, F-111Fs had been everywhere and attacked everything. They flew some 2,500 combat sorties and provided videotape confirmation that they had destroyed 2,203 targets, including at least 920 tanks, 252 artillery pieces, 245 hardened aircraft shelters, 13 runways, and 12 bridges (plus 52 more seriously damaged). Of over 8,000 precision-guided munitions dropped by USAF aircraft, 4,660 were carried by F-111Fs. (It was reported that one senior U.S. commander said during a raid briefing: "I want this target hit — give it

The fearsome armament of the Apache is prominent in this side view of Ol' Rigor Mortis. The standard AH-64 load was four AGM-114 Hellfire missiles on each inboard pylon and nineteen-tube rocket pods on the outboards. A 30 mm chain gun (M230) hangs beneath the nose. It fires High Explosive Dual Purpose (HEDP) ammunition at 650 rounds per minute and is capable of moving 86 degrees from side to side. The gun can be aimed by the copilot gunner using the TADS sensors, or by either pilot using the Integrated Helmet and Display Sight System (IHADSS).

OPPOSITE *A gun carriage for the 20th century. The Fairchild Republic A-10 was formally named Thunderbolt II, but is universally known as the "Warthog." It was designed to be highly maneuverable battlefield artillery and was built around the GAU-8 rotary cannon, which can deliver 30 mm depleted uranium rounds at a rate of 4,200 per minute. Up to 16,000 pounds of asssorted ordnance can also be carried. Heavy armor, multiple systems and widely separated engines high above the fuselage increase the Warthog's chances of survival when exposed to intense ground fire. The A-10 at the National Museum of the USAF is the one flown by Captain Paul Johnson on an epic eight-hour rescue support mission during Desert Storm. He was awarded the Air Force Cross.*

TOP *The inside of a bathtub is not usually like this. The A-10 cockpit sits within a protective titanium bathtub-shaped shield capable of withstanding a hit from a 23 mm shell. The windscreen is bulletproof glass, and the pilot sits on a "zero-zero" ejection seat — one that could safely be used when stationary on the ground.*

BOTTOM *On August 9, 1990, the 4th Tactical Fighter Wing at Seymour Johnson responded to the Iraqi invasion of Kuwait by deploying the F-15E Strike Eagles of the 336th Tactical Fighter Squadron to Saudi Arabia. The 335th TFS followed on December 27. During Operation Desert Storm, the 336th flew 1,088 combat missions and the 335th more than 1,200, attacking Scud missile sites, bridges and airfields. The 335th also made history by using a laser-guided bomb to down an enemy helicopter.*

to the F-111s.") As if to confirm their status, the Aardvarks finished the war in style, winning a fly-off with the F-15Es for the distinction of delivering the special GBU-28/B Deep Throat bomb, a weapon capable of penetrating over 100 feet of earth or 22 feet of reinforced concrete. On the last night of the war, two F-111Fs guided their new bombs into the hardened high command bunkers north of Baghdad, sending a message to Iraq's leaders that they were at personal risk even deep below ground.

As the days of February passed and the Coalition kept up its aerial assault on Iraq's military machine, the aircraft that formed the backbone of the USAF's front line flew combat sorties by the thousand, and some specialized types got a chance to demonstrate their true value. Among them were variants of the ubiquitous C-130. The EC-130H Compass Call added the final touches to the campaign to close the Iraqis' eyes and ears. With their computerized frequency scanning ability and batteries of jammers, Compass Call aircraft swamped the Iraqi airwaves, rendering reliable radio communication almost impossible for the enemy. First cousins to the EC-130H are the EC-130E PsyWar aircraft flown by the Pennsylvania Air National Guard. They can transmit over both commercial and military radio and television frequencies, and during Desert Shield / Storm they blanketed the Iraqis with broadcasts intended to demoralize both troops and civilians, simply by telling the truth about what was happening. Like the B-52s, they were credited with convincing large numbers of the enemy to surrender.

SWINGING WINGS

In the first phase of Operation Desert Storm, RAF Tornado GR 1s attacked Iraqi air bases at low level with Hunting JP233 airfield denial weapons. Later in the conflict they delivered Paveway II laser-guided bombs against other strategic targets. The RAF Tornado squadrons flew 1,500 operational sorties and lost six GR 1s in combat. OPPOSITE The aircraft on display at the National Museum of the USAF flew with 17 Squadron, RAF, from Dhahran, Saudi Arabia, where it took on desert camouflage and the name *Miss Behavin'*. BELOW Saudi Air Force Tornado F.3s, the air defense version of the aircraft, were on patrol over Saudi airspace immediately after Iraq's invasion of Kuwait. RAF F.3s were quickly deployed from the U.K. to join in, and remained in the region to fly patrols over the no-fly zones imposed on Iraq after the fighting stopped. Seen here are F.3s of 56 Squadron over eastern England.

ABOVE The F-111F Aardvark's long snout hides an AN/APQ-161 radar, with an AN/APQ-171 terrain-following set. The engine intakes on the 111-F were known as Triple Plow II, featuring three blow-in doors. Before engine start, the blow-in doors were closed. They opened as the TF30-100 turbofan engines powered up and gulped air. They remained open until after takeoff, when sufficient air could be provided by the intakes alone.

FORMIDABLE FIREPOWER

From front to rear, on the left of the fuselage, the Lockheed AC-130A carried an AN/ASQ-5 Black Crow vehicle ignition sensor, an AN/ASQ-24A stabilized tracking set, two M-61 six-barrel 20 mm cannon, an AN/AAD-4 FLIR (forward-looking infrarcd), two 7.62 mm machine guns, two 40 mm Bofors guns, an AN/APQ-133 beacon-tracking radar, and an AN/AVQ-17 searchlight. OPPOSITE The AC-130A on display at the National Museum of the USAF is the prototype gunship, which bears the name *Azrael*, Angel of Death.

RIGHT The AC-130A Hercules was powered by four 4,050-ehp Allison T56 turboprops and pulled along by square-tipped Hamilton Standard propellers.

BELOW Operation Desert Storm was the end of the A-7E Corsair II's twenty-four-year career with the U.S. Navy. Two squadrons of A-7Es (VA-46 and VA-72) deployed to the Gulf on board the carrier *John F. Kennedy*. In forty-two days of war, they flew 731 combat missions. The aircraft on display at Pensacola was flown by the squadron commander of VA-46 and logged thirty-seven combat missions over Iraq and Kuwait.

Colonel Harry M. Roberts is the Vice Commander of the 178th Fighter Wing, Ohio Air National Guard, located at Springfield-Beckley Municipal Airport in Springfield, Ohio. He was a member of the 401st Tactical Fighter Wing at Torrejon AB, Spain, where he served as a flight commander and flew combat sorties in operations Desert Shield and Desert Storm. Shot down over downtown Baghdad on January 19, 1991, he was captured and held as a POW for six weeks until combat operations ceased in March 1991.

"Hail Mary"

With the Iraqi Air Force reduced to impotence, and the enemy incapable of monitoring Coalition activities, General Schwarzkopf was able to set the desert stage for the final act of the Gulf War drama, secure in the knowledge that Saddam's forces were blind and deaf to his preparations. While maintaining a strong presence in front of Kuwait and trailing the coat of the U.S. Marines' assault ships as a distraction off shore, Schwarzkopf moved a huge force of U.S., British and French armored units westward into the desert, setting up a monstrous left hook to outflank the Iraqi Army and cut across its

The F-16 Fighting Falcon is a versatile aircraft, able to operate in all weathers, day or night. A total of 249 F-16s were deployed to the Gulf and they flew almost 13,500 sorties, the highest number of sorties for any system in the war. However, they were forced to fly at high and medium altitudes because of the AAA threat and, with a bombing system optimized for low-level attack, were not as effective overall as had been expected.

escape routes. As this was happening, the Coalition air forces pounded targets of all kinds, although attacks on enemy airfields were intensified for a while to insure against the possibility that the Iraqi Air Force might make one desperate concerted effort to respond to a ground offensive with chemical weapons.

Sepecat Jaguars were deployed to the Gulf in 1990 by both the RAF and the Armée de l'Air. They were assigned to battlefield interdiction duties using 1,000-pound bombs, cluster bombs and rockets against SAM sites, artillery, armored vehicles, troop concentrations and POL storage.

At 4 A.M. on the morning of February 24, 1991, strong Coalition ground forces, backed by overwhelming air support, thrust forward from their holding positions into Kuwait and southern Iraq. It was the largest combined offensive since World War II, involving as it did more than half a million troops. The frontal assault on Kuwait engaged the attention of the bulk of the Iraqi Army while the Coalition's armored columns raced across the desert far to the west. A-10s, helicopter gunships and Marine AV-8B Harriers came into their own, playing havoc with the enemy's armor, and in the west the inestimable value of plentiful tactical airlift was emphasized. The wettest weather for many years had turned extensive areas of the desert into a morass, and the army's supply convoys often got bogged down. C-130s, which had been heavily occupied already in moving troops and equipment to forward staging areas, now air-dropped tons of supplies to the rapidly moving spearheads, enabling them to maintain the momentum of their advance deep into enemy territory.

Their defensive plans unhinged by the crushing weight of the air campaign and by the speed and power of Schwarzkopf's armored left hook, most Iraqi troops either withdrew from their positions in confusion or surrendered in thousands. Those few who chose to stand and resist were comprehensively outgunned and outfought. Flushed from their carefully prepared bunkers and revetments, Iraqis attempting to scramble out of the battle area and escape were harried unmercifully by the Coalition's ever-present close air support. The road from Kuwait to Basra became a river of death and destruction, with the wreckage of hundreds of vehicles of all kinds scattered along it and in the desert nearby. By February 27, Coalition ground forces had advanced to place themselves across the escape routes from Kuwait and the Iraqi Army's resistance had effectively ceased. President Bush declared a ceasefire starting from 8 A.M. Baghdad time on February 28, exactly 100 hours after the ground assault began.

The Air Power Achievement

The Gulf War had lasted six weeks, all but four days of which was taken up by an air offensive against Iraq that was unrelenting in its severity. The Coalition air forces had flown 110,000 sorties, with the USAF claiming the lion's share. Losses had been remarkably light, totaling only thirty-five fixed-wing aircraft, fourteen of them from the USAF. All were attributable to ground fire. (They were two F-15Es, one F-4G, five F-16Cs, five A-10s, one EF-111A, and one AC-130H. A total of twenty aircrew were killed, fourteen of them in the AC-130H. Noncombat fixed-wing USAF accidents during the period of Desert Storm claimed a B-52G and two F-16Cs.) The Iraqi Air Force also lost thirty-five fixed-wing aircraft during combat sorties, but all of them were shot down in air-to-air engagements, thirty-one of them by F-15s of the USAF. Many more Iraqi aircraft were destroyed on the ground by air attack, and well over 100 others fled to the dubious haven of Iran.

Desert Storm was a crushing military victory, built on the often spectacular achievements of Coalition air power. From the speed of the initial response to Saddam's aggression and the creation of an air bridge thousands of miles long, to the imposition of air supremacy over Iraq and the effective destruction of the Iraqi Army as a fighting force, the Coalition's air forces demonstrated that air power properly used is a dominating factor in any major clash of arms. The USAF shouldered by far the greatest burden of any of the air forces involved in the Gulf War, and saw its dedication to advanced technologies justified in the performance of its newest and most complex systems.

Teamed with AWACS, the untried J-STARS provided unprecedented airborne battle control capabilities. The F-117As, F-15Es and EF-111As proved both effective and, to the surprise of some, extremely reliable, with serviceability rates approaching and occasionally exceeding an average of 90 percent. Precision guided munitions were a feature of the air campaign. Less than 8 percent of the 88,500 tons of bombs dropped were "smart," but they accounted for almost 80 percent of the targets known to have been destroyed by bombing. The Navstar Global Positioning System (GPS) and the Lantirn equipment were invaluable in enabling attack aircraft to maintain a round-the-clock, all-weather campaign against Iraq with astonishing (and for those on the receiving end, disturbing) accuracy.

None of this would have led to the remarkable results achieved if the available air power had not been properly used. The USAF's post-Vietnam insistence on recruiting the right people and giving them the best possible training paid off handsomely. In Desert Storm, the personnel of the Coalition air forces were notable for their professionalism. Perhaps just as significant was the political decision that, more than any other, exorcized the ghosts of Vietnam for the USAF — once it was determined that it was necessary to commit the military to action in the Gulf, the conduct of the campaign was left to the theater commander. He, in turn, had the advantage of dealing with a single air commander, who was able to use his air assets to the best possible effect. For once, it all came together for the airmen, who grasped their advantage and laid the foundations of a great victory. Wherever he is, Billy Mitchell must be smiling.

This skull and bomb badge decorates a B-52G appropriately named Nemesis.

After the Storm

In the 1930s, the RAF in the Middle East used a system of air control, policing the region from the air and taking punitive action against tribal leaders who disturbed the peace. In 1991, there was a sense of history repeating itself, if on a somewhat larger scale. Saddam Hussein was disinclined to accept the realities of his defeat and sought to challenge the postwar limitations imposed upon him. No-fly zones were established in the north and south of the country to prevent Iraqi aircraft from being used to persecute the people in those regions, and Coalition aircraft patrolled to enforce the restrictions. In the northern zone, above the 36th parallel, Coalition forces gave themselves the additional task of carrying humanitarian relief supplies to Kurdish settlements that had suffered under Saddam's regime. There was early evidence that the Iraqis intended to test the resolve of the Coalition. On March 20, 1991, an F-15C of the USAF's 36th TFW shot down an Su-22 within the northern zone. Two days later, it happened again, and this time the pilot of an accompanying Iraqi Pilatus PC-7 was so shaken that he bailed out before he was attacked. In 1992, an F-16 shot down a MiG-23 over the southern zone, and in the following year Iraqi SAM sites were attacked after Coalition aircraft had been regularly threatened during routine patrols. So it continued, establishing a role for international air power that is likely to become more prevalent in the years ahead. With the end of the 20th century, the air forces of the major powers could reflect that generally they still owed something of their size and shape to the doctrines of the Cold War. As air control measures, adopted by international agreement to enforce restrictions imposed on rogue states or renegade factions, increasingly become a fact of life for military aviation, they will have their effect on air forces, changing training, tactics and technology to take account of new priorities.

EUROPEAN TURBULENCE
The Caucasus

With the collapse of the Soviet Union and the unraveling of its Communist autocracy, latent unrest burst to the surface in a number of places on the fringes of the former Soviet empire. Nowhere was the upsurge more marked by violence than in the Caucasus. Armenia and Azerbaijan used MiGs and Sukhois inherited from the Soviet Air Force to pound one another as they struggled over the disputed enclave of Nagorno Karabakh. In Georgia, the recalcitrant Abkhazians were rocketed by Georgian Su-25s. It was in Chechnya, however, that air power was used to most punishing effect.

In December 1994, the Russians decided to regain control of the turbulent Chechen state by force. The Russian Air Force opened the campaign by attacking Grozny airport, where their Su-24s and 25s removed any possible opposition air threat by destroying a number of armed L-39 Albatross jet trainers and Mi-8 helicopters. They then moved on to attack widely spread targets in Chechnya, often with horrific results for the civilian population. Flying in all weathers, Mi-8 and Mi-24 helicopters used rockets and guided missiles against vehicles, bridges, and in close support of Russian troops. The Chechens fought back fiercely, shooting down several of the helicopters with SA-7s and machine guns and showing captured aircrew no mercy. Russian helicopters were heavily occupied in airlifting thousands of wounded

B-52s had to change with the times. Compare the cockpit of this B-52G with that of the B-52D on page 166-7. The throttle quadrant and the engine instruments are familiar, but video screens now confront the pilots.

soldiers back to field hospitals or in delivering ammunition to the forward infantry and artillery positions. In many months of relentless struggle, the Russian aircraft helped the guns of the tanks and artillery to wreak great destruction on Chechen towns and villages, and to impose a degree of control on Chechnya. However, as in Afghanistan, it became evident that massive application of sophisticated weaponry is not always a guarantee of achieving outright victory against a determined guerrilla enemy.

Break-up in the Balkans

The unraveling of the tenuous bonds that held Yugoslavia together began with the moves made by Slovenia toward independence in 1991. The Serbian leader, and then President of Yugoslavia, Slobodan Milosevic, reacted swiftly, sending tanks and troops across the Slovenian border. The army columns were preceded by a mixture of Yugoslav aircraft — MiG-21s, SOKO J-1 Jastrebs, J-22 Oraos, and G-4M Super Galebs — that attacked border posts and Ljubljana airport. The attacks accomplished little, and the Yugoslavian ground forces were effectively dealt with by the Slovenian Territorial Defense Force. By July 1991, Slovenia was independent and the focus shifted to neighboring Croatia, which was headed in the same direction. Serbia and Croatia were at war by September, and the Yugoslavian Air Force (JRV) was heavily engaged. MiG-21s were used to fire Maverick infrared missiles at the Croatian presidential palace, and from August onward the JRV made daily attacks on the besieged city of Vukovar. Against the relatively sophisticated JRV, the Croats cobbled together an air force of a few helicopters and an assortment of private aircraft. Later acquisitions included some MiG-21s bought from the

Ukraine or delivered by defecting JRV pilots. AN-2 biplanes were pressed into service as makeshift bombers, dropping homemade explosive devices made from old oil drums or gas cylinders. The Serb-Croat war died in its turn by the spring of 1992, replaced by an uneasy peace under the supervision of the United Nations Protection Force. In the course of the two conflicts, the JRV lost almost fifty aircraft; Yugoslavia lost Slovenia and Croatia.

Much worse was to come. In 1992, the Serbian minority in Bosnia, helped by the federal army, attempted to carve out enclaves for itself, laying siege to Sarajevo. By the time the United Nations imposed sanctions on Yugoslavia, some 20,000 people had died and up to two million had become refugees from fighting and "ethnic cleansing." NATO forces began monitoring flights in Bosnian airspace and by April

LEFT *The McDonnell Douglas F-15 Eagle was the dominant fighter in the air supremacy role during the last two decades of the 20th century. In Operation Desert Storm, F-15Cs scored thirty-four of the thirty-nine U.S. air-to-air victories. Two more F-15C kills were recorded by a Saudi pilot against Iraqi Mirage F1 fighters.* BELOW *The steeply raked engine intakes of the F-15 were capable of pivoting around the lower edge to point anywhere between 11 degrees below the horizontal to 4 degrees above. They did so to provide optimal air flow to the engines at all speeds and conditions of flight.*

1993, aircraft from France, the Netherlands and the United States were involved in Operation Deny Flight, flying combat patrols over Bosnia. As early as August, NATO began planning for air strikes against Serbian forces, but by February 1994, diplomatic efforts and the threat of air attack led to the withdrawal of Serb heavy weapons from around Sarajevo or the placing of them under UN control. However, that month, six Serb Galeb/Jastreb aircraft violated the no-fly zone. They were intercepted by F-16s and four of them were shot down. It was NATO's first combat action since it was founded in 1949.

From April 1994, NATO close support aircraft (Jaguars, A-10s, F-16s, F/A-18s) occasionally attacked selected targets to protect UN observers or discourage Serb aggression. In November, NATO began launching larger raids, and in May 1995, Serb ammunition dumps near Pale were destroyed by air attack. At the end of August, the market place in Sarajevo was shelled by the Bosnian Serbs. NATO responded with Operation Deliberate Force, a series of heavy air attacks on Serbian positions. In little more than two weeks, some 3,500 sorties were flown by bombers, fighters, AWACS, and ECM aircraft flying from bases in Italy and from U.S. aircraft carriers. The pressure brought to bear on the Serbian leadership by this air campaign was the decisive factor in forcing the Serbs to sign an agreement to cease their aggression and move their heavy weapons away from Sarajevo. Within a month, the Dayton peace accords were signed, bringing the Bosnian conflict to an end. Ambassador Richard Holbrooke of the U.S. was one of those who had no doubts about how this had been achieved, saying bluntly that "Airpower broke the back of the Bosnian Serbs, and directly led to the outcome in Ohio."

The Fairchild A-10A proved itself as an extremely effective battlefield weapon in the 1991 Gulf War. Between them, 144 A-10s flew 8,500 sorties and dropped over 23,000 bombs during Desert Storm. They are credited with destroying over 1,000 tanks, 1,200 artillery pieces, and 2,000 military vehicles. Besides all that, they hunted Scuds, attacked SAM and radar sites, and shot down two helicopters, so scoring the only aerial victories of the war attributed to guns.

Chaos in Kosovo

During the 1990s, Kosovo Albanian resistance to rule from Belgrade grew. The Kosovo Liberation Army (KLA) was formed and soon made clear that it was ready to use force to achieve its objectives. A campaign of attacks began against Serbian security forces, who responded with military repression of the population as a whole. In December 1997, NATO Foreign Ministers expressed concern at the escalating ethnic tension in Kosovo. Throughout 1998, diplomatic efforts were made to find a peaceful, negotiated solution, but the international community became aware that this might not be enough. In June 1998, NATO began planning for a range of military options, both ground and air, in support of the diplomatic process. NATO also undertook a series of air and ground exercises to demonstrate the Alliance's ability to project power rapidly into the region.

By September 1998 the Serbs were openly conducting a campaign of ethnic cleansing. An estimated 250,000 Kosovo Albanians were driven from their homes and some 50,000 were still in the open as the winter approached. It was clear many might die. The violence continued and, following a massacre in the village of Racak on January 15, 1999, NATO increased its state of readiness for action. The intransigence of the Serbs at the negotiating table, and evidence of a massive buildup of Serbian forces in and around Kosovo, led to the suspension of talks on March 19. Five days later, a NATO air campaign was launched that continued for seventy-eight days. Of 38,000 sorties flown, nearly 11,000 were strike sorties. The majority of the aircraft involved were from the United States, but as the operation continued greater numbers of allied aircraft were committed, until 829 aircraft from fourteen countries were available for

Twenty-eight countries (including many of the former USSR or satellites) have acquired export models of the impressive MiG-29 (Fulcrum). After the reunification of Germany in 1990, East Germany's MiG-29s were integrated into the German Luftwaffe. Seen here are two of the more than forty operated by the Polish Air Force.

tasking. The Serbs claimed to have shot down over seventy NATO aircraft, but only two (one F-117A and one F-16) were brought down by the Serb defenses, and both of the pilots were rescued.

The air campaign began with strikes aimed at neutralizing Yugoslavia's air defenses, and then widened to take in a limited range of military targets in Kosovo and southern Serbia. In late March 1999, when Milosevic showed no sign of responding to the opening phase, a much broader range of targets was included. It soon became clear that NATO was engaged in a major strategic bombing campaign. Oil refineries, radio and TV transmitters, and one of Milosevic's residences were hit, and the national power grid was disrupted on May 3. Every effort was made to keep collateral damage and civilian casualties to the minimum, but as in any air campaign it was inevitable that there would be tragic incidents, among them a mistaken strike on the Chinese Embassy and the destruction of a civilian train that happened to cross a bridge while it was under air attack. Overall, however, the air campaign achieved its aims. Well over 400 static targets were attacked, more than three-quarters of which suffered moderate to severe damage. There is also evidence that air strikes against the Serb field forces in Kosovo were successful in restricting their operations, and that the campaign did influence the thinking of the Serbian leadership. Milosevic ultimately agreed to the international community's conditions for ending the bombing, and the conflict ended on NATO's terms. Yugoslavia had to face the problems of a broken economy, a national infrastructure severely damaged by air attack, and a discredited political leadership. The wider world was left to ponder the use of air power as an instrument of international law, and its possible evolution in that role during the second century of powered flight.

The Boeing (formerly Rockwell) B-1B was designed to evade enemy radar by flying low level at near-sonic or supersonic speeds. With its buried engines, curved body, and radar-absorbent materials, the B-1B has a radar profile less than 1/100th that of the B-52. The B-1B at the National Museum of the USAF came from the 7th Bomb Wing at Dyess AFB.

On the morning of June 14, 1999, in the midst of NATO's efforts to halt ethnic cleansing in Kosovo, there was an incident that illustrated the difficulties of conducting a precise air campaign when the situation on the ground is confused. F-16s dropped bombs on a convoy between Rracaj and Gjakova that appeared to be led by a Serbian military vehicle. It was actually a convoy of refugees. Muharrem Alija's sister was among those killed and other members of his family were injured. Photographs of Muharrem in tears, the "boy in the yellow shirt," appeared on television and in newspapers and magazines worldwide, symbolizing the suffering of the people of the Balkans. NATO leaders said that the pilots had been hunting Yugoslav units burning out villages in western Kosovo, but accepted that the bombing had been a tragic mistake. Commander of the 31st Fighter Wing's F-16s, based at Aviano, Italy, in 1999 was Brigadier General Daniel Leaf. In the summer of 2005, Muharrem Alija traveled to the United States under the sponsorship of Lieutenant Colonel David McFarland, USAF Ret., and was invited to meet and talk with General Leaf.

FIGHTING TERRORISM
Terrorists and the Taliban

On September 11, 2001, four U.S. airliners on domestic flights were hijacked by Arab terrorists. Two were deliberately flown into the World Trade Center buildings in New York, a third struck the Pentagon, and the fourth crashed in open country in Pennsylvania. Responsibility for the attacks was claimed by the militant Islamic organization al-Qaeda, and by its leader, Osama bin Laden. The U.S. government rightly interpreted the attacks as acts of war, and made plans to strike back.

The declared aim of U.S. policy was to destroy Osama bin Laden and the al-Qaeda network, and Operation Enduring Freedom was the first step toward the achievement of that aim. Operation Enduring Freedom targeted the Taliban government in Afghanistan, which was known to have supported al-Qaeda and given its members safe haven. After U-2s had conducted reconnaissance sorties over Afghanistan, heavy bombers and aircraft from the U.S. Navy's carrier battle groups operating in the Arabian Sea began operations on October 7, 2001. Among the weapons systems included in the first wave of the air campaign against the Taliban were Tomahawk cruise missiles and, in the longest bombing raids ever conducted, several stealthy B-2 Spirits operating from their base in Missouri. B-1Bs and B-52s joined in, flying from Diego Garcia in the Indian Ocean. The strikes focused on the area in and around the cities of Kabul, Jalalabad, and Kandahar, aiming at runways, early warning radars, surface-to-air missile and gun sites, and concentrations of troops and armored vehicles. The

Taliban air force had about fifty aircraft, about half of which were ageing fighters and the rest transports or helicopters. All were swiftly destroyed, clearing the way for unarmed Coalition aircraft such as tankers and transports to operate over Afghanistan.

Within a few days, most al-Qaeda training camps had been severely damaged and the Taliban's air defenses had been destroyed. The campaign then focused on command and control centers, reducing the ability of the Taliban to coordinate an effective response. During this period and later, the success of the Coalition's ground forces in defeating their enemy was built on an unprecedented combination of massive air power using precision weapons and acting on information provided by special forces on the ground. With the effectiveness of the enemy command system seriously degraded, bombers struck at the Taliban's ground forces with "daisy-cutter" bombs of 15,000 pounds, and AC-130 gunships blasted enemy positions with cannon fire. The Taliban fighters had no previous experience of U.S. firepower, and often appeared on bare ridge-lines where special forces could see them and call in devastating air attacks.

As is now the case in any major conflict, transport aircraft were vital to the success of the operation. C-17s used unimproved dirt and gravel strips, functioning, according to one airlift pilot, "like C-130s on steroids." C-17s and C-130s dropped M-16 and AK-47 ammunition, warm clothes, and boots to U.S. and allied troops in the forward areas, and even dropped sacks of oats for the horses used by soldiers in mountainous regions. A transatlantic air bridge moved huge quantities of supplies through Europe and central Asia, helped by overflight and basing agreements with dozens of countries, including new allies Bulgaria, Azerbaijan, and Turkmenistan.

Once their grip on power had been broken, the Taliban and the al-Qaeda fighters retreated to a mountainous area southeast of Kabul, on the border with Pakistan. They took refuge in a network of caves and tunnels in an area of the White Mountains known as Tora Bora. It was widely believed that Osama bin Laden was there. The Coalition air forces pounded Tora Bora unceasingly, targeting cave mouths with the aid of imaging from aerial reconnaissance and in response to visual observations by troops on the ground. Hundreds of the enemy were killed in the Tora Bora complex, but bin Laden and many of his lieutenants managed to slip away across the border. The Taliban had been removed from power and al-Qaeda had been badly hurt, but the fight against terrorism was far from over.

Air power played a major part in the success of the Coalition intervention in Afghanistan. Unsurprisingly, the lion's share of the air campaign was borne by the United States, and the USAF's bombers led the way in terms of weapons delivered. Although USAF combat aircraft flew only about 20 percent of all strike missions in Afghanistan, they aimed some 6,100 tons of ordnance at their targets, or approximately 75 percent of the Coalition total. More significantly, at least 72 percent of the munitions used during the first two months of Enduring Freedom were precision-guided, a marked change since the 1991 Gulf War, when the figure for "smart" weapons was only 9 percent. President Bush later said that the blend of "real-time intelligence, local allied forces, special forces, and precision airpower has really never been used before." It had, he said, served to "shape and then dominate an unconventional conflict."

REMATCH IN IRAQ

The first Gulf War in 1991 ended with defeat for the Iraqi military, but with Saddam Hussein and the Baath Party still holding the reins of power in Iraq. Saddam's continued belligerence in the face of UN sanctions during the years that followed hardened the belief in the minds of many in the West that the problem of Iraq was not going to go away, and the terrorist attacks of September 11, 2001, against the U.S. brought matters to a head. Although there was no direct link apparent between Iraq and al-Qaeda, the attention of President George W. Bush and Prime Minister Tony Blair focused on Saddam's previous record in the production and use of weapons of mass destruction. Chemical weapons had been used by Iraqis in the war with Iran, and against the Kurds and the Shia of Saddam's own country. Before 1991, he had also shown more than a passing interest in developing a nuclear capability. All this was bad enough, but perhaps most threatening was the thought that the Iraqi government might have no inhibitions about passing weapons of mass destruction on to terrorists to use as they wished.

The assault on Iraq began in the early hours (local time) of March 20, 2003, over a day earlier than originally

The Northrop Grumman B-2 Spirit is a heavy stealth bomber with a range of more than 6,000 nautical miles unrefueled and over 10,000 nautical miles with one refueling, giving it the ability to fly to any point in the world within hours. A Generic Weapons Interface System (GWIS) allows the B-2 to carry variable loads of stand-off weapons and direct attack munitions on each sortie, enabling the aircraft to attack as many as four different types of target on a single mission. Twenty-one B-2s have been built and are based at Whiteman Air Force Base, Missouri.

planned. That morning, intelligence suggested that Saddam and his sons, Qusay and Uday, were with other Baathist leaders in a specific building in central Baghdad. Two F-117s were scrambled from Kuwait to take advantage of this information by attacking the building and killing those inside. Just before dawn, four 2,000-pound "bunker-busting" EGBU-27 bombs hit the target, but it was too late. The birds had flown. Saddam survived the intended assassination, but he had been sent a clear message. He was left in no doubt that he was a hunted man, liable to attract a direct and devastating attack if any one of his entourage ever dared to betray him by revealing his whereabouts.

The F-117 attack illustrated several characteristics of aerial warfare at the beginning of the 21st century. Reaction to intelligence received was swift (if not quite swift enough, in this case), with aircraft on their way less than two hours after the crews received their orders. (Given the mass of detailed planning normally associated with a precision strike launched from a distant base — target coordinates, weapon selection, enemy defenses, routes inbound and outbound, tanker aircraft holding points, radio frequencies, emergency briefings, aircraft and weapon preparation — this was no mean achievement.) The attacking aircraft were

"stealthy," designed to be almost impossible to detect on radar. The bombs were "smart," able to find their target either by laser guidance or GPS coordinates. The F-117s having offered this prologue of technological brilliance, the drama of the second Coalition war against Iraq began, with air power once again playing leading roles but this time reading from a more sophisticated script and using better props.

The lengthy air campaign that preceded the invasion of Iraq by ground forces in 1991 was not repeated in 2003. There was no need to spend weeks degrading the Iraqi air defenses because they were already largely ineffective. The Iraqi Air Force was a shadow even of its feeble 1991 self, and proved incapable of launching even one sortie against the Coalition's assault. SAM sites had been regularly struck by U.S. and RAF aircraft during their years of patrols over the "no-fly" zones of northern and southern Iraq, and these efforts had been intensified in the weeks leading up to the invasion. With Coalition air supremacy assured, U.S. and British troops crossed the Iraqi frontier and began to fight their way toward Basra and Baghdad less than 24 hours after the first F-117 strike. Pave Low and Chinook helicopters carried special forces deep into enemy territory, while

Black Hawks and Apaches ranged ahead of coalition armor. At first, however, much of the air campaign was strategic in character. In a televised address, President George Bush said that strikes had been launched against "targets of military opportunity" in Iraq. American and British warships opened the air assault by firing three dozen Tomahawk cruise missiles at Iraqi command and control centers, but Baghdad did not feel the full weight of Coalition air power until the night of March 21/22. U.S. Defense Secretary Donald Rumsfeld gave a hint of what was to come when he said: "What will follow will not be a repeat of any other conflict. It will be of a force and a scope and a scale that has been beyond what we have seen before."

"Shock and awe" was the term used for the massive air strikes on Baghdad. The term appeared in a 1996 U.S. Defense Department book entitled *Shock and Awe: Achieving Rapid Dominance*. The authors described shock and awe as a strategy "aimed at influencing the will, perception, and understanding of an adversary rather than simply destroying military capability." Recalling the ideas of early air power theorists, a primary war objective was seen as psychological rather than material dominance. There were aspects of "shock and awe" as it was applied in Iraq that were original, but the broad concept was not new. The Nazi blitzkrieg strategy of WWII and the dropping of atomic bombs on Japan are both examples of air power used with the intention of breaking the will of the enemy. The terror-

ist attacks on New York and Washington in 2001 were also aimed at inducing "shock and awe" in the U.S. population.

Seen round the world on live television, the night air assault on Baghdad was indeed an awesome experience for the viewers. Some 500 Tomahawks were fired from U.S. and British ships and submarines, and B-52Hs launched at least 100 AGM-86C CALCMs (Conventional Air Launched Cruise Missiles). An assortment of precision weapons delivered by over 700 strike aircraft, including F-117s, B-1s, B-2s, and Tornados, added to the destruction. Huge explosions lit the night sky one after another as government buildings in the center of the city were pounded incessantly. However, the timing of the attack and its unprecedented precision considerably reduced the element of shock. The buildings were almost empty of government officials, and the general population suffered hardly at all from "collateral damage." As a demonstration of air power precisely applied the assault of March 21/22 was impressive, but it is doubtful that it contributed much toward "achieving rapid dominance" by "influencing the will … of an adversary."

The capability to attack targets with great precision was one aspect of air power that had advanced markedly in the years since the 1991 Gulf War. Guided bombs had been used in small numbers both in WWII and in Vietnam. They were more widely used in the Gulf in 1991, but still accounted for less than 8 percent of the air weapons delivered. During the 23 days of the Iraq War's conventional phase (pre-insurgency), Coalition aircraft delivered almost 30,000 bombs and missiles of various kinds, two-thirds of which were guided by precision technology of some kind, which is a vast improvement in capability over the earlier

Looking like a machine from the Star Wars fleet, an F-117A Nighthawk crouches in its hangar, reflections creating pink eyes aglow. In this setting, its nickname of "Wobblin' Goblin" looks well deserved. The world's first aircraft designed using stealth technology, the F-117 achieved operational capability in October 1983. The first Allied air strike against Yugoslavia was made by Nighthawks on March 24, 1999, and they launched Operation Iraqi Freedom with a strike against Baghdad on March 20, 2003. F-117As are based at Holloman Air Force Base, New Mexico.

conflict brought about in little more than a decade.

Among the most notable air weapons used were the cruise missiles, fired from well outside the range of Iraqi defenses and flying to their targets at low level and high subsonic speeds. The ship/submarine-launched Tomahawk combines terrain-contour matching and inertial guidance to navigate, and is equipped with a scene-matching terminal guidance system, which reduces its CEP (Circular Error Probability) to a few meters. (However, a small number of errant Tomahawks did stray from their intended flight paths, several coming to earth in Saudi Arabia and Turkey.) The equally accurate AGM 86C, up to twenty of which can be carried by the venerable B-52H, holds to its track by using an onboard GPS (Global Positioning System) coupled to its INS (Inertial Navigation System). The Tornados carried the RAF's own stand-off weapon, Storm Shadow, which navigates by GPS and digital terrain-profile matching. As it nears the target, Storm Shadow jettisons its nose cone to reveal a high-resolution infrared camera. The target recognition hardware then compares what it sees with a stored image of the target. The warhead is in two parts — a penetration charge and a second larger charge, which is delayed by a fuse until after the target is penetrated.

Other precision munitions carried by Coalition aircraft included unpowered weapons such as JDAM (Joint Direct Attack Munition) and JSOW (Joint Standoff Weapon). The JDAM is a tail-kit conversion of standard "dumb" bombs. The "smart" tail unit contains an INS/GPS kit capable of taking a bomb to its target with great accuracy at night and in any weather. The JSOW, which has flip-out wings to allow a high-altitude launch from as far away as 40 nautical miles, also uses INS/GPS for midcourse navigation and adds imaging infrared and datalink for terminal homing. The anti-armor version of JSOW carries six BLU-108/B submunitions, each of which releases four projectiles that use infrared sensors to detect targets. Upon detonation, an explosively formed shaped charge is created, capable of penetrating armored targets. Both JDAM and JSOW are compatible with a wide range of combat aircraft, including the F/A-18, AV-8B, F-14, F-16, F-15E, F-117, B-1B, B-2 and B-52.

Precision weapons increased the effectiveness of strike aircraft by an order of magnitude in Iraq, but a very different application of air power was just as remarkable. UAVs (Unmanned Aerial Vehicles) were not new. They were considered by the U.S. in WWI (Kettering Bugs), served as target drones between the World Wars, and were used for reconnaissance in the 1991 Gulf War and later in the Balkans and Afghanistan. In Iraq in 2003, UAVs came into their own, making their presence felt both in reconnaissance and combat roles. Several types of UAV were used. One of the smallest is the U.S. Marine Corps' Dragon Eye, a 5-pound propeller-driven aircraft fitted with a video camera that can be assembled and hand-launched in no more than ten minutes. It operates at about 500 feet above ground and can fly for up to one hour. At the other end of the scale is the USAF's Global Hawk, which has a wingspan of 116 feet and can range as far as 12,000 nautical miles at altitudes up to 65,000 feet, cruising at over 300 knots for up to 35 hours. During a typical mission, Global Hawk can fly 1,200 miles to an area of interest and remain on station for 24 hours. In that time, its cloud-penetrating sensors can survey an area the size of Belgium, Holland and Switzerland put together and relay the imagery by satellite to battlefield commanders. Half Global Hawk's size, the Predator operates at lower altitudes, but can carry Hellfire missiles to add a strike capability to surveillance. (In November 2002, a Predator UAV operating over Yemen launched a Hellfire missile that destroyed a vehicle carrying al-Qaeda terrorists.)

Used in concert with satellites and reconnaissance aircraft such as the U-2 and E-8C JSTARS (Joint Surveillance and Target Radar System), UAVs provided Coalition commanders with a continuous stream of intelligence about Iraq and the movements of Iraqi forces. In 1991 bad weather had sometimes given the Iraqis temporary relief from aerial attack, but this time they discovered that even the dense shield of the *shamal* (sandstorm) was no protection. On March 25, the *shamal* began to blow and continued for three days. Iraqi ground forces moved to take advantage of the cover it offered, but that was a mistake. As they concentrated and began to deploy, they were closely watched by UAVs and JSTARS, which passed on the details to strike aircraft. The physical destruction then suffered by the Iraqis was considerable, but the psychological effects of the strikes were equally telling. Confident that they would be protected by the *shamal*'s apparently impenetrable blanket, Iraqi soldiers were horrified to find that they could be destroyed by weapons that came unheralded and out of nowhere.

At the peak of the Coalition's air campaign, close to 2,000 sorties of all kinds were being flown each day by manned aircraft. Such a high-intensity effort, carried out from bases and ships often considerable distances from the battlefield, could not have been attempted without substantial air tanker support. The tanker force comprised 268 aircraft (182 of them from the USAF), but they were hard-pressed to meet the demand. In the first three weeks of the air war, Coalition tankers flew over 7,500 sorties and delivered more than 46 million gallons of fuel to thirsty combat aircraft. In all, 1,800 Coalition aircraft (not counting army helicopters) flew a total of over 41,000 sorties of all kinds during the campaign, some 20,000 of which were individual strikes by combat aircraft. Almost 80 percent of the air effort was devoted to assisting the land battle by launching and supporting either interdiction or close support sorties. This wide-ranging and ever-present activity kept the Iraqi forces off-balance and was instrumental in allowing Coalition troops to maintain the rapid pace of their advance to Baghdad. The capital city fell on April 9, Saddam's army ceased to exist, and the role of the Coalition's forces became that of occupation. The conflict in Iraq nevertheless continued, but changed in character to that of an insurgency, in which the enemy is less obvious and air power's offensive role less certain.

CONCLUSION

The major air forces operating at the dawn of the 21st century were very different from those existing in the decade after WWII, when jet engines sparked revolutionary developments in military aviation, changing every aspect of air force life. Air power doctrine had to change, and so did recruiting, training, operations, flight safety, logistics, engineering, administration, and aviation medicine. At the same time, the appearance of nuclear weapons also had marked effects on the size and shape of air forces on both sides of the Iron Curtain. The competing nuclear powers had to create organizations and produce aircraft capable of posing a credible threat of delivering an apocalyptic blow. Air tankers were introduced to support the nuclear strike forces and quickly became a normal part of air force operations of all kinds. These Cold War developments brought

with them a heightened requirement to know what the other side was up to, and aircraft operating in the oldest air power role, reconnaissance, steadily increased in spying capability, by the 1960s flying at speeds and heights undreamed of only a few years before. Transport aircraft, too, made their mark early in the Cold War, during the Berlin Airlift, and remained a vital element of air force front lines everywhere, becoming ever more essential to the projection of power. However, despite vast improvements in aircraft performance, the effectiveness of individual combat aircraft for conventional warfare remained relatively low for many years, awaiting advances in weaponry.

By the turn of the century, technological progress had powered further dramatic changes in military aviation. The world's major air forces were much smaller but far more capable than they had been in the era of first generation jets. The USAF, for example, had less than 4,400 aircraft of all types on strength in 2003. In 1955, the figure was more than 28,400, almost seven times as large. Even so, the USAF of 2003 was a more effective force than its numerically superior predecessor. The airframes and engines in use were, of course, much improved. (In terms of pure performance, an F-100 is no match for an F-16.) However, they are only two items in the gallery of military aviation hardware. Important though they are, all aircraft can be regarded simply as transporters of one kind or another, designed to carry the weapons, cargo, people, cameras and so on that complete the assigned mission. In the second half of the 20th century, the basic airframes became increasingly regarded as secondary to other developments. The rate of airframe development slowed and aircraft remained in the front line far longer than earlier design generations. Priorities shifted to improving weapons and various systems, such as navigation aids, sensors, controls, and the avionics of the "glass cockpit." After WWII, the remarkable B-47 was in squadron service for seventeen years, far longer than the B-36, but the B-52 has been with squadrons in one form or another since 1954 and has survived innumerable modifications and rebirths to remain a formidable aircraft into the 21st century. The same is true of aircraft in other roles; compare the length of service of the F-86 with the F-15, and the C-124 with the C-130.

The ideas of the early air power theorists may not have been wholly borne out by developments in military aviation up to the end of the 20th century, but General Michael Dugan (former USAF Chief of Staff) was probably justified in claiming that "The technology finally caught up with the doctrine." The major air forces had proven aircraft established in their squadrons, and they were adorned with acronyms proclaiming their potency, including CALCM, JDAM, JSOW, FLIR, INS, GPS, ECM, HOTAS, LANTIRN.... Taking into account its stealthy characteristics, navigation and defensive systems, and the precision of its weapons, one conventionally armed B-2 could be as effective against selected targets as the hundreds of bombers launched on raids by the "Mighty Eighth" at the height of its powers in 1945.

If reform was in the air 100 years after the first flight of the Wright brothers, it came to air forces in the shape of UAVs (*Unmanned* Aerial Vehicles). The Wrights had given the world the glorious gift of human flight, but a century later Global Hawk, Predator and their like were the thin end of a rapidly growing wedge in flying operations. To the chagrin of pilots, UAVs threatened to eliminate the human element, because they held the promise of more cost-effective coverage of many reconnaissance and strike/attack tasks. Taken to what appears to be its logical conclusion, with the use of pilotless aircraft being extended to other roles, the development of UAVs would revolutionize military aviation, forcing significant change as did the jet engine in the years after WWII.

In 1945, General Carl Spaatz, USAAF, gave it as his opinion that: "Air power has evolved into a force

In a world where it is increasingly important to know what the opposition is doing, the Northrop Grumman E-8C JSTARS can provide commanders with up-to-the-minute intelligence about the situation on the ground. This "eye in the sky" is capable of determining the direction, speed and pattern of activity of ground vehicles and helicopters up to 150 miles away. Using secure data links, JSTARS can transmit this information to command posts and headquarters that could be thousands of miles from the area under surveillance.

co-equal with land and sea power, decisive in its own right and worthy of the faith of its prophets." In the years since WWII, air power has repeatedly confirmed his view. Aircraft have been involved in some way in every conflict, great and small, and have grown increasingly indispensable to military operations. The major air forces have been equipped with machines of staggering sophistication, but even minor third-world nations have felt it necessary to acquire a few jet fighters and turbo-prop transports. Coalition operations against Iraq and in Afghanistan emphasized that, while there may be no substitute for putting "boots on the ground" in the end, soldiers would find it much more difficult, and perhaps sometimes impossible, to conduct ground operations successfully without air power as a partner. Field Marshal Sir Bernard Montgomery was a controversial figure in WWII and often had harsh words to say about airmen, but even he admitted, "If we lose the war in the air we lose the war and lose it quickly." Spaatz and Montgomery gave their judgments in an era when military aviation was still a relatively blunt instrument. By the end of the 20th century, air power could be applied with awesome precision and devastating force. In the light of these developments, the generals would be justified in emphasizing their conclusions.

AVIATION'S IMAGE MAKERS

OPPOSITE TOP LEFT Keith Ferris, surrounded by his work in his New Jersey studio.

OPPOSITE TOP RIGHT Michael Turner in his Buckinghamshire studio. Michael is also well known for his motor racing illustrations.

OPPOSITE BOTTOM LEFT Ron Kaplan, before he was Executive Director of the National Aviation Hall of Fame, painting the artwork onto the nose of a B-25 in Dayton.

OPPOSITE BOTTOM RIGHT MotoArt is a collective of artists and marketers who create artwork and sculptural furniture created from airplane parts. Their escapades have been featured on a reality TV show. Dave Hall (left) and Donovan Fell III (center) are the founders and the creative spark behind the company. Rian Capaci is at right.

ABOVE Larry Godwin, Brundage, Alabama, works on a much larger scale, in full-size sculpture. One of his stainless-steel Wright Flyers is seen at Maxwell AFB in Alabama. His interpretation of the 1905 Flyer is seen here "flying" into place in downtown Dayton, Ohio. His sculpture of the Signal Corps Number 1 is on page 316.

ABOVE Aviation artist Gil Cohen has been a generous contributor to this project. His recent self portrait was done at the request of the authors.
LEFT TOP AND BOTTOM The EAA Airventure Museum holds the writing studio of Ernest K. Gann, which includes his typewriter, chair and associated aviation paraphernalia. He wrote such aviation classics as *The High and the Mighty* and *Fate is the Hunter.*
BELOW Ann Cooper writes about aviation and its rich history. She has featured aviation artists as well as the aviators. Ann is seen here facing the camera with one of her subjects, WASP pilot Dot Swain.

Top Erik Hildebrandt of Minneapolis, Minnesota, has made compelling images of warbirds, airshow performers and current military aircraft. He is pictured here above his image of the F-22.

Left Jim Dietz, also a frequent contributor to this project, played a fighter pilot in the 2006 film *King Kong*.

Top Donald Nijboer, Toronto, Ontario, at home in the cockpit of a Polish Air Force SU-7. Donald has created the *Cockpit* series, also published by Boston Mill Press.

Above Walter Boyne, former Director of the National Air & Space Museum, has published many aviation books and written hundreds of magazine articles. He also founded a cable TV channel dealing with aviation subjects.

running the engine and
propellers a few min-
utes to get them in work-
ing order, I got on the machine
at 10:35 for the first
trial. The wind according
to our anemometers at
this time was blowing a
little over 20 miles (corrected) 27 miles accord-
ing to the government an-
emometer at Kitty Hawk.
On slipping the rope
the machine started off
increasing in speed to
probably 7 or 8 miles. The
machine lifted from the
truck just as it was
entering on the fourth rail.
Mr. Daniels took a pic-
ture just as it left the
tracks. I found the

CHAPTER 2

Flight Safety

O N SEPTEMBER 17, 1908, Orville Wright and Lieutenant Thomas Selfridge took off from Fort Myer in the Wright Military Flyer. They were circling the field when a crack developed in the starboard propeller. The vibrations of the unbalanced blades caused the propeller to spin outside its normal arc and carry away one of the bracing wires supporting the rudder. The Flyer quickly became uncontrollable and dived steeply into the ground, severely injuring Orville and killing his passenger. Powered flight's honeymoon was over and Lieutenant Selfridge was assured of a place in aviation history, his name forever heading a list of aerial fatalities that would grow to engulf people from every nation and every walk of life in the century ahead.

The pioneers of flight were so excited by the idea of flying and its promise of freedom from earthly constraints that its dangers were largely ignored. It was an exhilarating adventure, an all-consuming miracle, and safety issues did not seem

ABOVE *On September 17, 1908, at Fort Myer, Virginia, Lieutenant Thomas Selfridge flew with Orville Wright in the Military Flyer. After four circuits of the field had been completed, a cracked propeller led to other structural failures and a crash. In the tangled mass of wreckage, Orville was found conscious but badly injured, having broken his thigh and several ribs. Selfridge had suffered a fractured skull and died after surgery, so gaining the morbid distinction of being the world's first fatality in a powered flying machine.*
LEFT *Wright brothers' artifacts held by the National Museum of the USAF include fabric from the 1903 Flyer, the splintered propeller from the 1908 accident that killed Lieutenant Selfridge at Fort Myer, a wing rib and an anemometer made by the Wrights, a U.S. flag given to Orville by the commander of Fort Myer in 1908, an original drawing by the Wrights, and copies of both the diary entry from December 17, 1903, and the telegram sent after the first flight.*

The Bristol Boxkite of 1910 was well named. It was kite-like in construction and, in common with most aeroplanes of the time, very flimsy. One advantage was that it was also very slow, so accidents, which were frequent, were not often fatal. (See text below.)

"It was warm and fine but rather suggestive of thunder; the air was perfectly still. I scarcely had occasion to move the control lever at all until I got to Bletchley, where it began to get rather bumpy. At first I thought nothing of this, but suddenly it got much worse, and I came to the conclusion that it was time to descend. A big black thunder cloud was coming up on my right front; it did not look reassuring, and there was good landing ground below. At this time I was flying at about 1,700 feet by my aneroid, which had been set at Oxford in the morning. I began a glide, but almost directly I had switched off, the tail of my machine was suddenly wrenched upwards as if it had been hit from below and I saw the front elevator go down perpendicularly below me. I was not strapped in, and I suppose I caught hold of the uprights at my side, for the next thing I realized was that I was lying in a heap on what ordinarily is the underside of the top wing. The machine in fact was upside down. I stood up, held on and waited. The machine just floated about, gliding from side to side like a piece of falling paper. Then it over-swung itself, so to speak, and went down more or less vertically sideways until it righted itself momentarily the right way up. Then it went down tail first, turned over upside down again and restarted the floating motion. We were still some way from the ground, and took what seemed a long time reaching it. I looked round somewhat hurriedly; the tail was still there, and I could see nothing wrong. As we got close to the ground the machine was doing long swings from side to side, and I made up my mind that the only thing to do was to try and jump clear before the crash. In the last swing we slid down, I think, about thirty feet, and hit the ground pretty hard. Fortunately, I hung on to the end, and, according to those who were looking on, I did not jump off till about ten feet from the ground." (See *Aviation Century The Early Years*, Chapter 2, "The Fokker Scourge," for a similar incident in, and out of, a Martinsyde Scout in World War I.)

worth bothering about. Aeroplanes did not even have such basic accessories as seat belts, an omission that occasionally had alarming consequences, as a young British Army pilot found out in 1911. In August of that year, No. 2 (Aeroplane) Company of the British Army's newly created Air Battalion, equipped with an assortment of Bristol Boxkites and Farman pushers, set out to exercise their skills by flying half a dozen of their biplanes from Salisbury Plain to fields in Norfolk, some 120 miles to the northeast. Only two of the machines completed the round-trip intact. There were no injuries because, unless a crash came at the end of a steep dive, the flimsy aeroplanes of 1911 generally hit the ground slowly and tended to crumple round their pilots, leaving them more humbled than hurt. However, Lieutenant Reynolds reported that he had an unusually exciting time after getting airborne one evening:

The ranks of the early aviators included a very high percentage of adventurers and thrill-seekers, people who tended to brush aside the thought that flying might be a hazardous business. They flew their flimsy machines alone most of the time, and personal safety was not something often at the forefront of their minds. Deaths were not uncommon as pilots lost control and crashed, suffered a structural failure in the air, or even fell out of their flying machines. Mishaps causing damage and injury were frequent, and men such as Louis Blériot and Cal Rodgers were constantly reported as mending wings, or broken bones, or both.

Aviation's character began to change with the dramatic developments of World War I. There were rapid improvements in aircraft structure and design, and in engine reliability. Cockpits began to carry a selection of basic instruments — compass, airspeed indicator, altimeter, tachometer, and gauges showing oil pressure, fuel contents and engine temperature. Experiments with radio were underway. Organized training systems were introduced to cope with the need to educate thousands of new pilots about flying. Seat belts appeared and in time parachutes were accepted, if not always welcomed, by pilots who saw them as some sort of reflection on their manhood. The number of training accidents remained distressingly high, but at least some flight safety aspects of military flying had begun to be addressed.

After World War I, those who were keen to see commercial aviation develop soon realized that progress depended on convincing the public that flying was safe enough to be considered a reasonable activity for rational human beings. One commentator observed that flying in the

In the late 1920s, Jimmy Doolittle made a significant contribution to flight safety when he designed a blind flying instrument panel and fitted it to a Consolidated NY-2. He made over one hundred simulated instrument flights "under the hood."

early 1920s was "unorganized, unregulated, unsafe and unprofitable." Until that changed, there could be no fulfillment of aviation's promise.

As knowledge of aerodynamics and structures increased, aircraft design improved. Engines continued to grow in power and reliability, and better materials became available, enabling manufacturers to produce machines that were stronger but lighter. Driven by the demands of the users, longer life was extracted from components and accessories such as oil and water pumps, generators, magnetos and spark plugs. Instruments improved in both sensitivity and reliability, largely due to the efforts of pilots such as Jimmy Doolittle. In the late 1920s, the Daniel Guggenheim Foundation funded the development of aircraft safety, with an emphasis on encouraging "perfection of control in a fog." The Full Flight Laboratory was set up at Mitchel Field on Long Island, with Doolittle at its head. The blind flying instrument panel he devised, fitted to a Consolidated NY-2, included a Kollsman sensitive altimeter, a turn-and-bank indicator, and a gyroscopically driven artificial horizon. The disadvantages of the magnetic compass were overcome by adding a gyroscopic direction indicator. In 1928 and 1929, Doolittle made over 100 simulated instrument flights "under the hood," with Ben Kelsey as safety pilot. Finally, on

TOP *The Boeing 307 Stratoliner was the world's first fully pressurized airliner. Only ten were built — three for Pan Am, five for TWA, one crashed, and one was supplied to Howard Hughes for use as his private aircraft.*

BOTTOM *On March 18, 1939, on its nineteenth test flight, the prototype Boeing 307 Stratoliner crashed, killing all on board. Boeing Chief Test Pilot Julius Barr was the pilot, and an engineer for a prospective airline customer was in the copilot's seat. That engineer had been pressing Boeing to find out what would happen if the 307 stalled with two engines on one side throttled back and the other two at takeoff power. Boeing refused to take such a risk but did agree to approach the condition cautiously. The airliner was seen to enter a spin, attempt a recovery and then start to break up, finally crashing on the slopes of Mount Rainier. What happened in the cockpit and what really caused the crash can only be a matter for speculation.*

September 24, 1929, he took off alone in fog, flew a wide circuit and completed a successful landing, all while relying primarily on instruments. Later that day, he repeated the performance for Daniel Guggenheim's benefit, this time under the hood and with Ben Kelsey in the other cockpit. This was one of the most significant flight safety advances in aviation history, effectively ending the time when pilots were forced to rely on flying "by the seat of their pants," whatever the conditions.

As aircraft became more sophisticated, so did the systems fitted to cope with emergencies. Retractable undercarriages needed a method of lowering in case they would not come down when selected. Fire, the aviator's most feared enemy, had to be detected and extinguished. Crews needed to be warned about other problems, too — hydraulic, pneumatic and electrical failures prominent among them — and

wherever possible had to be provided with alternatives. Multiple aircraft systems were introduced for essential services. Autopilots reduced crew fatigue on long flights. In time, as aircraft flew higher, pressurized cabins offered passengers and crews the artificial comfort of lower altitudes, introducing a requirement for emergency oxygen systems in case the pressurization failed. (Pressurization also created a structural problem at the beginning of the jet era, revealed by a series of disastrous accidents involving the world's first jet airliner, the de Havilland Comet.) In cockpits, klaxons and stick-shakers warned of an approaching stall, and voiced warnings (usually spoken by a woman) were fed into pilots' headphones. Systems developed that warned of imminent collision, with the ground or with other aircraft, and navigation using information provided by various forms of radar or by satellite largely removed any doubts about an aircraft's position.

Eventually, as computer technology developed, more and more aircraft operations were computer monitored or controlled. "Glass cockpits" were fitted, featuring screened displays in place of instruments, with finger-touch controls presenting selected flight information at will. Head-up displays projected essential details onto windshields so pilots would not have to lower their heads at critical periods of flight. Much of the flying in airliners was handed over to computers, and it became possible to land at major airports in zero visibility, the ground unseen until the wheels hit the runway. Information originally held on paper was stored in digital form, available when needed in the format required. Thousands of pages from countless manuals and charts were converted into compact disks. In the military, the pilots of combat aircraft exchanged their simple parachutes for ejection seats, and got used to going about their business while seated above powerful rockets. G suits helped to delay the onset of "blackout" during high G maneuvers, and pressure suits were worn by those operating at very high altitudes.

Martin-Baker is the world's longest-established manufacturer of ejection seats and related equipment made to safeguard an aviator throughout the escape, survival, location and recovery phases of an emergency. By 2005, Martin-Baker seats had saved well over 7,000 lives. The Martin-Baker Mk. 12 ejection seat seen here can be used with the aircraft stationary on the ground. In those circumstances, the parachute would be fully deployed in less than two seconds.

TOP *The Martin-Baker Mk. 16 ejection seat under test from a rocket sled. The seat's rocket has fired and the stabilizing drogue chute has deployed. The Mk. 16 is fitted to the Dassault Rafale and the Eurofighter Typhoon.*
BOTTOM *The Aces II ejection seat of this F-16 performed flawlessly and the pilot walked away from the crash. The subsequent inquiry found that the pilot (No. 6 of the Thunderbirds aerobatic team) had incorrectly set his altimeter for an air show at Mountain Home AFB, Idaho, on September 14, 2003, and had attempted to pull through from a split-S maneuver at 1,760 feet instead of 2,500 feet. He ejected just eight-tenths of a second before impact.*

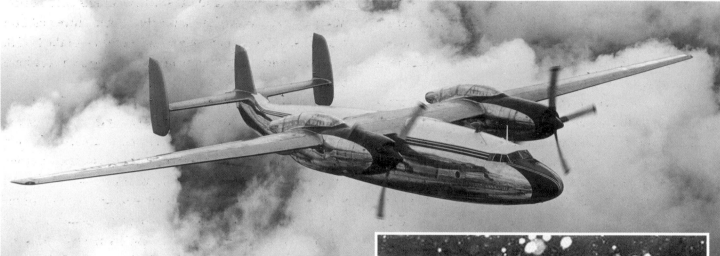

ABOVE *British European Airways operated up to twenty Airspeed Ambassadors between 1952 and 1958, calling them Elizabethans in honor of the newly crowned Queen. Graceful and reliable, this excellent airliner made the headlines for the wrong reasons in February 1958.* RIGHT *On February 6, 1958, Flight BE609, a British European Airways Elizabethan class Airspeed Ambassador (G-ALZU Lord Burghley), carrying players and staff of Manchester United Football Club, plus a number of journalists and supporters, crashed in a blizzard on its third attempt to take off from a slush-covered runway at Munich-Riem airport. There were twenty-three fatalities.*

Technology solved the problem of demanding low-level missions, allowing them to be entrusted to the autopilot and flown "hands off," by day or night and in all weathers.

On the ground, maintenance became highly organized, and technicians responsible for servicing aircraft were carefully selected and thoroughly trained. More and larger airfields were built, runways grew longer, and fire and rescue services were provided to meet any emergency. Navigation and approach aids were added to guide aviators more accurately and safely from place to place. Using just lights and radio beacons to start with, these systems eventually developed into a complex worldwide system of airways and airfield approaches, with aircraft carefully monitored and controlled on radar wherever necessary. Air traffic control, which before the days of radio relied on flagmen and light signals, became a science, demanding the highest standards from the responsible controllers, and air-to-ground communications went from the temperamental single-frequency

On January 14, 1951, a National Airlines DC-4 landed at Philadelphia. The aircraft overshot, ran into a ditch and caught fire. The pilot chose to land long, on a runway covered with wet snow instead of executing a missed approach. Seven of the twenty-eight on board died.

Morse code transmissions of the early 1920s to the clarity of multichannel UHF after World War II. Accurate weather forecasting, particularly once satellites offered comprehensive coverage, helped to diminish the risk of aircraft blundering into severe weather systems.

Less obvious, perhaps, were the advances made in aviation medicine that uncovered the facts about flight at high altitude or under high G loading, and warned of the hazards to be faced during ejection at high speed and of the disorientation pilots often suffered while flying without an external horizon. Rules were established to avoid aircrew fatigue. Stringent selection procedures were adopted for aircrew, both in military and civilian aviation, and flight training became more demanding, with flight simulators playing an increasingly important role in the later years of the century. It was a process that never stopped, as crews were subject to regular standardization checks both in the air and in flight simulators, where they could safely be confronted by almost every conceivable emergency they might have to face. Airline cabin crews were trained to meet all kinds of contingencies, ranging from fire in the air to childbirth, and including (after the rash of terrorist acts in the 1960s) dealing with hijackers. At the same time, security measures generally were tightened by the airlines and at airports, with passengers accepting the need for careful screening before boarding an aircraft.

"Tin-Kickers"

A vital element in the continued improvement in every aspect of flight safety has been the work of the accident investigation teams. Britain's Royal Flying Corps established an Accident Investigation Branch as early as 1915, and at the end of World War I, a Department of Civil Aviation was set up in the Air Ministry to investigate both civil and military accidents. After serving various parent ministries, the AIB passed to the Department of Transport in 1983, and in November 1987 its name was changed to the Air Accidents Investigation Branch. In the United States, the Civil Aeronautics Board was responsible for civil aircraft accident investigation until 1967, when the National Transportation Safety Board was formed. Before the century ended, the NTSB had investigated more than 100,000 aviation accidents and become the world's premier accident investigation agency. On call 365 days a year, NTSB investigators fly to anywhere in the world at a moment's notice. Many other countries have their own investigation branches, but they often rely on the expertise of the NTSB, at least in part because so many of the world's aircraft are built in the United States.

Accident investigators (commonly known as "tin-kickers" from their habit of wandering over crash sites turning pieces of wreckage over with their shoes) are multifaceted people. Primarily engineers operating as detectives, they must be knowledgeable about aviation and capable of working in harmony with their counterparts of other nationalities. Diplomatic skills are often needed, and the International Civil Aviation investigation manual adds such desirable characteristics as "inquisitive nature, dedication, diligence, patience, integrity, and humility." They also must be dispassionate about what they do. Aircraft accident sites are often horrifying scenes of death and destruction, and investigators have to be able to distance themselves from the carnage, gathering clues from the wreckage and the victims while retaining a sense of detachment.

"Black Boxes"

In the jet era, the "black boxes" became the most powerful tools of the accident investigators and the items most eagerly sought after an accident. There are two boxes (neither is black — orange is more easily seen), each of which keeps a record of events during a flight. Flight Data Recorders for airliners were introduced in the late 1950s, but could monitor only five flight parameters. Digital FDRs appeared in the 1980s, and in 1997 the U.S. Federal Aviation Administration required a minimum of eleven to twenty-nine parameters to be tracked depending on the size of the aircraft. These included time, heading, altitude, airspeed, vertical acceleration, longitudinal acceleration, pitch attitude, roll attitude, control column or pitch-control surface position, thrust of each engine, and time of each radio transmission.

The Cockpit Voice Recorder registers the conversations of the flight crew and all radio transmissions, as well as other sounds in the cockpit. Audio tracks are taken from the pilot's and co-pilot's headsets, and from a microphone in an overhead panel that records sounds such as engine noise, stall warning and landing-gear movement. To ensure that the most relevant information is made available to investigators, recorders must stop running once an aircraft has crashed. Generators power the recorders so that when the engines stop recording also stops.

The original design requirements for black boxes were that they had to withstand an impact equal to one hundred times the force of gravity (100G). They were installed with other ancillary equipment in the front avionics bay. However, after several recorders were destroyed in accidents, the Federal Aviation Administration increased the impact requirement to 1000G and the boxes were relocated in the rear of aircraft. The tests that recorders must now complete are severe: among them, surviving 3,400G for 6.5 milliseconds (equal to a deceleration from 360 mph to zero), resisting a heat of 1,100 degrees Centigrade for one hour and 260 degrees Centigrade for a further ten hours, and continuing to transmit "pings" for thirty days over a 2-mile radius while at a pressure equal to a depth of 20,000 feet below the surface of the ocean.

With such remarkable tools, crash investigators are able to reach conclusions about the causes of aircraft accidents more quickly and with far more assurance than was the case for most of the 20th century. In earlier years, their work was often slow and laborious, demanding an enormous amount of painstaking effort and single-minded dedication. Those are still essential qualities for investigators, but the information provided by black boxes has immensely eased their task in the majority of cases. Sometimes the cause of an accident is only too readily apparent, but many of the significant major accidents summarized here illustrate the value of the work done by investigators, both before and after the introduction of black boxes, and emphasize the importance of lessons learned from the findings of investigations.

TOP *On July 9, 1982, a Pan Am Boeing 727 took off from New Orleans in rain and gusty winds. It encountered severe windshear and reached a height of only 150 feet before descending steeply nose up. It clipped trees, struck a power line, and crashed into the suburb of Kenner, destroying six houses, damaging five more, and killing eight people on the ground. All 145 on board died. Investigators collected the wreckage and found very little of the aircraft intact.*

BOTTOM *Windshear was again the culprit at Dallas on August 2, 1985. An L-1011 of Delta Airlines was driven down while on final approach. It landed in a field, careened across a highway crushing a car, and bounced onto the airfield where it hit two large water tanks. There were 137 people on board killed.*

The de Havilland Comet 1 was the world's first jet airliner. It first flew in 1949 and then underwent exhaustive flight trials for three years before starting commercial services. Having gained a significant lead in building jet airliners, de Havilland then paid the price for being a pioneer. A series of crashes led to lengthy investigations. The Comet 1s were grounded and de Havilland was forced to go back to the drawing board to correct design problems that led to metal fatigue.

Weather Can Be Hostile

Bad weather has played a part in many aircraft accidents, especially those in the early days, when pilots still flew largely by the seat of their pants and relied on being in visual contact with the ground to find their way from one place to another. On April 7, 1922, a dull day with very poor visibility, the first midair collision between two airliners took place 60 miles north of Paris. A Daimler Airways DH-18 hit a Farman Goliath of Grands Express Aériens head on, and both aircraft crashed, killing seven people. The airliners were traveling in opposite directions on the route between London and Paris, with both pilots flying at only a few hundred feet, intent on navigating through the mist by following railways directly beneath their routes. Unfortunately, they chose the same railway lines.

In those early days, "major" aircraft accidents generally claimed few victims. It was not until after World War II, when jet engines made it possible for larger aircraft to cover more of the world, and air travel began to come within the budgets of more people, that the numbers of those killed per accident sometimes rose into the hundreds. However, one of the most startling crashes of the postwar years involved an aircraft that had neither jet engines nor the capacity to carry even fifty passengers. It generated banner headlines because the dead included several players from Manchester United Football Club. The team was on its way home from Belgrade after having qualified for the semifinal of the European Cup.

On February 6, 1958, an Airspeed Ambassador of British European Airways, carrying the Manchester United team, landed at Munich to refuel before flying on to London. The weather was wintry and the runway was covered in slush. By shortly after 2:30 P.M. the aircraft had been turned around and was ready to leave. Two takeoffs were attempted, but both were abandoned because of boost surging, an occasional difficulty with the Ambassador's engines. Half an hour later, after considering the problem, the pilots tried again. This time the surging was controlled and the aircraft gathered speed, but now the runway's slush became a factor. With copilot Ken Rayment at the controls, Captain Thain monitored the instruments: "I glanced at the airspeed indicator and saw it registered 105 knots and was flickering. When it reached 117 knots I called out 'V1' [the point after which it isn't safe to abandon takeoff]. Suddenly the needle dropped to about 112 and then 105. Ken shouted, 'Christ, we can't make it,' and I looked up from the instruments to see a lot of snow and a house and a tree right in the path of the aircraft."

Denied flying speed by the drag of the slush, the Ambassador plowed into the house and the tree and broke up. There were explosions and fire. Of the forty-four people on board, twenty-three died, including eight Manchester United footballers and copilot Ken Rayment. In the absence of informed opinion, blame for the crash fell squarely on Captain Thain. It was another ten years before the drag effect of slush was thoroughly tested and its dangers fully understood.

Thunderstorms and the violence they embody have been consistent killers throughout the history of aviation.

On January 13, 1982, an Air Florida Boeing 727 hit the 14th Street Bridge and crashed into the Potomac River on takeoff from Washington National Airport in heavy snow and frigid temperatures. Ice caused the engine instruments to show erroneously high thrust readings and it appeared that the crew attempted to take off using less than full power. Seventy-four of the seventy-nine on board perished and five more died in cars on the bridge.

On May 2, 1953, a storm caused the first loss of a jet airliner in passenger service. A de Havilland Comet 1 of the British Overseas Airways Corporation (BOAC) took off from Calcutta in thundery weather and six minutes later plunged to earth, killing all forty-three on board. It had broken up in the air, overstressed by severe vertical gusts. It was the beginning of a sad decline in the trailblazing airliner's fortunes, more fatal accidents following from different and unexpected structural problems. Similar proof of the power of turbulent air came on March 5, 1966, when another BOAC airliner, a Boeing 707, was torn apart by violent gusts while flying in clear air at 15,000 feet near Mount Fujiyama in Japan. The 124 people on board died when the 707 plummeted to earth, shedding its tail assembly, forward fuselage and all four engines on the way down.

Most serious accidents occur during the takeoff and landing phases of flight. At such times aircraft are low and slow, and especially vulnerable to the effects of severe weather. The phenomenon of wind shear is often associated with thunderstorms, and can produce downdrafts of close to 1,000-feet-per-minute vertical velocity. An aircraft suddenly encountering such a powerful gust near the ground can be forced into a situation from which it is impossible to recover. On June 24, 1975, a Boeing 727 of Eastern Airlines approached New York's John F. Kennedy Airport in heavy rain. About a mile from the runway it encountered a severe downdraft and was driven into the approach lighting tow-

ers, bursting into flames and disintegrating: 115 of the 124 people on board died. On the other side of the world, near Alma Ata, Kazakhstan, on July 8, 1980, all 166 persons flying in a Tu-154 were killed when it was forced down by a microburst shortly after takeoff, just as its high-lift devices were retracting and when it was close to its maximum weight. Two years later, a Boeing 727 of Pan American Airways took off from New Orleans in heavy rain and crashed into a residential area less than thirty seconds after getting airborne. The heavily laden airliner never got higher than 150 feet and was unable to climb against the strength of a fierce downdraft, striking trees before destroying a dozen houses. The dead included 145 on the aircraft and another eight on the ground. On August 2, 1985, 137 more victims were claimed by a savage microburst at Dallas. A Lockheed L-1011 of Delta Air Lines was forced down into a plowed field a mile short of the runway, crushed a car as it crossed a highway, and finally disintegrated in a fireball on hitting a water tank. Remarkably, twenty-eight people survived from the rear of the passenger cabin. Examination of the readings from the Tri-Star's DFDR revealed the strength and the rapidity of the changes in gust velocities that had caused the disaster. Accidents such as these encouraged research into wind shear, and led to the development of improved detection systems both for aircraft and airports. Terminal Doppler weather radar and the low-level wind-shear alert system (LLWAS) have been generally effective in countering the threat of severe weather near major airports. Airlines also intensified aircrew training on how best to cope with or, better still, avoid the worst thunderstorms and their associated wind shear.

Fear of Freezing

Ice and snow are particularly unforgiving enemies of flying. Perhaps the most dramatic demonstration of their destructive power was given on January 13, 1982, within walking distance of the U.S. capitol in Washington, D.C. It had been a harsh winter and the Potomac River was frozen over. An Air Florida Boeing 727 received clearance for takeoff from National Airport nearly an hour after de-icing procedures had been completed. There had been continuous moderate snowfall during the waiting period and the temperature remained below freezing. Ice had once again accumulated on the aircraft, a fact of which the pilots were apparently aware, as the CVR later showed. As the aircraft gathered speed on the runway, the pilots' remarks, captured on the CVR, revealed growing unease, beginning with a comment by the copilot (who was at the controls) on the indicated airspeed:

Copilot: God, look at that thing. That don't seem right, does it? Uh, that's not right.

Captain: Yes it is, there's eighty.

Copilot: Naw, I don't think that's right…. Ah, maybe it is.

Captain: Hundred and twenty.

Copilot: I don't know….

Captain: V1 … easy … V2. [Sound of stick-shaker warns of approaching stall]

Tower: Palm 90 contact departure control.

Captain: Forward, forward, easy. We only want five hundred. (500 ft/min rate of climb)

Come on forward … forward, just barely climb.

Captain: Stalling — we're falling!

Copilot: Larry, we're going down, Larry….

Captain: I know it. [Sound of impact]

The captain's casual assurance up to the point of the aircraft rotating to break ground abruptly changed to alarm when the stick-shaker indicated that the angle of climb demanded could not be maintained. The 727 was unable to hold altitude and, after hitting the 14th Street Bridge, crashed into the frozen Potomac River. Seventy-four of the seventy-nine persons on board died, and the five survivors owed their lives to the heroics of the crew of a U.S. Park Police helicopter and of a man who dived into the icy waters to help a woman when a rescue line slipped from her grasp. The disruptive effect of ice on the airflow over the wings was undoubtedly a major factor in the crash, but when the FDR was recovered, its evidence added another. It showed that the engines had not delivered sufficient power during the takeoff. The engine power indicators had given false information to the crew because of ice blocking air-inlet sensors in the engine intakes. The throttles had never been fully opened, the copilot checking their advance when the gauges indicated that the required takeoff thrust was being delivered. It seemed the crew had chosen to crash rather than overspeed the engines.

The fatal consequences of ice accretion were not confined to operations at low level. On October 31, 1994, an ATR-72 turboprop of Simmons Airlines crashed near Roselawn, Indiana, killing all sixty-eight people on board. The DFDR and CVR were recovered and their evidence made it possible to reconstruct the sequence of events leading to the crash.

An ATR-72 of Simmons Airlines crashed near Roselawn, Indiana, on October 31, 1994, killing all sixty-eight people on board. Ice accretion was the basic cause. The aircraft struck the ground almost vertically at over 400 mph, leaving a pathetically small scar in a plowed field.

Apparently there had been a buildup of ice on the wings while the aircraft had been in a holding pattern in cloud at 10,000 feet. During a descent to 8,000 feet, the ATR-72 began a series of uncontrolled rolling maneuvers, on one occasion completing a complete roll to the right, at the same time increasing its angle of descent. At 5,000 feet, in a 70-degree dive, the captain said "Nice and easy" as he tried to recover, but at 1,700 feet and an indicated airspeed of 430 mph (some 130 mph above the aircraft's limit) the ATR-72 shed its outer wing sections. It then slammed into a field partially inverted and disintegrated. Among other things, the accident investigation determined that the de-icing boots on the leading edge of the ATR-72's wing did not prevent the formation, aft of the boot, of an ice ridge that could seriously disturb the airflow over the ailerons. In the months that followed, ATR-72s (and the smaller 42s) were modified with larger de-icing boots.

Coming Together

Aircraft generally do not respond well to colliding with solid objects, be they other aircraft or stationary obstructions on the ground. On July 28, 1945, in one of the most sensational collisions ever, a USAAF B-25 flew into New York's Empire State Building, some 900 feet above street level. As it had been in the 1922 airliner collision over France, fog was a major contributing factor, with visibility in the New York area reduced to no more than an eighth of a mile. Maneuvering to get in line for a landing at Newark, the B-25 wandered blindly over Manhattan and was seen from the streets below weaving its way through the city's skyscraper forest before slamming into the 79th floor of

the Empire State. The impact punched a huge hole in the building, and wreckage tore through the offices, one engine emerging on the other side to fall on the penthouse of a neighboring apartment block. An elevator shaft was penetrated and the cable cut, sending the elevator car plunging to the basement. Its female attendant survived the terrifying experience because of giant springs fitted in the bottom of the shaft. The CAA subsequently raised the minimum altitude allowed over Manhattan to 2,500 feet.

Another celebrated American location was the setting for a midair collision on June 30, 1956. Two airliners, a Douglas DC-7 of United Airlines and a TWA Lockheed

TOP A Pacific Southwest Airlines Boeing 727 moments after colliding with a Cessna 172 of Gibbs Flight Service while making a visual approach to Lindbergh Field, San Diego, on September 25, 1978. BOTTOM On December 16, 1960, a United Airlines DC-8 collided with a TWA Constellation after entering a holding pattern for Idlewild Airport, New York, at more than twice the normal speed. The DC-8 crashed into the streets of Brooklyn. Six people died on the ground and another 128 in the two airliners.

Super Constellation, came together about 21,000 feet above Grand Canyon, apparently while both were concentrating on the wonders of the scenery far below. The burned-out wreckage of the two aircraft was found the following day deep inside the canyon. All 128 passengers and crew were killed. The disaster focused attention on the inadequacies of the U.S. air traffic system and forced the government into raising funds to improve control on the nation's aerial highways. It was perhaps ironic that the continuing limitations of the system should be exposed by the same two airlines in December 1960, this time over New York. A United DC-8 jetliner overtook a TWA Super Constellation in cloud at 5,000 feet, its wing slicing into the Connie's fuselage. The TWA airliner broke into three main pieces, which fell blazing onto Idlewild Airport. The DC-8, minus half of its starboard wing and an engine, carried on for another 8 miles before crashing into a Brooklyn street. As in the Grand Canyon accident, 128 people died on the two airliners, plus another six on the ground, a remarkably light additional casualty list considering the destruction of buildings in the area. After this, there was a major revision of air traffic regulations. The principle of "positive control" was introduced for all aircraft flying above 24,000 feet, and down to 8,000 feet on many airways. Speed limits were imposed within 30 miles of airports, and aircraft weighing more than 12,500 pounds were required to carry both transponder and DME equipment.

Military aircraft and civil air traffic sometimes did not mix well, and there were accidents as a result. On June 6, 1971, a U.S. Marine Corps F-4 sliced through a Hughes Air West DC-9 over Los Angeles. Both aircraft were destroyed and the sole survivor was the occupant of the F-4's rear seat, who ejected safely. The following month, a Boeing 727 of All Nippon Airways ran into an F-86 of the Japan Air Self-Defense Force flying as wingman in a formation that had strayed out of its military training area. All 162 people on the 727 perished, but the F-86 pilot managed to bail out. Both he and his leader were later sent to prison, convicted of involuntary manslaughter. In August 1979, another breach of the rules, this time by air traffic controllers in the Ukraine, brought together two Tu-134s of Aeroflot, killing 178, and in May 1985 they did it again with an Aeroflot Tu-134 and a Soviet Air Force

An-26, killing ninety-four in a head-on collision.

Not entirely without reason, airline pilots can be apprehensive about sharing airspace with private aircraft and critical of what they see as the unpredictable behavior of some private pilots, especially in the bustle of Californian skies. On September 25, 1978, the apprehension proved justified, but blame could not be attributed to the private pilots involved. A Boeing 727 of Pacific Southwest Airlines approaching Lindbergh Field, San Diego, overtook and struck a Cessna 172 practicing instrument approaches at the same airfield. The weather at the time was good, the tower was in contact with both aircraft, and each pilot had been informed of the other aircraft's presence, with the 727 captain saying more than once that he had the light aircraft in sight. Even so, a collision occurred, and 144 people died. Over Los Angeles, on August 31, 1986, it was simpler to apportion the major part of the blame to the pilot of a light aircraft when he wandered off course and into the Terminal Control Area. A Piper Archer, climbing out VFR from Torrance airport, collided at right angles with an Aeromexico DC-9 descending toward Los Angeles International. The airliner rolled onto its back and dived into a residential area, destroying eighteen houses and killing fifteen people on the ground. Sixty-four persons in the DC-9 and three in the Archer were killed. After the disaster, the FAA issued a requirement for all aircraft operating within 30 miles of a TCA's primary airport to have altitude-encoding transponders.

Two of the worst disasters in aviation history were collisions that resulted at least in part from misunderstandings between air traffic controllers and aircrew. On November 12, 1996, the crew of an Air Kazakhstan Il-76, inbound to the Indian capital of New Delhi, became confused over their let-down clearance and descended below their assigned height of 15,000 feet. An outbound Saudia 747 was level at 14,000 feet. Realizing the mistake, the Il-76 pilot, already below 14,000 feet, began to climb. Some 50 miles west of New Delhi, the transports met head-on, the engines of the 747 destroying the left wing of the Il-76. There were 349 people killed. Bad as it was, this figure was far fewer than that reached in the accident at Tenerife on March 27, 1977, involving 747s of KLM and Pan American Airways. Both "Jumbos," packed with passengers, had been diverted from their original destination of Las Palmas on the nearby island of Gran Canaria because of a terrorist bomb explosion in the terminal building there. After landing at Tenerife, the two 747s were parked next to each other, squeezed together in an area ill-suited to handling Jumbo jets. The Pan Am passengers, already late because of delays at Los Angeles, were kept on board while waiting for Las Palmas to reopen, but the KLM captain decided first to disembark his passengers and then to refuel his aircraft.

The diversion of traffic had overloaded Tenerife's small airport. Aircraft were parked on the taxiways and those intending to leave were forced to backtrack on the runway for some distance on their way to the takeoff point. When Las Palmas reopened, the Pan Am 747 was ready to leave immediately, but could not because the KLM aircraft was in the way, busy re-embarking passengers and filling fuel tanks. By the time these operations were complete and the 747s cleared to taxi, the local weather had deteriorated, with fog banks drifting over the airfield. As the KLM aircraft lined up for takeoff, the Pan Am 747 was facing it, less than a mile away and still taxiing to a turnoff point. Neither crew could see the other because of the fog, and the poor visibility made the Pan Am pilots miss a taxiway that would have allowed them to clear the runway quickly. Impatient to be off, the KLM captain began easing his throttles open, but was checked by his copilot. The transcripts of the CVRs, beginning with the KLM co-pilot's anxious intervention, and together with the tapes from the tower, reveal the confusion of the last fatal minute:

KLM copilot: Wait a minute, we don't have an ATC clearance.

KLM captain: No; I know that, go ahead — ask.

KLM copilot: Ah — the KLM four eight zero five is now ready for takeoff, and we're waiting for our ATC clearance.

Tower: KLM eight seven zero five — uh — you are cleared to the Papa Beacon, climb to and maintain flight level nine zero … right turn after take-off proceed with heading zero four zero until intercepting the three two five radial from Las Palmas VOR.

KLM copilot: Roger, sir, we are cleared to the Papa Beacon flight level nine zero, right turn out zero four zero until intercepting the three two five. We are now at takeoff.

(The brakes were released by the captain while the co-pilot was still transmitting.)

KLM captain: Let's go — check thrust.

Tower (answering the reading of the clearance): OK…. Stand by for takeoff … I will call you

Pan Am copilot: And we are still taxiing down the runway, Clipper one seven three six.

(These two transmissions were made together, causing only a shrill noise in the KLM cockpit.)

Tower: Papa Alpha one seven three six report runway clear.

Pan Am copilot: OK, will report when we're clear.

KLM engineer: Is he not clear then?

KLM captain: What do you say?

KLM engineer: Is he not clear — that Pan American?

KLM captain: Oh yes.

KLM co-pilot: V1

At about this time, the Pan Am captain saw the lights of the onrushing 747 and shouted "There he is! Look at him! Goddamn … that son-of-a-bitch is coming!" and his co-pilot screamed "Get off! Get off! Get off!" The Pan Am throttles were slammed open in an attempt to get clear, and the KLM aircraft reared up as its captain hauled back desperately on the control column, but it was too late. Four seconds after the call of "V1," there was an exclamation from the KLM captain, followed by the sounds of impact.

The KLM 747 did get airborne, but not enough to miss the Pan Am aircraft completely. The KLM fuselage skidded over the Pan Am aft fuselage, shearing off the top. It remained in the air for another 500 feet before crashing back to the runway and bursting into flames. All 234 passengers and 14 crew on board the KLM died in the intense fire. The Pan Am aircraft, too, burst into flames immediately, and many of those on the side of the aircraft which had been hit were killed instantly or quickly by the resulting fire. Those that were fortunate enough to escape the flames had to risk injury by jumping 20 or more feet onto wreckage. Of the 396 people on board the Pan Am flight, only 61 survived.

The root cause of the accident was that the KLM 747 started to take off before it was cleared to do so. However, the chain of events leading to the crash was complex, and a number of "what if…" questions begged for answers. Changing any one of a host of contributing factors would have avoided the accident. What if the Pan Am flight had not been late leaving Los Angeles and had reached Las Palmas before the bomb went off? What if there had been no bomb at Las Palmas? If the Pan Am captain had been allowed into a holding pattern over Gran Canaria (as he requested) instead of being diverted? If the KLM captain had not decided to refuel, delaying departure of both aircraft until after the fog rolled in? If the Pan Am crew had not missed the turnoff and had left the runway sooner? If the tower and the Pan Am copilot had not transmitted at the same time? If the KLM co-pilot had said "We are now taking off" instead of "We are now at takeoff"? Isolated factors in themselves, they came together to kill 583 people.

The aftermath of the worst single disaster in commercial aviation history. On March 27, 1977, a Boeing 747 of KLM collided with a Pan Am 747 on the runway at Tenerife. The KLM captain initiated takeoff without clearance while the Pan Am aircraft was taxiing on the runway. The burned-out remains of the KLM aircraft mark the spot where 583 people died.

Machines Can Be Fragile

All machines are subject to failure, but aircraft are among the few in which the consequences of even a minor failure can become catastrophic very quickly. Modern airliners and front-line military aircraft are among the most complex machines ever assembled, and the medium in which they operate can be terribly unforgiving. It is an unfortunate fact that in an aircraft comprising millions of component parts, the failure of a single item or the emergence of a tiny crack can lead to a major accident, despite years spent on research and development, the most rigorous testing, and meticulous maintenance procedures. Machines are always capable of giving the people who make and operate them a nasty surprise.

Perhaps the aircraft industry never received a greater shock than that of the mysterious losses of de Havilland Comet 1s in 1954. As the first jet airliner, the Comet was pioneering passenger-carrying operations at speeds and altitudes previously unknown to the airlines, and until 1954 it was a great success. The breakup of a Comet near Calcutta in 1953 was attributed to overstress in unusually severe weather conditions and therefore unlikely to be repeated. The picture began to change on January 10, 1954, when a BOAC Comet left Rome for London and climbed to 26,000 feet. At that point, the captain made a radio transmission that was never finished. Soon afterward, fishermen near the island of Elba saw wreckage plunging into the sea. The Comets were grounded while de Havilland and the British government investigated the disaster. Royal Navy divers and local fishermen did their best to recover as much of the aircraft as possible from 500 feet of water, and some fifty modifications were made to the rest of the Comet fleet in a speculative attempt to cover the problem. (The modifications included the installation of shields between the engines and fuel tanks, reinforced fuel lines and new smoke detectors.) With these completed, the Comets were cleared to fly again on March 23. The reprieve was short. On April 8, another Comet took off from Rome and disappeared during a climb to cruising altitude. Once more, Comets were grounded worldwide.

Meanwhile, some two-thirds of the Elba Comet had been recovered and techniques were being devised by the Royal Aircraft Establishment, Farnborough, that would set the pattern for all future investigations into major aircraft accidents. Thousands of parts from the shattered Comet were painstakingly reassembled like a giant jigsaw and scrutinized for clues; forensic pathologists extracted crucial evidence from the bodies of the victims; and a giant tank was filled with water so that a Comet fuselage could be subjected to repeated pressure tests, simulating the effects of three hours of flight every ten minutes. When all the evidence was in, it became clear that the Comets had succumbed to metal fatigue. The Comet 1 was designed with square windows, and cracks had appeared at the corners, eventually leading to catastrophic failure of the pressurized fuselage, which exploded with great violence once a crack began to spread.

Following a series of crashes involving de Havilland Comet 1s in 1954, a Comet fuselage was subjected to tests in a pressurized water tank at Farnborough, U.K., to simulate the effects of three hours of flight every ten minutes.

De Havilland paid a heavy price for pioneering jet transports. The only solution to the Comet's problem was a complete redesign including round windows, and that took four years. Other companies were able to learn vital lessons from the Comet investigation, and by the time the Comet 4 appeared in 1958, the Boeing 707 was well on its way to dominating the world's airliner business.

Another airliner bedeviled by structural failures was the McDonnell Douglas DC-10. On March 3, 1974, a DC-10 of Turkish Airlines smashed at high speed into a forest north of Paris, scattering wreckage over an area half a mile long and 100 yards wide. In this first nonsurvivable crash of a wide-bodied jet airliner, 346 people died. The villain of the piece was the door to the cargo hold, which had blown off in flight. Unlike other airliner doors, which were designed to plug the holes in the fuselage they covered, the cargo door on the DC-10 opened outward and relied on latches and locking pins to keep it secure. In this accident (and on several previous occasions with happier endings) the door had been closed, but the latches were not fully home. As the DC-10 reached 11,000 feet on the climb out of Paris, the pressurization overcame the latches and blew the door open. The resulting decompression affected the cargo hold more severely than the passenger cabin above and the floor in between collapsed, disrupting the elevator and rudder control runs in the process. The aircraft pitched nose down and the crew were unable to regain control.

Five years later, on May 25, 1979, the DC-10 suffered another blow in the worst U.S. domestic disaster to that date. As the aircraft lifted off the runway at Chicago's O'Hare Airport, the No. 1 engine, complete with pylon, broke away from its mounting and was hurled up and over the left wing. As it went, it took a chunk of the wing with it and damaged a number of the aircraft's systems. The DC-10 struggled up to 300 feet, rolled to its left and plunged into a field about a mile from the end of the runway, where it disintegrated in a huge fireball. The 271 persons on board and two bystanders were killed. The problem, revealed by the NTSB's meticulous detective work, was traced to fatigue fracture in the engine pylon, brought on by amended servicing practices introduced by American Airways to save time. The investigation also pointed to deficiencies in the surveillance and reporting procedures of the FAA, and to quality-control shortcomings of the manufacturer.

Pieces of the shattered Comet 1 recovered from the sea off Elba were reassembled on a hangar floor at Farnborough so that investigators could look for clues to the cause of the disaster. Evidence was found of fatigue failure at the corners of the comet's square windows. The painstaking work

carried out on the Comet disasters set a pattern for all future aircraft accident investigation.

ABOVE *Just after takeoff from O'Hare Airport, Chicago, on May 25, 1979, the No. 1 engine and pylon broke away from the wing of an American Airlines DC-10. A break in the hydraulic lines then allowed the left wing slats to retract, while the right wing slats remained extended. The left wing stalled and the aircraft rolled over. All 270 people aboard the DC-10 died, plus two more on the ground.* TOP RIGHT *Scars left on Sioux City Airport after the valiant attempt at a forced landing by the crew of an almost uncontrollable United Airlines DC-10 on July 19, 1989.* LOWER RIGHT *The aft fuselage of the United Airlines DC-10 after it came to rest at Sioux City. Of the 296 people on board, 184 survived.*

Engine Failure

At least one DC-10 mechanical failure led to an extended drama, with the crew struggling to control an aircraft that had become almost uncontrollable. On July 19, 1989, a United Airlines DC-10 was at 37,000 feet over Iowa when it was shaken by an explosion. The fin-mounted engine had suffered catastrophic failure, the huge fan disc at the front shattering and tearing away from the aircraft, damaging the tail and destroying lines in all three hydraulic systems. With total hydraulic failure, there was no way to operate the flying controls — ailerons, spoilers, elevators, rudder, flaps and slats were all useless. The DC-10 began to oscillate in pitch and had a strong tendency to roll to the right. Helped by a training captain who happened to be on board, the crew began a diversion to Sioux City Airport, learning on the way down how to gain some rough measure of control by juggling the power of the two good engines. In a remark-

able feat of airmanship, they managed to reach the airfield and line up with the runway, but they lacked the fineness of control needed to accomplish anything like a normal landing. Descending at 1,800 feet per minute, the DC-10 dropped its right wing just before hitting the ground and cartwheeled off the runway, rolling upside down and breaking into three pieces. That the aircraft arrived over the airfield under any sort of control at all was a wonderful achievement, and the sterling efforts of the crew saved the lives of 184 of the 296 people on board.

None of those traveling on an Il-62 of the Polish airline LOT on March 14, 1980 were so fortunate. As it approached Warsaw at the end of its flight from New York, the left inboard engine disintegrated, the flying fragments damaging two more engines and cutting the control lines to both the rudder and the elevator. Out of control, the Il-62 crashed into the moat of a castle, killing all eighty-seven on board including fourteen members and eight officials of the U.S. amateur boxing team. The accident was intitated by the failure of a turbine disc in the No. 2 engine, caused by metal fatigue.

Malfunctions Miscellaneous

Thousands of accidents have resulted from failures of aircraft components large and small, and every kind of system used in aircraft operation. Many have proved extremely costly in human lives. On June 28, 1982, a Yak-42 of Aeroflot, flying over southern Belorussia, had the screw-jack mechanism on the horizontal stabilizer run away, forcing the aircraft into a vertical descent that reached 1,000 feet per second. At about 19,000 feet and an indicated airspeed of over 500 mph, the Yak-42 began to break up: 132 people died. On August 12, 1985, the rear pressure bulkhead ruptured on a Japan Air Lines 747 some ten minutes after takeoff from Tokyo, allowing cabin air to rush into the unpressurized fin. A large part of the vertical stabilizer broke away and hydraulic lines powering the flying controls were severed. The crew reported the 747 "uncontrollable" several times before it crashed into a forested ridge. In the world's worst-ever single aircraft accident, 524 people were killed. Incredibly, four injured survivors were pulled from the rearmost section of the 747's wrecked cabin. In May 1991, 223 died when a Lauda Air 767 crashed in Thailand. A thrust reverser on the aircraft's left engine deployed in flight. On September 8, 1994, another control movement unselected by the pilots led to the destruction of a U.S. Air 737 with the loss of 132 lives. The longest airline accident investigation in history came to the conclusion that the basic cause was an uncommanded, rapid movement of the rudder to the left.

The shocking breakup of a TWA 747 off Long Island with the loss of 230 lives on July 17, 1996, gave rise to a host of alarming theories — there had been a bomb on board; a terrorist SAM had found its mark; perhaps the Jumbo had even been the victim of friendly fire from a U.S. Navy ship on an exercise. However, the wreckage showed no evidence of any form of explosive device. Indeed, there was no satisfactory evidence to support any of the theories advanced to explain the catastrophe, though it was believed that something, perhaps frayed wiring, had sparked and ignited the combustible fuel/air mixture in the almost-empty center fuel tank, setting off an explosion that destroyed the 747. Exhaustive examinations of the suspect wiring (and fuel pumps, valves, and any fittings likely to become hot) in all other 747s validated their systems and revealed no obvious culprits, but 747 operators were told to ensure that the center fuel tank was not left empty in flight.

Almost more shocking, because the drama was shown on television and involved the world's only operating supersonic airliner, was the blazing crash of an Air France Concorde near Paris on July 25, 2000. Just before the aircraft rotated on takeoff, a tire on the left main landing gear was destroyed when it ran over a piece of metal that was eventually shown to have fallen off a Continental Airlines DC-10 a few minutes earlier. Large pieces of rubber from the bursting tire were thrown against the underside of the Concorde's wing, causing a fuel tank to rupture. Escaping fuel ignited in seconds, and flames from an intense fire streamed out behind the aircraft as it lifted from the runway. Failure of the No. 2 engine was followed by loss of power to No. 1 and a call from the pilot that he was "trying for Le Bourget." A few seconds later the Concorde crashed into a small hotel and was destroyed. A small metal strip, of no particular importance to the aircraft that had lost it, had reduced a Mach 2 airliner to scrap and killed 113 people.

Smoke and Flame

Fire! Few dangers are as terrifying to imagine or as inexorably lethal as uncontrolled fire in the cabin of an airliner in flight. The first hint of trouble usually comes in the form of smoke carrying toxic fumes, after which the time for the crew to get the aircraft on the ground and evacuated is limited. How limited was made horrifyingly clear in a Boeing 707 of Varig (Brazil) on July 11, 1973. As the aircraft was prepared for a descent into Orly Airport (Paris), a transmission was made declaring an emergency and specifying that there was a fire on board. About 10 miles from touchdown, the pilot said there was "total fire." By this time, passengers were already being

> *"There are no new types of air crashes — only people with short memories. Every accident has its own forerunners, and every one happens either because somebody did not know where to draw the vital dividing line between the unforeseen and the unforeseeable or because well-meaning people deemed the risk acceptable."*
>
> STEPHEN BARLAY, *THE FINAL CALL: WHY AIRLINE DISASTERS CONTINUE TO HAPPEN*, MARCH 1990

TOP *No commercial aircraft was more controversial than the supersonic BAe-Aérospatiale Concorde. Economically a failure, it was nevertheless one of the finest technological achievements in 20th-century airliner history.*

BOTTOM *On July 25, 2000, an Air France Concorde caught fire after takeoff from Charles de Gualle Airport, Paris. Control was lost and the plane crashed into a hotel. Investigation revealed that the aircraft had run over a metal strip that had earlier fallen from a Continental Airlines DC 10. At least one of the Concorde's tires exploded and flying pieces ruptured fuel tanks. Escaping fuel ignited seconds later. In the smoking ruins of the hotel, five people died to add to the 109 on board the Concorde.*

overcome by fumes and the cockpit crew had put on oxygen masks and goggles. Smoke entered the cockpit in such dense clouds that the pilots had difficulty seeing the instruments, even though they had opened their side windows. Realizing that he had little hope of reaching the runway, the captain elected to put the aircraft down in open country. The 707 came to rest on its belly with the fuselage reasonably intact, but was soon engulfed by flames. Only one passenger and ten of the seventeen aircrew survived the crash; 123 people died, but they were already dead by the time the fire swept through the cabin, killed by the toxic gases they inhaled. It was believed that the fire had been started by human carelessness with a cigarette in one of the aft toilets. A similar fate befell a 707 of Pakistan International Airlines in Saudi Arabia on November 26, 1979. All 156 people on board died, and this time it was thought that the fire could have been started by a leak from a small kerosene stove. The passengers were mostly Muslim pilgrims returning from Mecca, and they were very fond of tea.

Less than a year later, Saudi Arabia was the scene of another fiery disaster. Smoke was detected in the aft cargo hold of a Saudia L-1011 seven minutes after takeoff from Riyadh. The crew reversed course and made a successful emergency landing at the airport, but the captain did not apparently realize the extent of the danger and the need for haste. He did not stop on a taxiway until almost three minutes after touchdown, and then kept the engines running for another three minutes. No evidence could be found that any attempt had been made to evacuate the aircraft, and the rescue crews had neither the equipment nor the training to force an entry. A door to the cabin was not opened until twenty-three minutes after the engines had shut down, and by that time it was far too late. All 301 persons on board were dead, most probably from the effects of various noxious gases — carbon monoxide, nitrous oxide, hydrogen cyanide, ammonia, and formic acid fumes. The fire eventually gutted the fuselage, burning away the roof but leaving the charred ruins smoldering on intact wings and undercarriage.

FLIGHT SIMULATOR
SAFETY TRAINING

The United Parcel Service air cargo division based in Louisville, Kentucky, operates a fleet of heavy and very heavy jet aircraft. They also operate and maintain full-motion aircraft simulators for currency training for all of their fleet. The simulator seen here is for the Airbus A300-600R. The complete cockpit of this airliner is perched on top of hydraulic supports, which give the occupants of the simulator all the "reality" necessary to complete the sensation of flight. Visual cues create the sensation of flight, the large computer-controlled video "environment" filling the vision of the pilot.

ABOVE The cockpit of the simulator. Behind the pilot's seat, the computer station where the simulator operator can program challenging flight situations into the training. OPPOSITE TOP Cliff Hicks is one of the UPS Flight Simulator technicians at the Louisville, Kentucky, facility. OPPOSITE INSET Below the simulator, the hydraulic legs and the very thick electrical cables which feed the machinery.

LEFT *On May 11, 1996, a ValuJet DC-9 crashed into the Everglades soon after leaving Miami International Airport. Improperly packed oxygen generators ignited, leading to a fire that burned through control cables and filled the cabin with smoke. There were no survivors from the 110 people on board.* RIGHT *A mangled oxygen generator recovered from the wreckage of the ValuJet DC-9.*

The contents of a cargo hold also featured in the destruction of a ValuJet DC-9 in Florida on May 11, 1996. Only ten minutes after taking off from Miami, the airliner buried itself in the mud and sawgrass of an Everglades swamp, killing all 110 people on board. After almost 80 percent of the aircraft's structure was recovered and put back together, it could be seen that a catastrophic fire had started in the DC-9's forward cargo hold. NTSB investigators determined that the fire began with the actuation of one or more oxygen generators that were being improperly carried as cargo. Criticism was directed at ValuJet and its contractor, Sabre Tech, for allowing the generators to be loaded in an unsafe condition, and at the FAA itself for its failure to insist on the fitting of fire detection and suppression systems in airliner cargo holds despite previous incidents involving oxygen generators.

Human Fallibility

Despite all the efforts made to promote flight safety and ensure that aircrews are well trained, there has never been a time in the history of aviation when a mistake was not being made in a cockpit somewhere in the world. Most are of little consequence, and others lead to near misses or minor incidents, but occasionally poor judgment ends in disaster. On July 5, 1970, the copilot of an Air Canada DC-8 deployed the spoilers inadvertently on an approach to Toronto. As the aircraft sank, the captain applied full power to cushion the impact with the runway, but the DC-8 hit the ground hard, tearing off the No. 4 engine and puncturing a fuel tank. As the aircraft climbed away to come round again, escaping fuel ignited and there were several explosions. Fatally crippled, the DC-8 dived into the ground, killing all 109 on board. Confronted with an unexpectedly difficult landing brought on by his copilot's mistake and initially unaware of the severe damage to his aircraft, it is perhaps not surprising that the captain elected to go round again, but hindsight suggests that if he had closed the throttles and stayed down, this fatal accident would have been limited to a incident involving no more than damage to the aircraft and a shaking for his passengers.

Less understandable was the behavior of an Eastern Airlines L-1011 crew that led, late on December 29, 1972, to the first fatal crash by a wide-bodied airliner. When the undercarriage was selected down for landing at Miami International, the green light for the nosewheel failed to come on. The approach was abandoned and the Tri-Star cleared the airport area while the crew tried to sort out their problem. The undercarriage was recycled to no effect, so the autopilot was engaged to hold 2,000 feet while other measures were tried to ensure that the nosewheel was down. Both pilots and the flight engineer, together with a maintenance specialist who was traveling as a passenger, became wholly involved in solving the puzzle. The CVR later revealed that a tone alarm, warning that the aircraft was leaving its selected altitude, failed to attract the attention of the crew. Neither pilot monitored the aircraft, but one of them must have nudged the control column, causing the autopilot to disengage. In the darkness over the Everglades, no one noticed that the Tri-Star was drifting downward. The last words spoken by the two pilots, recorded on the CVR, are a testament to the golden rule of dealing with emergencies when airborne — first fly the aircraft:

Co-pilot: We did something to the altitude.
Captain: What?
Co-pilot: We're still at two thousand feet, right?
Captain: Hey! What's happening here?

A few seconds later the Tri-Star's left wing struck the marshland of the Everglades at 230 mph. Wreckage was strewn over an area 1,500 feet long and 300 feet wide. Incredibly, 73 of the 176 persons on the flight survived the accident. It was later found that the source of the pilots' concern was a burned-out bulb. The nosewheel had been locked down all the time.

"Controlled flight into terrain" is a bland description of the sort of accident that often seems to defy logical explanation. Investigators have to ask themselves how a healthy crew could possibly have managed to fly a serviceable aircraft into an unyielding obstacle. On U.S. airlines between 1970 and 1975, almost 700 people died in nine such crashes. The last straw came on December 1, 1974, in an accident that was the catalyst for significant changes. A TWA 727 was diverted to Dulles International Airport because of high crosswinds at its intended destination, Washington National. The approach controller contacted the flight with "TWA 514, you are cleared for a VOR/DME approach to Runway 12." (A VOR/DME approach is an instrument approach using Very-high-frequency Omni-directional Range/Distance Measuring Equipment.) The crew took this as a clearance for immediate descent, although they were still over 30 miles from Dulles Airport. Weather at the time was wintry, with low cloud obscuring the ground. Not long afterward, the 727 brushed through some trees before slamming into Mount Weather at a little less than 1,800 feet. All ninety-two on board were killed. The investigation gave the probable cause as "the crew's decision to descend to 1,800 feet before the aircraft had reached the approach segment where that minimum altitude applied." It was believed that decision "was a result of inadequacies and lack of clarity in the air traffic control procedures which led to a misunderstanding

on the part of the pilots and of the controllers regarding each other's responsibilities during operations in terminal areas under instrument meteorological conditions." A particularly pertinent comment drew attention to "the issuance of the approach clearance when the flight was forty-four miles from the airport on an unpublished route without clearly defined minimum altitudes." The accident had important repercussions, among them an instruction that controllers would issue altitude restrictions to pilots making non-precision instrument approaches, and a requirement for all U.S.-registered airliners to be fitted with a ground proximity warning system (GPWS). In the years that followed, GPWS units became standard equipment on airliners worldwide.

Premature initiation of a descent when not sure of the terrain being flown over also led to the crash in the Andes most remembered for its epic (yet gruesome) story of survival. On Friday, October 13, 1972, a Fairchild FH-227D turboprop chartered from the Uruguayan Air Force by the members of a rugby team set out to cross the cloud-covered Andes en route to Santiago. Affected by an unexpectedly strong headwind, the pilot began his descent into Chile through cloud, assuming that he was clear of the mountains. At about 14,000 feet, the right wing clipped a ridge and the aircraft broke up, throwing several people out to their deaths. The main fuselage slid down the mountain slope and came to rest in a snow bank at 12,000 feet. Thirty-two of the forty-five people on the aircraft were still alive after the crash, but many of them were badly injured and some later died. Ten weeks later, in an astonishing feat of endurance that included being forced to eat the flesh of their dead comrades and see eight more of their party killed in an avalanche, sixteen survivors were rescued after two of them had found the strength to trek out of the mountains for help.

Following the introduction of GPWS systems, the number of "controlled flight into terrain" accidents fell, but they were still a threat for the unwary, as was demonstrated in Antarctica on November 28, 1979. On that day an Air New Zealand DC-10 on a sightseeing flight over the spectacular scenery of Antarctica ran into the lower slopes of Mount Erebus, a 12,500-foot active volcano on Ross Island, killing the 237 passengers and 20 crew. The immediate cause was the captain's decision to let down to 1,500 feet to get under low cloud cover and give his passengers a better view, in flagrant

An investigator approaches the wreckage of Air New Zealand Flight 901 on the slopes of Mount Erebus, Antarctica. The DC-10 struck the mountain on November 28, 1979, after descending through low cloud to give passengers a better view of the scenery. The dead numbered 257.

disregard of a company rule stating that aircraft were to maintain at least 6,000 feet, whatever the weather. Complicating the issue was the fact that neither of the pilots had flown over Antarctica before and were not familiar with the phenomenon of "white-out," in which the snow and ice below appear to merge with the cloud above, producing a white fishbowl effect and making it almost impossible for the human eye to judge how close an aircraft is to the surface. Another factor was that the route programmed into the DC-10's navigational system was changed just before the flight without informing the crew, and the new track led directly toward Mount Erebus instead of over the relatively low ground of previous flights. In the last moments of the flight, some members of the crew expressed their unease at the conditions and the captain made the decision to begin a climb. Seconds later, the GPWS sounded and the captain applied full power, but he could not outclimb the mountain.

The GPWS is an admirable flight safety aid, but it cannot always help those who are determined to go their own way and trust to luck. In the darkness of the early hours on November 27, 1983, an Avianca 747 was cleared to land at Madrid off an ILS (Instrument Landing System) approach. At the time, the captain was far from certain of his aircraft's position, but he set out to intercept the ILS centerline without bothering about the preceding instrument approach procedures. Bedeviling the situation was an incorrect outer marker crossing altitude of 2,383 feet given by the copilot — it should have been 3,283 feet. Eventually the GPWS sounded a warning, which was initially ignored by the captain. He then disconnected the autopilot and began to

reduce the rate of descent. It was too little, too late. The 747 hit a hill over 7 miles from the airport and 181 people died. Eleven surviving passengers were pulled from the wreckage, all seriously injured. A similarly disastrous ending to a 747 flight happened on August 7, 1997, during a night approach to Guam International Airport. Of the 254 people on board Korean Air Flight 801, 228 lost their lives when the aircraft struck a ridge about 3 miles from the airport at a height of 700 feet. The captain was conducting an ILS approach but had been informed that the glideslope was inoperative. Perhaps confused by spurious glideslope signals, the captain allowed the aircraft to descend below minimum altitudes on the approach, and appeared not to react to GPWS warnings in the later stages. Six seconds after the copilot advised that they should "make missed approach" the CVR recorded the first sounds of impact with the ground.

Human Frailties

Accidents caused by a breakdown in the human body are fortunately rare, but they do happen. On April 22, 1966, a Lockheed Electra of the American Flyers Airline Corporation crashed near Ardmore Airport, Oklahoma, during an attempted visual circling approach at night under a solid cloud base of 1,000 feet. Having just overshot from a missed approach, the Electra was in a right turn with undercarriage and flaps down when it hit a hill about a mile and a half from the airfield. Only fifteen of the ninety-eight people on board survived. An autopsy on the fifty-nine-year-old captain, who was also president of the airline, showed that he had severe coronary arteriosclerosis and probably died of heart failure before the crash. On the day of his fatal flight, he had been on duty for sixteen hours, and was undoubtedly both tired and under stress as he coped with the difficult flying conditions. It was later found that his medical records had been falsified, concealing both a long history of heart trouble and of diabetes, either of which would have made him ineligible for a first-class medical certificate, and therefore for an Airline Transport Pilot Rating.

It is possible that failure of a captain's heart also doomed a British European Airways Trident at Heathrow, London, on June 18, 1972. Less than two minutes after take-off, the Trident stalled and hit the ground hard after falling in a flat attitude from some 2,000 feet. None of the 118 persons on board survived the crash. A postmortem on the captain revealed that the arteries round his heart were seriously restricted and that one of them had hemorrhaged a short time before the flight, possibly as a result of a heated argument with another pilot in the BEA crew room. It was thought likely that he was in considerable pain by the time the Trident took off. That could have had something to do with his retraction of the airliner's slats and flaps at too low an airspeed in the climb, and the subsequent over-riding of the stick-shaker as the heavy Trident threatened to stall. It may be that the captain collapsed over the controls, leaving the inexperienced copilot to deal with an impossible situation. In the absence of a CVR, it was not possible to confirm all this conjecture, but the tragedy did lead to more stringent medical inspections for British pilots and to a requirement for CVRs to be fitted in all large commercial aircraft registered in the United Kingdom.

A collapse of another kind may have been behind the loss of an Egypt Air 767 in the Atlantic some 60 miles from Nantucket Island on October 31, 1999. The aircraft was cruising at 33,000 feet when it suddenly entered a steep dive, during which it reached a true airspeed of 660 mph and descended to 17,000 feet. It then zoomed back up to 24,000 feet before diving again, this time without any sign of recovery. Fifteen aircrew and 202 passengers died in the crash. Bound for Cairo from New York, the 767 carried a relief flight-deck crew to cover the long journey. The evidence of the CVR suggests that the relief captain took the controls and was left alone in the cockpit while the first captain went back into the main cabin. The relief captain then repeated a phrase several times, placing himself in the hands of God. The autopilot was disconnected and the aircraft began its dive. It then appeared that the first captain returned to the cockpit and that something of struggle for control ensued. Structural failure may have contributed to the final fall. Somewhat confusing though the evidence was, it suggested that the crash was caused by the mental break-down of the relief pilot, an experienced and respected airline captain who may have become seriously depressed about matters that had little to do with flying. It would not have been the first time that a pilot's state of mind had contributed to an accident.

Blunders, Luck and Judgment

Not every bad mistake leads inexorably to a fatal accident. Occasionally, an incident with all the hallmarks of a disaster is retrieved by the skill of the pilot, aided by a generous helping of good fortune. The story of the "Gimli Glider" shows that even when a Boeing 767 runs out of fuel in the air, a sad ending is not necessarily inevitable.

On July 23, 1984, an Air Canada 767 left Ottawa for Edmonton without serviceable fuel gauges. The amount of fuel on board had been checked before flight by dipping the tanks, but a confusion between the standard U.S. and metric systems of measurement left the aircraft with only half as much fuel as was needed to reach its destination. The first sign of trouble came at 41,000 feet over Red Lake, Ontario. A fuel-pressure warning light came on. A second light illuminated soon after, and the captain made the decision to divert to the nearest major airport at Winnipeg. A gradual descent had begun when matters took a far more serious turn. More warning lights came on and then the engines flamed out, turning the 767 into a 130-ton glider. Without engines, most of the aircraft's main services stopped working. An emergency ram air turbine (RAT) was dropped into the slipstream, supplying sufficient hydraulic pressure to allow the flying controls to be operated, but the aircraft's computers were off line and only small, basic standby instruments were left to the pilots. At a glide speed of 220 knots, the 767 was losing height at about 2,500 feet per minute and it soon became apparent that Winnipeg was too far away. The only possible alternative was Gimli, an abandoned RCAF base with twin 6,800-foot runways.

Unknown to the pilots, Gimli had been converted into a drag-racing strip, and this day was a "Family Day" for the Winnipeg Sports Car Club. Cars and campers were lined up along the edges of the runways and hundreds of people were on hand to enjoy the racing. As the 767 dropped rapidly toward Gimli, the crew discovered that their RAT supplied hydraulic power only to the flying controls; there was none to operate the landing gear, flaps or slats. With the airfield in sight, the captain ordered the landing gear dropped under gravity, but only the main wheels locked down. The nosewheel, held back by the slipstream, refused to lock. With 6 miles to go, the captain (an experienced sailplane pilot) realized that he was high and fast, and did what would have come naturally to him in a glider — he sideslipped the 767, losing both height and airspeed. Still traveling at 180 knots (50 knots faster than normal), the 767 crossed the runway threshold and touched down on the main wheels, as startled competitors and spectators scattered for their lives. The captain stood on the brakes, the main wheel tires burst, the nosewheel collapsed, and the 767's nose scraped along the runway trailing showers of sparks. The airliner ground to a halt only 100 feet from an area packed with campers, barbecues and families.

There was no time to relax. Fire broke out in the nose and dense smoke poured into the cabin through the cockpit. An emergency evacuation was ordered, and everyone on board left the aircraft safely, the only injuries (none of them serious) resulting from the use of the rear escape slides, which were nearly vertical because of the collapsed nosewheel. There were no injuries at all among the people enjoying "Family Day" at Gimli. Winnipeg Sports Car Club members used their fire extinguishers to put out the blaze, and the 767 was so little damaged that it was flown out of Gimli only two days later. What had begun as a catastrophe looking for somewhere to happen had been saved from disaster by the skill and judgment of the pilots. An odd coincidence added a footnote to their remarkable story — the Air Canada mechanics dispatched to repair the 767 ran their van out of fuel on the way and found themselves stranded in the backwoods of Manitoba.

Members of a rescue team survey the pieces of a BEA Trident that came to earth on June 18, 1972, soon after takeoff from London's Heathrow airport. The aircraft's wing slats had been prematurely retracted. Postmortem examination of the Captain showed that he had severe coronary artery disease, and had suffered an arterial hemorrhage just before the accident. The crash killed all 118 on board.

General Aviation's Fatal Attractions

The term "general aviation" broadly embraces all of the aviation world apart from the military and the major commercial enterprises. By its very nature, general aviation includes a vast range of aircraft types and aviators of every possible age, qualification and capability. It is hardly surprising therefore that it has always maintained a higher accident rate than either the military or the civil airlines. This is most obviously apparent in the United States, which hosts the majority of the world's general aviation activity. Even in the world's most air-minded nation, however, general aviation accidents do not attract much public attention unless a celebrity is involved. Aircraft crashes have claimed the lives of many famous people, and each time the event has been reported in terms reflecting shock and surprise that such things can happen. Among the names that have put flying obituaries on the front pages have been John F. Kennedy Jr., John Denver, Buddy Holly, Carole Lombard, Payne Stewart, Mike Todd, Guido Cantelli, Graham Hill, Patsy Cline, Rocky Marciano, Audie Murphy, Will Rogers, Jim Reeves, Ricky Nelson, Dag Hammarskjold, and many more. Their tragic deaths, however, have told only a small part of the story.

Immediately after World War II, there were more than seventy general aviation accidents per 100,000 flying hours in the United States, and in 1947 that produced a total number of 9,253 accidents. By the early 1980s, the figures were hovering around ten per 100,000 hours and 3,000 accidents, and in 1999 they had fallen respectively to seven and 1,908. Great though the statistical improvement has been over the years, and small though the figures seem when compared to those of some other forms of transportation, the bare statistics say little about the misery and

AUTHOR RON DICK'S PERSONAL EXPERIENCE

During the preparation of this volume of the *Aviation Century* series, I made my own small contribution to the statistics of general aviation accidents. On May 19 and 20, 2005, I flew a de Havilland Tiger Moth several times from Gum Creek, a small grass strip in rural Georgia. The aircraft performed perfectly, and on May 21, I made plans to fly it to Virginia with my son, Gary. Low cloud prevented an early start, but by 11 A.M. there was an improvement. The Tiger Moth was rolled out of the hangar, we strapped in, and started the engine without difficulty. After taxiing to the takeoff point, a few minutes were spent warming up the engine before completing the preflight checks. Engine oil pressure and temperature were normal, but the first test of the magnetos revealed a drop of 150 rpm on one of them. However, this discrepancy disappeared after more engine running, including bursts to full power, so the takeoff was started at 11:48 A.M.

Soon after takeoff, with the aircraft at about 100 feet AGL, it became clear that we were no longer accelerating. An airspeed of 55 mph was all that the Tiger could manage, and the engine was failing. The rpm had fallen to 1,750. We were going down. A line of tall trees was directly ahead and, to hold 50 mph, height was being sacrificed. I edged the aircraft to the right to make for a small gap in the trees, through which passed the local road. With the Tiger down to 50 feet or so, the end tree was barely avoided, the left wing brushing the branches. However, waiting alongside the road was a power line. It resisted the Tiger's attempt to enter the gap with determination. In a few violent seconds, the flying machine was reduced to a crumpled wreck, plucked from the air and dumped nose first on the front lawn of a small country house. There was no fire and both of us were able to climb out of the cockpits without further hardship, having suffered little more than cuts and bruises. Fire and rescue crews and the sheriff were on the scene very quickly, having been summoned by a 911 call by the lady in the nearby house. We were whisked away for further treatment at the local hospital, and the lady was left to admire her new and somewhat bizarre lawn ornament.

During May 2005, the NTSB reported on this aircraft accident and ninety-nine others in the US. Twenty-two of them were fatal. After an examination of NX82QC's engine by NTSB and FAA inspectors, it was believed that the cause of the partial power loss was the failure of a magneto at a very critical stage of flight. I was left contemplating our good fortune at surviving a very nasty accident, the first in a flying career that began in 1950. It can happen to anyone, anywhere, at any time, no matter how experienced the pilot. In some cases, a crash may be unavoidable, but nevertheless it would be as well for all pilots to take as their motto: "Be Prepared."

Plucked from the air and dumped nose first on the front lawn of a small country house. Note the power line that brought Ron and Gary Dick to earth still wrapped round the aircraft, and the proximity of the country house.

the all-too-frequent deaths behind the individual accidents. At the beginning of the 1980s, there were over 1,000 general aviation fatalities each year, and in 1999 there were still more than 600. In 1983, at least one fatal general aviation flying accident was recorded in the U.S. on 287 days of the year, and by the end of the century, that figure had fallen no lower than 258. On five days every week, there are people dying in general aviation accidents somewhere in the United States.

Military Mayhem

Generally speaking, military aircraft accidents, unless they result in the deaths of innocent bystanders and the destruction of their property, do not command as many headlines as do those involving civilian airliners. Sad though it is when any aviators die while practicing their profession, there is perhaps a recognition that military aviation, even in peacetime, has special risks, and that anyone who climbs aboard a military aircraft accepts them as facts of life. There are also factors of scale and human drama to consider. Military accidents may often be spectacular, but they rarely claim many lives, and those who die are usually young professionals doing their jobs. By contrast, in civilian airliner crashes the death toll is likely to be high and comprised mostly of persons from all walks of life who are merely passengers. The tragedy of people being carried helpless and in numbers to their doom offers a vicarious thrill of horror that is irresistibly fascinating to those of us who can read about it in the morning paper. In the non-flying field, a comparison might be the difference between the public reaction to the death of a little-known racing motorcyclist and a fatal passenger train wreck. The first might appear in a local

The "Gimli Glider" on its nose with escape slides extended, having come to rest on a disused airfield being used for car racing. A serious error in calculating the fuel available to the Air Canada Boeing 767 led to a four-engine flame-out, a desperate situation saved from disaster by the skill of the pilots in carrying out a successful dead-stick landing at Gimli. No lives were lost and there were no serious injuries.

newspaper, but the second could well be reported by the press of many countries. Nevertheless, there have been occasions when military misfortunes have reached front pages worldwide.

Too Close for Comfort

Although not strictly a military aircraft, Andrei Tupolev's ANT-20, the *Maxim Gorky*, was built to serve the purposes of the Soviet government and was brought to grief by an air force fighter pilot. In the mid-1930s, the *Maxim Gorky* was the largest heavier-than-air flying machine in the world. Powered by eight engines, it was 207 feet across the wing and weighed over 50 tons at takeoff. It was intended for use as a propaganda tool, and was equipped with a radio station, a printing press, a photographic studio, a film projector and a screen. On the outside, hundreds of lights could flash out a message, backed up if need be by powerful loudspeakers. Its cabins and sleeping berths could accommodate nearly 100 people. It was an aeronautical wonder of the age. On May 18, 1935, the *Maxim Gorky* was flying as usual in company with fighter escorts, tiny I-4 biplanes, which served to emphasize its great size for the benefit of awestruck crowds below. One of the fighter pilots, Nikolai Blagin, decided to put on a show of his own and began to fly aerobatics round the larger machine. That his self-confidence exceeded his judgment became obvious when the little fighter struck the monster's wing, sending both aircraft crashing to the ground. Blagin, forty-eight people on the *Maxim Gorky*, and three spectators were killed. It was aviation's worst disaster up to that time. Shortly afterward, a new word joined the Russian language — Blaginism was defined as "selfish exhibitionism."

Personal flights can come to unfortunate ends as well. The variables of weather, mechanical trouble and pilot error are factors considered by investigators of all types of crashes. Generally flying at lower altitudes than commercial flights, the pilots of the general aviation universe must be alert for everything from migrating birds to fast-changing weather.

Thirty-one years after the *Maxim Gorky* disaster, the drama of a small aircraft being fatally attracted to a large one was reenacted high over the Californian desert. The North American XB-70 Valkyrie was originally intended to be a Mach 3 strategic bomber, but by the early 1960s the concept had been overtaken by events. Only two XB-70s were built and both were used for high-altitude, high-speed research. On June 8, 1966, the second XB-70 took off on an airspeed calibration sortie, with a secondary task of completing a photographic session for the General Electric Company. Several aircraft powered by GE engines were to be photographed in formation. When the formation joined up, the XB-70 was in the lead with an F-4B and a T-38 off its left wing, and an F-104 and a YF-5A to the right. For nearly three-quarters of an hour, photographs were taken from an accompanying Learjet. Then the F-104, flown by Joe Walker, closed on the XB-70. The jet fighter's tail touched the Valkyrie's wingtip, and the powerful vortex generated by the huge delta wing rolled the F-104 to its left, dragging it through the bomber's twin fins. The F-104 exploded and, some seconds later, the XB-70 began to tumble. Struggling with a malfunctioning escape capsule, Al White eventually managed to eject from the doomed bomber, suffering serious injuries in the process, but copilot Carl Cross was killed in the crash. Joe Walker, a much-respected NASA test pilot, died in the collision. The invisible hazards of vortices generated by large aircraft had been tragically demonstrated.

Powered by eight engines and weighing 50 tons at takeoff, the Maxim Gorky *was the largest heavier-than-air flying machine in the world when it appeared in 1934. Inside it was equipped with a radio station, a printing press, a photographic studio, a film projector and a screen, while an exterior system of lights, backed up by powerful loudpeakers, could flash out propaganda messages.*

The sad end to a photographic session. Seconds after test pilot Joe Walker's F-104 was sucked into the B-70 Valkyrie by its powerful wingtip vortex, the evidence of disaster is clear in the cloud of burning fuel. B-70 pilot Al White escaped with serious injuries, but copilot Carl Cross and Joe Walker were killed.

Ever since armed services first took to the air, there have been midair collisions. During World War II, they were accepted as an almost unavoidable cost of fighting the war. The vast Allied bomber fleets engaged in the assault on Germany lost many aircraft through collision when hundreds of bombers were climbing out through cloud to join their daytime formations, or on the way to the target in a bomber stream at night. Peace brought that particular form of collision carnage to an end, but formation hazards lay in wait for aviators in peacetime, too. One of the first post-WWII flying accidents to attract worldwide attention occurred in the Atlantic in an area that gained notoriety as the Bermuda Triangle. Five Grumman Avengers took off from the U.S. Naval Air Station at Fort Lauderdale, Florida, on an over-water formation navigation exercise and disappeared. Faint radio transmissions suggested that the leader believed he was having trouble with his compasses and that the flight was lost. Search-and-rescue aircraft, including two Martin Mariners, were dispatched to the area, but without success. The five Avengers (and one of the Mariners) were never heard from again. Their disappearance fueled the fires of imaginative speculation about the Bermuda Triangle. Other losses of ships and aircraft in the area were linked together and used to embellish legends of alien intervention, a time warp, or an earthly "black hole." Hollywood took advantage of the stories in several movies, including the classic *Close Encounters of the Third Kind.*

Most visible to the public eye have been the rare accidents suffered by air force aerobatic teams. Accomplished though the professional military aerobatic teams are,

they do occasionally make mistakes. The fact that the teams have the role of representing their services to the world guarantees that, when the mistakes lead to accidents, they attract considerable attention. On July 18, 1982, four of the USAF Thunderbirds crashed during a practice display at Indian Springs, Nevada. The team went over the top of a loop in line abreast at what appeared to some onlookers to be an unusually low height. As the four T-38s approached the vertical during the second half of the loop, it became clear that recovery would not be possible. The Thunderbirds were destroyed by their own proficiency, crashing together in formation. In the official statement on the cause of the accident, it was attributed to a mechanical failure in the leader's T-38, not recognized until it was too late for all of them. The accident led to a public debate on the need for military aerial demonstration teams, but they received support at the highest level. On January 26, 1982, a statement was placed in the *Congressional Record*: "The Congress hereby reaffirms its strong support for the continuation of the Thunderbird program."

Even more catastrophic was the crash involving the Aermacchi MB-339s of Italy's Frecce Tricolori in 1988. Performing in an air show at Ramstein, Germany, on August 28, the Italian team had almost reached the end of a spectacular demonstration. The formation had split up to perform their "pierced heart" maneuver, with two major elements pulling up in opposite directions and a solo aircraft looping at right angles. They intended to complete their loops with a high-speed three-way crossover at 200 feet, but the solo pilot struck the formation leader and carried him into his right-hand wingman. The leader and his No. 2 crashed on open ground, but the solo aircraft plunged into the crowd. The three pilots and seventy spectators died, with hundreds more injured.

Facts of the Military Aviator's Life

It does not denigrate the standard of training nor the quality of the aircrew concerned to say that military flying accident rates have always been higher than those recorded by the commercial world. Far from it. It is the nature of the beast that armed services fly many aircraft to the edges of their performance envelope and operate in regimes where commercial angels have no need (or wish) to tread. The exhilaration of high-speed, low-level flying, the excitement of rehearsing for combat, the euphoria of taking a machine of pulse-racing performance to its limits in three dimensions — these things come with a price. It is a price that modern air forces have fought to reduce (with considerable success) by improving training and maintenance standards, and by making a conscious effort to educate aircrew about flight safety matters. It was not always so. Flight safety did not rate highly on the list of military priorities during World War II, and a casual attitude persisted during the immediate postwar years, which was unfortunate because this was the period when air forces were opening the door to the jet era.

One fact about flying jets in the decade immediately following World War II is inescapable — the accident rate in all air forces was appallingly high. Primitive air-craft, low experience levels, loose discipline, "press on" attitudes, a lack of understanding of the need for fundamental change that led to the perpetuation of outdated techniques and practices — all these came together to compile some horrifying statistics. In the years 1952/53, for example, the RAF fatal accident rate for jets was four times as high as it was for piston-engined aircraft, and there were some 200 fatal accidents involving the deaths of more than 300 aircrew. In peacetime, these were shocking figures, but they were not untypical of air forces generally as they learned the hard way about the realities of the jet revolution. By the late 1950s, matters were improving, but even in 1957 there were 463 major accidents in the RAF, of which 326 were in jets. Sixty-eight of these were fatal crashes in which 149 aircrew died, and the fatal accident rate for jets remained four times that for pistons. Bad though this was, it was getting better. In 1953, 405 aircraft were destroyed. By 1957, the figure was down to 157. This merciful decline has continued in the RAF and in other air forces ever since. In 1975, the RAF lost twenty-three aircraft of all types; in 1998, the total was six. In the USAF, the aircraft destroyed rate fell from 1.3 per 100,000 flying hours in 1974 to 0.3 in 1996.

The USAF's Thunderbirds aerobatic display team flew the T-38 Talon from 1974 to 1982. In one of the worst disasters ever suffered by a display team, all four T-38s crashed in formation when they failed to pull out of a loop at Indian Springs, Nevada, on July 18, 1982.

ACTS OF VIOLENCE
Aggressive Defenses

There have been an alarming number of cases in which civilian aircraft have found themselves in the wrong place at the wrong time and have been shot down by the military of another nation. The first civil airliner lost to air attack was a China National Aviation DC-2, shot down by Japanese fighters between Hong Kong and Chungking on August 24, 1938. The Chinese had taken the risk of flying a civilian aircraft in a combat zone and paid the price, as did KLM (Royal Dutch Airlines) in 1943. Operating in exile during World War II, a KLM DC-3 was intercepted and destroyed by Luftwaffe Ju-88s en route from Lisbon to London on June 1, 1943. Among the passengers killed was the British actor Leslie Howard, known for his role in *Gone With the Wind*. On July 23, 1954, a Cathay Pacific DC-4 was shot down by Chinese MiG-15s off Hainan, and on July 27, 1955, Bulgarian MiG-15s accounted for an El Al Constellation near the frontier with Greece. Israeli F-4s were the attackers on February 21, 1973, when they intercepted a Libyan airliner over Sinai. After the Libyan pilots appeared to ignore the warnings of the Israeli fighter pilots, the F-4s opened fire, forcing the 727 into a crash landing in the desert that killed all but five of the 113 people on board.

Cold War tensions and the provocations of intrusive reconnaissance flights lay behind the loss of a Korean Air Lines 747 on August 31, 1983. Leaving Anchorage bound

On July 3, 1988, the Vincennes *(CG-49), a U.S. Navy Aegis cruiser, shot down Iran Air Flight 655, killing all 290 passengers and crew as the Airbus A-300 flew over the Strait of Hormuz in the Persian Gulf. The crew of the* Vincennes, *in battle with Iranian gunboats at the time, misidentified the airliner as an Iranian Air Force F-14.*

for Seoul, Korean Flight 007 drifted to the right of its intended track. Flying at 33,000 feet, it entered Soviet airspace over the Kamchatka Peninsula, some 250 miles displaced from the established route. Soviet fighters scrambled from Kamchatka failed to intercept the airliner and it continued unmolested until it reached Sakhalin Island, where more Soviet fighters were waiting. Just before sunrise, the pilot of an Su-15 Flagon made visual contact with the intruder. It was later claimed that he initiated IFF (Identification Friend or Foe) procedures and then fired a warning burst of cannon fire across the 747's nose. These actions drew no reaction from the Korean crew, but the 747 began to climb. This was because it had been cleared to do so by Tokyo air traffic control, but it may have been interpreted by the Soviets as an attempt to escape, so the Su-15 pilot was instructed to attack. The fighter was positioned behind the Korean aircraft and two missiles were fired, one of which hit the 747 in the left wing. As the stricken airliner fell away, the Soviet pilot reported "The target is destroyed." The 747 crashed into the sea about 50 miles southwest of Sakhalin and all 269 people on board were killed.

At the time, the Soviets insisted that the Koreans had been involved in an espionage operation, working in concert with a USAF RC-135 that was known to have been in the area. Conspiracy theorists on both sides of the Cold War speculated on the fact that the 747 had overflown a number of sensitive military sites. Not until the FDR and CVR were released by the Soviets more than seven years later was it possible to confirm that the explanation for the transgression had more to do with carelessness than conspiracy. It seemed most likely that the 747's diversion from its planned track had been brought about by the Korean crew's failure to notice that the autopilot was not selected to INS mode and was therefore following a constant magnetic heading rather than the track programmed into the inertial navigation system. In another part of the world the mistake might have proved to be little more than temporarily embarrassing, but at the borders of the Soviet Union it was fatal.

Five years later, at the height of the war between Iran and Iraq, an action by the U.S. Navy shook the civil aviation world. U.S. naval forces were in the Persian Gulf to convoy Kuwaiti oil tankers through the war zone. A few days after their arrival in 1987, thirty-seven American

The Grimes Flying Lighting Laboratory is now undergoing restoration at the Urbana, Ohio, airport named for Warren Grimes. Grimes produced his first airplane lights in his garage in 1933. By World War II, Grimes Manufacturing Company had grown to produce lighting for the needs of military aviation. Today, Grimes continues to design, develop and manufacture lighting systems for aviation, aerospace and transportation industries.

sailors were killed when the frigate *Stark* was attacked (supposedly in error) by an Iraqi Mirage. The rules of engagement for U.S. ship commanders were consequently revised to give them more discretion about how to react to a "hostile threat." On July 3, 1988, the USS *Vincennes* (an Aegis class cruiser) became engaged in a battle with Iranian gunboats. In the middle of the action, while the *Vincennes* was maneuvering violently, the ship's radar registered an aircraft taking off from Iran's Bandar Abbas airfield. Believed by the ship's crew to be an Iranian Air Force F-14, it flew directly toward the *Vincennes*. Several warnings were transmitted from the ship on international frequencies. The captain of the *Vincennes*, already heavily involved in the engagement with the gunboats, accepted the advice of his anti air warfare officer that the target was accelerating and descending as it came closer. Concluding that the threat of attack from the air was real, the captain ordered the launch of two missiles. Moments later, an Iran Air A-300, climbing through 13,500 feet, was hit by both missiles. Minus a wing and its tail, the air-

liner plunged into the Strait of Hormuz, killing all 290 people on board.

Investigations into the disaster were conducted by both the U.S. Navy and ICAO (the International Civil Aviation Organization). In the process, it was found that, though a military transponder (possibly from an F-14 on the airfield) had been detected by the ship at the time that the A-300 took off, the airliner's civilian mode transponder had been operating as it climbed away. It was also apparent from the ship's recorded data that the Iranian aircraft had maintained its climb and had never descended toward the *Vincennes*. It seemed that the missiles had been fired based on assumptions made in the heat of the moment rather than on the information available. Once again, the danger of flying a civilian aircraft in the vicinity of a war zone was made tragically clear.

Airborne Terrorism

Explosions and fire on airliners have not always been caused by human carelessness. All too often they have resulted from deliberate acts. There had been occasional instances of aircraft being attacked by terrorists between the wars, but it was not until the 1960 and 1970s that airliners became targets of choice for those wishing to claim the world's headlines with violence. On the morning of October 12, 1967, a de Havilland Comet 4 of British European Airways flying from Athens to Nicosia, Cyprus, disappeared. Some hours later, small pieces of wreckage were seen scattered on the surface of the Mediterranean about 100 miles east-southeast of Rhodes. In view of the Comet's early history, it was at first thought that it had suffered another structural failure, but examination of some seat cushions showed that the aircraft had broken up because of an explosion. Those responsible were never traced, but it was believed that the conflict in Cyprus might be behind the attack, perhaps because one of the passengers had been incorrectly identified as the leader of the Greek Cypriot forces. Other suspicions focused on two passengers carrying unusually high levels of insurance coverage, one policy having been taken out just before the flight. (An attempted insurance claim had been behind an earlier crash. On November 1, 1955, a United Airlines DC-6 was destroyed by a bomb placed in his mother's luggage by John Graham. Minutes before the aircraft left Denver, he bought policies worth $37,500 on his mother's life.)

Among the victims of explosive devices in the 1970s were a Convair 880 of Cathay Pacific that crashed in the jungles of Vietnam in 1972, and an Aeroflot Tu-104 lost, together with a hijacker and his bomb, to the east of Lake Baikal in Siberia on May 18, 1973. Another

hijacker took the lives of himself and everyone else on a Malaysian Airlines 737 in December 1977 when he forced his way into the cockpit brandishing a revolver. He went on to seal the aircraft's fate by shooting both pilots. In a disaster bearing some similarity to that of the Comet 4 in 1967, a TWA 707 went down in the Ionian Sea after leaving Athens in September 1974. Once again, only small amounts of debris were recovered, but that included seat cushions showing clear evidence of high explosive. A Palestinian organization claimed responsibility for the bombing. In October 1976, a Cuban DC-8 crashed into the Caribbean after the crew transmitted "We have an explosion on board!" and a similarly terrified Gulf Air crew rode their 737 into the desert northeast of Abu Dhabi in September 1983. It was later found that some pieces of luggage had been put on board in Pakistan by a ticket-holder who was not on the aircraft.

Unaccompanied baggage also accounted for an Air India 747 crash on June 23, 1985. Apparently in retaliation for the 1984 attack on the Sikh Golden Temple by the Indian Army, plans were made by Sikh extremists to place bombs on two Air India aircraft on the same day, one bound for Bangkok from Tokyo and the other for London from Montreal. The bomb in Tokyo detonated prematurely, killing two baggage handlers, but the other exploded when the 747 was at 31,000 feet over the Atlantic to the west of Ireland, killing 329 passengers and crew. A little over two years later, on November 29, 1987, 115 people died when a Korean Air 707 was blown out of the sky off the coast of Burma while en route from Abu Dhabi to Bangkok. North Korean enmity lay behind the mass murder. An equally senseless deed, later attributed to Libyan terrorists, destroyed a UTA (France) DC-10 over Niger on September 19, 1989, killing 170 people.

One of the most infamous (and among the most exhaustively reported) acts of airline terrorism was that

The nose of Pan American 747 Maid of the Seas *lies buried in the mud near Lockerbie, Scotland, after being brought down by an explosion in the forward cargo hold. The attack was attributed to Libyan terrorists and was seen as an assault on a symbol of the United States. Two hundred and seventy people from twenty-one countries died, including eleven people on the ground.*

Smoke pours from the burning Pentagon on September 11, 2001, after American Airlines Flight 77, a Boeing 757, slammed into the building between corridors four and five and cut a wedge that extended from the outer E ring through to the B ring. Sixty-four people died in the 757, and another 125 were killed in the Pentagon.

which tore the Pan American 747 *Maid of the Seas* apart over Lockerbie, Scotland, on December 21, 1988. Large pieces of wreckage plummeted into the little town, destroying over twenty houses and killing eleven people on the ground. All 259 passengers and crew of the 747 died, probably very quickly, from the effects of explosive decompression at an altitude of 31,000 feet. The trail of debris, carried by the wind, stretched back some 80 miles. Investigators soon discovered evidence of a powerful explosive, identified as Semtex, and eventually traced the origin of the blast to a Toshiba radio cassette recorder inside a suitcase. It was estimated that the force of the explosion had been sufficient to separate the fuselage forward of the wings from the rest of the aircraft within three seconds. A minute portion of a timing device, manufactured in Switzerland and sold to Libya in 1985, was enough to point the finger of blame at the probable perpetrators. It was deduced that Libyans had managed to arrange for the suitcase containing the bomb to be carried from Malta to Frankfurt on an Air Malta flight. From there it joined a 727 bound for London, before being transferred to Pan Am 103. In 1999, two Libyan agents were taken to The Hague to stand trial for the bombing before a trio of Scottish judges, and in February 2001, more than twelve years after the atrocity, the court freed one defendant for lack of evidence, but convicted Abdelbaset Ali Mohmed al-Megrahi of mass murder, sentencing him to life imprisonment.

Suicide as an Act of War

Airborne terrorism as practiced in the later years of the 20th century was a frightening and horrifying phenomenon that raised worldwide consciousness of the threat and forced passengers to endure the necessary inconvenience of intrusive security measures. However, none of this had prepared people, either at the level of government or the general public, for the catastrophes inflicted on the cities of New York and Washington, D.C., on September 11, 2001. In a disaster unparalleled in the history of commercial flight, three jet airliners, a Boeing 757 and 767 from American Airlines and a 767 from United Airlines, were hijacked and deliberately crashed into the Twin Towers of New York City's World Trade Center and into the Pentagon outside Washington, D.C. A fourth aircraft, a 757 belonging to United Airlines, was hijacked and crashed in open country in western Pennsylvania. Both towers of the World Trade Center were heavily damaged and subsequently collapsed, engulfing the southern tip of the island of Manhattan in smoke, ash and mountains of rubble. The Pentagon sustained severe damage, with fires raging on for more than a day. Over 3,000 people died in the attacks, including all 266 aboard the four airliners.

The aircraft chosen by the hijackers were all on transcontinental flights and therefore carried heavy fuel loads. When they hit their targets, the 757s would each have been holding up to 9,000 gallons of aviation fuel, and the 767s could have held as much as 20,000 gallons. In effect, in the hands of men determined to die, these peaceful instruments of commerce and communication became guided missiles of enormous destructive power. As individual acts of aerial destruction, they ranked below only the nuclear strikes on Japan by single B-29s at the end of World War II.

MARTHA LUNKEN

The Federal Aviation Administration maintains a network of Flight Standards District Offices involved in airman, aircraft and air carrier certifications. Inspectors perform routine surveillance functions as well as the investigation of accidents and violations of aviation regulations. Each office also sponsors programs aimed at keeping pilots up to date on safety issues. The Cincinnati district's Safety Program Manager, Martha Lunken, is a familiar figure to pilots in southern Ohio and surrounding states. Her seminars and workshops encourage pilots to interact in a friendly atmosphere with the sometimes monolithic FAA, providing a vital link between "the Feds" and the aviation community.

Martha is also one of a tiny cadre of FAA inspectors assigned to give checkrides in the Douglas DC-3, testing for initial type ratings as well as recurrent checks for pilots operating under various FAA regulatory categories. She loves the airplane and, oddly, perhaps, for a federal inspector, is almost universally beloved by the pilots who operate them.

TOP Martha Lunken at the controls of a DC-3 she refers to as "the Goon."
RIGHT   Starting the P&W 1830s requires cross-handed operation of various switches.

Top Left The classic lines of the DC-3. This one has over 35,000 flying hours Above Martha turns the "Goon" onto final approach. Bottom Left Martha Lunken savors the joy of flying a DC-3, the window open and her elbow resting on the window frame. Bottom Right The DC-3 has enormous fabric-covered control surfaces, all of which make for fantastic slow speed control and the ability to fly in and out of just about any airfield.

THE FUTURE OF THE PAST

TOP Dr. John Burson, a surgeon living in Carrollton, Georgia, has a passion for classic aircraft, especially those made by de Havilland. He flies them from a little grass strip known locally as Gum Creek International. Seen here in the background are two Tiger Moths and two Chipmunks from his beautifully prepared collection. John Burson is one of those enthusiasts who maintains the spirit of the Golden Age and flies for the love of it in an open cockpit. At Gum Creek, the man flies the machine, defying the technological wonders of the 21st century's aeronautical world, where the machine increasingly flies the man. CENTER Two of John Burson's splendid de Havilland Tiger Moths, standing in the Georgia sunshine and ready for flight at the end of Gum Creek International's grass strip. BOTTOM The Great War Aeroplane Association is an organization that builds, flies and preserves World War I airplanes. At the Greenville Municipal Airport in Pennsylvania, Fred Murrin, president, stands in front of his newly built exact replica of a Sopwith Camel and Rick Bennet stands before his Nieuport 23.

CARS WITH WINGS

DAN PATTERSON WITH JAY MILLER, ON JIM HALL

Machines that go really fast, make a lot of noise and have wings. No, not airplanes, but race cars. A few years ago, I was shooting an assignment at the Indianapolis Motor Speedway, and found myself marveling at the all-consuming sound of the big engines on Indy cars. The last time I had seen anything going that fast, it was airborne and had wings. It was then I remembered when I first learned that these machines also had wings.

When I was in seventh grade, I had a paper route, and there was a contest to sign new subscribers to the *Journal Herald,* the morning paper. One of the sales incentives was a scale-model electric slot car of the new and revolutionary Chaparral race car. The use of aero technology in a race car was fascinating to a kid who was already a "propeller head." Once I had achieved the model car, I was much more interested in building it and racing it to glory than I was in gaining subscriptions for the newspaper.

The Aviation Century books are about aviation and how it changed the world. The use of aerodynamic principles forever changed the design of cars, those that race and those we drive on the road every day. The fins and chrome "mammaries" of General Motors designer Harley Earl were inspired by the fighter planes of World War II, and the progression to wings and "downforce" to improve cornering in cars was natural. Automobiles are even now wind-tunnel tested for efficiency, using an aeronautical design technique that dates back to the Wrights.

Fellow aviation photographer and historian Jay Miller of Forth Worth, Texas, had the opportunity to work with the man behind the innovations of the Chaparral, Jim Hall. Miller tells us that Mr. Hall is the "real deal. Jim was — and still is — greatly admired in the upper echelons of the world's automotive community. His propensity for technological innovation and his willingness to experiment have brought him many honors, more than a few victories, and the greatest of respect in a world chockfull of talented car people. Unlike most race car drivers, he was as intent on solving engineering

Jim Hall's Chaparral.

problems and overcoming design anomalies as he was in taking the checkered flag."

According to Miller, "Less well known is the fact that Jim was not only a world-class competition driver, but also a master automobile engineer. A graduate of Pasadena's esteemed California Institute of Technology with a mechanical engineering degree, he was no simple, self-educated garage mechanic. By the time he first stepped into racing in 1954, he was deep into the more esoteric aspects of automobile materials, propulsion, handling, and performance, and he fully intended to put that knowledge to work at the earliest possible point in his proposed career."

The Midland, Texas, story of the birth of the famous Chaparral cars is "long and complicated," says Miller, but he adds: "Arguably the most technologically important of all the Chaparrals was the 2E. The first of the series to be equipped with the famous down-force-generating wing, two were completed, but raced only six times. The wing — the origins of which can be traced back not only to Jim's engineering ticket but also to his strong peripheral interest in aviation and flying (he was, at one time, the owner and pilot of a North American P-51D Mustang) — was an archetypal engineering tour de force that sat on two vertical struts, high over the aft-mounted engine. In turn, the struts transmitted the wing's aerodynamic loads directly to the rear tires via the rear wheel hub carriers. Brilliant in both conception and execution, the design permitted large downloads on the tires without compressing the suspension system."

At the time of its debut at Bridgehampton, New York, on September 17, 1966, the Chaparral 2E was arguably the first race-car body optimized from birth to take advantage of aerodynamic downforce. As such, it was a precedent-setting form that would quickly and irrevocably set the standard for all other race cars to follow."

Jay Miller is the founder of the International Society of Aviation Photographers. He has published countless articles and many books about the history of aviation, and is an expert on aviation history and photography. In 2006 he received the Harry B. Combs Award for Excellence in the Preservation of Aviation History from the National Aviation Hall of Fame.

CHAPTER 3

What Next? 21st Century Wings

IN AVIATION'S EARLY YEARS, courageous fliers braved a new frontier, exploring the horizons of their three-dimensional freedom, but within a century it had become almost impossible to climb into an aircraft with the intention of doing something not already accomplished by someone else. Given the advantages inherent in operating the sophisticated machines of the 21st century, even the prospect of a nonstop solo flight around the world over both poles would not stir the public imagination as did the trail-blazing flights of the 1920s and 1930s. It is inconceivable that an airman could now be honored with a New York ticker-tape welcome like that given to Lindbergh. In future the real challenges for human fliers will be faced in space. Those that remain for flight within the atmosphere will be more obviously the concern of researchers, engineers, designers, airport planners and air traffic controllers. More often than not, pilots will take to the air (even on a type's first flight) knowing that most of the questions about whether and how the machine will fly have already been answered on the ground. Indeed, by the time the second centennial of the Wright brothers' first flight is celebrated, even the pilot's presence may become superfluous in other than a monitoring role.

By contrast, when the Wright brothers opened the door to the Aviation Century, the world of aeronautics was uncharted territory. Few people in the early years of aviation could have believed that while exploring the realm of human flight within the Earth's atmosphere such astonishing advances would be made in so short a time. The flimsy Wright Flyer bears little resemblance to a Boeing 747, and an F-16 is a far cry from a Fokker Eindecker. Technological progress was undoubtedly rapid, but was nevertheless largely evolutionary. The term revolutionary, often used to describe achievements in aeronautics, is probably justified only when applied to the effects on aviation of jet propulsion and, in later years, of computer-driven technology.

The composite wing of a Cirrus 22, a 21st-century marvel of materials and efficiency.

Wonderful aeronautical advances may still be made, but truly revolutionary change is now an unlikely event for flying machines — barring the invention of an anti-gravity shield. In designing and building aircraft, the basic challenges of lift and weight, thrust and drag, remain the same. Materials may become lighter and stronger, and engines more efficient. New fuels may provide the power, and sleeker airframes of unfamiliar shapes may offer less resistance to the air. New weapons and developments in unmanned flight may force dramatic changes in air power doctrine. These things may come to pass, but the principal secrets of flying in air were unraveled during the 20th century, in little more than one average human lifetime. Although predicting developments in atmospheric aviation may not be as uncertain an activity as it was in 1903, however, it would be unwise to believe that there are no surprises waiting in the future's wings.

A SECOND CENTURY OF AIR POWER

Immensely capable though they had proved to be, by the dawn of the 21st century the front-line fighters in service with the world's leading air forces were showing their age. The USAF's F-15 was taken on strength in 1974 and the F-16 in 1979. The U.S. Navy's fighters were of the same era, the F-14 making its debut in 1972 and the F/A-18 in 1981. The European air forces faced similar situations, with such aircraft as the Russian MiG-29 and Su-27, French Mirage 2000, Swedish Viggen, and British Tornado ADV all being products of the 1970s and 1980s. It is true that by 2000 none of these aircraft were quite the same machines as they had been when they first saw service. The combat capabilities of all had been considerably improved. Nevertheless it was time to take advantage of technology's relentless onward march and introduce aerial platforms able to make the most of developments in air warfare that had already had a marked influence on events during conflicts in the Balkans and the Middle East.

The Changing of the U.S. Guard

The U.S. requirement for an aircraft to succeed the F-15 arose as early as 1981, after intelligence revealed that the Soviet Union was testing new fighters, the MiG-29 (Fulcrum) and the Su-27 (Flanker), both of them with the potential to match or even surpass the performance of U.S. front-line aircraft. In 1986, two contractor teams, Lockheed/Boeing/General Dynamics and Northrop/McDonnell Douglas, were selected to produce prototypes of an Advanced Tactical Fighter (ATF). The prototypes were designated YF-22 and YF-23 respectively, and two of each were successfully flown in 1990. They were the first aircraft ever designed to combine stealth with agility and a supersonic cruise capability, but they had their differences. The radical design of the YF-23 emphasized stealth and maneuverability at high speed; the less unconventional YF-22 was less stealthy and not quite as fast, but used mobile, thrust-vectoring exhaust nozzles to improve subsonic maneuverability and was constructed with ease of maintenance and development potential particularly in mind. Both aircraft were twin-engined and were tested with competing engines, the Pratt & Whitney YF119 and General Electric YF120, each producing over 32,000 pounds of thrust, sufficient to allow the aircraft to super-cruise (fly supersonically without afterburner) at Mach 1.5.

OPPOSITE TOP LEFT *Tom Burbage was named executive vice president of Lockheed Martin Aeronautics Company in March 2000. Earlier, he served as Aeronautical Systems F-22 vice president and general manager and headed the Lockheed Martin-Boeing F-22 Team Program Office. He served in the U.S. Navy, became a test pilot, and logged more than 3,000 hours on over thirty types of military aircraft. Burbage received his bachelor's degree in aerospace engineering from the U.S. Naval Academy, and also holds master's degrees in aeronautical systems and business administration from UCLA.*

OPPOSITE TOP RIGHT *The supersonic F/A-22 is the product of a team effort by Lockheed Martin, Boeing and Pratt & Whitney. The end result is a stealthy air supremacy fighter, capable of taking on air-to-ground missions, that combines long range with high maneuverability. The F/A-22's integrated avionics gives it first-look, first-shot capability that should ensure U.S. air dominance for 40 years.*

OPPOSITE BOTTOM *The F-22 gets its power from two Pratt & Whitney F119-PW-100 advanced-technology engines with reheat. The F119-PW-100 is the most powerful fighter engine ever designed, with a maximum thrust of 39,000 pounds. The F-22 is capable of supercruising — flying at speeds of up to Mach 1.5 without using the afterburners.*

In 1991, the Lockheed team's F-22 was selected as the winning ATF design. The first F-22 fighter aircraft was rolled out in 1997 and was named Raptor. In September 2002, the USAF changed the designation to F/A-22 to reflect the fighter's multimission capabilities. Some indication of the complexity of developing a 21st-century combat aircraft can be gained by contemplating the passage of twenty years between the 1986 selection of contractors and 2006, the year when the F/A-22 achieves its initial operating capability at Langley AFB, Virginia, and is committed to a full production rate of ninety aircraft per year. (Compare the P-51 Mustang, which went from design start in May 1940 to RAF squadron delivery in January 1942.)

The F/A-22 is not a small aircraft. It is 62 feet long, spans 44.5 feet, and with a typical load weighs over 60,000 pounds at takeoff. (The P-51 Mustang had a length of 32 feet, wingspan of 37 feet, and takeoff weight of 12,000 pounds.) Power is supplied by two Pratt and Whitney F119-100 low-bypass afterburning turbofans fitted with thrust-vectoring nozzles. Together they produce over 70,000 pounds of thrust. The cockpit has six liquid-crystal color displays. A Kaiser multifunction display provides plan views of the air and ground tactical situation, offering priorities for potential threats and giving tracking information. Five other displays are available for communication and navigation, air and ground threats, and details of stores on board. Hands-on throttle and stick controls (HOTAS) are provided for the pilot, who also has a BAe Systems head-up display (HUD) to show target and weapon status and give cues for weapon launch.

The Raptor has four hard points on the wings, each of which can carry an AIM-120A Advanced Medium-Range Air-to-Air Missile (AMRAAM) or an external fuel tank. There are three internal weapon bays. The main bay can carry six AIM-120C AMRAAMs, or two AMRAAM plus two 1,000-pound GBU-32 Joint Direct Attack Munitions (JDAM). Bays on each side can be loaded with one Lockheed Martin/Raytheon AIM-9M or AIM-9X Sidewinder all-aspect short-range air-to-air missile. A variant of the M61A2 Vulcan cannon, installed internally above the right air intake, has 480 rounds of 20 mm ammunition that is fed to the gun at a rate of 100 rounds per second. The electronic warfare system includes a radar warning receiver and a missile launch detector. Also fitted are a plethora of systems for communicating

and navigating, including JTIDS (joint tactical information distribution system), IFF (identification friend or foe), GPS (global positioning system), plus an intraflight data link and a microwave landing system. All that sophistication brings the estimated 2005 fly-away unit cost of the F/A-22 to $133 million. (The P-51 cost $52,000 in 1944.)

A 21st-century combat aircraft of wider application than the F/A-22 grew out of a number of studies being undertaken separately in the 1980s and early 1990s in order to find eventual replacements for the U.S. Navy and Marine Corps's F/A-18, the U.S. Marine Corps' AV-8B, the USAF's F-16, and the Royal Navy's Sea Harrier. By 1995, the U.S. Congress had mandated that the U.S. efforts be merged as the Joint Strike Fighter (JSF) program, and in October 2001 it was announced that Lockheed-Martin's proposal had won the competition to produce the aircraft. It was the largest military contract ever awarded. Lockheed-Martin teamed with Northrop Grumman and British Aerospace for the project, which was estimated as eventually costing some $200 billion.

The first operational JSF, now designated F-35, could be delivered in 2009. To address the needs of the five principal customers (USAF, USN, USMC, RAF and RN) the F-35 is to be developed as a family of three aircraft. The basic airframes will have much in common, but there will be three major variants and considerable differences in the systems fitted to each. The USAF's F-35A will be the version produced in the greatest numbers, with over 1,760 aircraft required to replace the F-16 and A-10 in the conventional strike-fighter role. For its carrier operations, the USN will need some 460 F-35Cs to complement the F/A-18E/F Hornet and replace both the A-6 and older models of the F/A-18. The USMC is to receive over 600 of the F-35B STOVL (Short Take-Off Vertical Landing) variant as AV-8Bs are phased out, and the RAF and RN are planning to get 150 F-35Bs to replace the Tornado GR.7 and the Sea Harrier. A number of other nations, including the Netherlands, Belgium, Norway, Italy, Turkey and Australia are interested in the program, so the total production could reach well over 4,000 aircraft, at an estimated fly-away cost of $45 to 55 million (2003) each.

The principal F-35 power unit is the Pratt & Whitney F-135 engine capable of delivering 40,000 pounds thrust with afterburner. An equally powerful alternative is available

The Lockheed Martin F-35 Joint Strike Fighter is being produced in three main versions.
TOP The U.S. Navy will receive the F-35C, a navalized variant. Note the arrester hook. LEFT The F-35A will be flown by the USAF. BOTTOM The USMC, RAF and RN will fly the F-35B STOVL (Short Take-Off and Vertical Landing) version, which employs a lift fan powered by the aircraft engine via a clutched driveshaft. It is seen here hovering with the lift fan doors open. Two engines are being developed for the F-35 — the Pratt & Whitney F135 of 37,200 pounds thrust, and the General Electric/Rolls-Royce F136 of 40,000 pounds thrust. The 20,000-pounds-thrust lift fan for the F-35B is designed by Rolls-Royce.

in the F-136, produced by a General Electric / Rolls-Royce team. The F-35B STOVL version is also fitted with a large shaft-driven lift fan (SDLF) designed by Rolls-Royce, mounted vertically just behind the cockpit. The SDLF generates a column of cool air that provides nearly 20,000 pounds of lifting power, which combines with the thrust from the downward-vectored exhaust at the rear to enable the aircraft to rise vertically.

Designed by Lockheed-Martin, the F-35 gains from the company's experience with the F-22, and its similar systems will benefit accordingly. The F-35 is intended to provide its pilot with unsurpassed situational awareness, and with positive target identification and precision strike in any weather, by day or night. Mission systems integration and over-the-nose visibility are designed to enhance pilot performance dramatically, and the communications suite will be the most comprehensive of any fighter ever built. Beyond-line-of-sight communications will be integrated via satellites, and tactical data links will allow the sharing of data among flight members as well as with other airborne, surface and ground-based platforms. A variety of U.S. and Allied weapons will be carried, including JDAMs, Sidewinders and the Matra BAe Dynamics Storm Shadow.

The Sukhoi Su-37 is an example of the aeronautical wonders Russian industry can produce. Described as a "fifth-generation super maneuverability aircraft," the Su-37 has AL-37FU turbofan engines for thrust vectored control.

The Russian Response

The Russian front-line fighters in service at the turn of the century were the impressive MiG-29 and Su-27. Both were formidable combat aircraft that had drawn much applause for their spectacular performances at air shows, repeatedly demonstrating maneuvers at high angles of attack not attempted by their Western counterparts. The Su-27, in particular, clearly had great development potential, and Sukhoi has succeeded in keeping it at the forefront of the world's fighters with a series of upgrades. The aircraft's outstanding characteristics have attracted the attention a num-

ber of Asian customers, including India, China, Malaysia, Indonesia and Thailand. Sukhoi believes that the Su-30 derivative exported to India has a claim to being the most capable all-round fighter aircraft anywhere, since it "is capable of performing all the tactical tasks of the Su-24 deep interdiction tactical bomber and the Su-27 air superiority fighter while having around twice the com-bat range and 2.5 times the combat effectiveness."According to Alexey I. Fedorov of Sukhoi "[The Su-30] comes close to the fifth generation aircraft … it must have a long life. We can upgrade it to the fifth-generation standard."

Moves to design fifth-generation fighters began in the mid-1980s. One strong contender was MiG's Multi-role Tactical Fighter (MFI, or Mnogofunktsionahll'nyy Frontovoi Istrebitel), work on the prototype of which was finally begun in 1989. In 1994, the aircraft was rolled out and given the designation MiG 1.44. Unusually for a Russian design, it was of cropped-delta configuration with canards. Intended to be a match for the F-22, the MiG 1.44 appeared to place more emphasis on speed and agility than stealth. Nevertheless, it incorporated plasma stealth technology, based on electromagnetic wave–plasma interactions. The theory is that a plasma generator would envelop the aircraft in a film of ionized gas, which would be impervious to radar pulses, theoretically rendering the warplane electronically invisible. Promising though its potential seemed to be, the MiG 1.44 suffered an apparently fatal blow in 2001, after the Russian government abandoned the MFI program. The Future Air Complex for Frontal Air Forces (Perspektivnyi Aviatsionnyi Kompleks Frontovoi Aviatsyi, or PAK-FA) program was announced, specifying the need for an aircraft that could enter service beginning in 2010 and compete with the U.S. F-35 Joint Strike Fighter. MiG and Yakovlev teamed to bid for the contract, but they faced strong competition from Sukhoi.

While MiG had been working on the 1.44, Sukhoi had set off in an interestingly unconventional direction. Designated S-37 during its initial stages, the Su-47 Berkut (Golden Eagle) first flew in 1997. It is a very large aircraft for a fighter; 73 feet long, 74 feet across the wing, and with a maximum takeoff weight of 75,000 pounds. To power this monster, two Aviadvigatel D-30F6 afterburning turbofans of 34,000 pounds thrust each are fitted. The big surprise, however, was that Sukhoi elected to employ not only canards but also wings that are swept forward. The result is an aircraft that is extremely agile at subsonic speeds, able to alter its angle of attack and flight path very quickly, and more than adequately maneuverable in supersonic flight. Compared to a swept-back wing of the same area, forward sweep offers several advantages: a higher lift/drag ratio; superior maneuverability, longer range at subsonic speed, better stall resistance and antispin characteristics, a lower minimum flight speed, and a shorter takeoff and landing distance. In flight at high angles of attack, the stability and controllability of the Su-47 are impressive. All this having been taken into account, however, the Russians came to the conclusion that, great though the benefits of forward-swept wings are, they are not worth the extra cost and complexity associated with their design and manufacture. (Compare the similar conclusions reached in the United States during the Grumman X-29 program.)

When the PAK-FA was announced, Sukhoi entered the competition, proposing to build on the experience gained with the Su-47 to design a fighter of similar performance, but smaller and with a conventional wing. In late April 2002, the Russian government announced that the Sukhoi group had been awarded the contract. MiG and Yakovlev were promised workshares in developing the aircraft, but the loss of the competition was still a blow to MiG, leaving the company without its traditional leading role in a Russian fighter program.

The new fighter is intended to be about the same size as the U.S. F-35 JSF, featuring long range, supersonic cruise, low radar cross-section, supermaneuverability, and short takeoff and landing capability. The PAK FA's normal takeoff weight should be about 20 tons and it will be powered by two Saturn AL-41F thrust-vectoring engines of 40,000 pounds thrust each. India and Russia have agreed to develop the fighter jointly, and a highly ambitious timetable has been proposed, with a prototype flying in 2006, and production beginning in 2010. That being so, delivery could begin to front-line squadrons in 2011–12.

Evolution in Europe

In the 1980s, development work began on three European aircraft for the 21st century, the Swedish Gripen, the French Rafale and the Eurofighter. All three design teams opted for aircraft of very similar planforms — delta wings with foreplanes (canards). In Sweden, after an evaluation of the F-16 and F/A-18, the government decided to support local industry and authorized SAAB to go ahead with the JAS-39 Gripen, which eventually entered service with the Swedish Air Force in 1996. The Gripen is much smaller than its European rivals, single-engined rather than twin and with a loaded weight only about half that of the other two. Nevertheless, the Gripen offers high agility, a powerful multirole radar, modern weapons, a low environmental signature and a comprehensive electronic warfare suite. It is also much cheaper to buy and operate, which was undoubtedly a factor in the decision of the governments of South Africa, the Czech Republic, Hungary and Brazil to place orders for the aircraft. Interest has also been shown by Chile and the Philippines. In marketing the aircraft, Saab insists that "The operational cost of Gripen is 50 percent lower than any other aircraft in its class that is currently, or planned to be, in service. It is twice as reliable and easier to maintain than its competitors."

The Dassault Rafale is a twin-jet combat aircraft capable of carrying out a range of missions including ground and maritime attack, air defence and air superiority, reconnaissance, and nuclear strike.

The four-nation (Germany, Italy, Spain, U.K.) Eurofighter Typhoon is designed to be capable in many roles, but is principally intended as an air superiority fighter with surface attack capability. The Typhoon is agile at supersonic speeds and can fly at sustained speeds of over Mach 1 without the use of afterburner. Orders have been placed for well over 600 Typhoons. Seen here is a Typhoon in the markings of 17 Squadron, RAF, nominated as the Typhoon Operational Evaluaton Unit.

The French considered joining a European consortium to build a new fighter, but then rejected the Eurofighter as too heavy for carrier use and too costly for export. They elected to go it alone with the proven team at Dassault. The result is the Rafale, the A-model prototype of which first flew in 1986. There are three versions: single- and two-seat fighters (models C and B) for the Armée de l'Air and a single-seat carrier-borne fighter (M) for the Aéronavale. Political and economic uncertainties led to delays, and it was not until 1999 that a production Rafale M flew. The marine version has priority since it is replacing some venerable aircraft, including the decades-old Vought F-8 Crusader. Service deliveries of the M began in 2001 and the first squadron became operational on the carrier *Charles de Gaulle* in 2002.

Carrying a combat load, the Rafale could weigh close to 50,000 pounds at takeoff and is powered by two SNECMA M88-2 afterburning turbofans of 16,860 pounds thrust each. Like its rivals, the Rafale is designed to be aerodynamically unstable to provide agility, and it features a digital fly-by-wire system to make it flyable. The fighter also has excellent short-field capabilities. All versions of Rafale are fitted, in the side of the port engine duct, with a Giat 30 mm cannon, which fires at a rate of 2,500 rounds per minute. There are fourteen stores attachment points, all external: two on the fuselage centerline, two beneath the engine intakes, two astride the rear fuselage, six under the wings and two at the wingtips. The maximum external load is 17,600 pounds. In the strike role, one Aerospatiale ASMP standoff nuclear weapon can be carried. As an interceptor, the Rafale can take up to eight Mica AAMs and two underwing fuel tanks. The air-to-ground load is typically sixteen 500-pound bombs, two Micas and two fuel tanks; or two Apache standoff weapon

dispensers, two Micas plus external fuel; or a FLIR pod, Atlis laser designator pod, two 1,000-kilogram (2,205 lb) laser-guided bombs, two AS.30L laser ASMs, four Micas and a single fuel tank. In the antishipping role, two Exocet or ANS sea-skimming missiles, and four Micas could be carried, plus external fuel tanks. All this capability has not helped Rafale in the export market, where it has consistently lost out to rivals in the United States and Europe, in spite of Dassault's claim that "Rafale has been engineered not just to guarantee supremacy in the air, it has been engineered to achieve supremacy affordably, over the full duration of its service lifetime. By design, Rafale is easier and less costly to maintain than any current or proposed rival aircraft, and significantly cheaper than cold-war pedigree aircraft now being promoted as 'late-generation' Rafale competitors."

The last of the European deltas to appear was the multinational Eurofighter 2000, now known as the Typhoon. Government vacillations, differences in national requirements and shifting partnerships helped to delay the program for years. A demonstrator aircraft was flown by British Aerospace as early as 1986, and subsequently the United Kingdom, Germany, Italy and Spain agreed to form the Eurofighter collaborative project. Even then, German doubts about costs led to a temporary suspension of the program until a further agreement was reached in December 1992 and Eurofighter 2000 was officially launched. On March 27, 1994, at Manching, Germany, test pilot Peter Wegel at last took Eurofighter DA1 into the air for a forty-minute flight covering handling and systems checks. Ten days later, DA2 got airborne at BAe Warton with Chris Yeo at the controls. Both pilots were enthusiastic about the aircraft's qualities.

More ructions between the partners occurred in 1995 because of cuts in each nation's orders and the resultant need to adjust the national workshares. The final numbers of aircraft and workshares were set at: 232 (37.5 percent) to Britain, 180 (29 percent) to Germany, 121 (19.5 percent) to Italy and 87 (14 percent) to Spain. Subsequent progress was relatively smooth, and the Royal Air Force began taking deliveries of the Typhoon in 2003, when 17 Squadron became the first RAF squadron to receive the aircraft, tasked to evaluate the machine and see it through to front-line service.

The Typhoon is the largest of the European deltas, with a maximum takeoff weight of over 50,000 pounds. The combined thrust of its two afterburning Eurojet EJ200 engines is 40,000 pounds. In the cockpit, the pilot is provided with a voice-throttle-and-stick system (VTAS). The stick and throttle tops house twenty-four fingertip controls for sensor and weapon control, defense aids management, and in-flight handling. The direct voice input allows the pilot to carry out mode selection and data entry procedures using voice command. The Helmet Mounted Symbology System (HMS) and head-up display (HUD) show the flight reference data, weapon aiming and cueing, and the FLIR imagery. There are three multifunction color head-down displays (MHDDs), which show the tactical situation, systems status and map displays.

The Typhoon is fitted with an internally mounted Mauser BK 27 mm gun and has thirteen hard points for weapon carriage, four under each wing and five under the fuselage. An Armament Control System (ACS) manages weapons selection and firing and monitors weapon status. A bewildering mix of weapons can be carried as required for the air superiority, interdiction, defense suppression, close air support,

Looking as if it should be going the other way, the Sukhoi Su-47 Berkut was an intriguing attempt to produce a high performance fighter in defiance of convention. Although a large, heavy aircraft, the Su-47 proved very maneuverable, with impressive control response at extreme angles of attack. Cost and complexity were against it being approved for production.

and maritime strike roles, including BVRAAM (Beyond Visual Range), AMRAAM, ASRAAM, ARM, GBU-24 Paveway, Storm Shadow, Brimstone anti-armor, and anti-ship missiles.

Typhoon's DASS (Defensive Aids Sub-System) includes an electronic countermeasures / support measures system (ECM/ESM), front and rear missile-approach warners, supersonically capable towed decoys, laser warning receivers, and chaff and flare dispensers. There is a multi-mode X-band pulse Doppler radar and the PIRATE (Passive Infra-Red Airborne Track Equipment) system; in the air-to-air role, PIRATE functions as an infrared search and track system (IRST), providing passive target detection and tracking. In an air-to-surface role, it performs multiple target acquisition and identification, as well as providing a navigation and landing aid. PIRATE also provides a steerable image to the pilot's helmet-mounted display.

Typhoon is undoubtedly a very capable aircraft, but it is far from cheap. Depending on the steadfastness of the Eurofighter partners over the numbers to be bought and the systems selected for each variant, the cost of a single aircraft could be close to $90 million.

Asia Advances

While most Asian countries in the market for fighters in the later part of the 20th century were content to buy from the established aviation powers, acquiring such proven aircraft as the F-16 or Su-27, Japan, India and China encouraged their domestic industries in the production of combat aircraft. The Japanese settled for an aircraft based on the F-16, to be

Sweden's SAAB Gripen fourth-generation multi-role fighter aircraft was first flown in December 1988 and entered operational service with the Swedish Air Force in 1997. The aircraft seen here is in Hungarian markings. Hungary became the second country in NATO after the Czech Republic to select the Gripen to fulfill national, NATO and European defence requirements.

built by Mitsubishi with Lockheed-Martin as a major sub-contractor. The Mitsubishi F-2 program has been controversial, because the aircraft's unit cost is roughly four times that of an F-16, but Japan's commitment to its aerospace industry overrode financial concerns. The F-2 is noticeably different from the F-16 in a number of ways. It has a 25-percent larger wing area, radar-absorbent materials on the wing leading edges, a longer nose to accommodate a phased-array radar, and a larger tailplane. It also has the capacity to fire antiship missiles besides the normal array of weaponry. The F-2 first flew in 1995 and began entering service in 2001.

India began pursuing its Light Combat Aircraft (LCA) project in 1983 seeking a low-cost replacement for its ageing fleet of MiG-21s. Hindustan Aeronautics Limited was given responsibility for most LCA design and fabrication work and for integrating the efforts of subcontractors. The resulting delta-wing design features many advanced modern technologies, including a digital fly-by-wire control system, integrated avionics, extensive use of composite materials, and glass cockpit displays. The LCA is fitted with multimode radar, a laser designator pod and FLIR system, a ring laser gyro inertial navigation system, a comprehensive electronic warfare suite, and jam-resistant communications systems. A setback occurred in 1998 when India's nuclear tests prompted the United States to place sanctions on the sale of the LCA's intended engine, the General Electric F404 turbofan. Lockheed Martin's assistance in developing the flight controls also came to an end. India then decided to go ahead

alone, a decision that led to delays and cost overruns while developing the new engine, known as the Kaveri and producing 20,000 pounds thrust. Nevertheless, the first LCA prototype flew in 2001, and the LCA should begin to enter service by about 2010. It is a small aircraft, weighing less than 20,000 pounds with a typical load and with a wingspan of only 27 feet. Armament includes a 23 mm twin-barrel cannon, and there are seven hard points for the carriage of external stores.

The Chinese effort to design and build a new front-line combat aircraft began in the early 1980s, and was aimed at countering the fourth-generation fighters then being fielded by the USSR, the MiG-29 and Su-27. Initially designed as an air-superiority fighter, it was later modified to become a multirole aircraft capable of both air combat and ground attack missions. Built by Chengdu Aircraft Industry Corporation (CAC), the J-10 promises to be a most capable aircraft, and will be operated alongside China's fleet of J-11s (Su-27s built under license) and imported Su-30MK Flankers.

The J-10 is a single-seat delta, powered by a Russian-designed AL-31FN turbofan, producing 27,600 pounds thrust in afterburner. First flight of the J-10 was in 1996, but a fatal accident in 1997 caused by a fly-by-wire system fault led to delays. A redesigned prototype flew in 1998 and service entry began in 2005. The J-10 has a digital, quadruplex fly-by-wire system and HOTAS (Hands-On Stick And Throttle) controls. Three liquid-crystal multifunctional displays convey information to the pilot. The wings have eleven hard points for up to 9,900 pounds of weaponry, fuel tanks, and ECM equipment. Built-in armament consists of a 23 mm cannon, and external armament can include short-range infrared air-to-air missiles (Chinese PL-8, or the Russian R-73), medium-range radar-guided air-to-air missiles (Chinese

PL-11 and PL-12, or the Russian R-77), laser-guided bombs, antiship missiles (Chinese YJ-9K), and antiradiation missiles (YJ-9).

With the J-10, China took a major step forward in fighter development. As a lightweight multirole fighter-bomber, the J-10 will be a considerable asset to the front line of the Peoples Liberation Army Air Force (PLAAF) and could have export potential, particularly since it may be more affordable than its U.S. and European counterparts. With an eye even further to the future, China is also studying a fifth-generation multirole jet in the class of the F/A-22, with the aim of flying it by 2012 and having it in service by 2015.

Armchair Aircrew

Pilotless aircraft are not new. Designed and tested but not used in the closing stages of World War I, the Kettering "Bug" (then known as an Aerial Torpedo) was a small wooden biplane masquerading as a flying bomb. In World War II, thousands of Fieseler Fi-103s, better known as V-1s (*Vergeltungswaffe*, revenge weapon), were launched against the Allies by Nazi Germany. On the Allied side, the Aphrodite Project used old B-17 aircraft loaded with explosives and set on course by a pilot, who then bailed out. A second B-17 assumed radio control of the unmanned aircraft and directed it into a target. After WWII, drone B-17s were used to monitor atom bomb tests in the South Pacific.

Dozens of aircraft have also been adapted or designed for use as target drones or for unmanned reconnaissance missions. In the 1960s and 1970s, during wars in Southeast Asia and the Middle East, Ryan Firebees provided valuable intelligence and, in the Yom Kippur War of 1973, even acted as decoys, inducing Egyptian SAM sites to expend their

One of the earliest UAVs (Unmanned Aerial Vehicles) was the Kettering Bug, a wooden biplane with a bomb for a fuselage, powered by a 40-horsepower Ford engine. The number of engine revolutions needed to reach a target was calculated using target distance and forecasts of wind speed and direction. When the engine had turned the set number of times, a cam dropped into position, retracting bolts that held the wings to the fuselage. The wings then detached and the bomb fell. The Bug was demonstrated to the U.S. Army Air Corps in Dayton, Ohio, in 1918, but WWI ended before it could be put into production. This reproduction Bug was built by personnel at the National Museum of the USAF.

missiles before Israeli strike aircraft arrived. Tupolev 143 drones were used by Syria for reconnaissance over Israel, and they were also flown by the Soviets in Afghanistan.

Encouraged by the success of their Firebees, Israel began development of a new generation of UAVs (Unmanned Aerial Vehicles). In 1978, Israel Aircraft Industries produced Scout, an inexpensive piston-engined aircraft made of fiberglass that emitted an extremely low radar signature. Together with Scout's very small size (13-foot wingspan), this made it almost impossible to shoot down. Using a television camera mounted in a turret, Scout could transmit real-time, 360-degree surveillance data. In 1982, in the Bekaa Valley, Scouts were used to seek out Syrian missile sites and lure the Syrians into activating their radars. Israeli strike aircraft then attacked and destroyed all but two of the missile sites. Israel followed up with the Pioneer UAV in the late 1980s, and twenty of these were acquired by the U.S. military. Pioneers carried out surveillance both in the 1991 Gulf War and in Bosnia, working effectively with the USAF's JSTARS (Joint Surveillance Target Attack Radar System). In one celebrated incident during the Gulf War, Iraqi soldiers surrendered to a Pioneer, expecting accurate gunfire to follow their detection by the UAV.

The Predator UAV was first flown in June of 1994, and became operational when deployed to support Bosnian operations in 1996. It is a light, slow-moving vehicle powered by a four-cylinder Rotax engine of 100 horsepower. Over Bosnia, Predator proved capable of carrying out missions lasting more than twenty-four hours, loitering at 70 knots and flying at medium altitude. Predator was designed as a system, not merely an aircraft. The system consists of four aircraft, a ground control station (GCS), a primary satellite link, and about eighty-two people to allow for twenty-four-hour operation. A pilot and two sensor operators fly Predator from the GCS. The aircraft is equipped with a color nose camera, TV camera and infrared cameras, and a synthetic aperture radar (SAR) for looking through smoke, clouds or haze. The cameras produce full-motion video and the SAR still-frame radar images. A Multispectral Targeting System gives Predator the capability of firing two laser-guided Hellfire antitank missiles from under-wing pylons. Real-time data can be provided to other platforms, such as the JSTARS battlefield surveillance aircraft or submarines. Having repeatedly demonstrated its worth over the Balkans, Afghanistan and Iraq, Predator has become firmly established in the USAF, which operates more than sixty. The aircraft was initially fielded simply as a reconnaissance vehicle

under the designation RQ-1, but that was changed in 2002 to MQ-1 in recognition of Predator's multirole capabilities. At some $5 million each, Predator is a battlefield bargain.

Global Hawk is the product of a team led by Northrop Grumman's Ryan Aeronautical Center. It is a large machine with a wingspan of 116 feet, but its weight is kept down to 25,600 pounds at takeoff because more than half of the aircraft's structure is made up of lightweight, high-strength composite materials, including the wings, wing fairings, empennage (tail assembly), engine cover, engine intake and three radomes. Global Hawk is powered by a Rolls-Royce turbofan of 7,000 pounds thrust, and has an impressive operational envelope. The service ceiling is above 60,000 feet and it can stay airborne for over forty hours cruising at 340 knots. Global Hawk's ferry range is a phenomenal 14,000 miles. In May 2000, a prototype (RQ-4A) flew up the Atlantic coast of the United States from Eglin AFB, Florida, transmitting radar images to a U.S. Army ground station at Fort Bragg, North Carolina, and to the aircraft carrier USS *George Washington*, docked at Norfolk, Virginia. The RQ-4A then crossed the Atlantic, monitoring shipping on the way, and surveyed an amphibious landing exercise near Setubal, Portugal. That complete, the Global Hawk retraced its steps and landed at Eglin after a sortie lasting twenty-eight hours. That performance earned Global Hawk the Collier Trophy for the most significant aeronautical achievement of the year.

Global Hawk is an autonomous UAV, rather than a remotely piloted vehicle. Missions are prepared and the details loaded into the vehicle's navigation and mission computers before takeoff. Even so, the UAV still requires multiple satellite and line-of-sight links to allow

Flying at altitudes up to 65,000 feet, the Global Hawk UAV can survey, in one day, 40,000 square nautical miles while providing imagery with a three-foot resolution. For a typical mission, Global Hawk system could reach a target area 3,000 nautical miles away, and stay airborne for 24 hours. Demonstration reconnaissance exercises have included a nonstop crossing of the Pacific to Australia, and a double crossing of the Atlantic.

for in-flight route changes or aborts, as well as for relaying sensor data. Global Hawk has a mission-control element that is responsible for flight planning, sensor control and processing, and long-range control. Four operator stations communicate with the UAV by satellite, or via an X-band common datalink. During takeoff and landing, the aircraft is controlled by two operators in a dedicated van.

Global Hawk's sophisticated suite of long-range sensors allows it to operate outside the reach of hostile air defenses, and give it the capacity to survey as much as 40,000 square miles of terrain in a day. Through satellite and ground systems, the imagery can be relayed in near real time to battlefield commanders. Although it was still an experimental UAV in 2001, Global Hawk was rushed to Afghanistan to take part in Operation Enduring Freedom and proved to be an invaluable asset to U.S. forces. Later, in Iraq, it also played a pivotal role, providing timely information on targets such as the Republican Guard for strikes by Coalition air forces. Just one prototype was used in Iraq, and it flew only 3 percent of the intelligence imaging missions, but it was estimated that it accounted for 55 percent of the time-sensitive targets identified.

In some quarters, enthusiasm over Global Hawk's performance led to talk of adding wing pods to allow the housing of a full SIGINT (signal intelligence) suite, so rendering the manned U-2 redundant and retiring that aircraft by 2005. This suggestion was resisted by the U.S. Congress and the U.S. commanders-in-chief. The U-2 has a sensor/communications payload of 4,700 pounds, compared to the 2,000 pounds of Global Hawk. The turbofan of the U-2 has far greater thrust and drives genera-

The General Atomics RQ-1 Predator UAV is a medium-altitude, long-endurance, remotely piloted aircraft designed to provide intelligence, surveillance, and reconnaissance information to U.S. forces. The MQ-1 version of the Predator can be armed with AGM-114 Hellfire missiles for interdiction sorties. Dan Patterson photographed the Predator and the Global Hawk on the previous page at the National Museum of the USAF.

tors that provide more power for the sensors. The maximum altitude of the U-2 is about 15,000 feet higher than the Global Hawk, it climbs more readily above 50,000 feet, and it carries ECM protection. Being manned, the U-2 can theoretically react more quickly to changing threat or target situations. On the other hand, it takes three U-2s to provide twenty-four-hour coverage, as opposed to a single Global Hawk, and U-2 pilots are expensive to train and support, especially for such high-altitude flying, which requires full pressure suits. At least 90 percent of any manned combat aircraft's flying life can be expected to be devoted to flights other than combat. They are flown primarily on training missions. With UCAVs, the requirement for training in the air should be far less. Promising though it is, however, Global Hawk is not going to be acquired as cheaply as had once been hoped. The USAF plans to buy fifty-one aircraft at a cost estimated in a 2003 report for the U.S. Congress at $57 million. This figure takes into account the air vehicle, sensors, mission control elements, launch and recovery systems, spares, and associated equipment.

The Black Widow Micro-UAV has flown for 30 minutes, reached out to 10 miles from the controller, and cruised at airspeeds up to 30 mph. The control system was capable of autohold for heading, altitude and airspeed.

Pilotless Prospects

In the first few years of the 21st century, military UAVs demonstrated conclusively that they will have increasingly important roles to fill in any conflicts during the decades ahead. The inexorable advance of technology will ensure that they will become ever more capable. The successors to Global Hawk will be able to fly longer sorties at higher altitudes, and they will carry improved sensor packages. Operating above 60,000 feet and using fuel cells or solar-electric propulsion units, they could maintain 360-degree coverage of vast areas and stay on station for weeks if necessary. Flying missions of that kind, they might be regarded almost as low-orbit satellites, but unlike assets in fixed orbits they would retain the flexibility of aircraft.

For the immediate future, it is planned that the USAF's next unmanned combat aerial vehicle, the Boeing X-45, will be introduced in about 2010 to take over many of the missions aimed at suppressing enemy air defenses and attacking electronic facilities. Two X-45A prototypes were flown in 2002, but the stealthy X-45C version for the front line will be much larger. Its wingspan will be 48 feet, one and a half times that of the X-45A, and at 35,000 pounds, it will be almost three times as heavy. Two 2,000-pound Joint Direct Attack Munitions will be carried in internal weapon bays.

At the other end of the scale are miniature UAVs. The U.S. Army, for example, has had the Raven (RQ-11A) since 2003, using it in Afghanistan and Iraq with infantry and special forces troops. The Raven weighs just over four pounds and costs $25,000. Battery powered, it can stay in the air for 80 minutes at a time, flying up to 10 miles from the operator and cruising at 30 to 50 mph. Controlled through a laptop computer, the Raven transmits images taken by a color day video camera or a two-color infrared night camera. Launching the little UAV could hardly be more simple — start the engine and throw it in the air. Smaller still are the Micro Air Vehicles (MAVs), such as the propeller-driven AeroVironment Black Widow, which has a 6-inch wingspan and weighs only 2 ounces. It can fly for up to 30 minutes a mile from its controller, sending back live color video images of whatever is on the other side of the hill. Future MAVs brought into service are likely to be even tinier, bee-sized creatures capable of monitoring anything from troop movements to chemical contamination.

One of the problems to be overcome as UAVs are introduced to air forces is cultural. For a century, every pilot worthy of the name has enjoyed commanding exotic machinery, and has jealously guarded the privilege of strapping into a cockpit. Even though the facts are self-evident, it is hard for a fighter pilot to accept that a computer can withstand more violent maneuvers than the human body, and that microchips "think" faster than the human brain. Initially at least, pilots are unlikely to be happy about sitting back at base controlling their aircraft by looking at video screens or by using sensors on a head-mounted visor. Later in the century, as the "brains" of UAVs develop, even that form of control might be superfluous. They could become completely autonomous, thinking for themselves and communicating with others while flying in swarms of thousands.

Over thirty countries are working on the development of hundreds of UAVs of all shapes and sizes. Most of them are intended for reconnaissance duties, but as time goes by, more and more will be designed to include combat roles. Increasing shares of military budgets will be devoted to UAVs and it is possible that the fifth generation of manned fighters now being designed and built will be the last, at least for several decades. It is even possible to imagine that human military pilots will be part of history by the end of the 21st century as UAVs gain more capabilities. The problem of air-to-air refueling may be solved relatively quickly, and a long-range stealthy tanker could be developed to launch, control, rearm, refuel and recover UAVs, operating in the role of a flying aircraft carrier. Designers are already working with self-repairing materials capable of scaling holes in flight, and advanced concepts such as morphing, the capacity to change an aircraft's form by using stretchable skins and materials that remember shapes, are being considered to allow role-changing in flight.

Weapons Weird and Wonderful

Precision weapons had a significant effect on the way air power was applied in the later years of the 20th century. Future weapons are likely to have similarly profound consequences. Many will not rely on traditional explosive warheads. Directed energy weapons are among those beginning to emerge as options for military commanders. The Airborne Laser Laboratory of the 1970s laid the foundations for the Airborne Laser program, in which a weapons-class chemical laser is flown aboard a modified Boeing 747-400 freighter. Its mission is to destroy enemy ballistic missiles shortly after launch while they are still in the boost phase of flight. Advanced electrical power and thermal management technologies are beginning to make it possible for high-power laser weapons to be used on fighter aircraft.

Another directed-energy technology, employing high-power microwaves, can destroy without being lethal. This system has potential for command and control warfare, in suppressing enemy air defenses, against tactical aircraft or unmanned aerial vehicles, including missiles, and in airbase defense. When high-power microwaves are used on micro-electronic systems, they can cause them to burn out or function improperly. Short bursts of high-power microwave energy will have little effect on humans while being lethal to the electronics. The heavy military reliance on electronic components makes microwave weapons attractive for a wide range of missions, especially since there is small risk of collateral damage.

Scramjet-powered precision weapons will also have their effect on the air war. A fast-reaction, long-range, air-to-ground missile would be launched using a rocket booster to accelerate it up to Mach 4. Then the scramjet would continue its acceleration to a cruising speed above Mach 6. The duration of flight might be no more than ten minutes, but since the weapon flies seven times faster than a conventional cruise missile it would cover hundreds of miles quickly to reach time-critical targets. An aircraft launching a hypersonic weapon can cover an area almost fifty times greater than that reachable with a more conventional missile.

THE WINGS OF FUTURE TRAVEL

In the 1960s and 1970s, more than a dozen aircraft manufacturers from several countries were building major airliners. Thirty year later, the number was down to Airbus and Boeing, who dominated the world market for large airliners between them. Antonov, Ilyushin, Tupolev and Yakovlev were still active in Russia. As the 20th century drew to a close, Airbus and Boeing drew different conclusions about future trends in commercial aviation and chose to develop very different designs for their new flagship aircraft.

Larger or Sleeker?

Although the new Airbus and Boeing designs derive from contrasting interpretations of commercial aviation's future, neither of them will differ significantly in general layout and appearance from their predecessors. They will have swept wings, podded engines, and tubular fuselages. They will be the result of an incremental approach to jet airliner design that has its roots in the Boeing 707 of the 1950s. The euphoria that followed the introduction of the 707 fueled predictions that by the end of the century airline travelers would be flying in supersonic darts, but the harsh realities of commercial aviation forced operators and manufacturers to turn away from innovative, very high-performance designs and take a steadier, more evolutionary line, shaped by slim profit margins. Dreams of high speed and spacious cabins gave way to subsonic cruise and high-density seating. Whatever the advertising says, airlines are businesses, so profits and stock prices necessarily carry more weight in the boardroom than do passengers.

This is not to say that there have not been changes. Half a century after the appearance of the 707, airliners are built using lighter but stronger materials and their various parts may be manufactured by hundreds of companies in several countries. Glass cockpits deliver information from sophisticated avionics to pilots more concerned with monitoring an aircraft's performance than flying it by hand. Environmental regulations have helped to produce engines that are both far more powerful and significantly quieter. In the passenger cabins the in-flight entertainment systems have been vastly improved, but the legroom in coach class still presents a challenge for most human beings.

The Boyd Group of Evergreen, Colorado, a leading aviation and consulting company, has always had forthright opinions about the shortcomings of airline travel. They and others have commented on the tendency for airlines to treat passengers as just another form of cargo, packing their customers into fuselages more suited for containers than people. Aircraft manufacturers understandably react to the wishes of their customers, the airlines, and so produce cargo-carrying aircraft. It is no accident that one of the Airbus 340's selling points is said to be its "tremendous operating efficiency ... enhanced by voluminous underfloor holds for generating cargo revenue, with room for 60 to 100 percent more freight than the largest competing aircraft on the market. The unrivaled operating economics of the A330/A340 family mean that an aircraft can even operate profitable cargo flights without a single passenger on board." A former vice-president of Boeing, Robert B. Brown, has supported the view that cargo has been the principal factor determining airliner design, giving that as the reason why passengers are forced to try stuffing their bags and belongings into inadequate overhead bins high above their heads, are then crammed into tightly packed rows of seats, and left breathing recycled, germ-laden air for hours on end.

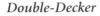

Double-Decker

The Airbus studies of air travel's immediate future led to the A380, which first flew from Toulouse, France, on April 27, 2005. At takeoff for its first flight the A380 weighed 928,300 pounds, so conclusively establishing itself as heir to the title of world's largest commercial aircraft. Airbus began to consider a very large airliner in the early 1990s, making a conscious bid to end Boeing's dominance of the very large airliner market. Engineering development work on an aircraft then designated the A3XX began in June 1994. Numerous configurations were examined, including one for a single-deck aircraft that would have had twin vertical tails and seated twelve abreast. A full-length twin-deck configuration was finally decided upon largely because of the significantly lighter structure required. Once the fiftieth order for the aircraft had been received, the A3XX was redesignated A380 and officially launched on December 19, 2000. In early 2001 the general configuration design was frozen, and metal cutting began on January 23, 2002. On January 18, 2005, the A380 was introduced to the world in a lavish ceremony attended by 5,000 invited guests including the French president, the German chancellor, and the British and Spanish prime ministers, representing the countries that had invested heavily in the $13-billion program, and the CEOs of the fourteen airlines that between them had placed firm orders for 149 aircraft by then.

Key aims of the project included retaining the ability to use existing airport infrastructures with minimal modification, and keeping operating costs to at least 15 percent less than those of the 747-400. With 49 percent more floor space and only 35 percent more seating than the 747, Airbus is hoping to combat some of the criticisms of airline passengers by providing wider seats and aisles. Making the most of 21st-century technologies, the A380 is also designed to be quieter, and to

In designing the 787 Dreamliner, Boeing have taken the view that airlines will prefer to operate a midsize airliner that is extremely efficient and is capable of very long range flight. Composite materials are being used to a much greater degree than in any previous passenger aircraft.

have a more efficient fuel burn and lower emissions than the 747-400.

Several A380 models are being prepared. The basic aircraft is the 555-seat A380-800. The freighter version, A380-800F, will be able to carry a 150 tonne payload and is due to enter service in 2008 with FedEx. Potential future models will include the shortened 480 seat A380-700, and the stretched A380-900, with 656 seats. Power will be provided by four Rolls-Royce Trent 900 or Engine Alliance (General Electric / Pratt & Whitney) GP7200 turbofans of 68,000 to 84,000 pounds thrust each. The A380 is a prominent example of a truly international product. The prime contractors are in France, Germany, the United Kingdom and Spain, but components for the A380 airframe will also be manufactured in Australia, Austria, Belgium, Finland, Italy, Japan, South Korea, Malaysia, Netherlands, Sweden, Switzerland and the United States.

The first customer to place a firm order for the A380 was Emirates, followed by Air France, International Lease Finance Corporation (ILFC), Singapore Airlines, Qantas and Virgin Atlantic. Together these companies completed the fifty orders needed to launch the program. Later, they were joined by FedEx, Qatar Airways, Lufthansa, Korean Air, Malaysia Airlines, Etihad Airways, Thai Airways and UPS. The first passengers to experience travel by A380 will be those of Singapore Airlines. Commercial service is expected to begin in the second quarter of 2006 on the Kangaroo route, flying between London, Singapore and Sydney.

Dreamliner

It is Boeing's claim that it is responding to the overwhelming preference of airlines generally by focusing its development efforts on the 787 Dreamliner, designed for super-efficiency and intended to "provide new solutions for airlines and passengers." Taking an entirely different view from Airbus of future possibilities, two Dreamliner models, the 787-8 and 787-9, will carry 223 to 259 passengers in tri-class configurations on routes up to 8,500 nautical miles. A third variant, the 787-3, will accommodate 296 passengers in two classes over routes of 3,500 nautical miles. By jet airliner standards, the new aircraft is mid-size, but it is planned to provide airlines with long-range capability

The double-decker Airbus A380 first flew on April 27, 2005, from Toulouse, France. Commercial flights begin with the delivery of the first aircraft to Singapore Airlines in late 2006. According to Airbus, "The A380 burns fuel per passenger at a rate comparable to that of an economical family car."

through unmatched fuel efficiency. Boeing's promise is that "passengers will see improvements with the new airplane, from an interior environment with higher humidity to increased comfort and convenience." However, freight has not been forgotten. It is claimed that "Airlines will enjoy approximately 45 percent more cargo revenue capacity" than other aircraft in the 787's class.

Boeing has announced that the 787's advances will be possible because the majority of the primary structure, including the fuselage and wing, will be made of composite materials. The aircraft will also incorporate "health-monitoring systems that will allow the airplane to self-monitor and report maintenance requirements to ground-based computer systems." General Electric and Rolls-Royce have been selected to develop the engines, and it is expected that advances in engine technology will contribute as much as 8 percent of the aircraft's increased efficiency. It is hoped to gain further improvements in efficiency in the way the aircraft is designed and built.

Launch of the 787 program occurred in April 2004 with an order from All-Nippon Airways. Two months later Air New Zealand placed an order, and Blue Panorama and First Choice Airways became the first European customers in July 2004. The first U.S. order came in October 2004 from Primaris Airlines, and this was followed in December by orders from Continental,

TOP *Piaggio Aero's pusher-turboprop P180 Avanti is a phenomenon in the business aircraft world. It offers customers the speed of a light jet aircraft and the comfort of a large, quiet cabin. Fuel efficiencies are nearly 40 percent less than most business jets and 25 percent less than the most efficient twin turboprops. A non-cylindrical, low-drag fuselage developed through extensive wind-tunnel testing allows a large cabin cross-section without a big drag penalty, and Piaggio's three-lifting-surface configuration permits a 34-percent reduction in total wing area over more conventional designs, thereby reducing weight and drag.* LEFT *The Avanti's power is provided by two Pratt & Whitney Canada PT6A-66Bs rated at 850 shaft horsepower. Novel, high-performance five-bladed pusher propellers, designed at Ohio State University, are instrumental in giving the Avanti jet-like speed and good fuel economy.*

Is Your Journey Really Necessary?

Not all aviation visionaries have a rosy view of the future for commercial aviation. Innovative designer Burt Rutan is one of those who is skeptical, even suggesting it as possible that airline travel as we know it could fade to a shadow of its present self before the end of the 21st century. Rutan and others have floated the idea that advanced communications, coupled with extremely high-resolution images augmented by realistic sound, smell and touch sensations, could diminish the desire of people to fly, especially since airline travel is likely to remain something of a challenge for most passengers. Are the airlines (and Boeing and Airbus) listening? At this stage in the evolution of air travel, do they care? Rutan has said that, in his opinion, "business travel will be the first to disappear." At his company, Scaled Composites, e-mail and video-conferencing have already cut travel by about 50 percent. However, for the immediate future, Rutan does see advantages in developing an air travel system involving smaller aircraft "that are safe, pilot-friendly, and compatible with a future airspace and airport infrastructure that allows door-to-door travel. You can go where you want to go, when you want to go, and at about the same cost as the airlines."

JAL and Vietnam Airlines. Customers kept coming in January 2005, with six Chinese carriers — Air China, China Eastern Airlines, China Southern Airlines, Hainan Airlines, Shanghai Airlines and Xiamen Airlines. By April, Ethiopian Airlines, Icelandair, Korean Air, Air Canada and Air India had joined the waiting list. Production of the 787 will begin in 2006. First flight is expected in 2007 with certification, delivery and entry into service occurring in 2008.

This is the idea behind the Small Aircraft Transportation System (SATS) proposal in the United States, which is based on the belief that the infrastructure of hub-and-spoke airports and interstate highways is saturated and incapable of handling the increases in numbers of passengers projected for the early decades of the 21st century. While the 600 or so hub-and-spoke airports in the United States are badly congested, more than 5,400 other public-use airports are underemployed. Some 98 percent of the U.S. population lives within a 30-minute drive of one of the public-use airports, and there are over 18,000 more landing fields in reserve. Taking all this into account, NASA has set a goal of "reducing public travel times by half in 10 years and two-thirds in 25 years," while keeping a new system cost-competitive with existing choices and meeting public expectations for safety. Jerry Hefner, NASA's SATS project manager, has said: "SATS is a vision for a new kind of air travel that will complement today's airline system. Cockpit technologies already being developed will allow new classes of aircraft including very light jets and other advanced small planes to use neighborhood airports to fly people from place to place."

It is NASA's view that SATS technologies could lead to an advanced generation of "smart aircraft" and "smart airports," designed to make virtually any runway end or helipad in the nation accessible to aircraft that have jet performance at propeller-like prices. Desirable though such a system might be, it would have a number of hurdles to clear. The investment needed to improve regional airports would be considerable, as would the cost of providing small jet aircraft with the technologies required for them to operate into those airports without radar and adequate air traffic control. Environmental objections to increased traffic in rural areas would have to be expected, and it would seem inevitable that the integration of regional services with the airline traffic at hub airports would place further demands on an already stressed system. It would also be a challenge to bring the cost of using sophisticated small jets within reach of the ordinary non-business traveler. The end result envisioned in the SATS proposal might well be something to be desired, but is it worth the effort and the costs necessary for its achievement? That remains to be seen.

At the other end of the scale from the aerial minibus idea is the use of large, long-range jet aircraft for luxury travel to exotic places. Following in the wake of the boom in ocean cruising, an increasing number of companies are offering those who have the time and the money what amounts to a flying cruise-ship experience. Generally, a Boeing 757-sized aircraft is fitted with fewer than 100 very comfortable passenger seats instead of the more usual tightly packed 200-plus. On board are lecturers, a chef, a doctor, and a highly professional multilingual staff to ensure that the journey is one to remember.

Pilot Mark Rogers leans into the turn taking off from the airport at Boyne City, Michigan. The glass cockpit of the Cirrus SR 22 illustrates the stark differences in the technology available to aircraft designers of the 21st century. The large flat-panel displays give Mark all the information he needs for safe flight. The panel on the right shows a moving map of the area; the panel on the left provides the flight and aircraft data in real time. Note the artificial horizon and the corresponding angle of the real world outside the cockpit.

THE FUTURE OF AVIATION IS IN THE CLASSROOM

Nick Wahl from the Dayton, Ohio, area is a passionate young student of the Wright brothers, and plans to make a career out in the aerospace industry. Nick is also a volunteer worker at the Wright Brothers Aeroplane Company (see pages 334–5). Nick built a 1/12 scale working model of the 1903 Wright Flyer, and has test-flown it under controlled conditions while tethered. Nick is seen here with his model in front of the full-size replica built and flown by the WBAC.

The Warren County Aerospace Academy is a part of the Warren County Career Center, a vocational education school that draws from all of the high schools in this county. This unique school is the brainchild of Dr. Vince Roesnner. His belief that providing interested students with hands-on learning experiences and instruction from qualified aviation professionals would motivate the students to not only learn this industry, but also to excel in their regular studies, has been proven correct. TOP One of the FAA's honored instructors, John Lane, shares some of his extensive knowledge about aviation and how it works with students attending the Warren County Aerospace Academy. CENTER School director Terry West, on the wing of one of the school's Piper Arrows, talks about the basics of aviation.

BOTTOM Aviation education begins each morning when the yellow school bus stops under the flag and motivated students walk toward the hangar and the classroom.

HANDS-ON EDUCATION
STARTS WITH REAL AIRPLANES

The National Aviation Hall of Fame has created an educational program for kids called SkyReach. For the program, they selected famous aircraft from different eras in aviation history and created characters for them, drawn by Columbus artist Mitch Carly. The Hall of Fame has also arranged with owners of these types of airplanes to bring those characters to life. Bob Odegard of Fargo, North Dakota, has transformed his DC-3 into *Duggy*, the first flying character of the series.

Duggy attended airshows across the United States in 2005, bringing the concept of aerospace education into airports across the country and was met with huge interest. Executive Director Ron Kaplan says that the goal of SkyReach is to educate and inspire kids about aviation. It is entirely possible that the next great national hero — perhaps the man or woman who first travels to Mars or explores an as yet unknown world — could credit his or her first interest in aviation to meeting *Duggy* at an airshow.

OPPOSITE *Duggy* on the ramp along with a replica 1903 Wright Flyer. The early-morning sun casts a long shadow from these icons of an earlier age. Artist Mitch Carly and the full-size result of his creative ideas. ABOVE *Duggy* smiles across the tarmac. A 1902 Wright glider replica is silhouetted in the foreground. LEFT *Duggy* beams down on school groups that came to learn about flying.

In 2006, a company called Starquest Expeditions was among those flying a typical round-the-world route, carrying its customers from Washington, D.C., to Peru (Machu Picchu), Easter Island, Samoa, Australia (the Great Barrier Reef), Cambodia (Angkor Wat), Tibet (Lhasa), India (Taj Mahal), Tanzania (Serengeti), Egypt (Luxor and the Pyramids), and Morocco (Marrakech), all in twenty-four days. Starquest's brochure includes an invitation to explore "the world's most treasured and legendary places — places that define the human experience, where natural splendor merges with the majesty of human achievement. Travel by private jet with a team of world-class scholars and professional staff for a level of service, comfort and convenience that makes *Around the World by Private Jet* a truly extraordinary journey." All of which is a far cry from what the average coach-class passenger must endure on a scheduled flight with one of the world's airlines.

Where's the Joy?

Luxury air touring may continue to offer pleasurable travel for the privileged few in the 21st century, but enjoying the sheer exhilaration of flight for its own sake is likely to be a much rarer experience than in earlier years. In the 1930s, the Imperial Airways flying boat route from the United Kingdom to South Africa took the best part of a week, touching down for overnight stops on such legendary waters as the Nile and Lake Victoria. The aircraft flew at relatively low level, so passengers could see the pyramids and African wildlife from above and were conscious of the earth moving by beneath. The flight was an adventure in itself. Cocooned in a metal tube at 30,000 feet or more, most passengers now pay little attention to the apparently motionless scene outside and console themselves with video entertainment while they wait for the boredom to end. In modern jet travel, the destination is important; the flight is an experience to be endured.

For pilots of commercial aircraft, too, flying is much less of a challenge than it once was. Flight safety, quite rightly, is paramount in airline travel, but as flying has become safer it has necessarily become more humdrum. The commercial pilot's role is evolving steadily into that of monitoring an aircraft's progress instead of controlling it. Indeed, another generation may see pilots becoming flight managers on board wholly automated aircraft, machines capable of taking off, flying a route and landing without the touch of a human hand. The job then becomes just that — a job rather than a calling. The responsibilities may be just as great, but young men looking for the thrill and challenge of flight will have to look elsewhere.

No doubt military aircraft will remain more exciting. Flying a machine of fearsome power, that responds as fast as thought and offers uninhibited freedom of movement in three dimensions, is exhilarating. However, relatively few pilots reach squadrons that operate in the fighter/attack roles. Most military aircrew fly in larger aircraft and experience job satisfaction rather than sheer exhilaration. In the 21st century, even fighter pilots are considerably restricted by weighty rules and regulations, and are constantly responding to outside control, even during the relatively short periods when they may be in combat. Then there is always the possibility that the future will see increasing numbers of front-line aircraft flying unmanned. Where is the thrill of controlling a high-performance aircraft from the comfort of a plush chair in an operations room? Perhaps by then generations brought up with the virtual reality of computer games will find both thrill and satisfaction aplenty in operating a combat aircraft from a distance.

Whatever the difficulties, it seems certain that many people will still want to experience the delights of general aviation, either with flying clubs of some kind or in aircraft privately owned. However, in an era when the threat of terrorism is ever present, even private flying is feeling the weight of increased regulation, with such commercial activities as crop-spraying and banner-towing being particularly affected. Then there are rising fuel and insurance costs that impose restrictions by limiting the number of people who can afford to fly, as does the price of a typical light aircraft. In 2005, a basically equipped new Cessna 172 Skyhawk was priced at $164,000; a used 1977 Skyhawk could be had for about $57,000. A private pilot's license could be obtained from scratch for between $4,000 and $5,000, and a Cessna 172 could be rented for about $58 per hour. These costs are unlikely to reduce. The understandable desire of aviation authorities is to improve flight safety, and that means better avionics — enhanced vision systems, communication data links, satellite navigation systems, transponders and so on. All of which costs money, and hints at a long-term future when even private aircraft might be capable of autonomous flight. Where would be the joy in that? Since general aviation is looked upon as the breeding ground for most professional pilots, the aviation industry as a whole could suffer from the effects of these various factors in the long run.

There are ways of flying more cheaply and simply, of course, and it is probable that these alternatives will continue their already impressive rates of growth in the years ahead. In the opinion of many, gliding is the purest form of human flight and is within reach of those with only moderately deep pockets. Microlights, too, are relatively inexpensive to own and operate. In 2005, the simplest machines, in kit form complete with engine, could be built and put into the air for less than $10,000. Sophisticated microlights might cost $100,000 or more. Many homebuilt kits for more substantial aircraft could be bought for similar sums, but machines at the top end of that market, like some of the Lancair IV series, could set the customer back half a million U.S. dollars. There will always be enthusiasts who will find ways to indulge their passion for flight, but the 20th-century dream of having an aircraft in every garage seems likely to remain a dream.

> "We have been trying to tell people for years that the theoretical framework does suggest gravity can be interacted with. The limited results we have also point in that direction. The main point is that even if our assumptions are wrong, given the sheer implications of the proposal it should be investigated. What if it does work? This is the question I'd like to answer."
>
> VICTOR ROZSNYAY, CEO,
> GRAVITY CONTROL TECHNOLOGIES

Airport Anguish & Terminal Trouble

In an edition of *The Aeronautical Journal* published in 1966, Sir Peter Masefield wrote: "No one can believe that the airport of 2066, or the aircraft which fly into them, will even remotely resemble those of 1966." How true. Even by the time of Masefield's comments, airports had changed dramatically in the two decades since the end of World War II. In 1946, *Fortune* magazine commented on "Chicago's filthy little airport" handling 1.3 million passengers. However inadequate that was, it was at least an airport with its own terminal buildings. In the late 1920s, Universal Air Lines System's terminal was in downtown Chicago. It had wicker furniture, a fireplace, and restaurant service. After lunch, since weight was particularly important on early aircraft, passengers were required to step onto scales for weighing before boarding an airline bus to the airfield.

By 2004, the figure for Chicago O'Hare had reached 74.5 million, well clear of the 67 million at London's Heathrow, which has more international movements than anywhere

else, but O'Hare still had to settle for second place. Hartsfield-Jackson airport in Atlanta was the busiest passenger airport in the world, handling more than 83.6 million passengers in 2004, an average of close to a quarter of a million every day. Almost as impressive were the airport's other statistics, including a passenger terminal complex covering 130 acres, with 83 retail stores, 77 food and beverage outlets, 30,000 parking spaces, 1.7 million square feet of cargo handling space, 25,000 chairs, 53,000 lightbulbs, and 1,296 toilets. Vast though they are, the major airports continue to grow. In 2005, Heathrow's huge Terminal 5 was well on the way to completion and the Atlanta airport management was contemplating a $5.4-billion expansion, adding a fifth runway, another terminal, improved transportation and additional parking. In 2005, the Airports Council International of North America announced that, up to 2009, airport capital development costs in the United States will total more than $71.5 billion.

The impressive scale of these enterprises is matched by the immense problems confronting the commercial aviation industry as it struggles to cope with its further development. The aviation industry and the airlines have become essential elements of the world's economy, but it is obvious that they must be profitable if they are to flourish. The investments made in aircraft production and maintenance, air traffic facilities, runways, hangars, terminals and the infrastructure surrounding airports are vast and forever rising. The need to ensure the safety of passengers both in the air and on the ground, heightened security requirements in the face of terrorism, and the relentless increase in the costs of fuel, materials and labor, all add to the burden to be borne by commercial aviation while trying to maintain profitability. Passengers rightly expect flying to be as safe and comfortable as possible, and they want it to be convenient, with untroubled access to domestic and international flights and rapid handling of baggage. The problem is that these various factors tug in opposite directions. The cost of providing commercial air transport and its infrastructure is unlikely to fall; demand will certainly increase in the next decade

Burt Rutan's designs have been at the cutting edge of aeronautical innovation for many years. Here his graceful White Knight *straddles the miniature* SpaceShipOne, *the first privately funded spacecraft to reach an altitude of 100 kilometers, on June 21, 2004, with Mike Melvill at the controls.*

(estimates suggest that it will double by 2015); and passengers will continue to resent rising air fares, high-density seating, and crowded terminals with their inevitable delays. While airports need to take account of passengers' discontent, from the management's point of view, delays are not entirely a bad thing. Airports are evolving from drab depots to glittering gateways for the cities they serve, drawing much of their income from airlines' takeoff and landing fees, car parks, retail rent, and advertising, but increasingly from their shops, and when people wander the terminals they often use the time to spend more money.

Besides the purely commercial aspects of airports, there are political angles to consider. The major airports need to expand to survive, but in the developed countries any expansion usually meets with strong opposition. Some people welcome any development that encourages local business, but others object to seeing their land swallowed up by runways, terminals and roads. They deplore the increased traffic, both road and air, that brings with it higher levels of congestion, noise and pollution. The political and legal struggles involved in overcoming these objections can drag on for years. This is generally not the case in the developing world, where airport construction is given every encouragement and commercial air activity is booming. While the West's major airports were able to report steady growth in passenger traffic during 2004 (Atlanta 5.7 percent, Chicago 8.7 percent, Heathrow 6.1 percent), some of the figures from the Far East were far more dramatic. Bangkok rose by 25.8 percent and Beijing by a staggering 43.2 percent.

In 1926, all the scheduled passenger airlines in the United States together used only twenty-eight aircraft. Even with all of them full and in the air at the same time, only 112 passengers would have been flying. One Airbus 380 has the capacity to carry five times that number. By the end of the 20th century, U.S. airlines were handling some 700 million passengers each year. The worldwide total was approaching a staggering 2 billion, a figure almost as great as the total populations of China, the United States and the European Union countries combined. Commercial air transport has more than its share of problems, but it is difficult to imagine the world without its services, at least for the foreseeable future. From a few flimsy fabric machines to a world-changing force in one century? Wilbur would be astonished.

The Perils of Prediction

Nevil Shute Norway was not a man ignorant of aeronautical matters, nor was he devoid of imagination. He was an aeronautical engineer and he wrote novels under the name Nevil Shute. Among them was the aviation classic *No Highway,* a tale about catastrophic metal fatigue in airliners that was published in 1948, six years *before* similar problems led to the Comet disasters. In 1929, he wrote: "The commercial aeroplane will have a definite range of development ahead of it beyond which no further advance can be anticipated." He predicted that with the benefit of another half century of aeronautical progress (by about 1980), aircraft would be achieving speeds of 130 mph, would be able to fly for 600 miles, and would have reached maximum weights of 20 tons, of which the payload would be 4 tons. Well before Shute's half century was up, an X-15 reached Mach 6.7 (1967), a P2V Neptune flew 11,236 miles nonstop (1946), and a Boeing 747 took off weighing 375 tons with a payload of 90 tons (1976). Anyone contemplating the future of atmospheric aviation in the 21st century would do well to remember that a man of Nevil Shute

Norway's accomplishments could be that far off in forecasting 20th-century developments.

Bearing that in mind, there is nevertheless an irresistible urge to peer into the crystal ball. The interior may be murky, but it is possible to discern that aeronautical developments in the 21st century will include progress, or at least research, in the following fields, among others:

- Unmanned military aircraft, seeking improvements in range, endurance, survivability, lethality, stealth characteristics, and cost
- Civil transports with flight managers instead of pilots, the business of operating the aircraft being left to automatic systems harnessing the vast power of advanced lightweight computers
- Computer-controlled "intelligent" engines, making use of metal matrix composites, more electrical components, and new combustion systems
- Blended wing and lifting body aircraft
- Supersonic business jets
- Fire-suppression systems in all aircraft areas
- Wing-morphing to allow in-flight configuration change, and to replace flaps and slats
- Hypersonic boost/glide vehicles, scramjets and hybrid engines
- Reductions in the environmental impact of aircraft, especially with regard to noise, local air quality and climate change
- Alternative fuels, including hydrogen and methane
- Increasingly realistic flight simulators, both for crew training and for aircraft development
- Air traffic systems to improve safety through collision and terrain avoidance, severe weather and wake-vortex detection, and synthetic vision technology
- Airports and terminals that can handle passengers by the million, plus their baggage. This to be achieved while meeting security requirements, but without causing undue stress to the passengers or straining the surrounding infrastructure

The young Wrights began in the late 1800s with very active imaginations. Their father brought them a windup toy that flew around the rooms of their home. After hearing the story of how the Wrights went flying, Lawrence thought about that for a moment, placed his model of the Flyer on the launch rail at Huffman Prairie, and away he flew.

Then there are prospects for change that might be described as beyond the fringe:

- Virtual environments, reducing the need to travel
- Tele-transporters, eliminating the need for aircraft, initially for cargo, but later for people too
- The almost unintelligible theory behind Spin Wave Technology, which deals with the possibility of controlling electromagnetic interactions between subatomic particles, so apparently ushering in the prospect of developing aircraft that are much larger, travel faster, fly higher, stay airborne longer, and who knows what besides

Predicting trends and possibilities is necessarily an inexact science, so we can assume with confidence that there will be surprises waiting for us in the 21st-century world of aeronautics. The promise of aviation's future is great, but so are the challenges to be faced. Those who live to celebrate the bicentennial of the Wright brothers' first powered flight and look back on the achievements of aviation's second century will no doubt have wondrous tales to tell. If they are as remarkable as those of the 20th century, they will be wondrous indeed, and aviation will once again have helped to change the world.

Rediscovering the Wrights

OCTOBER 4, 2005

ONE HUNDRED YEARS AGO today, in a small pasture east of Dayton, Ohio, Orville and Wilbur Wright were on the edge of immortality. They were about to perfect the solutions to manned flight on which they had been working for six years.

In that relatively short time the Wrights had solved the problems of balance and control, corrected the mistaken aerodynamic theories of previous experimenters, and invented aerial propellers from first principles. They had taught themselves to fly, conducting thousands of glides and hundreds of powered flights (and crashes), and had developed sensible procedures for preflight inspections and preparation for flight. They accomplished all this while running a thriving bicycle business in Dayton. They flew successfully at Kitty Hawk on December 17, 1903, having spent about $1,000, all self-funded. Compared with Samuel Langley's ill-fated efforts, which were supported by the federal government and cost almost $100,000, the Wrights' achievement was remarkable.

They knew that the 1903 aeroplane was proof of the concept, but was far from being a practical aircraft. They also knew that they needed to continue their flying trials from a site closer to their Dayton workshop, and to the mechanical expertise of Charlie Taylor, their engine builder. Orville recalled a pasture he had visited while in high school. It was east of Dayton and was owned by Torrence Huffman. It was relatively close to home, next to the interurban streetcar tracks, and fairly secluded. The Wrights approached Huffman about continuing their flying experiments there. He agreed, but asked that they not hurt any of the cattle grazing on what was known as Huffman Prairie. They promised to take care and often had to shoo the cows away before attempting any flying.

The 1903 machine was damaged after its fourth flight, so they had to build a new aeroplane. The 1904 Flyer II was in most ways a duplicate of its predecessor, although Charlie Taylor managed to get better performance from the engine. However, progress toward the goal of a practical aircraft was slower than anticipated. In 1903 they had flown in a straight line at sea level, in cold weather and into a stiff wind. In Ohio, nearly 1,000 feet above sea level and in much warmer weather, they found by trial and error that air is not the same

Sculptor Larry Godwin's (see page 247) stainless-steel representation of the Wright Signal Corps No. 1 stands at the entrance to Wright Field, outside Dayton, Ohio.

First flight stone marker at the Wright Brothers National Memorial, Kill Devil Hills, North Carolina.

Once again the brothers found a simple solution. They felt that they had proved the concept of manned flight in 1903, but were now wasting an enormous amount of time laying down and moving long tracks. They devised a launch system, a catapult that would give them flying speed at the end of a shorter track and that was not totally dependent on the direction of the winds. They built a large, tall tripod, into which was hoisted a heavy weight. The weight was attached to the Flyer by a rope that ran under the track, through a wheel and back along the top of the track to the Flyer's skids. When the weight dropped, it would accelerate the Flyer down the track and into the air. From a series of trials, they concluded that about 1,600 pounds would provide them with a good steady pull. The takeoff problem was solved.

everywhere. They discovered that the molecules of air grow further apart as altitude and temperature increases. Compounding the problem was the fact that Ohio winds are variable in speed and direction. As a result, the Flyer II did not perform at all like the 1903 Flyer. In fact, if it weren't for the conditions they faced in December of 1903 on the Atlantic coast, the Wrights might never have flown at all. They made a 60-foot launching rail at Kitty Hawk and left the ground well before the end. At Huffman Prairie they set out tracks as long as 240 feet and often failed to reach flying speed.

That done, they concentrated on the more serious issues of center of gravity and flight control. At the same time, they squeezed additional power from the engine and developed more efficient propellers. The 1904 Flyer showed some improvement by the end of the flying season, by when

Orville and Wilbur Wright and their 1904 Wright Flyer II, at Huffman Prairie east of Dayton, Ohio.

both pilots were managing longer flights with more sustained turns. Wilbur flew the first full circle in the 1904 Flyer, thanks in part to the cooler conditions and "thicker" air of autumn. Even so, the brothers concluded 1904 somewhat discouraged, their successes offset by unforeseen problems. They had crashed frequently and the Flyer had spent too much time on the ground for repairs. As they prepared for another year, the 1904 Flyer was disassembled and its reusable parts employed in the construction of a new machine.

The 1905 Flyer III was a much more robust aircraft. The better propellers and improved engine performance allowed the Wrights to build an aircraft that was heavier and structurally stronger. The landing skids were heavier, and had a more gradual curve to allow for smoother landings. The canard/elevator was much larger and further out in front, and the rudder was also larger and further to the rear. These extensions began to solve the issues of balance. The larger surface area of the controls also made them more responsive at the relatively slow flying speeds of the Flyer.

From the outset, the 1905 Flyer was noticeably better and easier to control than the earlier aircraft, but it would still occasionally become very unstable and dart to the ground. On July 14 of that year, the Flyer III was severely damaged in a crash that came close to killing Orville. However, the brothers felt that they were close to the solving the problems of practical flight. They analyzed the Flyer's performance and decided to extend the control surfaces even further both front and back, and once again to increase the surface areas. A series of summer storms soaked Huffman Prairie, and it was the end of August before flying was again possible, but then the results of their modifications were stunning and immediate. They flew with much more authority and reliability, soon completing circles and figure eights, and remaining airborne for as long as an hour – or until the gasoline in the small tank was used up and they were forced to land. The flights of September and early October of 1905 were milestones

The enlarged canard of the 1905 Wright Flyer III, on display at Carillon Historical Park, Dayton, Ohio. The vertical half-moon shaped vanes were an attempt by the Wrights to add stability. They called them "blinkers."

in the history of flight, proof positive that the Wright brothers had achieved their goal of building and flying the world's first practical aeroplane.

One hundred years after these momentous events, the aviation community is rediscovering the Wrights. There is no doubt about their place in history or that they solved the basic problems of manned flight. Now the question is, how did they do it? Orville and Wilbur were generally methodical and precise about their notes and calculations, and their approach to the science of aeronautics. They also made hundreds of photographs of their machines and experiments. What is lost to history are the conversations they had. We know the results of their efforts, but questions still remain — what did not work so well, and what did work well that wasn't recorded?

In the early 21st century, many efforts were underway to recreate the experiments. These were aimed at gaining a better understanding of the Wrights and how they solved their problems. From their writing in letters and in journals it can be seen that they were funny and wry, serious and dedicated.

ABOVE The Wrights at Huffman Prairie, 1905, *by Gil Cohen.*
LEFT *An archival image of the 1905 Flyer over Huffman Prairie.*

Their sister Katherine emerges from their letters and from her own writing as a significant influence on the brothers, especially after Orville's crash at Fort Myer and Wilbur's successes of in Europe during 1908. After climbing up and down the dunes hauling replica gliders at Jockey's Ridge near Kill Devil Hill in 2002, U.S. Navy pilot Claus Ohman commented that, besides being accomplished aviators and writers, the Wrights must have been splendid athletes. They hauled their gliders up and down the hills themselves, while he had lots of volunteer help.

A great number of people have tried to follow the trail blazed by the brothers and to uncover the secrets of their success. Attempts to build and fly Wright Flyers at the 50th and 75th anniversaries of the first flights were failures, and many then believed that the secrets would remain buried in the past. However, 21st-century builders and fliers thought otherwise. And as the 100-year mark approached, scholars and collectors searched for and found a new treasure trove of Wright photographs, letters and documents, filling in many of the empty spaces between the lines. All this helped to ensure that the centennial of the first flight in 1903 was widely noted and celebrated. The recent anniversary, in 2005, of the more strictly defined successes in practical flight during 1905 has meant even more to the aviation community, as the 1905 flights did a century ago to the origins of the aviation industry.

It is well known that after October of 1905 the Wrights did not fly for more than two years, while they attempted to protect and market their invention. It became obvious to them that public demonstrations would be necessary to

Wright and early aviation historian Betty Darst in front of the reproduction porch at 7 Hawthorn Street, in Dayton, Ohio. This was the location of the Wright home at the time of all their flying experiments. The original house was moved by Henry Ford to Greenfield Village, in Dearborn, Michigan, in 1936. Betty Darst works to remind the Dayton community just how valuable their existing Wright resources are and how much Wright sister Katherine contributed to the eventual successes the brothers enjoyed.

"make the sale." Early in 1908 they built two new aircraft based on the Flyer III design to use them in demonstrations for the U.S. Army and for interested investors in Europe. Wilbur went to France and Orville to Fort Myer, Virginia. The 1908 public flights silenced the skeptics and made the Wrights instant international media stars, the first of the new century.

The years that followed were filled with challenges, and the industry the brothers had founded literally flew past them in a very short time. Having solved the problems of controlled and practical flight, the Wrights were soon over-taken by other visionary pioneers who reached for new heights. In the 21st century, many of the groups who fol-lowed the Wrights did their best to adhere to their methods

Two archival images from the collection of Terrell Wright. TOP *Wilbur flying very low while demonstrating the Flyer at Pau, France, in 1909.* BOTTOM *Wilbur inspecting his aircraft at Governor's Island, New York, before one of his flights over New York Harbor in 1909.*

ABOVE Wright Signal Corps No. 1 *on the parade ground at Fort Myer, Virginia, during Orville's demonstrations of the* Flyer. LEFT *A marble marker notes the location at Fort Myer today. A century later, the trees have grown and some of the buildings remain.*

and techniques. However, the body of knowledge was also expanded by projects such as the Utah State University aeronautical engineering department's USU Flyer, a student project led by Dr. Dave Widauf. Their thesis was simple — if the Wrights were working today, they would have used the most contemporary materials available, just as they did 100 years ago. Dr. Widauf teaches composite manufacturing technology and the group used the specifications for the 1905 Flyer III as a basis for their aircraft.

They designed and built their Flyer based on a new computer analysis of the dynamics and stability of the 1905 machine. This helped them to decide how they could create an aircraft that was safe to fly, while using the methods of control and form of the original Wright Flyer. Built from carbon fibers and resins, the structural forms (wing ribs, spars and struts) employed the latest methods of composite construction. This included a "wavy pattern" of aligning the fibers, which were rolled into the shape of the Wrights spruce struts. The 6-foot-long struts weigh less than one pound each. The USU Flyer has made over 400 safe takeoffs and, most importantly, an equal number of safe landings.

DAYTON AVIATION HERITAGE

Dayton Aviation Heritage National Historical Park opened in 2003, the centennial year of manned powered flight. The park, made up of several locations including the Huffman Prairie Flying Field and interpretive center and the 1905 Wright Flyer III and exhibits at Carillon Historical Park, has as its centerpiece the neighborhood just west of downtown Dayton where the Wrights first lived and worked as printers, bicycle entrepreneurs and pioneers of aviation. The museum that stands behind one of their cycle shop locations details all of their early endeavors and offers a sampling of life in this thriving part of early 1900s Dayton.

TOP RIGHT Superintendent Larry Blake, at the very left of this portrait, and his capable staff have built this national treasure. *Rear, left to right:* Leonard Simpson, facility manager; Steve Sepeck, engineer; Bob Petersen, park ranger, and Tim Good, management assistant. *Second row, left to right:* LaVerne Sci, Paul Laurence Dunbar State Memorial; Julia Frasure, park guide; Ann Honious, chief, education and resources management; Mark Good, park guide; Mary Dagg, park guide; Jennifer Onufer, park guide; and Gregg Smith, visitor use assistant. *Front row, left to right:* Larry Blake, superintendent; Marty Anderson, administrative assistant; Judi Hart, educational specialist; Bill Yandle, park guide; Lisa Martin, park guide; and Mandy Murray, park guide.
BOTTOM RIGHT The cycle shop, as it would have been when the Wrights worked here at the end of the 1800s.

The museum and interpretive center were built and funded through Aviation Trail, a local group of community activists and passionate keepers of the flame that is the aviation heritage of Dayton, Ohio.

ABOVE *Two more archival images from the collection of Terrell Wright: Wilbur flying toward the camera in 1908 at Le Mans, France; Wilbur attends to the Flyer.*
RIGHT *The marker at les Hunadaires, the horse-racing track outside Le Mans, where on August 8, 1908, Wilbur Wright flew publicly for the first time in Europe and overnight changed international attitudes toward aviation.*

Although some of the traditionalists of Wright history have criticized this project, it has proved the value of the Wright's basic design theories and is a tribute to their experimental use of cutting-edge materials.

Dayton, Ohio, has a new national park in the West Third Street neighborhood where the Wrights lived and worked while solving the problems of manned flight. This long-neglected area of Dayton was the economic and living center of the community in the early 1900s and the restored buildings create the atmosphere of the period. The Wrights lived in a close community, where solutions to problems

Descendants of aviation pioneers in Dayton, Ohio, in October of 2005 for the Centennial of Practical Flight. Amanda Wright Lane is a great-grand niece of the Wrights. Visiting Dayton from France were Theiry Tissandier, Louis Sallenave and Gerard Bollee. Mr. Tissandier is the grandson of French pioneer Santos-Dumont, Mr. Sallenave's family supported Wilbur Wright in France, and Mr. Bollee's great uncle was the Wrights' French business partner.

were found across the street or down the block. After the 1913 flood devastated the inner city, the community began to change, and by the 1960s it was little more than a ghetto. The Wright family home on Hawthorn Street and the Wright Cycle Shop building had been moved away long before to Dearborn Village by Henry Ford. As it happened, that was just as well. During the tumultuous racial strife of the late 1960s, west Dayton was burned and the house and shop would certainly have been lost forever.

Local aviation historians found an earlier building that had been used as a cycle shop by the Wrights and a long process of acquisition and renewal began. "Wick"

ABOVE *In Wilbur Wright plaza in Le Mans, the monument to the Wrights, dedicated in 1920.*
RIGHT *As the centennial of the 1908 flights approaches, a dedicated group of aviators and historians are building a replica of the 1908 Flyer.*
BELOW RIGHT *Clement Guy, a project craftsman, and the French replica Flyer.*

Wright, their grand-nephew, and Ivonette Wright Miller, their niece, carried the message and the passion for many years, and finally federal approval was granted for a National Park of scattered sites across the Dayton area. Together with the neighborhood where they lived and worked, the park includes the Huffman Prairie flying field, now swallowed up by Wright-Patterson Air Force Base, and the real treasure in Wright history, the original 1905 Flyer III, on display at Carillon Historical Park. Orville Wright supervised the restoration of the aircraft before his death in 1948.

October 5, 2005, was the centennial of the moment of perfection the Wrights sought, a practical and safe flying machine. On that day in 1905 they felt that they had completed their experiments, achieved their goals, and it was time to take advantage of their knowledge. The rest is the history of the aviation century.

ACADEMIC FLYER

TOP RIGHT In 2001 the University Library at Wright State University installed a non-flying but exact replica in the atrium of the main library.
BELOW Project leader and Wright historian Howard DuFour. BOTTOM Careful handstitching is required to finish the wings. The talented hands are those of Dawne Dewey, head of the Special Collections and Archives department at the University Library. Dawne and her staff manage the Wright Collection. See the opening photograph of Chapter One, *Aviation Century The Early Years*, for a selection of objects from this unique collection. BELOW RIGHT The WSU Flyer being assembled on the floor of the library.

TOP Completed wings and control surfaces make the background for this illustration of how delicate and translucent Wright aeroplanes can appear. Darrell Sevy steadies the edge of one of the canards. ABOVE One of the handcarved replica 1903 Wright propellers before final assembly. RIGHT Jo Lucas, whose great-grandfather worked for the Wrights, did most of the sewing for the WSU project. She found that working on this project allowed her to connect with her family's past.

BACK TO THE FUTURE

Below The student and faculty design team from Utah State University, in front of their project, a Wright design aircraft, with their control system of wing warping, the "canard" elevator in front of the machine, and chain-driven propellers. The project was based on the theory that if the Wrights were working today, they would have used the latest and lightest materials; this Flyer is built of composites. Bottom A collection of the composite fiber and materials used to build the USU Flyer. The "wavy" pattern seen at right is used to create the struts. On the left is a cutaway segment of one of the struts. Top Right In July of 2003, the USU Flyer circled Huffman Prairie. It was the first Wright aircraft to do so in a very long time, and pilot Wayne Larsen felt he was fortunate to have the honor of making this flight. Bottom Right A unique silhouette is cast onto the runway — an image that can be seen only from a Wright-designed aeroplane.

LOOKS LIKE A WRIGHT FLYER

For many years, the Wright "B" Flyer was the only flying example in the entire world of a Wright aircraft. Built by a group of aviators and engineers in Dayton, this look-alike has never been represented as an original Wright aircraft, but up in the sky, it does represent the spirit of the Wrights.

This venerable flying machine has appeared at air shows in many countries, and has been flown by pilot John Warlick in a recreation of Wilbur Wright's famous circling of the Statue of Liberty in New York Harbor.

THE WRIGHT EXPERIENCE

RIGHT The Wright Experience, near Airlie, Virginia, is an organization dedicated to exact and meticulous research about the Wrights and early flight. Ken Hyde, front row right, and his talented team of experts have gone to extreme lengths to find the answers to some of the mysteries the Wrights left unanswered. Team members are:
Front row, L to R: Cliff Guttridge, Greg Cone, Debbie Albrecht, Ken Hyde. *Second row:* Bob Bollinger, Milt Cockrell, Weldon Britton, Beverly Hyde, Larry Parks. *Center:* Wendy Hyde
Third row: Steve Thal-Larsen, Bill Hadden, Cyndi Messick, Pete Piske, Paul Glenshaw. *Fourth row:* Dave Meyer, John Corradi, Ray Reilly.
BELOW An original Wright 1905 propeller in the collection at Wright State University, being measured digitally for the Wright Experience.
OPPOSITE Greg Cone, Wright motor expert at the Wright Experience, makes notes while studying original Wright Aeroplane Company wooden foundry patterns. These well-crafted shapes are made to very close tolerances to create the castings, then machined to final form. Greg explained that the paddle-shaped piece was a control arm and the piece with vanes standing vertically would be an impellor for a water pump. INSET Greg and his micrometer.

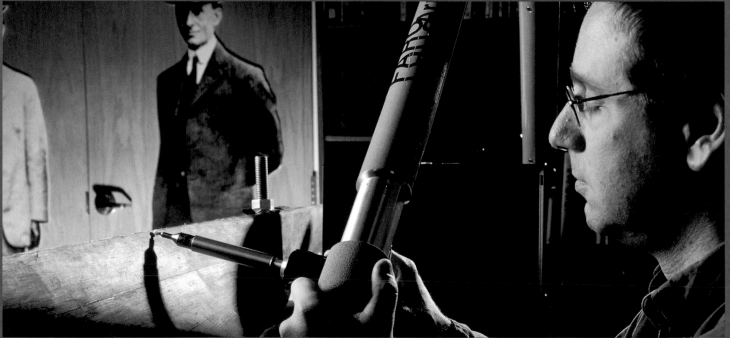

THE SPIRIT OF DAYTON

The Wright Brothers Aeroplane Company, of Dayton, Ohio, also studies and flies Wright aircraft. Led by Nick Engler, this small and intrepid group has followed Nick's goals to build and fly all the Wright experimental flying machines, starting with the kites from the late 1800s.

ABOVE In October of 2002, from the top of Jockey's Ridge, a few miles south of Kill Devil Hill where the Wrights flew in 1902, the glider built by Nick and his crew flies almost 100 years to the minute after the Wrights solved the problems of control.

RIGHT Major Dawn Dunlap flies the 1902 glider. INSET The outstretched fingers of one of the handlers releasing the glider. Major Dunlap is a test pilot in the USAF; in 2002 her other airplane was an F-15.

Kitty Hawk Kites and owner John Harris provided invaluable assistance to the efforts to recreate the soaring flights along the Outer Banks of North Carolina.

Longest Flight: Unknown

WRIGHT
BROTHERS
AEROPLANE Co.

1905
Wright Flyer III

ABOVE Nick Engler unconsciously replicates the pose of Wilbur Wright in the photograph from 1903. Nick Engler rests for a moment on a replica Wright wind tunnel. On his left is a 1905 Flyer III, behind him, Wright Bicycle replica, and to the rear, a 1903 Flyer flown successfully several times in 2003 and 2004. RIGHT A Wright kite flying against the setting sun along the Outer Banks. LEFT Launched into the wind, an experienced hang-glider pilot from Kitty Hawk Kites soars above the sand dune.

A FLYER OVER HUFFMAN PRAIRIE

Mark Dussenberry of Dover, Ohio, built this exact replica of the Wright Flyer III flown in 1905 by the Wrights. The Wrights believed that this was their successful airplane, a practical and reusable flying machine. In the fall of 1905 they demonstrated that the boundaries of flight were limited only by the imagination. In October 2005, Mark flew across the same grass fields the Wrights had a century before. Huffman Prairie Flying Field is now a part of the Dayton Aviation Heritage National Historical Park, on the grounds of Wright-Patterson Air Force Base, maintaining the tradition of aviation and research that the Wrights began in the Dayton area late in the 1800s.

TOP LEFT Mark Dussenberry climbs the launch catapult pylon. BOTTOM LEFT Mark lies prone on the lower wing as his assistants pull the propellers to start his replica Wright horizontal four-cylinder engine. TOP Mark Dussenberry, dressed for a film being made for the National Park Service. ABOVE As the cable holding the Flyer III is released, the machine outruns the assistants.

ABOVE On October 5, 2005, the Dussenberry Flyer leaves the launch rail. BELOW These flights were seen by a few thousand onlookers. As the Flyer soared majestically across the Flying Field, viewers had time to consider the significance of what was happening and where it was taking place.

A WRIGHT LEGACY

TOP RIGHT Great grand-niece of the Wrights, Janette Davis Yoreg of Edina, Minnesota, with some of her family's artifacts. The leather folder contains a remnant of the cloth of the 1903 Flyer, and another piece lies on top. The postcards at bottom were sent from Wilbur to their niece Leontine in France, inquiring about her studies.

BOTTOM RIGHT Keith Yoreg, great-great-grandnephew of the Wright brothers, now taking flight instruction, is the latest member of the Wright descendants to keep the family traditions alive. Keith is holding Orville Wright's NACA security badge. NACA is the National Advisory Committee for Aeronautics, active from 1915 to 1958 and the predecessor to NASA.

The Wrights received honors and awards from around the world. The Special Collections and Archives at Wright State University Libraries holds the Wright Collection and displays these medals in the reading room at the university. BELOW TOP Congressional medal presented to the Wrights at the homecoming celebration in Dayton, June 18, 1909, by General James Allen. BELOW CENTER Aero Club of America medals presented to the Wrights at the White House by President Taft, June 10, 1909. BELOW BOTTOM City of Dayton medals presented to the Wrights at the homecoming celebration in Dayton, June 18, 1909, by Mayor Edward Burkhart.

POSTSCRIPT
Stephen Wright

"For some years now I have been afflicted with the belief that flight is possible to man. My disease has increased in severity and I feel it will soon cost me an increased amount of money if not my life. I have been trying to arrange my affairs in such a way that I can devote my entire time for a few months to experiment in this field."

Those words were written by my great grand uncle Wilbur Wright on May 13th 1900. They were the words he chose to use in introducing himself to Octave Chanute, a man who would become a friend, counselor, champion and ultimately, through tragic miscommunication, detractor, over the course of the next ten years until his death in 1910.

The condition Wilbur Wright described as a disease would soon spread to infect his younger brother Orville and by the end of the first decade of the last century its reach would extend to hundreds if not thousands of people worldwide. Its origin is not clear but I would wager a guess that it is probably as old as mankind itself, and our ancient ancestors, weakened by envy, most probably contracted this insidious infection through their eyes as they watched birds in flight.

> "To say that the Wright brothers learned to fly in North Carolina is like saying that a teenager learns to drive by moving his parent's car 15 feet in the driveway. The dream and the advancement of flight was born in Ohio."
> — OHIO REPRESENTATIVE JOHN A. BOEHNER. A CONGRESSIONAL RESOLUTION PROCLAIMED DAYTON THE "BIRTHPLACE OF AVIATION," JUNE 2003. THE RESOLUTION PASSED THE HOUSE 378-3. THE SENATE VOTE WAS UNANIMOUS.

I'm pleased to report that after nearly a century of heavier than air flight no cure has been found for Wilbur's disease. I'm pleased because this condition's many and varied symptoms are often beneficial to its host. We have made progress with this chronic condition in 100 years in that for the most part we've learned how to manage the symptoms. Fatalities are fewer and farther between and usually those who catch this disease suffer only to the extent that they can't get enough of it and it's obvious that it carries with it an addictive component.

For those of you here who feel you may have Wilbur's Disease but aren't quite sure, allow me to run down a list of some of the most common symptoms. Common symptoms include but are not limited to: Looking skyward every time you here an aircraft overhead to see what kind it is.

Knowing what kind of aircraft it is before you look skyward just to confirm that what you heard was in fact what you thought it was.

Does the smell of 100 octane exhaust or burning JP4 bring about within you a feeling of euphoria? Do you become excitable and restless at the sound of a turbine spooling up?

Do you frequently have grease under your fingernails or do you enjoy the tingling sensation you get when you sand fiberglass with no gloves because you were too excited about going to work on your home built to put them on?

Does your spouse berate you for spending too much time at that damned airport?

Do you dream of flying all the time?

If you exhibit any of these symptoms I feel obligated to advise you to contact your physician for a qualified diagnosis although there is nothing he can do in terms of a cure. You've probably got Wilbur's Disease.

STEPHEN WRIGHT, DAYTON INTERNATIONAL AIR SHOW,
JULY 17, 2003

SOUVENIRS OF THE AVIATION CENTURY

When we began this project, we thought we should have a section about aviation as a lifestyle. The entire Aviation Century series has become that and we have amassed the evidence to prove it. People tend to accumulate artifacts and memorabilia whatever their interests. They have rooms dedicated to quilts, golf, wine, trains, stamps, books, music, theater and every personal interest and hobby imaginable.

Aviation is no exception. There are small personal items such as pilots' wings and squadron patches. Stamps and documents grow into drawers full of stamps and documents. Photographs and artwork become a revolving gallery as there just is not the wall space to display them all. Fleecy flight jackets consume closet space and pieces of airplanes really start to become an issue. Then there are books — hundreds and even thousands of books. Shelves must be very firmly anchored to the walls and even then the occasional disaster can happen. The photo to the left is just a sample of the "stuff" that our pursuit of aviation has generated. We hope you will enjoy searching among the items in this photograph. They represent our efforts of the past eight years, but they are a tiny fraction of whole.

In the center are some of our books — the four previous volumes of the Aviation Century series, *American Eagles,* and the Living History Series. On the shelves above are some of our favorites, including Ed Jablonski's *Flying Fortress,* Ernie Gann's *Fate is the Hunter,* Lindbergh's *Spirit of St. Louis,* and Pierre Clostermann's *The Big Show.* Behind the model of the Spad XIII is a portrait of Ron Dick and his wife, Paul, taken the last time he wore his RAF uniform.

Below the books there are two copies of *National Geographic,* one from December 1953, the 50th anniversary of flight, and the other from December 2003, the 100th anniversary. To the left of the magazines, there is a selection of international stamps created since the earliest days of flight. Inside the magnifier is Bleriot, and just to the left is a first day cover, carried by then Air Commodore Ron Dick in the B-17 he flew from the U.S. to the U.K. in 1983. Under the model of the F-100 is a set of his RAF wings and the squadron badge of IX Squadron. At the far left is a World War II escape map printed on silk. The goggles are RAF issue and the fleecy jacket is a B-3, Army Air Forces, World War II.

The wine to the right of the engine model comes from the Chandelle Wineries of Sonoma, California, whose labels are always aviation themes. Cheryl Patterson is seen under the fin of the Italian racer, the MC-72, and the model of the same floatplane has Italian Air Force wings beneath its wing. The books under the floats are among the many to have served as references throughout the project.

The U.S. Army Air Force "brass" insignia belonged to the late Dr. Louis Ryterband, a flight surgeon and lieutenant colonel during World War II. Finally, taped into one of the many sketchbooks filled during this project, a Polaroid, dated July 17, 1998. The portrait made that day of Patty Wagstaff was the first image made specifically for this history of aviation.

BIBLIOGRAPHY

Anderton, David A. *History of the U.S. Air Force*. New York: Military Press, 1981

Angelucci, Enzo. *World Encyclopedia of Civil Aircraft*. New York: Crown Publishers, 1982

Angelucci, Enzo. *Rand McNally Encyclopedia of Military Aircraft*. New York: Military Press, 1983

Apple, Nick and Gene Gurney. *The Air Force Museum*. Dayton, Ohio: Central Printing, 1991

Armitage, Michael. *The Royal Air Force*. London: Arms & Armour Press, 1993

Baker, David. *Flight and Flying: A Chronology*. New York: Facts on File, 1994

Baldry, Dennis, ed. *The Hamlyn History of Aviation*. London: Hamlyn, 1996

Bauer, Eugene E. *Boeing in Peace & War*. Enumclaw, WA: TABA Publishing, 1991

Bauer, Eugene E. *Boeing, the First Century*. Enumclaw, WA: TABA Publishing, 2000

Bergquist, Ronald E. *The Role of Air Power in the Iran-Iraq War*. Maxwell AFB, AL: Air University Press, 1988

Bickers, Richard Townshend. *A Century of Manned Flight*. Broadstone, UK: CLB, 1998

Bishop, Chris, ed. *The Aerospace Encyclopedia of Air Warfare, Volume 2*. London: Aerospace Publishing, 1997

Bonds, Ray, ed. *The Story of Aviation*. New York: Barnes & Noble, 1997

Bowman, Martin W. *The Royal Air Force at War*. Yeovil, UK: Patrick Stephens, 1997

Bowyer, Chaz. *History of the RAF*. London: Hamlyn, 1982

Bowyer, Chaz, and Michael Turner. *Royal Air Force*. Feltham, UK: Temple Press, 1983

Boyd, Alexander. *The Soviet Air Force since 1918*. New York: Stein & Day, 1977

Boyne, Walter J. *Boeing B-52*. London: Janes, 1981

Boyne, Walter J. *The Leading Edge*. New York: Stewart, Tabori & Chang, 1986

Boyne, Walter J. *Phantom in Combat*. Washington, DC: Smithsonian Books, 1985

Boyne, Walter J. *Silver Wings*. New York: Simon & Schuster, 1993

Boyne, Walter J. *The Smithsonian Book of Flight*. Washington, DC: Smithsonian Books, 1987

Boyne, Walter J., and Donald S. Lopez, eds. *Vertical Flight*. Washington, DC: Smithsonian Institution Press, 1984

Braybrook, Roy. *Air Power*. London: Osprey, 1991

Brooks, Andrew. *V Force*. London: Janes, 1982

Brown, David, Christopher Shores and Kenneth Macksey. *Air Warfare*. Enfield, UK: Guinness Superlatives, 1976

Bryan, C.D.B. *The National Air & Space Museum*. New York: Harry N. Abrams, Inc., 1980

Burge, C.G., ed. *Encyclopaedia of Aviation*. London: Pitman, 1935

Butowski, Piotr, and Jay Miller. *MiG*. Leicester, UK: Midland Counties Publications, 1991

Chant, Christopher. *20th Century War Machines (Air)*. London: Chancellor Press, 1999

Chant, Christopher. *The History of Aviation*. London: Tiger Books International, 1998

Chesnau, Roger. *Aircraft Carriers of the World*. Annapolis, MD: Naval Institute Press, 1984

Christienne, Charles, and Pierre Lissarrague. *Histoire de L'Aviation Militaire Francaise*. Paris: Charles-Lavauzelle, 1980

Cooksley, Peter G. *Air Warfare*. London: Arms & Armour Press, 1997

Cooling, Benjamin Franklin, ed. *Close Air Support*. Washington, DC: Office of Air Force History, 1990

Dick, Ron, and Dan Patterson. *American Eagles*. Charlottesville, VA: Howell Press, 1997

Divone, Louis and Judene. *Wings of History*. Oakton, VA: Oakton Hills Publications, 1989

Doganis, Rigas. *The Airline Business in the 21st Century*. London: Routledge, 2001

Donald, David, ed. *US Air Force Directory*. London: Aerospace Publishing, 1994

Dorr, Robert F. *Vought A-7 Corsair II*. London: Osprey, 1985

Dorr, Robert F., and Chris Bishop, eds. *Vietnam Air War Debrief*. London: Aerospace Publishing, 1996

Downey, Bob. *V Bombers*. London: Arms & Armour Press, 1985

Drury, Richard S. *My Secret War*. Fallbrook, CA: Aero Publishers, 1979

Dzhus, Alexander M. *Soviet Wings*. London: Greenhill Books, 1991

Ethell, Jeffrey, and Alfred Price. *Air War South Atlantic.* London: Sidgwick & Jackson, 1983

Faith, Nicholas. *Black Box.* London: Boxtree, 1998

Fessey, Wayne, ed. *One Hundred Years of Powered Flight.* Hadleigh, U.K: Brigade 2000, 2003

Flintham, Victor. *Air Wars and Aircraft.* London: Arms & Armour Press, 1989

Foster, Peter, R. *RAF Buccaneer.* Shepperton, UK: Ian Allan, 1987

Francillon, René J. *World Military Aviation 1995.* Annapolis, MD: Naval Institute Press, 1995

Francillon, René J. *Air National Guard.* London: Aerospace Publishing, 1993

Friedman, Norman. *U.S. Aircraft Carriers.* Annapolis, MD: Naval Institute Press, 1983

Friedman, Norman. *British Carrier Aviation.* Annapolis, MD: Naval Institute Press, 1988

Fritzsche, Peter. *A Nation of Fliers.* Cambridge, MA: Harvard University Press, 1992

Futrell, Robert F. *The United States Air Force in Korea.* Washington, DC: USAF History Office, 1996

Futrell, R. Frank; William H. Greenhalgh; Carl Grubb; Gerard E. Hasselwander; Robert F. Jakob; Charles A. Ravenstein. *Aces & Aerial Victories.* Washington, DC: Office of Air Force History, 1976

Gero, David. *Aviation Disasters.* Yeovil, UK: Patrick Stephens, 2000

Gibbs-Smith, Charles H. *Aviation: An Historical Survey.* London: Science Museum, 1985

Green, Geoff. *British Aerospace.* Wotton under Edge, UK: Geoff Green, 1988

Green, William, and Gordon Swanborough. *The Complete Book of Fighters.* New York: Smithmark, 1994

Greenwood, John T., ed. *Milestones of Aviation.* New York: Hugh Lauter Levin Associates, 1989

Grinter, Lawrence E., and Peter M Dunn, eds. *The American War in Vietnam.* Westport, CT: Greenwood Press, 1987

Gunston, Bill, ed. *Chronicle of Aviation.* London: Chronicle Communications, 1992

Gunston, Bill. *American Warplanes.* New York: Crescent Books, 1986

Gunston, Bill. *The Illustrated Encyclopedia of Aircraft Armament.* New York: Orion Books, 1988

Hallion, Richard P. *Legacy of Flight.* Seattle, WA: University of Washington Press, 1977

Harrison, James P. *Mastering the Sky.* New York: Sarpedon, 1996

Hastings, Max, and Simon Jenkins: *The Battle for the Falklands.* London, Michael Joseph, 1983

Heppenheimer, T.A. *A Brief History of Flight.* New York: John Wiley & Sons, 2001

Hoyt, Edwin P. *Carrier Wars.* New York: Paragon House, 1992

Isby, David C. *Fighter Combat* in the Jet Age. Harper Collins, 1997

Jackson, Robert. *Avro Vulcan.* Cambridge, UK: Patrick Stephens, 1984

Jackson, Robert. *V-Bombers.* Shepperton, UK: Ian Allan, 1981

Jackson, Robert. *Air Force: The RAF in the 1990s.* Shrewsbury, UK: Airlife Publishing, 1990

Jarrett, Philip, ed. *Modern Air Transport.* London: Putnam, 2000

Jenkins, Dennis R. *McDonnell Douglas F15 A/B/C/D/E.* Arlington, TX: Aerofax, 1990

Johnson, J.E. *The Story of Air Fighting.* London: Hutchinson, 1985

Jones, Barry. *V-Bombers.* Marlborough, UK: Crowood Press, 2000

Josephy, Alvin M. *The American Heritage History of Flight.* New York: American Heritage Publishing, 1962

Kern, Tony. *Flight Discipline.* New York: McGraw-Hill, 1998

Kinsey, Bert. *The Fury of Desert Storm.* Blue Ridge Summit, PA: Tab Books, 1991

Leary, William M., ed. *From Airships to Airbus (Vols 1&2).* Washington, DC: Smithsonian Institution Press, 1995

Macksey, Kenneth. *The Penguin Encyclopedia of Weapons & Military Technology.* London: Viking, 1993

Mark, Eduard. *Aerial Interdiction in Three Wars.* Washington, DC: Center for Air Force History, 1994

Marriott, Leo. *80 Years of Civil Aviation.* Edison, NJ: Chartwell Books, 1997

Mason, Francis K. *The British Fighter since 1912.* London: Putnam, 1992

Mason, Francis K. *The British Bomber since 1914.* London: Putnam, 1994

Mason, R.A. *Air Power*. London: Brasseys Defence Publishers, 1987

Mason, R.A. *War in the Third Dimension*. London: Brasseys Defence Publishers, 1986

Micheletti, Eric. *Air War Over the Gulf*. London: Windrow & Greene, 1991

Micheletti, Eric, and Yves Debay. *Victory Desert Storm*. London: Windrow & Greene, 1991

Millbrooke, Anne. *Aviation History*. Englewood, CO: Jeppesen Sanderson, 1999

Miller, David and Chris. *Modern Naval Combat*. New York: Crescent Books, 1986

Miller, Roger G., ed. *Seeing Off the Bear*. Washington, DC: USAF History Office, 1995

Momyer, William W. *Air Power in Three Wars*. Washington, DC: US Government Printing Office, 1978

Mondey, David, ed. *Aviation*. London: Octopus Books, 1980

Morse, Stan, ed. *Gulf Air War Debrief*. London: Aerospace Publishing, 1991

Murray, Williamson, and Robert H. Scales. *The Iraq War*. Cambridge, MA: The Belknap Press, 2003

Musciano, Walter A. *Warbirds of the Sea*. Atglen, PA: Schiffer, 1994

Nijboer, Donald. *Cockpits of the Cold War*. Erin, Ontario: Boston Mills Press, 2003

Novosel, Michael. *Dustoff*. Novato, CA: Presidio Press, 1999

Nowarra, H.J., and G.R. Duval. *Russian Civil and Military Aircraft*. London: Fountain Press, 1971

Oakes, Claudia, ed. *Aircraft of the National Air & Space Museum*. Washington, DC: Smithsonian Institution Press, 1981

Oliver, David, and Mike Ryan. *Warplanes of the Future*. Osceola, WI: MBI Publishing, 2000

Pattillo, Donald M. *A History in the Making*. New York: McGraw-Hill, 1998

Peacock, Lindsay T. *Strategic Air Command*. London: Arms & Armour Press, 1983

Polmar, Norman, ed. *Strategic Air Command*. Annapolis, MD: The Nautical and Aviation Publishing Company, 1979

Prentice, Colin W. *Monino*. Shrewsbury, UK: Airlife, 1997

Rabinowitz, Harold. *Conquer the Sky*. New York: Metro Books, 1996

Rawlings, John D.R. *The History of the Royal Air Force*. Feltham, UK: Temple Press, 1984

Redding, Robert, and Bill Yenne. *Boeing, Planemaker to the World*. Greenwich, CT: Bison Books, 1983

Ross, Tony, ed. *75 Eventful Years*. Canterbury, UK: Wingham Aviation Books, 1993

Sabbach, Karl. *Twenty-First Century Jet*. New York: Scribner, 1996

Seagrave, Sterling. *Soldiers of Fortune*. Alexandria, VA: Time-Life Books, 1981

Serling, Robert J. *The Jet Age*. Alexandria, VA: Time-Life Books, 1982

Sharpe, Mike. *Air Disasters*. London: Brown Partworks, 1998

Shute, Neville. *Slide Rule*. Kingswood, UK: Windmill Press, 1954

Spick, Mike. *Fighters at War*. London: Greenhill Books, 1997

Steijger, Cees. *A History of USAFE*. Shrewsbury, UK: Airlife Publishing, 1991

Sturtivant, Ray. *British Naval Aviation*. Annapolis, MD: Naval Institute Press, 1990

Sweetman, Bill. *YF-22 and YF-23*. Osceola, WI: Motorbooks International, 1991

Taylor, John W.R., Michael Taylor and David Mondey. *Air Facts & Feats*. Enfield, UK: Guinness Superlatives, 1977

Taylor, John W.R., and Kenneth Munson. *History of Aviation*. New York: Crown Publishers, 1972

Taylor, Michael J.H. *Great Moments in Aviation*. London: Prion, 1989

Thetford, Owen. *Aircraft of the Royal Air Force*. London: Putnam, 1988

Thruelson, Richard. *The Grumman Story*. New York: Praeger, 1976

Tilford, Earl H. *Setup*. Maxwell AFB, AL: Air University Press, 1991

Trest, Warren A. *Air Force Roles and Missions: A History*. Washington, DC: USAF History Office, 1998

van der Linden, F. Robert. *Aircraft of the National Air & Space Museum*. Washington, DC: Smithsonian Institution Press, 1998

Vogt, William M., and Carl A Gnam. Eds. *Desert Storm.* Leesburg, VA: Empire Press, 1991

Walker, Bryce. *Fighting Jets.* Alexandria, VA: Time-Life Books, 1983

Walkcr, J.R. *Air to Ground Operations.* London: Brasseys Defence Publishers, 1987

Ward, Richard L. *Hunter Squadrons.* Vista, CA: Aeolus Publishing, 1985

Wragg, David. *The Offensive Weapon.* London: Robert Hale, 1986

Yonay, Ehud. *No Margin for Error.* New York: Pantheon, 1993

Young, James O. *Meeting the Challenge of Supersonic Flight.* Edwards AFB, CA: Air Force Flight Test Center, 1997

Young, Ralph B. *Army Aviation in Vietnam, Volumes 1 & 2.* Ramsey, NJ: Huey Corporation, 2000

Young, Warren R. *The Helicopters.* Alexandria, VA: Time-Life Books, 1982

BOOKS BY CORPORATIONS, MUSEUMS AND OTHER ORGANIZATIONS

Forty Years On ... London: Handley Page Ltd., 1949

National Museum of Naval Aviation. Pensacola, FL: Naval Aviation Foundation, 1996

Pedigree of Champions: Boeing since 1916. Seattle, WA: The Boeing Company, 1977

The Pratt & Whitney Aircraft Story. Hartford, CT: Pratt & Whitney Aircraft, 1950

United States Air Force Museum. Wright-Patterson AFB, OH: Air Force Museum Foundation, 1997

ANNUAL PUBLICATIONS

Jane's All the World's Aircraft. London: Jane's Yearbooks

Jane's Fighting Ships. London: Jane's Yearbooks

MAGAZINES

Aeroplane Monthly. London: IPC Media Ltd.

Aerospace International. London: Royal Aeronautical Society

Aerospace Professional. London: Royal Aeronautical Society

Air & Space Smithsonian. Washington, DC: Smithsonian Business Ventures

Air International. Stamford, UK: Key Publishing

Flight Journal. Ridgefield, CT: Air Age Inc.

Flypast. Stamford, UK: Key Publishing

GENERAL